Cases in Economic Development: Projects, Policies and Strategies

Internationally written and refereed, *Butterworths Advanced Economics Texts* seek to inform students and professional economists by providing clarity and rigour in economic analysis.

General Editor

Bruce Herrick
Department of Economics,
Washington and Lee University, USA

Consulting Editors

John Enos
Magdalen College,
University of Oxford, UK

Gerald Helleiner
Department of Political Economy,
University of Toronto, Canada

Michael Roemer
Harvard Institute for International Development,
Harvard University, USA

Pan Yotopoulos
Food Research Institute,
Stanford University, USA

Titles in preparation

Comparative Economic Development
Development Economics: Theories and Evidence

Other titles are under consideration

Butterworths Advanced Economics Texts

Cases in Economic Development: Projects, Policies and Strategies

Michael Roemer and Joseph J. Stern
Harvard Institute for International Development

Butterworths
London Boston
Sydney Wellington Durban Toronto

First published 1981

©Michael Roomer and Joseph J. Stern, 1981

HD
82
R6493
1981

British Library Cataloguing in Publication Data

Roemer, Michael
  Cases in economic development. –
  (Butterworths advanced economic texts)
  1. Economic development – Case studies
  I. Title   II. Stern, Joseph J.
  330.9   HD82

  ISBN 0–408–10729–4
  ISBN 0–408–10730–8 Pbk

Typeset by Scribe Design, Gillingham, Kent
Printed and bound by Robert Hartnoll Ltd, Bodmin, Cornwall

To our parents

Acknowledgment

Our experience in working with policymaking institutions in a number of developing countries made us sensitive to the difficulties of applying theoretical constructs to real life situations. While theoretical tools of economics provide a sound and consistent framework within which to analyze many development problems, in applying these tools one often needs to modify them to fit available data and take account of missing information. One also learns to temper conclusions to reflect uncertain information and the constraints imposed on policymakers by non-economic variables. In trying to convey this sense of complexity to our students, we decided there was a need both to teach the theoretical tools of development analysis and to show how such tools could be applied in a realistic setting. The material in this volume has grown out of a course we taught at Harvard University which tried to meet these objectives.

The development of new teaching materials is a time-consuming task. We were fortunate that Derek C. Bok, President of Harvard University, was sufficiently intrigued by our idea of how economic development might be taught to policymakers to give us a grant from the Innovative Teaching Fund which allowed us to invent the economy of Beracia in which all our cases are placed. A series of research assistants and teaching assistants struggled with us to cook up data for Beracia, then to make it conform to some standard of realism, and finally to revise the data when time and events rendered the original realism obsolete. David Ring first struggled with the task of making Beracia not too much like any one country, but not too different either. Subsequently, Jeffrey Lewis worked through a complex set of revisions and learned, to his chagrin, that a change in any economic variable had to be worked through virtually every piece of data in the manuscript. A grant from the EXXON Education Foundation paid for these activities and helped bring the project to fruition. Dani Kaufman helped to teach much of this material in our graduate course, and gave us advice on how to revise the material in light of students' reactions and comments.

Several colleagues at Harvard University and elsewhere helped us to improve the product. Richard Mallon bravely took on several of these cases for his own graduate course, worked through them carefully, and offered us incisive suggestions for improvement. Malcolm Gillis, Robinson Hollister, Jr, Malcolm McPherson, and Robert Klitgaard read and commented upon parts of the manuscript. The fact that we did not incorporate all suggestions for revision and change in no way diminishes our debt. Bruce Herrick, who read the entire manuscript, was instrumental in moving the project to publication and we are grateful for his enthusiastic support.

Several secretaries suffered through innumerable drafts, revisions, rearrangements, renumberings, and confusions, somehow keeping enough order to make this book possible. Mary Lavallee and Pamela Rowley bore the initial brunt of this effort; Audrey Cheong Sow Chang and Ann MacGowan completed the task.

Both authors are Institute Fellows in the Harvard Institute for International Development. We owe a special debt of gratitude to Lester E. Gordon, until recently the Director of HIID, who encouraged us in this and other projects over the years, as both a colleague and a friend.

Perhaps the greatest contribution to this project over the past five years came from our students who not only had to work through the first drafts of the cases and pay serious attention to them, but whose grades depended in part on their forbearance. We have taken their suggestions seriously but, more important, we would never have seen this project through without their encouragement.

Michael Roemer
Joseph J. Stern

Contents

List of Tables

Case 11 Income inequality and poverty

Appendix to Case 11

Introduction

This book is motivated by a simple premise: the experience of development is so remote from that of the classroom that every possible aid must be used to enable students to understand it. The cases in this book—on project analysis, sectoral planning and macroeconomic policies—place the student in the midst of vital development controversies, policy struggles that should ring true to those who have been involved. They were developed as the basis for a year-long graduate course in economic analysis for decision-making at Harvard University, and are sophisticated enough to interest advanced students and experienced policy analysts. If used as supplementary exercises in introductory courses, the cases can give new students the feel of battle, some sense of being involved.

It may seem suprising that, in order to introduce realism and specificity, we have invented an imaginary country, Beracia, and set all the cases there. We have several reasons for approaching reality through fiction. In order to simulate actual planning experience, a range of analytical issues must be set in a single economy. This helps students appreciate that each development problem is part of a tightly tied knot; oosening a single loop affects the tautness of all others. If students analyze agricultural investment in Ghana and a balance-of-payments crisis in Colombia, they are likely to miss the essential connections between breaking structural barriers to cash crop production and promoting export growth. These cases build upon each other, so that students gain most by working through several of them and thereby accumulating a knowledge of the economy.

But which country should be chosen? If students are to spend a semester or a year on a single economy, it should be one displaying a wide variety of problems typical of developing countries. No one country is typical and no single economy displays all the features that should be covered in a comprehensive course. Beracia has been designed with a greater-than-normal range of problems, so that it can encompass the features of mineral-rich countries such as Zambia and Peru, agrarian economies such as the Philippines and Ivory Coast, and aspiring exporters of manufactures, such as Colombia and Pakistan. A final corollary reason for inventing Beracia is that selecting any one real country for study tends to discourage students whose geographical interests lie elsewhere and to give undue advantage to the few who know the country well.

Our fictional country is introduced in Part II, which presents four reports similar to World Bank economic reports on developing countries. Sufficient data are elaborated to explain the economy's salient features and to provide the student with the background necessary to analyze the cases. These data are plausible, because they have been derived from the characteristics of several developing countries, and consistent, but only to the extent that national accounts and other data sources are consistent in practice. Because economics cannot be divorced from politics, a report provides the political context from which economic decisions will emerge and suggests political constraints within which economic analysis must fit. The viscissitudes of the international economy, especially since 1970, are transmitted realistically to Beracia's economy and the problems it faces in 1978 resemble those of real developing countries. Because Beracia is both representative of real countries and linked to actual economic events, students can use the literature on developing countries to support their analysis of Beracian problems and can use standard data sources, such as those on commodity prices and trends in world trade, to supplement the data provided on Beracia. Teachers may use the background description of Beracia as a standard, detailed source of data, as complete as that for most LDCs and much more readily available to all students, from which any number of illustrative exercises on economic analysis can be structured. Many of these have been suggested in the cases.

The cases in this collection are divided into project, sector and macroeconomic categories, but the division is to some extent artificial. Each case contains something of value for most of the other cases and the interconnections should be emphasized more than the divisions. The cases span many sectors—mining, agriculture, manufacturing, transport, education and health. Our intention has been to design exercises illustrating those kinds of investment planning and policy analysis that have received most attention from economists and that have been put to practical use in the third world. The heaviest concentration is on project analysis (Part III), because it is probably used (and is certainly taught) more widely than other planning techniques. The links between Part III and Part V are tight, however, because the estimation of shadow prices leads the student directly into macroeconomic analysis and the consideration of factor markets. Moreover, the sectoral cases in Part IV build upon the techniques of Part III.

Although many of the cases may seem complex to the student as they involve considerable computation, they are in fact highly simplified abstractions from real project studies, some of which run to several volumes.

The advanced student or experienced planner will find that the country descriptions of Part II and the cases are self-explanatory. A newcomer to development, however, will require some guidance before tackling the cases. Part I and the introductions to Part III, IV and V offer guidance to those students. They are not intended to substitute for textbooks on various aspects of planning. Rather, they help to orient the reader within the field of development, introduce some of the analytic techniques that will be useful in understanding the cases, and offer annotated bibliographies to texts and treatises.

Development Planning

Part 1

Development Planning

Development Planning

The economy of Beracia has been constructed to simulate the characteristics of a large group of developing countries and the cases have been designed to place the student in the middle of realistic planning controversies. In order to explain the theory and practice of development planning behind these cases, Part I explores the competing goals of development, the basis of all planning, and introduces the theory and practice of development planning.

Development goals and strategies[1]

In mixed economies—and this includes all developing countries except China, North Korea, Vietnam, Cambodia and Cuba—development planning has two distinguishable motivations. The first is to correct inherent flaws in the market mechanism to help the market allocate resources more efficiently. Interventions of this kind include controls over monopoly, taxation to correct external diseconomies, investment planning to capture external economies, protection of infant industries, and so forth. For this class of planned interventions, the underlying assumption is that market allocations are inherently consistent with accelerating growth, if only the market can be made to work more closely to its theoretical ideal. Planning has limited aims and the least intervention possible is the best outcome.

The second motivation is more common and covers more kinds of intervention. In this view development goals are presumed to be poorly served by the market. Governments try to control market forces as much as possible and point economic activity in directions it would not ordinarily go. Market allocations are generally thought to preclude goals such as income redistribution, basic needs and reduced international dependence. Accelerated growth and increased employment are frequently approached more through planned intervention than through market allocations, although there is a real question whether 3 this perception by governments is correct. In any case, the rationale for planning depends critically upon the goals of development and the ability of market mechanisms to achieve these goals. The purpose of Part I is to provide a framework for the cases and introductory texts of Parts III, IV and V. Before doing so, we need to review five major development goals—economic growth, income redistribution, employment creation, basic needs and reduced dependence—and their implications for planning.

ECONOMIC GROWTH

After World War II, stimulated by the reconstruction of Europe under the Marshall Plan and the increasing momentum of decolonization in Asia and Africa, economists returned to the theory of economic development. For most contributors, the central issue was growth: how to increase the endowments of productive factors available to a country and thus increase the annual production of goods and services at its disposal. The aim of growth was increased welfare for all citizens, and it was assumed (for reasons explored below) that if production could be increased, the distribution of income would take care of itself. The experience of thirty years and some searching criticism have cast a shadow over this assumption (World Bank, 1978, 1979; Morawetz, 1978), but growth remains central to all development plans.

Of the factors contributing to growth, *capital* received most attention after the war. The simplest and most durable model of economic growth is the Harrod–Domar model, which is a straightforward extension of Keynesian analysis. In it, capital is the only factor of production and growth depends on two parameters: the ratio of savings to national income and the productivity of capital, both of which must be increased to achieve higher growth with a given level of saving (see Part V for a presentation of the model). The simplicity and elegance of the model made it the basis for many later contributions to the theory of development. The model directed economists' attention to means of mobilizing domestic saving, increasing the flow of external aid that could supplement domestic saving, and planning investment to increase the productivity of capital. Development plans were directed principally to these issues and the popularity of project appraisal is perhaps a result of its particular facility for ensuring the most productive utilization of a given flow of investment.

The focus on *mobilization of saving* explains several concerns of planners. To induce the private sector—households and businesses—to save more, governments try to modernize banks and other financial institutions and, in a few cases, to raise interest rates so that savers obtain an attractive return net of inflation. To increase government saving, economists prescribe higher, more progressive tax rates and improved tax administration. Third world governments typically collect smaller fractions of their GNP in taxes than do industrial countries. Because higher revenues often appear to reduce resistance to higher expenditures, especially on civil servants' salaries and defense, control of current expenditures has also become a planning issue. Once government generates saving, it can be directed either to the private sector (through direct or indirect loans) or to the government's own development expenditures. In practice the latter benefits most and many early development plans were to a large extent multi-year budgets for government investment expenditure[2]. Fiscal issues are reflected in the descriptive materials on Beracia and Case 10 focuses on them.

Finally, if domestic saving is a constraint on growth, then *foreign saving*, whether private investment or official aid, can be used to increase growth. The Marshall Plan's success and the popularity of the Harrod–Domar view of growth both pointed to foreign capital as a way out of the bind created by inadequate saving. Foreign aid programs have been devised to a considerable extent on this reasoning. The need for aid reinforces the concern for development planning, because donors believe that national plans are essential to ensure that their aid is used productively and does not substitute for domestic saving (Papanek, 1972).

The Harrod–Domar model reflects only one constraint on growth. During the 1950s, Prebisch and other students of Latin American development noted the structural bind into which many of these economies had fallen. Unable to increase their export earnings because they depend on slowly growing demand for raw materials and foodstuffs, yet dependent on imports of capital and intermediate goods, these countries cannot grow because they lack adequate foreign exchange earnings. The *foreign exchange constraint* to growth was enshrined as an impediment equal to the savings constraint in series of 'two-gap' models by McKinnon (1964), Chenery and Strout (1966) and others in the early 1960s. In these models, described in Part V, some economies seem restricted primarily by their lack of domestic saving and others more by their inability to earn foreign exchange (the two gaps). Planning models and project appraisal techniques account for both factors. Two-gap models have influenced donors to expand their rationale for aid: even if a country has adequate domestic saving to finance its target growth, it might still need aid to finance imports. Countries such as India and Colombia received large loans for several years aimed primarily at an increased flow of imports.

International trade has been intertwined with concern for economic growth ever since Adam Smith, and growth stategies centering on trade have been as prominent as capital-centered theories throughout the postwar period. The classical theory of comparative advantage has been interpreted to mean that tropical countries should concentrate on producing foodstuffs and raw materials for export and use their proceeds to import manufactured goods. This strategy has worked for a few countries that are well endowed and fortunate in their choice of product and market. For the most part, however, it has led to inadequate export growth, because the demand for tropical foods and raw materials has not grown rapidly enough to finance the imports needed for accelerated growth. The strategy has also led to structural rigidities that make it difficult for countries to shift from one export to another as world market conditions change. In the plantation and mining sectors, export orientation has created enclave economies which employ much capital and few workers. The high wages paid to these workers set a pattern for the rest of the economy that in turn discourages employment, while the input requirements of these export industries do not encourage the development of linkages to other sectors[3].

Impatience with slow export growth led several Latin American countries to begin a process of *import substitution* during the 1930s and 1940s. It has since become the dominant mode of industrial development throughout the third world. The standard pattern is to begin by producing consumer goods at home, shifting from imports of these goods towards imports of the capital equipment, raw materials and intermediate goods needed to produce them. If the process continues from there to substitute for producer goods, it could lead to a complete, well-balanced and integrated industrial structure. However, to protect domestic producers from international competition, governments typically erect high tariffs for consumer goods and keep duties low on imported inputs. The result—high protection for domestic factors of production—creates little incentive for initial import substituters to become efficient or to expand their markets through exports. The next step—producing capital goods and other inputs at home—raises the costs of these inputs and damages the original import substituters, so that step is often resisted for some time. For small countries in particular, this dead end is reached rather quickly and import substitution ceases to be an engine of growth[4].

Disenchantment with both primary export-led growth and import substitution has led several countries to attempt a transition from the export of resource- and labor-intensive raw materials to export of labor-intensive manufactures, a process Ranis (1973) calls *export substitution*. The most successful practitioners of this strategy have been Taiwan and South Korea, although Pakistan, Brazil, Colombia and others have pursued it also. (Hong Kong and Singapore have promoted manufactured exports successfully, but had no agricultural base from which to start). To make this strategy effective, it is necessary to follow policies that create an 'open' economy, in the sense that protective barriers are kept low and the price regime does not discriminate against exports. This implies market-oriented exchange rates, interest rates and wages, moderate and uniform tariffs, and few quotas. To earn profits, producers are forced to compete under world market conditions, to be efficient and to achieve economies of scale by exporting. The reinforcing benefits of efficiency and scale combine to permit the backward integration and industrial diversification which are so difficult to attain under import substitution regimes. With diversification comes the ability to shift export produces in the face of changing market conditions, 'the capacity to transform'[5], and thus keep exports and the economy growing. Korea's remarkable growth performance since 1960, which has survived the oil price increase and continued into the late 1970s, is the best current example of this strategy in action. But this is not an easy path to development. It takes entrepreneurship, strict discipline by industrialists and workers, and a strong government to permit competition to determine outcomes. It may be very difficult to switch from a protected regime to an open one without major and politically risky disruptions[6]. Moreover, increasing protectionism by industrial countries against labor-intensive manufactures from LDCs has begun to place this strategy in jeopardy.

Even if savings and export earnings were abundant, as they are in the petroleum exporting countries, economic development would be constrained by the availability of the human skills necessary to direct these material inputs. The term *absorptive capacity* was coined for this skill and management constraint and in two-gap models it can be represented by a limit to the growth of investment. A more fundamental concept, *human capital,* has emerged to explain the role of education, as well as health and nutrition, in economic development. It is based on the observation that expenditure of time and money on education of individuals enhances their ability to participate in and contribute to development (even though their immediate motives may be different). Hence education creates human capital in much the same way that savings creates physical capital and both are required for development. This concept has reinforced the faith placed by most governments in formal education, especially secondary and higher education. However, the high incidence of unemployment among the educated in countries such as India and some searching critiques of the market for educated labor have raised serious doubts that an advanced, formal educational system is central to the growth process[7]. Case 7 examines these issues.

The need to mobilize scarce resources has led to the almost universal resort to economic planning to guide development. Several historical reasons have been advanced for this worldwide trend: the rapid development of the Soviet Union under comprehensive planning; the intellectual legacy of British socialism to the many British colonies receiving independence after World War II; and the requirement by aid donors, especially the World Bank and the United States, that plans be developed to ensure the productive use of their assistance. Economists have provided additional rationales for planning. One school of thought, popular since World War II, is that growth must proceed as a balanced advance on all fronts, so that each industry benefits from the markets and external benefits created by all the other industries and expands in tandem. Clearly such balanced growth requires central planning. The unrealism of balanced growth in countries with little managerial capacity is evident, but other economic arguments also favor planning. Markets for labor and capital function poorly and face many structural rigidities; important investments are so large that private capital will not finance them; industry is so primitive that the external benefits of infrastructure and inter-industrial markets do not exist and have to be created, presumably by central direction; small markets and economies of scale imply monopoly in many industries; and large parts of the population do not regularly enter markets, but deal in the subsistence economy. Each of these flaws in the market mechanism seems to point towards central planning.

Although planning is now an accepted part of the development scene, it has not been without critics. At a theoretical level, the most telling case against planning has been Harry Johnson's observation (1962) that most of the points given in favor of planning are really arguments about imperfections of the market system. If the diagnosis is correct, Johnson argues, the prescription ought to involve improvement of the market mechanism so it can function better as an allocator of resources[8]. In any case, most of these imperfections are at least partially caused by government interventions such as overvalued exchange rates, controlled interest rates and minimum wage legislation, for which the corrective policies are obvious, though not necessarily easy to implement. Given the myriad of allocational decisions to be made; the extreme sophistication and complexity of models that would enable planners to make those decisions; the severe shortage of professional and managerial personnel available to government; and the poor record that many governments have in the direct management of resources for economic purposes; there remains a *prima facie* case to utilize the market mechanism as much as possible and to reserve for direct government management only those activities whose characteristics make private implementation infeasible or disadvantageous. However, this maxim is rather vague in its details and to a large extent the desirable scope for direct government allocation and management depends upon the goals other than growth that each activity is supposed to serve. We now turn to these other goals.

INCOME REDISTRIBUTION

Advocates of growth-oriented strategies have assumed that increased income would be shared by the poor as well as the rich. Once incomes rise, it is argued, even if among the advantaged groups, their increased demand for goods and services provides opportunities for the poorer members of society to obtain wage employment or to sell more of their farm output (the 'trickle-down' effect). Also, market-oriented growth proceeds by employing the most abundant and cheapest resources, of which unskilled labor—provided by the poorest members of society—is the most important. This gradually increases wages, small farm incomes and other returns to these factors. Finally, governments concerned with redistribution of income are better placed to use fiscal mechanisms to distribute the gains of development, the more rapid the growth of output. Kuznets' (1963) observations from cross-country data, that income distribution seems first to grow less equal with growth and to begin to grow more equal only after considerable development has taken place, have raised doubts about these assumptions. Over time, observation of the development process seems to confirm that in most countries with low average incomes, even rapid growth does not benefit the poor very much, certainly not as much as the rich.

Once it became evident that the growth process is more likely to concentrate wealth and power than to equalize them, redistribution of income began to receive consideration as a separate goal of development. This raises some obvious questions: are there inevitable conflicts between growth and income equalization? If so, how can equalization be achieved with minimal sacrifice to growth, or vice versa? And what is the trade-off between these two goals[9]?

One of the apparent conflicts between growth and distribution centers on saving. Much of the saving is done by the wealthier members of the community, whose incomes are large enough to permit saving; whose enterprises earn profits that are reinvested; and whose incomes and expenditures account for a substantial share of the taxes upon which government saving depends. If the poor save a much smaller fraction of their incomes than the rich, and if growth is constrained by a lack of saving, then one way to spur growth is to put more income at the disposal of the wealthy. However, the premise that redistribution of income would lead to decreased savings has been challenged[10].

A second apparent conflict concerns management and entrepreneurship, which are scarce factors in developing countries. Under competitive conditions, those farms and enterprises that are managed more innovatively and efficiently will earn higher profits than others, and will also lead economic development. If growth is the goal, nothing should be done to discourage such enterprises from continuing to accumulate wealth. Yet distributional goals would give a different prescription, blunting the incentive for successful units to continue expanding. Of course, many high incomes in LDCs have been earned, not as the result of successful competition, but through exploitation of protection and other government policies that reduce competition.

Third, the external economies of industrial development are most evident in the cities, which have received the lion's share of industrial and infrastructural investment. Yet the urban population on average has higher incomes than the rural population and continued emphasis on urbanization would widen that disparity. One of the most enduring models of development, originated by Lewis (1954) and elaborated by Ranis and Fei (1961), suggests that growth proceeds as the modern (industrial or urban) sector absorbs surplus labor and savings from the traditional (rural) sector. Once surplus labor is eliminated by industrial growth, both sectors can grow together. But until that happens, modern sector incomes grow more rapidly than rural incomes, worsening income distribution.

The strongest prescription for income redistribution is a radical reform of asset holdings, especially land reform. Four of the most notably egalitarian developing countries accomplished a radical land reform under military or revolutionary conditions: China, Taiwan, South Korea and Cuba. Once accomplished, such radical reforms appear to reduce the conflict between equality and growth. However, the political and economic risks of radical reforms need no elaboration and, viewed from the pre-reform situation, asset redistribution poses the conflict between equity and growth in as sharp a form as any. For countries unable to contemplate asset redistribution but wishing to improve income distribution, it is necessary to structure investment programs and price policies so that increases in income are distributed more favorably for those with lower incomes.

This concern for redistribution has renewed and intensified interest in *rural development*. The greatest disparity within most developing countries is between rural and urban populations. Industrialization strategies worsen this disparity for long periods. But agriculture itself has growth potential and, if small farms receive inputs, credit and supporting infrastructure investment, agriculture may help stimulate growth without worsening income distribution[11]. A parallel strategy is that advocated by the ILO Employment Mission to Kenya (1972; one of a series of ILO missions on employment). Many small firms have grown up on the fringes of the modern economy. These utilize semi-skilled labor to produce simple, inexpensive goods and services which are accessible to the lower income groups. If these 'informal sector' units are encouraged in the development process, they may help reduce the conflict between growth and distribution.

An introduction to the data and issues of income distribution is provided by Case 11.

EMPLOYMENT CREATION

The legitimacy of job creation as a separate goal has been questioned. When it was thought that rapidly growing income meant satisfactory job creation there seemed no need to aim specifically at the latter. Even when it was recognized that jobs were not being created rapidly enough to absorb the growing labor force, many argued that the real problem was not jobs as such, but income distribution. If incomes can be redistributed by fiscal means, then it is better to maximize growth and redistribute than to sacrifice growth to create more jobs. If, on the other hand, employment is a key ingredient to equitable distribution, then it is not a final goal, but an instrument to achieve the underlying goal of greater equality.

Our knowledge of the employment problem is based on conventional western concepts and measures: a person is usually considered employed if he or she has worked for cash income at some time during the period covered by the typical survey and is considered in the workforce if she or he has actively sought a job during the period. By these definitions, measured unemployment can be high enough, e.g. 14 percent in Bogota in 1968, 12 percent in Philippine cities in 1965 (Turnham, 1970). But that is not the whole story. Even the casual observer notes a high degree of under-employment in third world countries, people who are in the formally defined workforce but who are (i) working at full capacity a small fraction of the available time; (ii) working long hours at very low incomes; and (iii) working at tasks well below their educational attainments. Simultaneously, and perhaps paradoxically, one also observes a large fraction of the population, especially rural housewives, who are (iv) not in the formal labor force but fully employed at very low productivity tasks. Much of the perceived employment problem is really about these four groups, yet their condition is not reflected in conventional statistics[12].

These considerations all point to employment as either a subsidiary goal, an instrument instead of a goal, or an irrelevant concept as conventionally measured. Despite this, governments do behave as if job creation were itself a basic aim. People value work for its own sake and employment remains the most satisfying way of participating in development. Hence governments undertake programs to provide wage employment for as many as possible.

Whether employment is a separate goal or an instrument to other goals, its achievement raises some interesting strategic issues of both supply and demand. To deal with labor supply first, the most obvious and all-consuming problem is *population growth*. With limited supplies of complementary factors of production, rapid population growth means more underemployment and lower incomes. The debate over population growth, ably summarized by Todaro (1977, Chapters 6 and 7), has been complex, wide-ranging and intense, and this brief review cannot do justice to it. It is clear that the demographic transition, which in the developed countries took place relatively smoothly, is occurring in the third world through a rapid decline in mortality rates and either an increase or very slow decline in birth-rates, resulting in the so-called population explosion. The research and policy issues facing both scholars and governments is what can be done within the limits of morally acceptable measures to reduce birth-rates as rapidly as possible.

To oversimplify considerably, an early approach was to provide family planning facilities—i.e. contraceptive techniques and medical advice on using them—to populations that were assumed to want smaller families. Foreign aid programs of the 1960s favored this approach. In the past decade, however, it has been recognized that the fertility issue is far more complex. Desired family size can be influenced by income levels, growth and equality, by opportunities for female employment, and by the health status of both mother and child. It appears that development, especially if accompanied by greater income equality, tends to reduce birth-rates. But the response may not be fast enough to avoid extreme population pressure. Moreover, the precise mix of development policies, including the availability of traditional population programs, may itself influence the speed with which the demographic transition takes place.

A second supply issue is the quantity and relevance of *education*. If educated workers spend long periods searching for jobs to match their expectations, part of the answer must lie in the kinds of education provided. Education systems are often captives of colonial legacies in which general education predominated; vocational education often meant training for clerkships; and the admired professions were doctors and lawyers. Rural primary schools may teach little to prepare students for the employment most readily available to them, farming. Technical education may be aimed at technologies unsuitable for labor-abundant countries (see below) or for positions more exalted than useful in countries in the early stages of industrialization. Put simply, too many students may be encouraged to seek higher education than can be absorbed into the labor force in positions commensurate with their resulting expectations.

Granted that the supply of labor is increasing rapidly and its control is likely to be effective only in the long run, what can governments do about increasing the *demand for labor*? Income growth rates have been high by most standards. Why then has employment creation been so much slower than income growth and why has unemployment risen? If unskilled labor is abundant and cheap, while capital is scarce, investors should attempt to use production methods that employ more labor and less capital. Yet we observe highly capital-intensive projects where more labor-intensive ones would have been feasible. There are several reasons for this paradox. First, labor may be abundant, but it has not been cheap, because governments have legislated minimum wages, social insurance and other devices that, while protecting the incomes of those employed, also make it expensive to hire workers. Urban, employed workers are politically strong, so the impetus for such protective legislation is clear. However, it is the migrant from rural areas or the marginal, under- or unemployed urban worker who suffers when employers are not willing to increase their workforce at the high, legislated cost of wages and benefits. To compound the problem, governments have both controlled interest rates at low levels and kept exchange rates overvalued and duties low on imported capital goods in an attempt to reduce the cost of investment and thus to encourage it. The results, however, have been contrary. First, saving is discouraged by low interest rates. Second, these policies make it relatively attractive to substitute cheap capital for expensive labor in all productive activities. This bias in favor of capital affects not only the ratio of labor to capital in any given venture, but the choice of investment and output: those sectors using capital more intensively are favored by investors over labor-intensive sectors.

Government's distortion of the market mechanism is not the only problem. As long as developing countries remain dependent on imported capital equipment, they will be forced to use technologies developed in industrial country markets, where factor endowments make labor expensive and capital relatively cheap. Even if developing countries get their factor prices 'right'—i.e. get them to represent real scarcities—they may find it difficult to purchase plant and equipment that uses labor intensively. Some intermediate technology is available, especially from larger LDCs such as China, India and Brazil, but it is not always easy to coordinate such technology with finance and management. If multinational corporations are making the investment, their decision may be determined more by factor prices in their home markets and by proprietary interests in their own technology than by factor market conditions in the host country. Export markets may require standards that can be delivered only by sophisticated machinery. Finally, even if labor-intensive techniques were available and economic, it is not clear that entrepreneurs will always choose them. They may find it easier and more comfortable to manage fewer workers and depend on engineers to keep their equipment running, since labor-intensive techniques involve more complex management problems. Alternatively, they may simply prefer modern, capital-intensive equipment because it gives them greater satisfaction to be at the forefront of technology, a syndrome identified by Wells (1975) as 'engineering man' (as opposed to economic man).

This recitation of barriers to labor-intensive growth suggests a strategy to increase job creation without reducing growth potential. Because many of the problems stem from government controls over prices and quantities (licensing of imports and investment, which tends to favor the influential, large-scale and capital-intensive producers over others), the key to the counter strategy is liberalization and a more market-dependent system. Wages and interest rates should be determined by market forces, for these will reflect factor scarcities and tend to make labor-using and capital-saving techniques and goods more profitable than others. Exchange rates should be determined more by competitive conditions in world markets, which will almost invariably mean devaluation, and tariffs should be made more uniform. These measures will make it more profitable to export simple manufactures and agricultural commodities, both of which tend to be more labor-intensive than much protected, import-substituting industry. If markets are liberalized and access to inputs is determined more by competitive conditions than by bureaucratic allocation, then the small, politically weaker but more labor-intensive units in the urban and rural areas will have a better chance to survive and grow. Where government intervention may remain necessary, as in the distribution of agricultural inputs, small units should be favored—or at least given equal access—to promote labor-using production. This neoclassical strategy, based on market allocation and comparative advantage, has been tried successfully in a few countries, notably Taiwan, South Korea, Hong Kong and Singapore (now known as the 'Gang of Four'). In these cases, rapid output growth has induced rapid employment growth to the extent that market-determined real wages have risen substantially and the income distribution has either improved or at least not worsened. Market forces are no panacea, for many of the reasons mentioned above, and the successes of the Gang of Four will not be easily duplicated. But in the mixed economies, market-based solutions generally offer more hope for growth with employment creation than interventionist approaches[13].

BASIC NEEDS

If the emphasis on distributional goals can be labeled 'beyond economic growth', then the newly developing emphasis on basic human needs may be labeled 'beyond income distribution'. Basic needs may be defined as those goods and services that create a minimum standard of living and upon which higher human aspirations depend. These include sufficient food to provide minimum nutrition for productive work; housing; water supplies and health services to reduce the incidence of endemic diseases and mortality, especially among infants and the young; and primary education to prepare people for a productive and satisfying adulthood. The concern for basic needs stems from four reservations about distributional goals and strategies[14]. First, proponents of the basic needs approach argue that it is the very poor— say, for example, those in the lowest one-third or so of the income distribution—who are least able to benefit from development and that redistributional strategies are not likely to be effective in reaching this group. They are disenfranchised in every sense, with little local or national power and little capacity to take advantage of development opportunities, even if offered to them. To give them this capacity, society must provide the very poorest with the basic necessities of life.

Second, even if redistribution could reach this group, its emphasis on income transfers is misplaced, because the very poor are either not willing or not able to use additional cash productively to relieve their poverty. The most familiar manifestation of this doubt is the claim that additional income tends to be spent on ceremony and drink, rather than on basic needs. This observation is consistent with a paternalistic approach to helping the poor, one which argues that the poor do not know how to help themselves as well as others in society know how to help them. It is antagonistic to the classical economists' view that, granted consumer sovereignty (and ignoring externalities), the socially optimal disposition of any cash transfer is the consumption pattern chosen by those receiving it. However, as Harberger (1978) has pointed out, human societies have consistently acted as if they prefer to help the indigent through transfers in kind for specified purposes, rather than transferring cash and trusting consumer sovereignty. But it has also been observed that target groups are adept at substituting goods provided in kind, at least in limited quantities, for their consumption needs (e.g. when school lunches are given, school children get less to eat at home). If so, then a basic needs approach may be effectively transformed by the poor themselves into transfer of generally disposable income.

Third, and more fundamentally, the poor may simply be unable to benefit from income transfers. Lacking political power and the economic and social services infrastructure enjoyed by the advantaged members of society, the very poor have no means of applying this additional income to improve their lives. To take only two obvious examples: if access roads are not in place, the poor farmer cannot count on marketing his produce and may not then invest in producing cash crops; and if water and medical services are too far away, there is little opportunity to transfer higher income into better health.

The fourth reservation about income distribution involves the comparative effectiveness of the two approaches. Redistribution of income is likely either to be especially costly and disruptive, if assets are redistributed (especially through land reform), or to be slow and marginal in its effect, as when redistribution takes place by channeling more of the benefits of growth towards the poor. Basic needs strategies, however, are seen as a means of targeting investments precisely to improve the welfare of the poor and increase their productivity. Consumption of certain goods and services—more nutritious food, improved housing, piped water, health services and primary education—is then expected to yield long-term benefits, just as investment does. There are many assumptions behind this position and a good deal of evidence on both sides of the consumption-as-investment argument. If confirmed by further investigation and future experience, it would be the strongest argument in favor of a basic needs approach.

The practical effect of a basic needs approach would be to place greater emphasis on food (as opposed to cash crop) production, housing investment and the provision of social services, including water supplies. Presumably, with resources limited, these investments would come at the expense of cash crop agriculture, industrialization and large-scale infrastructure (trunk roads, power plants, etc.). Unless the consumption-as-investment argument is substantiated by evidence, there would be an obvious trade-off between growth, at least as conventionally measured, and the welfare of the very poor. And if provision of basic needs is not accompanied by greater productivity of the poor and economic growth, it will be difficult to sustain the strategy very long. Advocates of a basic needs strategy point out that China achieved basic needs without sacrificing growth, albeit in a revolutionary situation. At the same time its opponents point to Sri Lanka which also provided for basic needs but has been stagnant ever since. We need much more data on these and other cases before drawing conclusions.

That brings us to a final point. The advocacy of basic needs as a development strategy is a fairly recent phenomenon[15]. Its most vociferous proponents now seem to be part of the international aid establishment, who would like more LDC governments to adopt the strategy. However, except for a few countries like China, Sri Lanka, Cuba and Tanzania, not many governments have embraced this approach. Indeed, it is not even clear precisely how a basic needs strategy should be implemented in any given case and the World Bank, among others, is trying to elaborate practical approaches. Because a basic needs strategy is in its infancy as a systematic approach to development, this case book has not been designed to focus on it. However, two cases—Case 5 on control of schistosomiasis and Case 7 on educational strategy—are addressed to investment choices very much like those that might surface in a basic needs strategy, and Case 11 includes questions of poverty alleviation which are central to meeting basic needs.

REDUCED DEPENDENCE

In an earlier guise, reduced dependence has been a goal of development since at least the industrial revolution, which inexorably transformed warfare until it became clear that a military nation must first be an industrial nation. The rise of Germany, Japan and the Soviet Union as modern industrial states was inextricably linked with their aspirations to become military powers. Most developing countries in the last half of this century do not aspire so openly to military might, although that motivation has not altogether disappeared. However, many third world spokesmen and scholars have emphasized other forms of dependence from which their countries would like to escape. They object to the dependence on a few raw material exports for most of their foreign exchange earnings; on imported capital goods and embodied technology for their investments; on foreign capital to supplement domestic saving; and on foreign managerial and technical skills to run their modern industrial plants.

Although political independence formally ended the colonial era in Africa and Asia after World War II, it has only changed the form of economic dependence. Under colonialism (and, in Latin America, even afterwards, until the 1940s) the metropolitan country bought raw materials and foodstuffs from the colony and sold it manufactures, mostly consumer goods, but also some capital equipment. After independence (in Latin America, after the onset of World War II), former colonies began to industrialize by substituting for imports, especially of consumer goods. We have already discussed how backward integration was discouraged under import substitution, so that these countries traded dependence on consumer good imports for dependence on producer good imports, a state in which most of the third world remains.

The same policies that encouraged import substitution also discouraged export diversification, leaving many third world countries heavily dependent on exports of a few raw materials (e.g., copper, tin, rubber, cotton) and foods (e.g., tea, coffee, cocoa, rice) to pay for imported producer goods. Because the world markets for these exports grow relatively slowly and suffer severe cyclical fluctuations, the entire development effort is slower and less stable than it might be if exports had been diversified. A country capable of producing a wide range of manufactured and agricultural products at competitive costs is able to shift its exports to take advantage of changes in market conditions. This capacity to transform reduces dependence on a few exports for foreign exchange earnings and on critical imports of intermediate and capital goods. It does not necessarily mean less trade, however. South Korea and Taiwan, for example, have gained a substantial capacity to transform while increasing the ratio of trade to GNP. The ability to produce capital goods also enables a country to develop technologies more suitable to their own factor endowments. The key to this concept of reduced dependence is flexibility.

Writers concerned with dependence on world trade have offered a competing strategy, not to create export flexibility, but to reduce imports by creating a more fully integrated industrial sector. In contrast to the colonial trade regime or its post-independence, import-substituting replacement, in which primary exports are transformed by trade into final goods, this 'basic industry' strategy would transform domestically available resources directly into final goods through local production[16]. This would be achieved by promoting basic or heavy industries, such as metal, chemical, pulp and capital goods industries, precisely those goods that are now imported. With import dependence reduced, exports of raw materials can also be de-emphasized. This strategy is less concerned with competitiveness in world markets than with the structure of domestic industry (and, to a lesser extent, with the structure of demand). With industry, agriculture and mining linked as completely as possible, the economy should be a replica, though on a smaller scale, of the industrial structure of a developed country. However, because developing countries are unlikely either to generate the domestic saving required for such capital-intensive development or to develop the technical skills required for some time, this strategy is likely to increase dependence on foreign capital and manpower. And, because it depends during its early years on intensive use of a scarce factor—capital, it is likely to result in lower growth for a considerable period.

Theorists of dependence would argue that the phenomenon cannot be understood on the level of economics, but requires a Marxist sociological interpretation. Frank (1972) starts with the notion, originated by Prebisch (United Nations, 1950) and used by most dependence theorists, of a *center* consisting of industrial, developed countries that import raw materials and export manufactures and a *periphery* of underdeveloped countries that export the raw materials and depend on imports of manufactures. Frank, however, looks more closely at the periphery and observes within it another center-periphery structure. The center consists of the capitalists, the educated elite, the military, workers in the modern sector and other politically and economically advantaged groups. The periphery comprises marginal urban workers, small farmers and tradesmen, landless laborers and similarly disadvantaged groups. This dual economy and society is similar to that observed by many neoclassical economists. The Marxist interpretation is that the third world's own center has developed an economy so much like, and so dependent upon, the economies of the industrial world that their interests lie closer to the center countries than to the periphery of which they are nominally a part. Policies towards wages, interest rates, foreign exchange rates, tariffs and foreign investment have been rigged to serve these advantaged classes and they also serve the industrial center countries. They discriminate against the marginal, poor groups, as many neoclassical economists have also argued. Frank's particular contribution is to see this discrimination as deliberate and self-serving, reinforced by intercourse with the industrial world and thus almost impossible to change under existing political and social structures. This conclusion may be too strong, given examples of countries such as South Korea that have achieved egalitarian and dependency-reducing development, but probably has wide application in the third world[17].

The Frank view has interesting implications for the New International Economic Order (NIEO), the attempt by third world countries to improve the terms upon which they trade and obtain capital and technology on world markets. The NIEO, as most efforts connected with development, is being conducted on the assumption that the relevant unit of analysis is the nation-state. Thus improvements in the terms of trade, access to industrial country markets, and the flows of aid and private investment are all being negotiated to benefit countries, rather than particular groups within those countries. However, Frank's dependency analysis suggests that the benefits of such improvements in trade and capital flows would be captured by the already advantaged groups within each developing country and would be unlikely to benefit the poorer groups in society.

Planning theory and practice

THE PROCESS OF PLANNING

A consensus among political leaders on the goals of economic development is a prerequisite for national planning. In the ideal situation, each goal would be approximated by some measurable indicator, such as GNP growth or employment creation, a task for the economic planners. Then political leaders and planners may agree upon targets for each goal, such as a desirable GNP growth rate or minimal acceptable level of employment creation. Political leaders, working with the planners, would then ideally translate national priorities into relative weights for each of the important goals. The result would be a *social welfare function*, a mathematical expression which combines each of the relevant goal measures into a single indicator. This expression is the *objective function* of programming models, explained in Part IV. It is the measure by which the development plan will be judged: the higher the value of the objective function, the better the plan.

Armed with goal targets or a welfare function, economists can then undertake the next three steps in planning. First, they assess the availability of scarce resources—skilled labor, capital, foreign exchange, natural resources—over the plan period; these are the *resource constraints* on the development plan. Then planners survey all the possible *activities* that could be undertaken over the plan period in order to achieve targets or fulfill goals. Investments (development projects) are the usual focus of interest, but broadly specified programs (e.g. agricultural credit) and policies (e.g. investor incentives) are also relevant.

The third step is to select development activities for inclusion in the plan. In doing so, the resource constraints cannot be violated. Within these limits, planners select projects and policies that will satisfy the development targets or, if a welfare function has been specified, they select activities to maximize its value. When targets have been set, this is called *consistency planning*. It answers the question, can our targets be met within the limits of resources? When targets require resources in excess of the estimated constraints, there is a gap of the kind characteristic of the 'two-gap' models discussed above. When planners try to achieve a maximum value for the objective function, this is called *optimality planning*, for which programming models are used. Part IV discusses both consistency and optimality models, and its two cases (Cases 6 and 7) give students a chance to apply them to industrial and educational planning[18].

Although this theoretically correct sequence has been advocated by most writers on economic planning, there is increasing skepticism that it is workable within any political decision-making process. The politicians who are responsible for government policies seldom are willing to specify their goals precisely enough for the purposes of economic planners. Moreover, they really need some of the results of planning, namely the trade-offs between achieving some goals at the expense of others, in order to make intelligent choices about goal priorities. Finally, it often turns out that the constraints and available investments so limit the choices that long debates about goal priorities in advance of planning work would not be productive. To overcome these problems with the traditional planning sequence, it may be advisable for planners not to assume that goals and priorities are determined, but to produce a set of alternative plans or strategies, each designed to emphasize a different goal or set of goals. For example, one strategy might maximize growth while a second is designed to redistribute income to rural areas. From these alternative strategies, political decision-makers can see precisely what the trade-offs are among achievement of competing goals and then can decide not only what goals to emphasize, but at the same time what activities to undertake to achieve those goals (Loucks, 1975; Roemer, 1976). Case 6 provides an opportunity to plan alternative strategies for industry.

The nature of the political process raises still more fundamental doubts about the efficacy of medium- to long-range economic planning. Killick (1976) suggests a reorientation of economic planning to suit the realities of political decision-making. He points out that economists' planning models deal in discrete, long-term periods and attempt to solve purely economic problems. In contrast, political leaders must continually make decisions, usually are forced to concentrate on short-term issues, and must satisfy political constraints that often lead to apparently irrational results when viewed from the economist's perspective. In such a context the relevance of sophisticated planning tools is dubious at best. Economists' most productive role may then be to demonstrate to political leaders that knowledge gained from planning—especially the limitations of resources and the trade-offs among goals—is valuable for short-term decision-making. Eventually planners may be able to insinuate rational economic considerations into the political process. Planning becomes a medium for a dialogue between technicians and politicians in which each can educate the other. Cases 9 and 10 are examples of short-term, partly political problems in which economists have a major contribution to make.

LEVELS OF PLANNING

Every level of government can and ought to use planning to improve the allocation of resources under its control. This holds for central government and each of its sectoral ministries, for regional and local governments, and for public enterprises in every field. At each of these levels, the underlying aims and processes of planning are the same: define goals, identify means, estimate constraints, then choose activities to achieve those goals within the limitations of resources. It is theoretically possible that central planners could undertake these functions for all government agencies and public enterprises. They would have to build a large general equilibrium model, probably of the inter-industry type, with sufficient detail (that is, a large number of minutely defined sectors) so that model solutions could be converted directly into detailed instructions for implementation at all levels of government. Then, once the welfare function has been determined, detailed national planning would be a mechanical process.

Only a few of the advanced socialist countries have even approached this degree of centralization, sophistication and detail. No market-based developing countries have done so, nor would they be advised to attempt it in the foreseeable future. Existing models are not capable of generating reliable results at the needed level of disaggregation. In most LDCs, it would be extremely costly to train sufficient professional staff to operate the most sophisticated of existing models, and costly to divert them from other planning jobs. Much important information about local needs and conditions will never be learned by highly centralized planners. And such plans would probably not be implemented in any case.

A less precise approach to planning is more practical. Under it, the central planners are responsible for helping policy-makers to define the welfare function and for estimating the major resource constraints. Analyses of macroeconomic, balance-of-payments, fiscal, and distributional conditions, of the kind suggested in the cases of Part V, are necessary to carry out this stage of planning. Resource constraints include the government budget, and planners have to allocate a portion of this to each of the ministries, local governments and public enterprises for planning purposes. Under the best practice, not yet widely adopted, central planners would also indicate *shadow prices* at which each of the scarce resources would be valued when appraising development projects. Shadow prices, or opportunity costs, represent the real cost to society of using a factor—land, labor, capital or foreign exchange—in one project instead of another. In other words they measure the effect additional resources will have on the social welfare function. (This concept is explained more fully in Part III on project appraisal.) Partial indicators of goal achievement—value added per unit invested, net foreign exchange saved or earned, employment, etc.—are more commonly suggested to ministries and local governments to measure their proposals.

Each decentralized planning unit then uses the objective function, shadow prices (or partial indicators) and budget, handed down by central planning, to make up its own development plan. It identifies investment projects or more broadly defined programs, evaluates them using shadow prices and the rules of project analysis (see Part III), then selects the projects and programs that best achieve the goals of the welfare function within the limits of the budget. The results are presented to central planners, who may then alter budget allocations if it appears more likely that national goals could be achieved by permitting some units to undertake more projects than originally planned. The contributing units could then be asked to redo their planning under revised budget allocations, although this is seldom done.

If a process of trial-and-error were carried out, then government, with its decentralized planning units, would generate a plan similar to one that might emerge from a large model programmed to maximize the social welfare function, assuming the model had the same information as the various planners. But decentralized planning, even without a second round, has important advantages over centralized planning. Most fundamentally, it involves each of the responsible government agencies in the planning process. These agencies must implement the plan, and it is important that they feel committed to its success. Their participation helps to incorporate local conditions and technical considerations in decisions about the plan. It also has educational value: the planning process is a good model for decision-making in any agency or enterprise and informs planners, politicians and implementers about the constraints and trade-offs in development. Decentralized planning has its costs, especially in the large number of professionals at all levels of government who must be involved. But the benefits of improved planning are likely to justify the cost.

In the past few years, some planners have advocated greater decentralization, to the point of inviting the populace to participate in formulating plans that affect them. Thus villages would be consulted by local government planners about agricultural projects, roads, schools, and health services in their areas. This is the logical extension of the argument that planning requires contributions from those with local knowledge and commitments from those who must implement the results. The process between local government planners and the populace is similar to that between central planners and the other government agencies. To make participation effective, it is important that the view of participants be taken seriously and that proposals be changed to reflect those views. This makes the planning process more open, less controlled and sometimes frustrating to planners whose 'rational' designs may have to be scrapped or changed. But it also brings the benefits of planning to a much wider group and can help ensure the plan's success, especially if a widespread development is an important goal.

The cases in this book deal with planning and policy analysis rather than implementation. Unfortunately, economic planners frequently ignore issues of implementation, although their work means little if plans are not carried out. Decentralized planning avoids the most obvious split between central planners and implementers. Even within agencies, however, planning generally takes place in units divorced from operational activities. This has seemed advantageous, indeed necessary, because the exigencies of daily operations make it difficult to find the time for long-range planning and generate attitudes inimical to planning. But the divorce has costs, in that isolated planners usually have little feel for the barriers to successful implementation of otherwise excellent plans. These barriers are not only technical, but bureaucratic and political as well. The country's managerial and engineering capacity may be inadequate to implement extensive, intricate or technologically complex projects. When new programs imply changes in procedure and control, elements of the civil service may well be opposed to the change and in a position to retard, subvert or prevent it. Similarly, some political interests are inevitably damaged by change and may be in a position to frustrate development plans. In some instances the conflicts are inherent and difficult to avoid, but in others they may be avoided by deft planning, with particular attention to implementation problems. The point is that planning cannot be divorced from implementation and more attention needs to be paid to the link between the two. (See Pressman and Wildavsky, 1974, for a case study of the difficulties of implementing national plans at the local level; Warwick, 1979, discusses political, social and bureaucratic barriers to implementing technically sound plans.)

Notes

1   The organization of this section and several of its propositions owe much to a presentation by Paul Streeten at Boston University in May, 1978, which helped to crystallize the authors' thinking on many of the issues presented.
2   A good source for background on savings mobilization, capital markets and the fiscal system is McKinnon (1973).
3   For a summary and two samples of the vast literature on primary export-led development, see the articles in Meier (1976), pp. 707–723.
4   For an admirable summary of the experience with import substitution, see Bruton (1970); excerpts appear also in Meier (1976), pp. 747–752.
5   See Kindleberger (1962), Chapter 7.
6   The most recent complete treatment of the Korean experience with outward-looking development is by Krueger (1979).
7   For a systematic treatment of education and development, see Blaug (1972).
8   Johnson's article is reprinted in Meier (1976), pp. 787–792.
9   These issues are thoroughly explored in the collection by Chenery et al. (1974). Cline (1975) provides a useful review of the literature.
10   See Cline (1972) for a simulation approach to measuring the effect of income redistribution on saving.
11   Lipton (1976) argues that urban elites pursue policies ensuring continued rural poverty. Recent works incorporating the new emphasis on small-scale agriculture and industry include Johnston and Kilby (1975) and Mellor (1976).

12   This paragraph owes much to Bruton (1978).
13   For a review of the burgeoning literature on employment, see Morawetz (1974).
      Edwards' (1974) collection covers the topic as completely as any single volume and
      his opening article is a comprehensive review of issues. Todaro's (1977) Chapter 8
      provides a brief but good textbook treatment of employment, as do his Chapters 6
      and 7 on population.
14   Much of this section is drawn from seminars given by Arnold Harberger and Paul
      Streeten, at Harvard and Boston Universities, respectively, during 1978.
15   For this reason there is little published and readily available on the subject. For an
      early statement of advocacy and a later collection of introductory articles, see the
      two volumes by the International Labour Office (1977a; 1977b).
16   Thomas (1974) provides an articulate case for the basic industry strategy.
17   For a neoclassical critique of dependency arguments, see Cohen (1973).
18   For fuller explanations of planning techniques, see Hagen (1963), Heal (1973) and
      Waterston (1965).

References

DEVELOPMENT GOALS AND STRATEGIES

BLAUG, M. (1972). *An Introduction to the Economics of Education*. Baltimore, Penguin

BRUTON, H. J. (1970). The Import-Substitution Strategy of Economic Development. *The Pakistan Development Review* **10,** 123–146 (excerpts reprinted in Meier (1976) 747–752)

BRUTON, H. J. (1978). Unemployment Problems and Policies in Less Developed Countries. *American Economic Review   Papers and Proceedings* **68,** 50–55

CHENERY, H. B. and STROUT, A. M. (1966). Foreign Assistance and Economic Development. *American Economic Review* **56,** 679–733

CHENERY, H. B., AHLUWALIA, M. S. *et al.* (1974). *Redistribution with Growth*. London, Oxford University Press

CLINE, W. R. (1972). *Potential Effects of Income Redistribution on Economic Growth: The Latin American Cases*. New York, Praeger

CLINE, W. R. (1975). Distribution and Development: A Survey of Literature. *Journal of Development Economics* **1,** 359–400

COHEN, B. J. (1973). *The Question of Imperialism*. New York, Basic Books

EDWARDS, E. O. (1974). *Employment in Developing Nations*. New York, Columbia University Press

FRANK, A. G. (1972). *Lumpenbourgeoisie: Lumpen Development*. New York, Monthly Review Press

HARBERGER, A. C. (April 1978). On the Use of Distributional Weights in Cost–Benefit Analysis. *Journal of Political Economy* **86-2,** part 2, S87–S120

INTERNATIONAL LABOUR OFFICE (1972). *Employment, Incomes and Equality: A Strategy for Increasing Productive Employment in Kenya*. Geneva (excerpts reprinted in Meier (1976))

INTERNATIONAL LABOUR OFFICE (1977a). *The Basic Needs Approach to Development: Some Issues Regarding Concepts and Methodology*. Geneva

INTERNATIONAL LABOUR OFFICE (1977b). *Employment, Growth and Basic Needs: A One-World Problem*. New York, Praeger

JOHNSON, H. G. (1962). *Money, Trade and Economic Growth*. London, George Allen and Unwin, pp. 152–163

JOHNSTON, B. F. and KILBY, P. (1975). *Agricultural and Structural Transformation*. New York, Oxford University Press

KINDLEBERGER, C. P. (1962). *Foreign Trade and the National Economy*. New Haven, Yale University Press

KRUEGER, A. O. (1979). The Developmental Role of the Foreign Sector and Aid. Harvard East Asian Monograph No. 87. In *Studies in the Modernization of the Republic of Korea, 1945–75*. Cambridge, Harvard University Press for the Council on East Asian Studies

KUZNETS, S. (1963). Quantitative Aspects of the Economic Growth of Nations: VIII. Distribution of Income by Size. *Economic Development and Cultural Change* **11,** 1–80

LEWIS, W. A. (1954). Economic Development with Unlimited Supplies of Labour. *Manchester School* **22,** 139–191

LIPTON, M. (1976). *Why Poor People Stay Poor: Urban Bias in Development*. Cambridge, Harvard University Press

McKINNON, R. I. (1964). Foreign Exchange Constraints in Economic Development. *Economic Journal* **74,** 388–409

McKINNON, R. I. (1973). *Money and Capital in Economic Development*. Washington, D.C., Brookings Institution

MEIER, G. M. (1976). *Leading Issues in Economic Development*, third edn., New York, Oxford University Press

MELLOR, J. W. (1976). *The New Economics of Growth: A Strategy for India and the Developing World*. Ithaca, N.Y.: Cornell University Press

MORAWETZ, D. (1974). Employment Implications of Industrialization in Developing Countries: A Survey. *Economic Journal* **84,** 491–542

MORAWETZ, D. (1978). *Twenty-five Years of Economic Development, 1950 to 1975*. Baltimore, Johns Hopkins University Press

PAPANEK, G. F. (1972). The Effect of Aid and Other Resource Transfers on Savings and Growth in Less Developed Countries. *Economic Journal* **82-327,** 934–950

PREBISCH, R. (1963). *Towards a Dynamic Development Policy for Latin America*. New York, United Nations

RANIS, G. (1973). Industrial Sector Labor Absorption. *Economic Development and Cultural Change* **21,** 387–408

RANIS, G. and FEI, J. C. H. (1961). A Theory of Economic Development. *American Economic Review* **51,** 533–546

THOMAS, C. Y. (1974). *Dependence and Transformation: The Economics of the Transition to Socialism*. New York, Monthly Review Press

TODARO, M. P. (1977). *Economic Development in the Third World*. London, Longman

TURNHAM, D. (1970). *The Employment Problem in Less Developed Countries*. Paris, OECD

UNITED NATIONS (R. Prebisch) (1950). *The Economic Development of Latin America and its Principal Problems*. Lake Success, N.Y.

WELLS, L. T. Jr. (1975). Economic Man and Engineering Man: The Choice of Technology in a Low-Wage Country. In C. P. Timmer *et al.*, *The Choice of Technology in Developing Countries. Some Cautionary Tales*, Harvard Studies in International Affairs No. 32, pp. 69–94. Cambridge, Center for International Affairs

WORLD BANK (1978). *World Development Report 1978*. Washington, D.C.

WORLD BANK (1979). *World Development Report 1979*. Washington, D.C.

PLANNING THEORY AND PRACTICE

HAGEN, E. E. (ed.) (1963). *Planning Economic Development*. Homewood, Ill., Richard D. Irwin

HEAL, G. M. (1973). *The Theory of Economic Planning*. Amsterdam, North Holland

KILLICK, T. (1976). The Possibilities of Development Planning. *Oxford Economic Papers* **28–2,** 161–184

LOUCKS, D. P. (1975). Planning for Multiple Goals. In *Economy-Wide Models and Development Planning* (ed. by C. R. Blitzer *et al.*). London, Oxford University Press

PRESSMAN, J. and WILDAVSKY, A. (1974). *Implementation: How Great Expectations in Washington are Dashed in Oakland*. Berkeley, University of California Press

ROEMER, M. (1976). Planning by 'Revealed Preference': An Improvement upon the Traditional Method. *World Development* **4–9,** 775–783

WARWICK, D. P. (June, 1979). Integrating Planning and Implementation: A Transactions Approach. Development Discussion Paper No. 63. Cambridge, Harvard Institute for International Development

WATERSTON, A. (1965). *Development Planning: Lessons of Experience*. Baltimore, Johns Hopkins University Press

Part II

The Economy of Beracia

A note to the reader

These reports are intended to introduce Beracia and to provide data that will be useful in analyzing the cases in Parts III, IV and V. The reader who expects to work through several of the cases will find it helpful to read these reports first, both to become familiar with the economic and political context of Beracia and to note the kinds of data that are available for later use. A reader who expects to work on only one or two of the cases, however, need not invest much time in studying these reports beforehand. For that purpose, the needed data can be pinpointed by reference to the List of Tables and a cursory look through the relevant reports. In any case, it is not necessary to become thoroughly familiar with the data before analyzing the cases. It would be more efficient to delve into this material in detail only as it becomes necessary to analyze particular cases.

Fact sheet for Beracia

Population (1977): 20.37m
Area: 295 000 square miles (755 000 square kilometers)
Gross national product (1977, at factor cost): US$ 6029m (or $ 296 per capita)
Share of GNP produced by industry: 20%
Income share of the poorest 40 percent (households, 1975): 12%
Exports (fob, 1977): $ 690.6m
Major exports (fob, 1977): copper ($ 243.7m), cotton ($ 126.2m), rice ($ 70.8m), timber ($ 87.5m)
Imports (cif, 1977): $ 825.5m
Reserves (1977): $ 41.9m
Currency: Lepta (Lp)
Official exchange rate: Lp 8.69 per $

Beracia

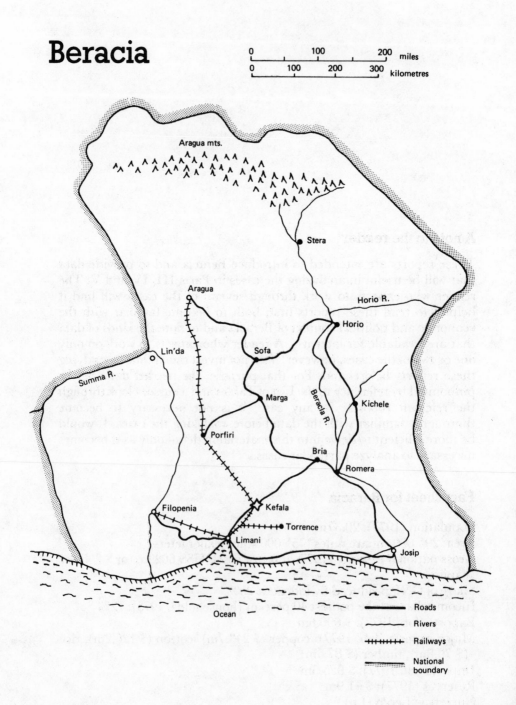

0   100   200   miles
0   100   200   300   kilometres

Aragua mts.

Stera

Horio R.

Aragua

Horio

Lin'da

Sofa

Summa R.

Marga

Beracia R.

Kichele

Porfiri

Bria

Romera

Filopenia

Kefala

Torrence

Limani

Josip

Ocean

——————— Roads
——————— Rivers
++++++++ Railways
——————— National
            boundary

Economic and Political Developments in Beracia, 1956–1977

Ever since Beracia gained independence in 1955, its political and economic fortunes have been so inextricably connected that it is difficult to discuss one without the other. The government that took Beracia into independence had been elected a year before to govern over internal matters, while the colonial power still controlled external affairs. Most members of the government were established political leaders who had led the fight for independence and spent much of their adult lives either in political agitation or in jail; their experience in government was minimal. The Prime Minister, Jamal Negara, was 70 years old at independence and was considered the father of his country. A scholar and politician, he had never been part of a government before he became Prime Minister. Fortunately, the euphoria of independence served to keep civil peace for the first year.

The first economic crisis struck in 1957, when world prices of copper, Beracia's principal export, fell sharply. The mines, which were then privately owned, rejected longstanding union demands for pay increases. Towards the end of 1957 the miners struck and the government was forced to use the army—still commanded by colonial officers— to put down civil unrest and protect the mines from sabotage. Although the miners went back to work in early 1958, world copper prices remained depressed for another year. However, agricultural and industrial output were buoyant and the economy recovered rapidly from the 1957 recession. National income grew substantially for two years and, despite some political squabbles, the government seemed secure. Aid donors, led by the United States, began to tout Beracia as an example of a country launched on the path to self-sustaining growth.

Then, in 1960, Beracia suffered one in a series of shocks to which the country has always been prone: severe drought. The rainy season, which usually begins sometime from mid-December to mid-January, failed completely in early 1960 and grain production was cut in half that

year, compared with 1959. After almost five years in power, the government had become adept in several aspects of managing the economy. It
was able to respond effectively to reduce non-food imports by imposing
strict but allegedly temporary licensing, negotiating substantial
increases in aid, and purchasing large quantities of grain on world
markets. Despite these moves, the effect on incomes was inevitable: per
capita income fell dramatically, as did investment; private consumption also declined. Ironically, the government's improved management
capacity merely shifted the effect of the drought and, in a sense, may
have contributed to the government's downfall.

As 1960 wore on and the full effects of the drought became apparent,
civil unrest became widespread and the Prime Minister was forced to
resign. A scuffle among ministers for the position led to governmental
paralysis. Finally, the defense minister, General Arrides, stepped in
with army support, forced most of the contending ministers to resign,
cancelled elections scheduled in 1961, and ruled as a military dictator
for almost six years. Although the government was technically civilian
and had civilian ministers, there was never any doubt that only the
army's allegiance to Arrides kept it in power.

The period of political stability was used to good effect economically.
Investment was sustained at reasonably high levels; a large new copper
mine was opened in late 1962 and other exports grew steadily during the
early 1960s so that growing imports could be financed; and, as a
consequence, GNP grew at the unprecedented rate of almost 10 percent
a year from 1960 to 1965. Unfortunately, the boom was ended abruptly
by a drought in 1966, less severe than that in 1960, but damaging
enough: food grain production fell by about 20 percent and income per
capita fell for the first time since the 1960 drought. Only a fortuitous
increase in copper prices prevented a serious balance-of-payments
crisis. During the five years of growth, members of the military were
becoming disenchanted with the growing power and independence of
General Arrides. At the first sign of a turn in economic fortunes, the
army intervened again, this time to force Arrides to hold elections in
1967. A panel of officers effectively governed during the interim as a
'Committee of Regents' until elections were held; Arrides became a
figurehead.

The newly elected parliament was rather splintered and it required a
coalition of three parties to form a government. Fortunately, one of the
most popular leaders was given both the finance and planning portfolios and under his stewardship economic development resumed at a
satisfactory pace for the rest of the 1960s, although growth was slower
than during the first half of the decade. The economy exhibited several
strengths that carried it through the decade. The copper exploration
and investments initiated during the Arrides regime, together with
favorable prices, helped propel a relatively diversified set of exports to a
12.5 percent annual growth rate in current prices, enabling imports to

grow by 10 percent a year. Investment in industry continued to grow as the government emphasized import substitution and provided protection to make it profitable. Agriculture recovered rapidly from the drought, demonstrating that Beracian farmers could probably feed the country if only water supplies could be assured.

However, water supplies were not assured and in 1971 the third post-independence drought hit Beracia, producing the familiar set of reactions: grain output dropped by a third, exports fell as imports rose, causing a foreign exchange crisis that was compounded by the world monetary crisis of 1971; and per capita income again fell, this time by 15 percent. The coalition government, which had limped along for five years, seemed impotent to deal with the dual crisis of weather and world trade. Paralyzed by indecision, the government temporized throughout the fall of the year. Finally, in early 1972 the military, in a bloodless coup, dismissed the government and for the first time ruled in its own name. For a time the military held its own in economic management, as high prices for raw materials favored Beracia's exports sufficiently to pay for imports which were becoming very expensive in the face of worldwide inflation. The government opted to replenish reserves after the 1971 debacle. To do so, they restrained outlays on imports, which threatened to get out of hand with world inflation, and thus reduced the real value of goods imported. Hence income growth was restrained and by 1974 per capita income had recovered to a level only slightly above its 1970 peak of Lp 1319 ($ 167 at the 1970 exchange rate).

This tentative and rather fragile recovery was brought to a halt by the oil crisis and price increase of 1974. Beracia is almost totally dependent on imported petroleum for its fuel needs and its fuel import bill nearly quadrupled in one year. The effect on the balance of payments was mitigated somewhat during 1974 by peak copper prices, but in 1975 the copper boom collapsed and Beracia was plunged into a foreign exchange crisis from which it has not emerged. Despite a doubling of official aid, some of it from the OPEC countries, and full use of IMF facilities, Beracian reserves virtually disappeared in three years. Even this abysmal situation would have been far worse had not strict import controls been imposed and the volume of imports reduced, so that in the period 1975–1977 the real value of imports was about 20 percent below the 1972 peak and at the lowest level in a decade. Given the growth of the economy since the mid-1960s, this represented severe import starvation. This scarcity of goods alone would have been inflationary, but Beracia also imported its share of world inflation, so that the GNP deflator, for example, doubled from 1971 to 1977. Not surprisingly under the circumstances, real income per capita declined by 7.5 percent from 1974 to 1977, the first such decline in the absence of a drought in Beracia's short history as an independent nation.

The military government has been widely blamed for this deplorable state. Only a few governments in the developing world have handled the oil crisis smoothly and it may have been too much to ask that Beracia's government overcome such a severe external disequilibrium in three years. However, the government has often seemed paralyzed, its only reactions being to impose more strict controls which, however necessary in the short run, contain no long-run remedies. By late 1976 the military had had enough of governing and announced its intention to hold elections in mid-1977.

Once more a three-party coalition emerged with a majority of seats in Parliament and the new government represented a spectrum from moderate leftists to moderate rightists. The coalition is led by Mahmet Negara, son of the first Prime Minister, himself now 70 and a patriarch whose strongest asset is his family name and a position above the struggles for political power. He ran for election without any benefit of issues or promises. The key members of the cabinet were strong representatives of each of the participating parties: a conservative businessman for Finance; an economist of moderately socialist leanings for Planning; and a former general with close ties to the outgoing military government for Home Affairs.

The new government has made economic development a primary objective, but has also warned of the need for difficult measures to overcome the now chronic balance-of-payments crisis before the growth path of the 1960s can be attained again. The Prime Minister has given the Finance Minister a year to demonstrate that he can solve the structural trade problems facing Beracia. In the interim, the Planning Commission is to develop a set of plans for renewed growth, once the payments problem is on the way to solution, and to institute a series of rolling plans covering five-year periods. For the first of these plans, a longer term perspective of twenty years is to be developed. In briefing the Cabinet on the approach the Commission would take in its planning exercise, the Planning Minister proposed a pragmatic combination of controls and reliance on the market. He favors a gradual move towards socialism, emphasizing nationalization of major industries with majority foreign ownership. He also expressed concern about continued high unemployment levels and the evidently growing gap between the upper 20 percent of the income earners and the lower 40 percent. Even during the period of rapid growth, when all groups seemed to be benefiting, the gap was probably growing. During the stagnation of the past seven years, it seems likely that the average income of the lowest 40 percent has fallen. Despite sporadic attempts since independence, meaningful land reform remains a platitude without a program. Although several governments, including the new one, have pledged to reduce industrial concentration, the industrial families remain strong and one of their number is now Finance Minister. Unions have attained considerable power, but their membership is restricted to the relatively few favored workers in modern industry. The Cabinet accepted the

TABLE R1.1 Growth rates for GDP and major sectors[a] (percent per annum)

Sector	1956–60	1960–65	1965–70	1970–75	1975–77	1956–77
Agriculture, *of which*	−5.4	10.7	5.8	1.0	3.6	3.3
Foodgrains		−15.5	17.6	6.3	1.6	2.8	3.2
Other crops		− 0.7	6.4	10.0	0.3	5.7	4.3
Livestock, forestry and fishing		5.6	3.7	3.1	0.2	4.1	3.1
Mining and quarrying	5.1	8.1	4.6	2.4	1.8	4.7
Manufacturing, *of which*	6.5	11.0	7.4	3.2	3.3	6.7
Large-scale[b]		8.2	13.5	8.4	3.3	3.3	7.8
Small-scale[c]		2.6	2.6	2.6	2.6	2.6	2.6
Construction	0.6	12.9	7.9	2.1	2.8	5.6
Utilities	8.9	7.9	2.2	4.6	4.6	5.6
Wholesale and retail trade	5.5	10.9	7.0	2.1	−0.3	5.7
Transport and communication	2.2	8.1	8.6	−0.7	5.1	4.6
Services, other	7.2	6.8	7.0	2.5	−0.3	5.2
Gross Domestic Product	1.2	9.7	6.5	1.9	2.0	4.7

Notes: [a]Based on constant 1970 price data at factor cost.
[b]Large-scale industries are defined as manufacturing establishments using power and employing 20 or more workers.
[c]The growth of small-scale industries is extrapolated at the population growth rate.
Source: Derived from *Table R1.5.*

priorities of the Planning Minister, but it is clear that income redistribution will depend on income growth if political resistance is to be manageable.

As part of his brief, the Planning Minister reviewed the growth record of Beracia since independence. Gross domestic product has grown at 4.7 percent a year on average, with GDP per capita growing at 2.1

TABLE R1.2 Distribution of Gross Domestic Product by major sectors (percent)

Sector	1956	1960	1965	1970	1975	1977
Agriculture, *of which*	44.5	34.0	35.7	34.5	33.1	34.1
Foodgrains		26.6	14.2	20.2	19.9	19.6	20.0
Other crops		5.4	5.0	4.3	5.1	4.7	5.0
Livestock, forestry and fishing		12.5	14.8	11.2	9.5	8.8	9.1
Mining	6.1	7.1	6.6	6.0	6.2	6.2
Manufacturing, *of which*	9.3	11.4	12.1	12.6	13.5	13.8
Large-scale		6.4	8.3	9.9	10.8	11.6	11.9
Small-scale		2.9	3.1	2.2	1.8	1.9	1.9
Construction	4.1	4.0	4.6	4.9	5.0	4.9
Utilities	1.3	1.7	1.6	1.3	1.5	1.6
Wholesale and retail trade	11.6	13.7	14.5	14.8	15.0	14.4
Transport and communication	5.3	5.5	5.1	5.6	4.9	5.2
Services, other	17.9	22.5	19.8	20.2	20.8	19.9
Gross Domestic Product[a]	100.0	100.0	100.0	100.0	100.0	100.0

Note: [a]Totals may not add to 100.0 percent because of rounding.
Source: Derived from *Table R1.5.*

TABLE R1.3 Economic characteristics, 1956–1975

	1956–60	1961–65	1966–70	1971–75	1956–77
Fixed investment to GDP[a]	0.166	0.161	0.173	0.169	0.164
Incremental capital–output ratio[b]	3.2	3.7	4.4	4.1	4.1
Trade ratio[c]	0.213	0.199	0.185	0.168	0.182
Savings rate[d]	0.177	0.178	0.157	0.179	0.176

Notes: [a] At 1970 market prices.
   [b] One-year lag, i.e. fixed investment summed for years t to $t + 4$ divided by the increase in GDP from year t to $t + 5$.
   [c] Average of exports and imports divided by GDP.
   [d] Investment plus exports less imports as share of GDP, each in constant 1970 market prices.
Source: Derived from *Table R1.7*.

percent, but this of course masks the large swings in income growth which have already been noted: GDP hardly grew at all during the first four years, mainly because of the drought of 1960, then rose by 10 percent annually from 1960 to 1965 and by 6.5 percent for the next five years. From 1970 to 1977, GDP grew by about 2 percent, but per capita income fell by about 0.6 percent a year. The leading sector for the entire period has been large-scale manufacturing, which has grown at 7.8 percent a year, while construction, utilities and trade have grown at rates from 5.6 to 5.7 percent. Agriculture has turned in a creditable performance, growing at 3.3 percent, enough to increase per capita food production, but its problem remains its susceptibility to drought.

TABLE R1.4 Price indices (1970 = 100)

Year	Consumer Price index	Import price index			Domestic wholesale price index	Capital goods price index	Implicit GDP deflator
		Total	Capital goods	Others			
1956	50.5	57.0	58.7	55.9	66.7	63.9	51.7
1957	51.8	60.2	62.9	57.5	68.1	66.3	52.5
1958	54.5	60.1	64.2	58.9	68.3	66.9	54.8
1959	56.3	62.2	65.6	60.0	67.1	66.6	55.5
1960	63.4	63.2	66.1	61.4	71.4	69.5	60.6
1961	60.5	63.7	66.0	62.2	73.6	70.9	56.9
1962	64.3	74.0	75.8	72.8	74.8	75.1	63.5
1963	69.0	83.9	82.8	84.6	74.9	77.7	65.7
1964	72.5	84.5	83.3	85.3	74.7	77.8	69.5
1965	78.0	85.8	84.3	86.8	80.3	81.7	75.3
1966	81.9	87.8	86.9	88.2	84.0	85.0	81.1
1967	86.3	92.1	89.8	93.6	87.4	88.2	85.1
1968	91.1	93.9	92.6	94.8	91.8	92.1	90.9
1969	95.6	96.6	95.6	97.2	95.1	95.3	96.1
1970	100.0	100.0	100.0	100.0	100.0	100.0	100.0
1971	113.9	105.9	103.7	107.3	105.3	104.7	107.0
1972	114.6	122.6	105.8	132.1	116.2	112.5	108.3
1973	123.9	143.6	109.2	163.8	128.4	120.7	123.8
1974	143.7	201.2	125.1	235.3	163.6	144.5	140.8
1975	178.3	216.9	144.9	250.8	180.4	159.7	160.4
1976	203.7	210.7	153.4	237.9	198.9	177.3	186.7
1977	224.1	–	–	–	215.0	185.6	208.6

Source: Beracia Central Bureau of Statistics, *Monthly Statistical Bulletin*, various issues.

TABLE R1.5 Gross Domestic Product by economic activity, 1956–1977 (factor cost, constant 1970 prices, lepta million)

Sector	1956	1957	1958	1959	1960	1961	1962	1963	1964	1965	1966
Agriculture, *of which*	4395.2	4425.7	4815.5	5145.7	3528.3	5019.0	5346.3	5902.4	5815.0	5864.8	5230.0
Foodgrains	*2628.8*	*2658.5*	*2759.0*	*3040.2*	*1475.3*	*2833.8*	*3057.1*	*3403.3*	*3274.1*	*3312.4*	*2642.8*
Other crops	*535.0*	*547.6*	*603.5*	*587.9*	*520.4*	*579.3*	*591.8*	*610.4*	*667.4*	*710.1*	*719.7*
Livestock, fishing and forestry	*1231.4*	*1219.6*	*1453.0*	*1517.6*	*1532.6*	*1605.9*	*1697.4*	*1888.7*	*1873.5*	*1842.3*	*1867.5*
Mining and quarrying	600.1	590.8	566.4	610.5	733.4	792.4	717.2	1093.6	1068.7	1084.4	1042.9
Manufacturing, *of which*	916.6	921.2	1095.0	1308.2	1181.3	1371.9	1434.4	1647.9	1870.2	1987.8	2009.2
Large-scale	*628.6*	*625.6*	*791.8*	*997.1*	*862.0*	*1044.5*	*1098.4*	*1303.1*	*1516.5*	*1625.1*	*1636.7*
Small-scale	*288.0*	*295.6*	*303.2*	*311.1*	*319.3*	*327.4*	*336.0*	*344.8*	*353.7*	*362.7*	*372.5*
Construction	403.2	430.5	496.2	548.2	413.1	565.0	573.7	629.1	675.8	755.7	613.5
Electricity, gas, water and sanitary services	127.8	130.2	157.9	186.9	180.4	188.7	195.6	224.7	267.2	262.8	230.1
Wholesale and retail trade	1150.8	1151.5	1355.8	1582.4	1422.2	1559.6	1656.0	1947.5	2184.5	2382.1	2239.3
Transport, storage and communication	521.1	550.7	575.1	6479	568.3	641.5	652.0	734.0	754.4	837.8	812.9
Other services	1769.9	1812.3	2154.0	2429.6	2336.8	2439.4	2464.5	2801.4	3080.4	3252.7	3159.5
Gross Domestic Product	9884.7	10 012.9	11 215.9	12 459.4	10 363.8	12 577.5	13 039.7	14 980.6	15 716.2	16 428.1	15 337.4
Net factor income from abroad	−233.9	−229.9	−233.5	−234.4	−231.0	−230.8	−274.1	−269.4	−300.3	−270.3	−261.6
Gross National Product	9650.8	9783.0	10 982.4	12 225.0	10 132.8	12 346.7	12 765.6	14 711.2	15 415.9	16 157.8	15 075.8
Population[a] (millions)	11.914	12.236	12.487	12.894	13.191	13.526	13.807	14.194	14.646	15.107	15.542
GNP/capita (Lp)	810	800	880	948	768	913	925	1036	1053	1070	970

Notes: [a] The population estimates are based on an analysis of the 1970 census and the rate of natural increase of 2.6% per annum derived from this analysis was used to derive all population figures. See C.R. de Schell and M. Padua, 'Analysis of Beracian Census Data,' Research Report No. 4, Beracian Institute of Social Studies, 1976.

TABLE R1.5 (*continued*)

Sector	1967	1968	1969	1970	1971	1972	1973	1974	1975	1976	1977[b]
Agriculture, *of which*	5913.2	6445.9	7379.9	7777.0	5986.7	7226.0	7983.9	8243.3	8173.6	8396.6	8764.9
Foodgrains	*3128.1*	*3534.1*	*4337.3*	*4489.2*	*3025.1*	*4141.9*	*4731.1*	*4918.0*	*4851.2*	*4948.4*	*5126.8*
Other crops	*841.4*	*922.6*	*1049.0*	*1143.5*	*1114.3*	*1159.6*	*1201.2*	*1131.6*	*1157.9*	*1200.5*	*1294.3*
Livestock, fishing and forestry	*1943.7*	*1989.2*	*1993.6*	*2144.3*	*1847.3*	*1924.5*	*2051.6*	*2193.7*	*2164.5*	*2247.7*	*2343.8*
Mining and quarrying	1161.5	1285.3	1163.0	1360.3	1306.6	1424.3	1351.4	1443.0	1532.5	1555.2	1588.6
Manufacturing, *of which*	2287.8	2513.1	2706.7	2843.2	2827.6	3172.4	3403.6	3503.9	3331.4	3422.7	3551.1
Large-scale	*1905.8*	*2121.2*	*2304.4*	*2430.6*	*2404.1*	*2738.3*	*2958.0*	*3046.7*	*2862.4*	*2941.3*	*3057.3*
Small scale	*382.0*	*391.9*	*402.3*	*412.6*	*423.5*	*434.1*	*445.6*	*457.2*	*469.0*	*481.4*	*493.8*
Construction	792.0	901.7	1078.4	1104.6	975.0	1111.5	1276.4	1313.9	1224.5	1211.5	1259.7
Electricity, gas, water and sanitary services	264.0	268.6	296.1	293.0	273.0	289.0	350.4	373.2	366.7	381.4	401.5
Wholesale and retail trade	2569.4	2781.7	3087.3	3346.1	2905.6	3451.8	3703.9	3945.6	3716.5	3631.8	3697.4
Transport, storage and communication	967.9	1036.0	1141.9	1264.4	1111.5	1355.9	1501.6	1486.7	1219.7	1265.4	1346.5
Other services	3643.0	3951.9	4292.6	4553.5	4114.6	4610.9	5055.3	5412.4	5141.6	5151.6	5113.5
Gross Domestic Product	17 598.8	19 184.2	21 145.9	22 542.1	19 500.6	22 641.8	24 626.5	25 722.0	24 706.5	25 016.2	25 723.2
Net factor income from abroad	-258.8	-243.0	-240.4	-236.0	-233.5	-255.9	-219.5	-229.2	-238.2	-220.5	-197.2
Gross National Product	17 340.0	18 941.2	20 905.5	22 306.1	19 267.1	22 385.9	24 407.0	25 492.8	24 468.3	24 795.7	25 526.0
Population[a] (millions)	15.892	16.341	16.764	17.044	17.432	17.824	18.386	18.858	19.348	19.851	20.367
GNP/capita (Lp)	1091	1159	1247	1309	1105	1256	1327	1352	1265	1249	1253

b Provisional.
Source: Central Bureau of Statistics. *Monthly Statistical Bulletin* (various issues).

TABLE R1.6 Gross National Product by expenditure, 1956–1977 (current market prices; lepta million)

	1956	1957	1958	1959	1960	1961	1962	1963	1964	1965	1966
Private consumption	3908.3	4136.6	4911.6	5597.3	5686.6	6048.2	6992.1	8 420.5	9 342.8	10 265.6	10 857.0
Government consumption	511.3	539.7	579.0	624.7	651.8	685.9	762.2	909.4	1 084.2	1 253.1	1 402.9
Fixed investment	1089.7	1395.9	1406.4	1431.6	1256.4	1555.1	1698.7	1 907.9	2 063.1	2 788.4	2 349.7
Changes in stocks	+92.1	−149.0	+27.8	+189.2	−199.1	−25.2	+16.8	+56.1	+135.1	+11.8	−158.8
Exports of goods and non-factor services	1269.9	1261.4	1292.9	1405.0	1263.8	1445.3	1707.2	2 068.0	2 264.2	2 502.8	2 888.9
Imports of goods and non-factor services	−1261.7	−1386.5	−1460.3	−1619.3	−1683.6	−1811.2	−2030.9	−2 549.2	−2 787.3	−3 053.4	−3 161.1
Gross Domestic Product at market prices	5609.6	5798.1	6757.4	7628.5	6975.9	7898.1	9146.1	10 812.7	12 102.1	13 768.3	14 178.6
Net factor income from abroad	−121.4	−121.2	−128.6	−131.7	−130.1	−134.3	−174.9	−178.1	−209.2	−204.0	−213.6
Gross National Product at market prices	5488.2	5676.9	6628.8	7496.8	6845.8	7763.8	8971.2	10 634.6	11 892.9	13 564.3	13 965.0
Indirect taxes, net of subsidies	−483.8	−534.0	−604.9	−668.0	−724.4	−788.8	−873.3	−1 025.2	−1 235.2	−1 454.7	−1 693.1
Gross National Product at factor costs	5004.4	5142.9	6023.9	6828.8	6121.4	6975.0	8097.9	9 609.4	10 657.7	12 109.6	12 271.9

TABLE R1.6 (*continued*)

	1967	1968	1969	1970	1971	1972	1973	1974	1975	1976	1977
Private consumption	12 685.1	14 471.2	16 766.9	18 983.1	18 576.0	21 012.5	24 377.7	29 074.7	34 131.5	39 035.0	44 267.1
Government consumption	1 592.8	1 820.7	2 087.2	2 400.6	2 807.6	3 268.6	3 665.5	4 231.8	5 032.0	5 841.5	6 663.2
Fixed investment	3 223.3	3 841.4	4 505.3	4 082.7	4 077.1	4 837.5	5 828.2	7 302.0	7 360.2	8 330.8	9 098.9
Changes in stocks	+3.3	+99.5	+317.6	+418.7	−702.3	−275.4	+308.9	+632.8	−459.3	−747.3	−263.0
Export of goods and non-factor services	3 144.9	3 585.0	3 767.5	4 053.9	3 561.5	4 374.8	6 330.0	7 526.3	5 702.5	6 274.0	6 344.3
Imports of goods and non-factor services	−3 725.4	−4 057.4	−4 514.0	−4 584.1	−4 972.1	−5 676.3	−6 192.2	−8 179.5	−7 956.9	−7 749.0	−7 759.9
Gross Domestic Product at market prices	16 924.0	19 760.4	22 930.5	25 354.9	23 347.8	27 541.7	34 318.1	40 588.1	43 810.0	50 985.0	58 350.6
Net factor income from abroad	−220.6	−221.5	−230.9	−236.0	−237.6	−277.9	−278.7	−322.8	−382.2	−412.9	−406.9
Gross National Product at market prices	16 703.4	19 538.9	22 699.6	25 118.9	23 110.2	27 263.8	34 039.4	40 265.3	43 427.8	50 572.1	57 943.7
Indirect taxes, net of subsidies	−1 984.1	−2 282.1	−2 597.2	−2 812.8	−2 872.9	−3 153.9	−3 843.4	−4 468.5	−4 637.1	−4 663.7	−5 049.7
Gross National Product at factor cost	14 719.3	17 256.8	20 102.4	22 306.1	20 237.3	24 109.9	30 196.0	35 796.8	38 790.7	45 908.4	52 894.0

Source: Government of Beracia, Planning Commission, Economic Research Section.

TABLE R1.7 Gross Domestic Product by expenditure, 1956–1977 (constant 1970 market prices; lepta million)

	1956	1957	1958	1959	1960	1961	1962	1963	1964	1965	1966
Private consumption	7 739.2	7 985.7	9 012.1	9 941.9	8 969.3	9 997.0	10 874.2	12 203.6	12 886.6	13 161.1	13 256.4
Government consumption	1 012.5	1 041.9	1 062.4	1 109.6	1 028.1	1 133.7	1 185.4	1 318.0	1 495.4	1 606.5	1 712.9
Fixed investment	1 705.2	2 105.4	2 102.2	2 149.5	1 807.7	2 193.4	2 261.9	2 455.5	2 651.8	3 413.0	2 764.4
Changes in stocks	+144.1	−224.7	+41.5	+284.1	−286.5	−35.3	+22.4	+72.2	+173.7	+14.4	−186.8
Exports of goods and non-factor services	2 468.9	2 462.9	2 553.6	2 793.2	2 697.7	3 061.5	2 830.5	3 512.7	3 565.2	3 709.2	3 472.1
Imports of goods and non-factor services	−2 227.2	−2 327.4	−2 446.0	−2 632.4	−2 709.9	−2 469.0	−2 776.5	−3 095.6	−3 352.8	−3 611.1	−3 614.3
Gross Domestic Product at constant market prices	10 842.7	11 043.8	12 325.8	13 645.9	11 506.4	13 881.3	14 397.9	16 466.4	17 419.9	18 293.1	17 404.7
Indirect taxes, net of subsidies	−958.0	−1 030.9	−1 109.9	−1 186.5	−1 142.6	−1 303.8	−1 358.2	−1 485.8	−1 703.7	−1 865.0	−2 067.3
Gross Domestic Product at factor cost, constant prices	9 884.7	10 012.9	11 215.9	12 459.4	10 363.8	12 577.5	13 039.7	14 980.6	15 716.2	16 428.1	15 337.4

	1967	1968	1969	1970	1971	1972	1973	1974	1975	1976	1977
Private consumption	14 698.8	15 885.0	17 538.6	18 983.1	16 309.0	18 335.5	19 675.3	20 232.9	19 142.7	19 163.0	19 753.3
Government consumption	1 845.7	1 998.6	2 183.3	2 400.6	2 465.0	2 852.2	2 958.4	2 944.9	2 822.2	2 867.7	2 973.3
Fixed investment	3 654.4	4 170.9	4 727.5	4 082.7	3 894.1	4 300.0	4 828.7	5 053.3	4 608.8	4 698.7	4 501.2
Changes in stocks	+3.7	+108.0	+333.3	+418.7	−470.8	−244.8	+255.9	+437.9	−287.6	−421.5	−141.7
Exports of goods and non-factor services	3 766.8	3 850.0	3 741.1	4 053.9	4 384.4	4 859.7	4 316.3	4 243.5	4 758.5	4 737.9	4 627.0
Imports of goods and non-factor services	−4 071.5	−4 323.3	−4 661.2	−4 584.1	−4 762.4	−4 708.7	−4 306.1	−4 080.9	−3 736.9	−3 740.1	−3 736.6
Gross Domestic Product at constant market prices	19 897.9	21 689.2	23 862.6	25 354.9	21 819.3	25 393.9	27 728.5	28 831.6	27 307.7	27 305.7	27 976.5
Indirect taxes, net of subsidies	−2 299.1	−2 505.0	−2 716.7	−2 812.8	−2 318.7	−2 752.1	−3 102.0	−3 109.6	−2 601.2	−2 289.5	−2 253.3
Gross Domestic Product at factor cost, constant prices	17 598.8	19 184.2	21 145.9	22 542.1	19 500.6	22 641.8	24 626.5	25 722.0	24 706.5	25 016.2	25 723.2

Source: Same as Table R1.6.

Agriculture's share of GDP fell rapidly, from 45 to 36 percent during the first 10 years after independence (the 1960 level of 34 percent is unduly influenced by the drought), but there has been little structural shift since then.

The Planning Minister also analyzed Beracia's growth in terms of some commonly used indicators of effort and efficiency. Its investment rate has been remarkably constant since independence, varying from a low of 16 percent of GDP in the period 1961–1965 to a high of 17 percent from 1966 to 1970. The saving rate has also been steady over the period, averaging about 18 percent for the whole period. This overstates savings performance, however, because the constant-price calculation does not reflect the severe deterioration in Beracia's terms of trade which reduced Beracia's savings in the mid-1970s. Finally, the capital–output ratio has shown a tendency to rise from the efficient level of the late 1950s, 3.2, to levels exceeding 4.0 since 1965. The Minister has emphasized that improved allocation of investment resources could generate considerably more rapid growth without any increase in the savings effort.

Income and Employment

Average income

Gross domestic product (at constant factor cost) grew at 4.7 percent per year from 1956 to 1977, reaching Lp 52.9bn in 1977 (see *Table R1.6*). During that period, population rose from 11.9 to 20.4m, a growth rate of 2.6 percent per year, so that income per capita grew at 1.6 percent per year; GDP per capita was Lp 2600 ($ 300) in 1977. Thus Beracia ranks well below many of the developing countries of southeast and east Asia and Latin America in average income, but also well above the poorest of the third world countries. Its population growth rate, though on the high side, is not extreme and its per capita income growth, while progressing steadily in the 1960s and early 1970s, has slowed down and experienced near stagnation in the mid-1970s.

Income distribution

Although its average per capita income places Beracia in the middle rank of developing countries, a large fraction of the population must be considered among the poorest in the world. According to an unpublished survey of household income, completed in 1975 by the Central Bureau of Statistics, 28 percent of the households surveyed earned less than Lp 3000 a year, a level equivalent to only $ 89 per person per year. The poorest 60 percent of the households all earn less than $ 167 per person per year and account for less than one-quarter of total household income (*Table R2.1*).

Rural households are poorer than their urban counterparts, as *Table R2.2* shows. In 1975, 63 percent of rural households earned less than Lp 6600 in comparison with only 50 percent of urban income earners surveyed; at the other end of the distribution, 15 percent of urban households earned over Lp 13 200, compared to 10 percent of rural

TABLE R2.1 Cumulative distribution of household income shares, 1975

Number of households: percentage share of		Approximate cumulative income share (%)
Bottom	10	1
	20	4
	40	12
	60	24
	80	46
Top	5	27
	10	38

Source: Central Bureau of Statistics, 'Household Income Survey for Beracia, 1975', unpublished.

TABLE R2.2 Distribution of income, rural and urban households, 1975

Income range (Lp/month)	Percentage of households		
	Rural	Urban	All
0– 250	31.4	20.9	28.1
251– 550	31.8	29.2	31.0
551–1100	27.1	34.6	29.5
1101–2300	6.9	10.4	8.0
2301+	2.8	4.9	3.4

Source: As for *Table R2.1.*

households. Inclusion of subsistence production, estimated at about Lp 350 per person per year for rural dwellers (and considerably less for urban residents), would improve the picture for the rural population, but not alter the basic conclusion that the benefits of development have relatively favored city dwellers and have not closed the gap between them and the rural populace.

Wage employment

Of the total population of 17.0m in 1970, the most recent census year, some 6.4m are considered to be economically active and 1.2m of these worked for wages in establishments of five employees or more during that year. Although annual enumerations of wage employees only include firms with more than 10 employees, smaller samples of the other firms, together with the 1970 census data, permit the CBS to make annual estimates of wage employment in all establishments of five or more workers. These are shown in *Table R2.3.*

Wage employment grew by 2.9 percent a year from 1967 to 1976, reaching 1.29m in the latter year. Of these workers, 37 percent were in agriculture, mining, manufacturing, construction and utilities; the balance were in service sectors. The estimated total wage bill is shown

TABLE R2.3 Wage employment by sector (million)

Sector	1967	1970	1974	1975	1976
Agriculture	87	88	89	89	90
Mining	53	52	58	61	63
Manufacturing	135	151	167	168	170
Construction	100	116	136	135	137
Utilities	14	16	20	21	22
Wholesale and retail trade	163	181	222	221	224
Transport, storage and communications	83	100	117	118	120
Other services	366	403	459	463	465
Total	1001	1107	1268	1276	1291

Source: Central Bureau of Statistics. *Wage Employment* (various issues).

TABLE R2.4 Wages and salaries by sector (lepta million)

Sector	1967	1970	1971	1974	1975	1976
Agriculture	200	239	265	342	421	516
Mining	290	365	405	632	821	990
Manufacturing	557	795	879	1147	1 561	1 921
Construction	399	569	564	1008	1 294	1 534
Utilities	59	84	103	162	214	262
Wholesale and retail trade	556	745	769	1237	1 604	1 875
Transportation, storage and communications	346	516	576	823	1 071	1 284
Other services	1303	1856	2047	2844	3 719	4 450
Total	3710	5169	5608	8195	10 705	12 832

Source: As for *Table R2.3.*

TABLE R2.5 Wage trends

Sector	Average wages (Lp/yr)				Index of real wages[a] (1970 = 100)	
	1967	1970	1973	1976	1973	1976
Agriculture	2290	2710	3520	5 730	107	106
Mining	5460	7020	9640	15 720	123	122
Manufacturing	4130	5260	7120	11 300	118	116
Construction	3990	4900	6760	11 200	118	119
Utilities	4130	5260	7180	11 900	121	122
Wholesale and retail trade	3410	4110	5190	8 370	106	104
Transport, storage and communications	4160	5160	6690	10 700	112	109
Other services	3590	4610	5930	9 570	115	113
All wage earners	3720	4680	6150	9 940	115	113
Minimum wage	2400	3000	3840	6 000	111	106

Notes: [a]Deflated by the consumer price index: 1967, 86.3; 1970, 100.0; 1973, 123.9; 1976, 203.7.

in *Table R2.4*. Wage and salary payments rose by 15.0 percent per annum over the nine years, its share of GDP at factor cost rising from 24.8 percent in 1967 to 27.7 percent in 1976. *Table R2.5* shows that average wages rose from Lp 3720 per year in 1967 to Lp 9940 in 1976, an increase of 13 percent in real terms over the period, using the consumer price index as the wage deflator. The largest increases in real wages were in mining, utilities, manufacturing and construction, while agriculture and trade recorded the smallest. The average wage of Lp 9940 in 1976 compared with a minimum wage of Lp 6000 (for full employment) and per capita GDP at market prices of Lp 2662.

The government instituted a minimum wage in 1960, originally applicable only to mining, manufacturing and utilities. At first this statutory minimum was enforced only weakly, if at all. However, over the years its coverage has been extended, its level raised and its enforcement improved. Virtually all firms of 50 or more employees now adhere to the minimum, but compliance is not so extensive for smaller firms, especially those with 10 or fewer employees. The minimum wage has been changed frequently in the past several years, from Lp 200 per month in 1967 to Lp 250 in 1970, Lp 320 in 1973 and Lp 500 in 1976. This legal minimum is applicable to all employers except those in agriculture. Large farms and estates must pay at least Lp 400 a month or Lp 16 daily, although it is difficult to enforce this minimum; the statutory wage does not apply for small farms (10 hectares or less).

Casual and non-wage labor

Of the economically active population, 80 percent does not work regularly for wages, or at least was not so enumerated in the 1970 census. The bulk of this group are self-employed farmers, but most agricultural laborers, shopkeepers, self-employed artisans, and many urban casual workers are included in this group. A Center for Social and Economic Research (CSER) survey of farm workers, completed in 1976, showed that farmers pay a wide range of daily wages, which vary with the time of year, the kind of task and the region*. A wage rate range from Lp 5.0 to Lp 9.5 per day covers 90 percent of the responses to the survey, with a sample median close to Lp 7.0 per day. The sample showed that most casual farm laborers were able to raise some subsistence crops of their own, either by farming their own small plots or by squatting on vacant land.

An earlier project of the CSER surveyed casual urban workers, especially street hawkers and casual construction workers. *Table R2.6*

* G. Elon (1977). Rural Employment in Beracia: A Survey. Occasional Paper No. 14, Center for Social and Economic Research, University of Beracia

summarizes the results of that survey, taken in 1975, when the minimum wage was Lp 400 per month. It is clear from the table that the legal minimum is not effective for large groups of urban workers, even for some who evidently work for establishments, such as construction firms, that are legally covered by the minimum wage legislation.

TABLE R2.6 Distribution of earnings of casual urban workers, July 1975 (%)

Monthly earnings (Lp)	Street hawkers	Casual construction workers	All casual workers
0– 99	25	13	20
100–199	27	19	23
200–299	23	7	17
300–399	12	17	19
400–499	6	18	10
500–599	2	8	3
600+	5	18	8

Source: G. T. Marvin and G. Elon (1976). Earnings of Casual Urban Workers in Kefala. *Beracia Development Journal* **XI**, 81–103.

Unemployment

The concept of unemployment is an elusive one in a country such as Beracia. There has been a steady migration from rural areas into the major cities, as evidenced by the respective population growth rates: urban population has grown at about 5.5 percent per annum during the last 15 years, compared with a rate of 2.1 percent for the rural population. Wage employment has grown at only 2.9 percent a year since employment surveys began in 1967, so there is presumably a growing number of urban residents who do not have wage employment or who are not counted as employed by the surveys. However, many of these people are employed in the non-wage or casual (informal) sector in the cities. The 1970 population census indicated that urban unemployment—defined as those actively seeking work but having no source of income outside the family for the most recent three-month period—was about 9 percent of the economically active urban population. A follow-up survey completed last year showed that the unemployment rate may have risen to as much as 12 percent. However, the survey technique was different and the definition of unemployment was slightly broader than in the census: anyone not currently earning income was considered unemployed.

Income taxation

All wages, salaries, interest, dividends and profits are subject to income tax in Beracia. However, the only effective enforcement is through withholding by the employer, so in practice only those working for larger employers actually pay income tax. The rates are steeply progressive; a system of family allowances exempts up to the first Lp 7500 from income tax. The highest marginal rate is 70 percent, applicable to incomes in excess of Lp 100 000; the average rate at Lp 100 000 would be 37 percent. *Table R2.7* shows the tax rates applicable to a family of four, the maximum for which family allowance can be applied. The rates shown apply to all those who earn income in Beracia, whether residents or not. However, overseas aid agencies, both national and international, and some large investors are able to negotiate exemptions for their foreign personnel.

TABLE R2.7 Income tax rates, family of four

Income range (Lp/yr)	Marginal tax rate	Average rate at top of range
0– 7 500	0	0
7 501– 15 000	10	5
15 001– 25 000	20	11
25 001– 40 000	30	18
40 001– 60 000	40	25
60 001– 80 000	50	32
80 001–100 000	60	37
100 001+	70	

Source: Ministry of Finance (1976). *The Income Tax Code.*

Trade and Payments of Beracia, 1956–1977

Although Beracia's trade ratio has fallen from its post-independence high of 21 percent to around 14 percent over the period from 1975 to 1977, the economy remains an open one, dependent on imports for some foodstuffs, many raw materials and most capital goods. Hence the conditions of world trade and payments profoundly affect Beracian development. In fact, the most urgent task confronting the new government is to break the structural bottlenecks that characterize its international trade.

Exports

Beracia's 'big four' export commodities, which have comprised from two-thirds to four-fifths of total export value, are copper, cotton, rice and wood. Copper exports have more than doubled in volume since independence, as a result of the opening of the Torrence mine in late 1962 and the subsequent exploitation of smaller deposits in the Torrence area. However, there have been no new major discoveries since then and output (and therefore exports) has been relatively stagnant since 1972 (*Table R3.1*). Even during the years of growing copper exports, most of the variation in copper earnings was a consequence of swings in world prices. *Table R3.2* shows the unit values in dollars received by Beracia for its four principal exports. Copper prices rose fairly steadily from 1964 to 1970, but have been subject to wide swings without any cyclical trend during the 1970s. The 30 percent decline in 1971 was followed by a 90 percent increase in unit value from 1971 to 1974, after which prices settled back to 10 percent below their 1970 values. These swings are reflected in copper earnings, shown in *Table R3.3**, which have varied from as low as 16 percent of export earnings (1957) to as high as 46 percent.

---

* These values include the effects of two devaluations: from Lp 6.32 per U.S. dollar to Lp 7.90 per \$ in May 1962 and to Lp 8.69 per \$ in December 1971.

TABLE R3.1 Commodity exports by volume (thousand tons)

	Copper	Cotton	Rice	Timber
1956	75.3	55.4	486.7	419.5
1957	82.1	59.3	453.9	422.3
1958	79.8	62.1	478.1	487.6
1959	85.3	65.8	481.3	512.4
1960	100.1	51.2	217.6	501.5
1961	109.1	63.8	282.3	522.9
1962	92.0	67.7	302.8	564.0
1963	146.1	69.4	299.2	559.8
1964	143.1	71.3	306.9	491.7
1965	146.3	74.5	352.6	615.3
1966	143.1	63.4	297.4	678.2
1967	156.3	65.9	331.7	708.4
1968	172.4	69.4	344.2	645.2
1969	161.3	71.3	399.5	653.6
1970	178.7	76.0	407.0	629.9
1971	199.3	59.3	312.8	604.3
1972	208.5	71.3	398.7	672.5
1973	192.2	75.4	443.0	707.2
1974	207.5	70.3	417.8	713.2
1975	218.4	67.6	440.4	725.6
1976	219.7	75.9	393.9	747.9
1977	215.4	72.3	412.8	730.8

Source: Central Bureau of Statistics.

TABLE R3.2 Unit value indices (in U.S. dollars) for principal exports,
1956–1977 (1970=100)

	Copper	Cotton	Rice	Timber
1956	42.3	103.4	102.5	39.6
1957	30.4	109.5	106.1	40.0
1958	29.5	88.0	109.8	35.6
1959	45.5	78.9	99.1	38.1
1960	43.6	97.8	92.0	43.0
1961	41.9	92.3	95.8	48.5
1962	37.8	88.0	105.1	49.8
1963	41.3	86.2	101.7	62.3
1964	42.7	104.0	97.5	69.1
1965	50.5	99.4	96.5	67.8
1966	77.3	97.9	112.0	71.0
1967	72.8	82.6	132.5	86.2
1968	80.9	107.6	149.1	87.6
1969	99.9	96.6	121.0	91.5
1970	100.0	100.0	100.0	100.0
1971	71.2	113.6	77.9	101.1
1972	73.0	108.2	88.6	87.5
1973	115.8	172.4	182.3	140.4
1974	133.2	179.0	282.3	168.7
1975	80.0	136.9	192.8	137.5
1976	91.0	201.4	146.4	147.4
1977	90.6	229.9	150.4	151.7

Source: Central Bureau of Statistics.

Cotton exports have not shown much growth over the post-independence period, but cotton prices have risen by 130 percent since 1970, so earnings from this crop have more than doubled during the 1970s. In 1977 cotton accounted for almost one-fifth of export earnings. Rice exports are, like cotton, a residual of production after domestic consumption to some extent (although some exports are of a variety not favored by Beracian consumers). Thus consumption has grown more quickly than production and exports have fallen since the years just after independence, with large falls being accounted for by unfavorable growing conditions. Rice export prices have shown swings even greater than copper prices: in 1977 unit values were at the peak level attained during the 1960s, but still only just above half of the 1974 historic high. These gargantuan price swings are reflected in rice export values (*Table R3.3*), which have varied from 9 to 16 percent of total export earnings

TABLE R3.3 Commodity exports by value (fob prices; lepta million)

	Copper	Cotton	Rice	Wood	Other metals	Other agricultural products	Manufactures	Total
1956	251.5	274.9	359.6	82.8	132.1	106.8	5.1	1212.8
1957	194.7	311.6	347.0	84.1	134.6	115.0	10.1	1197.1
1958	185.9	262.3	377.9	86.6	156.1	135.2	18.3	1222.3
1959	305.3	249.0	343.8	97.3	165.6	134.6	32.2	1327.8
1960	344.3	240.5	144.2	107.5	176.8	98.6	73.1	1185.0
1961	350.1	282.5	194.7	126.4	182.0	116.3	111.9	1363.9
1962	343.2	357.2	286.7	175.2	197.6	143.4	118.7	1622.0
1963	595.7	358.7	274.1	217.2	174.6	152.5	203.0	1975.8
1964	602.8	444.8	269.4	211.7	249.6	138.2	247.3	2163.8
1965	729.2	444.0	306.5	259.9	263.9	143.0	243.3	2389.8
1966	1091.8	372.1	300.1	302.1	304.9	113.0	276.5	2760.5
1967	1120.2	326.3	395.8	380.8	317.6	125.6	335.8	3002.1
1968	1373.0	447.9	462.2	352.3	287.6	156.4	354.7	3434.1
1969	1588.7	413.2	435.3	372.9	278.1	160.4	352.3	3600.9
1970	1763.3	455.8	366.6	392.6	292.3	169.8	421.1	3861.5
1971	1399.3	404.1	219.6	380.6	313.8	137.5	503.3	3358.2
1972	1652.4	509.1	350.2	403.7	359.8	196.4	679.6	4151.2
1973	2416.7	857.7	800.3	680.7	346.7	223.3	700.4	6025.8
1974	3000.5	830.2	1168.6	820.8	371.9	301.7	729.1	7222.8
1975	1895.7	610.4	841.5	684.2	321.2	319.7	765.3	5438.0
1976	2170.6	1008.7	571.2	755.4	349.6	341.6	748.9	5946.0
1977	2117.4	1096.7	615.1	760.0	330.9	330.4	751.4	6001.9

Source: Central Bureau of Statistics.

since 1960. Further growth in either rice or cotton exports will have to come either from reduced acreage in other crops, especially wheat, or from heavy investments in irrigation. Finally, both timber export volumes and unit values have grown fairly steadily over the two decades. However, some of the price increase after 1960 may have been caused by the shift in the composition of timber exports from logs to lumber and other wood products. The share of wood exports has risen from under 7 to about 12 percent since independence.

TABLE R3.4 Structure of the value of commodity exports (percent)

	Copper	Cotton	Rice	Wood	Other metals	Other agricultural products	Manufactures	Total
1956	20.7	22.6	29.7	6.8	10.9	8.8	0.4	100.0
1960	29.1	20.3	12.2	9.1	14.9	8.3	6.1	100.0
1965	30.5	18.6	12.8	10.9	11.0	6.0	10.2	100.0
1970	45.7	11.8	9.5	10.2	7.6	4.4	10.9	100.0
1975	34.9	11.2	15.5	12.6	5.9	5.9	14.1	100.0
1977	35.3	18.3	10.2	12.7	5.5	5.5	12.5	100.0

Source: Derived from *Table R3.3*.

Even considering just the 'big four', Beracian exports are more diversified than those of many primary product exporters. In addition, the growth of non-traditional exports has been an encouraging feature of Beracian development. Other metals and agricultural products have yielded increasing revenues, although rising prices have probably accounted for all of this growth. The most promising feature, however, has been the sustained growth of manufactured exports. These have been encouraged by the government's bonus voucher scheme, discussed below, and have grown apace with industrial production. Manufactured exports now exceed 12 percent of the total.

As a result of these various trends and fluctuations, export earnings grew satisfactorily from independence until the peak in 1974, registering a 10 percent per annum rate of growth on average. However, much of the growth since 1970 was a result of the sharp rise in raw material prices and when these collapsed with the worldwide recession of 1975/76, Beracian export earnings fell with them. Earnings in 1977 were below the level achieved in 1972. Moreover, overall export earnings reflect the economy's susceptibility to drought, which affects cotton and rice production to the extent that export earnings fell substantially in both 1960 and 1971, the two worst drought years.

The government continues to levy *export duties* on a number of commodities. Copper is subject to a 15 percent tax. Windfall profits arising from higher world market prices have been partially captured by a surcharge of 25 percent on all revenues in excess of $900 per metric ton (tonne) and particularly by the corporate income tax. Other metals are taxed at 10 percent. Raw cotton exports were subject to a 5 percent export duty rate up to 1962, when an effort was made to divert some potential raw cotton exports to the growing domestic textile mills. The duty on raw cotton reached a peak of 20 percent just after the 1971 devaluation, but has been 10 percent since 1973. Timber, the only other commodity taxed, bears a 15 percent export duty. Duty collections are shown in *Table R3.5*.

Considerable credit for the growth in exports of manufactures can be traced to the *export bonus voucher scheme*, introduced in 1965. At that time,

TABLE R3.5 Export duties[a] (lepta million)

	Copper		Cotton	Wood	Other metals	Total
	Duty	Surcharge				
1956	35.4	–	13.0	11.8	18.2	78.4
1960	49.7	–	13.2	14.9	23.1	100.9
1965	106.4	–	64.6	36.9	24.4	232.3
1970	254.5	86.1	64.4	53.9	26.2	485.1
1973	347.5	196.7	82.8	109.1	31.7	767.8
1975	274.4	51.8	58.3	98.2	29.4	512.1
1977	303.4	98.9	99.7	109.2	31.6	642.8

Note: [a]Net of refunds.
Source: Ministry of Finance, *Economic Survey 1977*.

manufactured exports received a bonus voucher equivalent to 25 percent of the export receipts, a rate subsequently raised to 35 percent. The exporter can then sell the voucher to importers (or use it himself). Vouchers entitle importers to an allocation of foreign exchange equal to the face value of the voucher, although the foreign exchange must also be paid for. Because import controls have kept foreign exchange allocations below demand, bonus vouchers have always carried a substantial premium, running from 25 to 100 percent of the face value, depending on the scarcity of imports. Thus, for example, an exporter who sells Lp 100 of manufactures receives a voucher entitling the holder to purchase Lp 35 of foreign exchange. The exporter might sell the voucher for, say, Lp 50, thus earning a total of Lp 150 for Lp 100 of exports.

In 1966, the government extended the bonus voucher scheme to cover high quality (long grain) rice exports, which constitute about 95 percent of total rice exports. The decision created a certain amount of concern, since it was feared that growing rice exports would come at the expense of domestic consumption and might lead to greater imports*. Rice exports did rise sharply from 1966 to 1970 under the stimulus of a 15 percent bonus voucher, but rice production rose sufficiently to prevent an increase in rice imports. A considerable quantity of the new rice exports were of a variety not generally consumed in Beracia.

In late 1974 the voucher rates were further revised. Most manufactures continue to receive the 35 percent rate, but a few items, constituting 10 percent of manufactured exports, now receive a rate of 45 percent. Because of the sharp rise in the world price, the rate on rice exports was cut to 7.5 percent, substantially reducing the quantity of bonus vouchers in circulation and causing the premium to rise.

* The problem was further compounded by the fact that most food grain imports, including some quantities of rice, are purchased under U.S. PL 480 agreements which prohibit exports by the recipient country of 'like' commodities. Beracia has argued in the past that long grain rice is a distinct product, with a low substitution elasticity against regular rice or wheat, and that the demand for long grain rice, largely from the Middle East, is not in competition with demand for other food grains. This question is likely to arise again when Beracia develops her potential to export regular quality rice.

TABLE R3.6 Exports under bonus voucher (fob, current prices, lepta million)

	Bonus voucher exports (1)	Total exports (2)	Bonus voucher exports as a percent of total exports (3 = 1 ÷ 2)
1965	272	2390	11.4
1966	479	2761	17.3
1967	598	3002	19.9
1968	683	3434	19.9
1969	660	3601	18.3
1970	699	3862	18.1
1971	623	3358	18.6
1972	909	4151	21.9
1973	1409	6025	23.4
1974	1748	7223	24.2
1975	1511	5438	27.8
1976	1245	5946	20.9
1977	1351	6002	22.5

Source: *Bulletin of the State Bank of Beracia* (various issues).

Imports

Beracia's dependence on imports is indicated by the ratio of import expenditures (cif) to GDP at market prices, which has averaged 17 percent in constant prices since independence. The sharp drop to 13 percent from 1975 to 1977 is evidence more of export stagnation and the resulting stringent import controls than of import substitution. Nevertheless, within this high total, there has been a structural shift in imports which indicates some measure of import substitution. In the classic pattern of early import substitution, Beracia has reduced its share of import expenditures on consumer goods from 40 percent at independence to only 13 percent in 1977 and the decline has been fairly steady if drought years are excluded (*Tables R3.7* and *R3.8*). Concomitantly, expenditures on intermediate goods and raw materials have risen from 29 to 53 percent of import outlays since independence, as growing import-substituting (and some export) industries have remained dependent on imported materials. The share of capital goods imports has been about one-third over the entire period.

Although import price indices are not very reliable, data already presented (*Table R1.4*) shows almost a quadrupling of average import prices since 1956 and a doubling since 1970, with the increase less pronounced for capital goods and more so for other imports. The real value of imports, calculated from these price indices and the import values of *Table R3.7,* grew by about 4 percent a year over the first 20 years of independence, but has fallen by 22 percent over the period from 1971 to 1977, as import controls became increasingly stringent. The

TABLE R3.7 Structure of commodity imports (current prices; lepta million)

	Consumer goods					Raw materials and intermediate goods				Capital goods	Total
	Food grains	Other essentials	Semi-luxuries	Luxuries	Total	For capital goods	For consumer goods	Fuels	Total		
1956	270.1	119.4	25.7	34.6	449.8	75.0	157.4	80.2	312.6	353.7	1116.1
1957	277.0	125.8	30.2	41.1	474.1	76.8	172.2	86.1	335.1	400.5	1209.7
1958	283.1	117.3	35.0	52.6	488.0	117.7	190.5	107.1	415.3	444.8	1348.0
1959	270.1	95.9	40.7	59.5	466.2	141.9	248.0	121.3	511.2	475.0	1452.4
1960	619.1	70.0	22.2	34.7	746.0	114.9	170.5	108.4	393.8	365.8	1505.6
1961	343.9	86.4	60.3	88.0	578.6	158.2	247.9	139.9	546.0	505.3	1629.9
1962	369.1	106.4	28.0	44.5	548.0	200.8	325.7	153.5	680.0	575.7	1803.7
1963	397.1	145.9	34.2	57.0	634.2	276.1	438.2	183.7	898.0	747.8	2280.0
1964	428.2	128.5	42.0	64.2	662.9	289.7	470.8	210.0	970.5	837.8	2471.2
1965	446.9	118.1	48.3	75.1	688.4	305.0	505.6	239.9	1050.5	944.7	2683.6
1966	577.6	100.6	34.1	58.4	770.7	315.1	535.5	247.1	1097.9	835.5	2704.1
1967	488.7	178.6	61.2	83.6	812.1	384.3	659.2	280.5	1324.0	1100.5	3236.6
1968	489.5	165.5	67.4	85.9	808.3	412.4	714.8	305.7	1432.9	1305.9	3547.1
1969	474.0	164.6	77.6	91.4	807.6	467.3	813.9	339.5	1620.7	1554.1	3982.4
1970	467.3	132.9	80.9	97.8	778.9	489.3	797.6	356.4	1643.3	1572.1	3994.3
1971	901.5	100.0	68.1	86.3	1155.9	494.7	867.3	374.0	1736.0	1552.2	4444.1
1972	638.6	171.0	53.5	69.7	932.8	758.7	1182.2	378.1	2319.0	1811.6	5063.4
1973	851.3	142.4	59.4	76.2	1129.3	800.1	1224.5	455.0	2479.6	2127.0	5735.9
1974	1116.8	156.9	64.5	86.4	1424.6	925.7	1347.4	1615.3	3888.4	2378.9	7691.9
1975	939.3	181.3	65.4	65.9	1251.9	852.9	1384.6	1547.4	3784.9	2414.9	7451.7
1976	794.4	144.7	75.9	71.9	1086.9	811.4	1291.7	1495.6	3598.7	2500.7	7186.3
1977	612.2	152.6	88.4	82.3	935.5	856.8	1354.9	1554.5	3766.2	2471.8	7173.5

Source: Government of Beracia, unpublished Planning Commission data.

TABLE R3.8 Structure of commodity imports (percent)

	Consumer goods		Raw materials and intermediate goods			Capital goods	Total
	Food grains	Others	For capital goods	For consumer goods	Fuels		
1956	24.2	16.1	6.7	14.1	7.2	31.7	100.0
1960	41.1	8.4	7.6	11.3	7.2	24.3	100.0
1965	16.7	9.0	11.4	18.8	8.9	35.2	100.0
1970	11.7	7.8	12.2	20.0	8.9	39.4	100.0
1975	12.6	4.2	11.4	18.6	20.8	32.4	100.0
1977	8.5	4.5	11.9	18.9	21.7	34.5	100.0

stagnation of GNP from 1972 to 1977 is partly a consequence of this drop in imports.

To restrain the always strong demand for imports, successive governments have used the full range of policy instruments: tariffs, controls, voucher schemes and exchange rate adjustments. *Import duties* follow the pattern familiar in import-substitution regimes: very high on non-food consumer goods (125–250 percent) and moderate on raw materials (15–25 percent) and on capital goods (12.5 percent), so that effective protection is quite high for most commodities produced in Beracia. Duties were eliminated on fuels after the oil price increase in 1974 and have been lowered to only 5 percent on foods (*Table R3.9*). In addition, most imports are subject to sales or excise taxes of from 10 to 15 percent. Collections of all these taxes are lower than nominal rates because of exemptions and administrative irregularities.

Import controls were first instituted by the Negara government in 1960 and have been a feature of the exchange regime ever since, although with varying degree of severity. During the foreign exchange crises following the three droughts, when food grain imports rose and agricultural exports fell, and the oil price increase of 1974, import duties were adjusted to discourage demand. However, the government felt constrained not to raise manufacturing costs by substantially increasing

TABLE R3.9 Indicative nominal import duty rates (percent)

	1956	1960	1965	1970	1973	1975	1977
Capital goods	10	12.5	12.5	12.5	12.5	12.5	12.5
Fuel	50	50	16	16	16	0	0
Raw materials for capital goods	10	15	10	15	15	15	15
Raw materials for consumer goods	10	20	20	20	25	25	25
Food	10	10	14	14	10	5	5
Other essentials	52.5	67.5	82.5	97.5	97.5	125	125
Semi-luxuries	52.5	120	135	142.5	142.5	175	175
Luxuries	75	127.5	150	150	202.5	250	250

Source: Customs and Excise Department, *Manual of Custom Duties and Export Taxes in Beracia* (revised), September 1979.

duties on producer goods. By 1965 consumer goods other than food grains, which bear the highest duty rates, constituted less than 10 percent of imports and now constitute less than 5 percent, so there is not much that can be done to alleviate exchange shortages by cutting back on these items. Faced with the need to cut back producer goods, but unwilling to raise duties substantially above present levels, the government has depended mainly on controls to restrain import demand, especially during crises. There was a period of liberalization during the last half of the 1960s, when the bonus voucher scheme was introduced (see below) and export growth was encouraging. The 1971 drought necessitated a reversion to controls, but these were relaxed again after the devaluation in December 1971 and during the export price boom of 1973/74. Since the oil price rise, however, stringent controls have remained in force.

A study undertaken in 1976 by the research staff of the Central Bank of Beracia tried to measure the scarcity premium on imports created by licensing. After allowing for 'normal' mark-ups and distribution costs, the study found that for consumer goods other than food grains, which are all subject to licensing, the premium is about 45 percent; for those

TABLE R3.10 Import duty collections by type of commodity (percent in cif value)

Type of good	1956	1960	1965	1970	1975
Consumer goods					
Food grains	7.9	7.8	11.1	12.3	4.7
Essentials	44.0	54.2	63.8	99.6	119.4
Others	50.2	97.4	106.7	168.7	207.6
Raw materials					
for consumer goods	8.2	14.7	16.4	15.2	21.6
for capital goods	7.7	11.6	7.6	14.8	13.7
Capital goods	8.1	10.6	9.2	12.1	11.7
Fuels	42.0	34.0	13.0[a]	15.1	–

Note: [a]Subsequent to the establishment of a domestic refinery most import tariffs on fuel were changed to excise taxes and are no longer shown as import duties.
Source: M. Gralides (1976), 'The Structure of Indirect Taxes in Beracia,' *Beracia Development Journal* **XI**, 42–54.

raw materials and intermediate goods that are imported under license (about 60 percent), the premium averages about 40 percent; and for those capital goods that are under license (about 80 percent), the premium is about 50 percent. Commodities not under import controls—food grains, raw materials for industries producing 'essential' consumer goods such as textiles and footwear, and capital goods for replacement or maintenance—are imported under 'Open General License', a document that requires registration with the licensing authority in the Ministry of Trade, but is automatically granted for specified classes of commodity. Goods imported under bonus voucher also receive licenses automatically, but are included in the percentages of goods under license given above. However, the Bank study showed that bonus voucher imports carry virtually no premium resulting from licensing, since the voucher premium is large enough to absorb the licensing premium.

After three years of stringent controls, the system has begun to crumble. Importers are learning how to get around controls by various administrative means; smuggling has been on the rise; and rumors of bribery have become more insistent in recent months. The new government is split on how to approach controls. The Planning Minister would like to improve them, but has recognized the difficulties in doing so. The Finance Minister prefers to eliminate them and to use price incentives of various kinds to control demand. The Trade Minister would like to keep them, partly because they are the only real influence his ministry has on trade policy, but he is weak politically and not likely to be a factor in the final decision.

TABLE R3.11 Imports under bonus voucher (cif prices; lepta million)

	Bonus voucher imports (1)	Total imports (2)	Bonus voucher imports as a percent of total imports (3 = 1 ÷ 2)	Voucher price to importers (Lp)[a]
1965	58	2684	2.2	–
1966	109	2704	4.0	175
1967	175	3237	5.4	133
1968	190	3547	5.4	139
1969	180	3982	4.5	158
1970	205	3994	5.1	155
1971	190	4444	4.3	171
1972	275	5063	5.4	134
1973	360	5736	6.3	124
1974	403	7692	5.2	127
1975	317	7452	4.3	159
1976	314	7186	4.4	198
1977	327	7174	4.6	213

Note: [a]Price an importer pays to an exporter for a voucher that entitles him to purchase (and pay for) Lp 100 of foreign exchange.
Source: State Bank of Beracia, *Bulletin of the State Bank of Beracia*, various issues.

In 1965, as part of a trade liberalization program, the Arrides government introduced the *export bonus voucher scheme,* which was discussed above (pp. 52–53). The premium at which vouchers have sold on the market has varied widely depending on the scarcity of imports. The lowest premium, 24–27 percent over the face value, occurred during the 1973/74 export boom; the highest, from 71 to 113 percent, have occurred in drought years and during the recent foreign exchange crisis (*Table R3.11*). The premium was at an all-time high during 1977 when the new government took office. The bonus voucher represents a very high exchange rate for imports. For example, with the premium at 50 percent, the effective exchange rate for imports purchased under a

TABLE R3.12 Commodity composition of bonus voucher imports (percent)

	1967	1970	1975	1977
Consumer goods	31.4	50.4	47.9	46.3
Raw materials	35.2	34.7	35.1	34.8
Capital goods total	33.4	14.9	17.0	18.9

Source: As for *Table R3.11.*

voucher is Lp 21.73 per dollar, in comparison with the official rate of Lp 8.69*.

Exchange rate adjustments have also been employed to stem import demand (and to encourage exports). The first devaluation, by 25 percent to a rate of Lp 7.90 per dollar, was undertaken by the Arrides government in May, 1962, in an attempt to surmount the lingering effects of the drought 18 months earlier. On that occasion, some tariffs were reduced (only temporarily, as it turned out) and controls were eased. Exports rose substantially over the next two years, but the opening of the Torrence copper mine and an increase in the world price of cotton were principally responsible. Nevertheless, exports of wood and manufactures did seem to respond. Imports rose by 24 percent in 1963, which may not have been surprising in the wake of reduced controls, but by only 8 percent the next year. In 1971, following the drought and in the wake of the United States devaluation and the Smithsonian currency agreement, Beracia again devalued against the dollar, this time by 10 percent to Lp 8.69 per dollar. Again, exports boomed a year after the devaluation, but this time price increases clearly played the major role. Imports also grew strongly, once more responding more to reduced controls than to the higher exchange rate.

Balance of payments

The result of the trade trends and policy measures just discussed is clearly shown in *Table R3.13*. Through good times and bad, with very few exceptions, Beracia's demand for imports has exceeded its ability to export. Generally the trade deficit has been 3 percent of GDP or considerably less, even in the past two years. However, in the crisis years—1960, 1971 and 1975—the deficit reached 4.5 percent of GDP.

---

* Consider the following example. A manufacturer exports goods valued at Lp 100 for which he receives vouchers with a face value of Lp 35. The vouchers can be sold at a premium of, say, 50 percent, or for Lp 52.50. The exporter has thus earned Lp 152.50 for his exports. An importer who purchased the vouchers for Lp 52.50 can now buy Lp 35.00 of foreign exchange at a total cost of Lp 87.50 (= Lp 35.00 + Lp 52.50), a premium of 150 percent. To achieve the same import price without vouchers, the exchange rate would have to be devalued by 150 percent, from Lp 8.69 to Lp 21.73 per dollar.

TABLE R3.13 Commodity imports and exports (current prices; lepta million)

Year (1)	Imports (cif) (2)	Exports (fob) (3)	Surplus (+)/ deficit (−) (4 = 3 − 2)
1956	1116.1	1212.8	+96.7
1957	1209.7	1197.1	−12.6
1958	1348.0	1222.3	−125.7
1959	1452.4	1327.8	−124.6
1960	1505.6	1185.0	−320.6
1961	1629.9	1363.9	−266.0
1962	1803.7	1622.0	−181.7
1963	2280.0	1975.8	−304.2
1964	2471.2	2163.8	−307.4
1965	2683.6	2389.8	−293.8
1966	2704.1	2760.5	+56.4
1967	3236.6	3002.1	−234.5
1968	3547.1	3434.1	−113.0
1969	3982.4	3600.9	−381.5
1970	3994.3	3861.5	−132.8
1971	4444.1	3358.2	−1085.9
1972	5063.4	4151.2	−912.2
1973	5735.9	6025.8	+289.9
1974	7691.9	7222.8	−469.1
1975	7451.7	5438.0	−2013.7
1976	7186.3	5946.0	−1240.3
1977	7173.5	6001.9	−1171.6

Source: Government of Beracia, Central Bureau of Statistics.

Beracia, despite its relatively diversified export pattern and rapidly growing non-traditional exports, remains a chronic deficit country. Service payments, including interest, profit remittances and salaries paid to foreign workers, exceed Beracia's earnings of similar items, so that the balance on goods and services is more adverse than for merchandise trade alone. Beracia's net transfers, which are positive, are not large enough to change the picture: the current account balance has been negative in every year since independence except one, 1973 (*Table R3.14*).

Fortunately, Beracia has been able to attract enough foreign capital to cover these current account deficits in most years until recently. The country has remained attractive to investors, because of profitable opportunities in either mining or import-substituting industry. It has even been able to borrow small amounts in European and American credit markets. As a neutral in foreign affairs, Beracia has also been successful in attracting aid. In times of falling real values of concessionary aid, Beracia has been able to maintain an inflow equivalent to about 2 percent of GNP in most years since independence, with the notable exception of 1977. And in recent years it has begun to use trade credits increasingly to finance its trade deficit, primarily by stretching out payments due to foreign suppliers.

TABLE R3.14 Beracia balance of payments (current prices; lepta million)

Item	1956 Cr	1956 Dr	1957 Cr	1957 Dr	1958 Cr	1958 Dr	1959 Cr	1959 Dr	1960 Cr	1960 Dr	1961 Cr	1961 Dr
Goods and services												
Merchandise (fob)	1212.8	1011.0	1197.1	1102.4	1222.3	1222.8	1327.8	1313.5	1185.0	1372.9	1363.9	1478.0
Freight and insurance	3.4	105.1	4.1	107.3	4.6	125.2	4.9	138.8	4.6	132.7	5.0	151.9
Investment income	14.1	135.8	17.2	138.4	18.4	146.4	18.7	150.5	18.5	148.6	19.3	153.6
Other services	53.7	145.6	60.2	176.8	65.4	112.3	72.3	166.9	74.2	178.0	76.4	181.3
Total goods and services	1284.0	1397.5	1278.6	1524.9	1310.7	1606.7	1423.7	1769.7	1282.3	1832.2	1464.6	1964.8
Net goods and services	–	113.5	–	246.3	–	296.0	–	346.0	–	549.9	–	500.2
Transfer payments												
Private transfer (net)	77.0	–	79.6	–	80.7	–	80.7	–	71.9	–	72.5	–
Official transfers (net)	7.6	–	12.6	–	6.3	–	3.2	–	53.4	–	4.4	–
Net transfer payments	84.6	–	92.2	–	88.3	–	83.9	–	125.2	–	76.9	–
Balance on current account	–	28.9	–	154.1	–	207.7	–	262.1	–	424.6	–	423.3
Capital account												
Direct investment (net)	44.5	–	58.6	–	65.6	–	61.9	–	57.5	–	106.3	–
Commercial loans (net)	21.8	–	26.7	–	29.4	–	30.8	–	24.6	–	31.5	–
Central government (net)	42.6	–	70.8	–	90.1	–	135.8	–	224.8	–	307.3	–
Trade credits and arrears (net)	–	–	–	–	–	–	5.3	–	8.4	–	10.3	–
Net non-monetary	108.9	–	156.1	–	185.1	–	233.8	–	315.3	–	455.4	–
IMF (net)	–	–	–	–	–	–	–	–	6.2	–	4.3	–
Central Bank (net)	–	80.9	–	3.4	22.0	–	27.4	–	105.6	–	–	35.8
Net monetary sector	–	80.9	–	3.4	22.0	–	27.4	–	111.8	–	–	31.5
Net capital account	28.0	–	152.7	–	207.1	–	261.2	–	427.1	–	423.9	–
Errors and omissions	0.9	–	1.4	–	0.6	–	0.9	–	–	2.5	–	0.6

TABLE R3.14 (continued)

Item	1962 Cr	1962 Dr	1963 Cr	1963 Dr	1964 Cr	1964 Dr	1965 Cr	1965 Dr	1966 Cr	1966 Dr	1967 Cr	1967 Dr
Good and services												
1. Merchandise (fob)	1622.0	1629.2	1975.8	2083.6	2163.8	2249.9	2389.8	2434.7	2760.5	2452.6	3002.1	2935.8
2. Freight and insurance	5.6	174.5	6.0	196.4	6.3	221.3	6.6	248.9	7.0	251.5	8.2	300.8
3. Investment income	20.4	195.3	24.0	202.1	27.0	236.2	36.4	240.4	42.7	256.3	51.3	271.9
4. Other services	79.6	227.2	86.2	269.2	94.1	316.1	106.4	369.8	121.4	457.0	134.6	488.8
Total goods and services	1727.6	2226.2	2092.0	2751.3	2291.2	3023.5	2539.2	3293.8	2931.6	3417.4	3196.2	3997.3
Net goods and services	—	498.6	—	659.3	—	732.3	—	754.6	—	485.8	—	801.1
Transfer payments												
1. Private transfers (net)	116.4	—	130.3	—	148.7	—	146.3	—	159.5	—	168.7	—
2. Official transfers (net)	3.5	—	4.7	—	2.4	—	15.0	—	18.2	—	23.7	—
Net transfer payments	119.9	—	135.0	—	151.1	—	161.3	—	177.7	—	192.4	—
Balance on current account	—	378.7	—	524.3	—	581.2	—	593.3	—	308.1	—	608.7
Capital account												
1. Direct investment (net)	83.4	—	95.8	—	85.6	—	123.6	—	85.3	—	121.0	—
2. Commercial loans (net)	37.8	—	68.2	—	62.9	—	72.3	—	39.0	—	64.1	—
3. Central government (net)	210.8	—	300.6	—	314.7	—	369.1	—	390.2	—	406.7	—
4. Trade credits and arrears (net)	—	2.5	—	4.3	2.5	—	5.7	—	—	10.4	—	8.2
Net non-monetary	329.5	—	460.3	—	465.7	—	570.7	—	504.1	—	583.6	—
5. IMF (net)	10.4	—	—	—	—	7.4	—	7.7	—	7.9	—	—
6. Central Bank (net)	39.7	—	63.2	—	124.5	—	24.5	—	—	179.3	27.3	—
Net monetary sector	50.1	—	63.2	—	117.1	—	16.8	—	—	187.2	27.3	—
Net capital account	379.6	—	523.5	—	582.8	—	587.5	—	316.9	—	610.9	—
7. Errors and omissions	—	0.9	0.8	—	—	1.6	5.8	—	—	8.8	—	2.2

TABLE R3.14 (continued)

Item	1968 Cr	1968 Dr	1969 Cr	1969 Dr	1970 Cr	1970 Dr	1971 Cr	1971 Dr	1972 Cr	1972 Dr
Good and services										
1. Merchandise (fob)	3434.1	3226.0	3600.9	3614.7	3861.5	3635.0	3358.2	4036.4	4151.2	4605.2
2. Freight and insurance	8.6	321.1	9.9	367.7	10.7	359.3	11.0	407.7	12.8	458.2
3. Investment income	67.8	289.3	79.2	310.1	86.3	322.3	98.8	336.4	102.3	380.2
4. Other services	142.3	510.3	156.7	531.6	181.7	589.8	192.3	528.0	210.8	612.9
Total goods and services	3652.8	4346.7	3846.7	4824.1	4140.2	4906.4	3660.3	5308.5	4477.1	6056.5
Net goods and services	–	693.9	–	977.4	–	766.2	–	1648.2	–	1579.4
Transfer payments										
1. Private transfers (net)	179.5	–	184.7	–	185.5	–	186.3	–	233.5	–
2. Official transfers (net)	46.6	–	41.9	–	48.2	–	56.1	–	65.2	–
Net transfer payments	226.1	–	226.6	–	233.7	–	242.4	–	298.7	–
Balance on current account	–	467.8	–	750.8	–	532.5	–	1405.8	–	1280.7
Capital account										
1. Direct investment (net)	130.6	–	140.6	–	124.3	–	172.2	–	188.6	–
2. Commercial loans (net)	46.8	–	74.0	–	57.5	–	127.3	–	147.6	–
3. Central government (net)	380.6	–	432.3	–	423.9	–	610.7	–	640.3	–
4. Trade credits and arrears (net)	–	0.7	3.5	–	–	3.8	145.0	–	37.8	–
Net non-monetary	557.3	–	650.4	–	601.9	–	1055.2	–	1014.3	–
5. IMF (net)	–	–	–	–	–	–	51.2	–	27.8	–
6. Central Bank (net)	–	92.5	95.4	–	–	65.4	304.6	–	235.7	–
Net monetary sector	–	92.5	95.4	–	–	65.4	355.8	–	263.5	–
Net capital account	464.8	–	745.8	–	536.5	–	1411.0	–	1277.8	–
7. Errors and omissions	3.0	–	5.0	–	–	4.0	–	5.2	2.9	–

TABLE R3.14 (*continued*)

Item	1973 Cr	1973 Dr	1974 Cr	1974 Dr	1975 Cr	1975 Dr	1976 Cr	1976 Dr	1977 Cr	1977 Dr
Goods and services										
1. Merchandise (fob)	6025.8	5190.2	7222.8	6992.0	5438.0	6783.0	5946.0	6552.1	6001.9	6540.9
2. Freight and insurance	16.8	545.7	19.1	699.9	16.7	678.7	16.5	634.2	17.5	632.6
3. Investment income	122.6	401.3	128.6	451.4	104.3	486.5	115.7	528.6	112.8	529.7
4. Other services	287.4	456.3	284.4	487.6	247.8	495.2	311.5	562.7	324.9	586.4
Total goods and services	6452.6	6593.5	7654.9	8630.9	5806.8	8443.4	6389.7	8277.6	6457.1	8289.6
Net goods and services	–	140.9	–	976.0	–	2636.6	–	1887.9	–	1832.5
Transfer payments										
1. Private transfers (net)	215.2	–	247.8	–	293.9	–	309.7	–	316.3	–
2. Official transfers (net)	11.3	–	28.4	–	88.9	–	64.6	–	63.7	–
Net transfer payments	226.5	–	276.2	–	382.8	–	374.3	–	380.0	–
Balance on current account	85.6	–	–	699.8	–	2253.8	–	1513.6	–	1452.5
Capital account										
1. Direct investment (net)	165.4	–	241.6	–	192.8	–	183.9	–	199.7	–
2. Commercial loans (net)	105.0	–	131.4	–	129.6	–	147.8	–	153.5	–
3. Central government (net)	380.7	–	455.6	–	993.7	–	856.6	–	732.3	–
4. Trade credits and arrears (net)	–	65.3	37.3	–	195.8	–	112.4	–	147.5	–
Net non-monetary	585.8	–	865.9	–	1511.9	–	1300.7	–	1233.0	–
5. IMF (net)	–	29.3	41.6	–	115.4	–	395.8	–	94.7	–
6. Central Bank (net)	–	638.6	–	203.4	606.8	–	–	196.8	110.2	–
Net monetary sector	–	667.9	–	161.8	722.2	–	199.0	–	204.9	–
Net capital account	–	82.1	704.1	–	2234.1	–	1499.7	–	1437.9	–
7. Errors and omissions	–	3.5	–	4.3	19.7	–	13.9	–	14.6	–

Source: Research Department, Central Bank of Beracia.

TABLE R3.15 Beracia foreign exchange reserves
(as of December 31)

Year	Foreign currency (U.S.$ million)	Domestic currency (lepta million)
1956	116.4	735.4
1957	116.9	738.8
1958	113.4	716.8
1959	109.1	689.4
1960	92.3	583.8
1961	98.0	619.6
1962	73.0	579.9
1963	65.4	516.7
1964	49.6	392.2
1965	46.5	367.7
1966	69.2	547.0
1967	65.8	519.7
1968	77.5	612.2
1969	65.4	516.8
1970	73.7	582.2
1971	31.9	277.6
1972	4.8	41.9
1973	78.3	680.5
1974	101.7	883.9
1975	31.9	277.1
1976	54.5	473.9
1977	41.9	363.7

Source: State Bank of Beracia, *Financial Statistics*, various issues.

The resultant of these balance-of-payments transactions, reserve changes, is shown in *Table R3.15*. From independence until the mid-1960s, reserves fell, dropping to half of their 1956 value by 1965. The sharp increase in copper prices in 1966 helped restore reserves to the range of $ 65–78m for the next five years, until 1971/72 when drought and the collapse of copper prices all but wiped out reserves. The world commodity price boom of 1973/74 again restored reserves, this time to nominal values higher than ever before ($ 102m by 1974), only to have the oil price increase and the recession of copper prices threaten to eliminate reserves once again. Only increased drawings from the IMF, especially during 1976 under the new oil facility, kept reserves from falling well below the current (1977) level of $ 42m, equivalent to only 0.6 months of imports.

Fiscal and Financial Developments, 1956–1977

Fiscal development

One encouraging feature of Beracian development has been the government's steady handling of the fiscal situation throughout the post-independence period, despite changes in government and the vicissitudes of drought and shifts in the terms of trade. *Tables R4.1* and *R4.2* contain fiscal data for financial years from 1956/57 to 1976/77. Although the tax effort was unexceptional just after independence, a concerted effort by the Negara and Arrides governments bore results and during most of the 1960s tax revenues exceeded 17 percent of GDP. However, the tax ratio has fallen sharply in the last two fiscal years, 1975/76 and 1976/77, to under 15 percent. The Finance Minister believes this dip to be temporary and forecasts a recovery to the levels of the early 1970s within two years.

The structure of taxation remains that of an underdeveloped economy. The share of tax revenues from duties on trade has fallen substantially, from one-third in the first 15 years after independence to under one-fourth in the mid-1970s. To some extent this may reflect the shift from consumer goods imports to raw material imports, as the latter carries much lower duty rates. However, the decline in copper export values is the chief cause of this drop in trade tax revenues. While the share of taxes on traded goods has fallen, other indirect taxes have risen enough to offset the decline, so that Beracia's heavy dependence on indirect taxes remains. At independence, 62 percent of tax revenues came from indirect taxes. The ratio peaked at over two-thirds in the early 1970s, then fell back to 61 percent in the mid-1970s.

The largest direct taxes are on mining and other corporate income. One of the few fiscal reforms enacted by the colonial government was the shift from a sliding export tax on copper revenues to a larger profits tax on the copper companies. The intention was both to raise revenues, since a fixed 15 percent rate replaced the sliding duty, and to collect windfall profits through the profits tax. In 1966 the government added a surcharge of 25 percent on all revenues exceeding an average price of $ 900 per tonne, but otherwise has retained the copper tax structure, even after nationalization of the large mines. Indeed, the Beracia Copper Company is the largest single taxpayer in the country, a position it is proud of publicly but complains about within government circles. The steady growth of other direct taxes (12 percent a year since

TABLE R4.1 Consolidated government expenditures (current prices; lepta million)

Fiscal year[a]	Goods and services	Debt service, transfers	Gross capital formation	Subsidies	Total
1956/57	536.9	91.6	343.8	6.3	978.6
1957/58	542.5	117.5	397.7	7.1	1064.8
1958/59	615.4	126.4	441.2	7.6	1190.6
1959/60	633.9	145.3	472.6	8.3	1260.1
1960/61	669.6	140.6	477.7	10.8	1298.7
1961/62	702.1	143.3	532.8	13.4	1391.6
1962/63	822.2	185.6	564.3	15.1	1587.2
1963/64	996.6	218.3	663.0	16.8	1894.7
1964/65	1171.7	254.1	771.8	19.9	2217.5
1965/66	1334.5	272.6	743.7	22.7	2373.5
1966/67	1471.2	318.3	868.7	25.8	2684.0
1967/68	1714.4	361.6	1083.9	29.8	3189.7
1968/69	1927.0	428.0	1262.7	40.0	3657.7
1969/70	2247.4	522.9	1330.0	50.9	4151.2
1970/71	2553.8	657.1	1452.8	62.0	4725.7
1971/72	3061.3	640.2	1543.9	79.6	5325.0
1972/73	3475.8	668.4	1564.5	101.3	5810.0
1973/74	3855.2	781.0	1853.4	150.5	6640.1
1974/75	4608.4	889.7	2082.3	163.6	7744.0
1975/76	5455.6	1074.0	2133.0	142.0	8804.6
1976/77	6227.3	1135.0	2032.1	151.8	9546.2
		Analysis (percent)			
1956/57	54.9	9.4	35.1	0.6	100.0
1960/61	51.6	10.8	36.8	0.8	100.0
1965/66	56.2	11.5	31.3	1.0	100.0
1970/71	54.0	13.9	30.7	1.3	100.0
1975/76	62.0	12.2	24.2	1.6	100.0
1976/77	65.2	11.9	21.3	1.6	100.0

Note: [a] July 1–June 30.
Source: Ministry of Finance, *Detailed Estimates of Expenditure and Receipts* (various years).

independence) is largely a consequence of the corporate profits tax. Protection, growth of import-substituting industries and, in recent years, rapid inflation have combined to yield a rapidly growing tax base. Attempts to reform the personal income tax have been sporadic and ineffectual. The tax gains most of its revenue from earnings withheld from regularly employed workers, that is, from the middle income groups. Entrepreneurial and investment income is taxed under the code, but evasion—both legal and illegal—is the rule and the wealthy pay very little income tax. Moreover, neither agricultural land nor agricultural incomes are subject to tax, so that a growing group of middle income and wealthy farmers pays no income tax at all.

TABLE R4.2 Consolidated government revenues (current prices; lepta million)

Fiscal year[a]	Import duties	Export duties	Sales and excise taxes	Direct taxes on mining	Direct taxes others	Other revenues	Total	Surplus (+) deficit (−)
1956/57	200.3	82.8	231.3	61.5	239.7	8.4	824.0	−154.6
1957/58	228.4	74.3	264.3	66.5	272.8	9.8	916.1	−148.7
1958/59	263.6	90.8	303.0	78.6	310.1	12.1	1058.2	−132.4
1959/60	266.0	101.8	326.7	84.3	298.3	13.8	1090.9	−169.2
1960/61	315.2	109.4	348.7	95.8	319.0	16.1	1204.2	−94.5
1961/62	301.7	119.1	407.6	100.5	368.0	17.8	1314.7	−77.0
1962/63	314.2	159.2	473.2	103.4	409.2	19.0	1478.2	−109.0
1963/64	373.8	203.5	558.4	118.0	457.1	19.9	1730.7	−164.0
1964/65	442.7	227.6	701.0	139.8	515.1	20.9	2047.1	−170.4
1965/66	522.3	268.2	790.2	213.9	581.9	23.4	2399.9	+26.4
1966/67	625.5	300.5	927.9	253.5	651.1	27.7	2786.2	+102.2
1967/68	746.3	330.3	1093.3	277.5	709.2	36.6	3193.2	+3.5
1968/69	854.3	370.2	1239.5	360.4	756.9	46.7	3628.0	−29.7
1969/70	917.6	454.6	1449.0	431.9	809.2	58.3	4120.6	−30.6
1970/71	947.0	437.7	1532.6	336.2	866.1	72.7	4192.3	−533.4
1971/72	870.3	413.5	1686.3	283.6	959.5	93.1	4306.3	−1018.7
1972/73	943.0	629.7	1945.8	573.3	1108.5	109.2	5309.5	−500.5
1973/74	1194.7	877.2	2348.2	719.5	1386.8	124.1	6650.5	+10.4
1974/75	1327.4	750.4	2753.2	575.7	1621.6	237.2	7265.5	−478.5
1975/76	1247.7	577.4	2925.2	389.8	1857.5	404.8	7402.4	−1402.2
1976/77	1200.3	643.1	3027.7	398.8	2156.7	530.3	7956.9	−1589.3

				Analysis (percent)				Share of GDP (%)	
								Revenue	Deficit
1956/57	24.3	10.0	28.1	7.5	29.1	1.0	100.0	14.4	2.7
1960/61	26.2	9.1	29.0	8.0	26.5	1.3	100.0	16.2	1.3
1965/66	21.8	11.2	32.9	8.9	24.2	1.0	100.0	17.2	–
1970/71	22.6	10.4	36.6	8.0	20.7	1.7	100.0	17.2	2.2
1975/76	16.9	7.8	39.5	5.3	25.1	5.5	100.0	15.6	3.0
1976/77	15.1	8.1	38.1	5.0	27.1	6.7	100.0	14.6	2.9

Note: [a]July 1–June 30.
Source: As for Table R4.1.

Government expenditure, including investment, has grown at 12 percent a year, slightly faster than GDP; allowing for inflation, the real growth is just over 5 percent a year. The share of government expenditure in GDP has changed very little since independence, growing from 17 percent in 1956/57 to 19 percent in 1970/71, then retreating to 17.5 percent in 1976/77 (*Table R4.3*). The disturbing feature of expenditure performance has been the shift from public investment towards public consumption and debt service. Government's gross capital formation accounted for from 33 to 40 percent of expenditures in the years just after independence, but for only 21 to 27 percent in recent years.

Although rising public debt accounts for some of this shift, a larger and more rapidly growing absorber of revenues has been wages and salaries paid to government workers: the rise of wages and salaries has outstripped the growth of current price GDP. Wage control is a major item on the agenda of the incoming Finance Minister and one of the most politically sensitive he will have to deal with.

TABLE R4.3 Government expenditure by function (as a percent of GNP)

	General services	Defense	Economic services	Social services	Unallocated	Total
1956/57	3.2	1.3	5.7	4.2	2.8	17.2
1960/61	3.5	1.1	5.8	4.8	2.2	17.4
1965/66	3.2	1.2	5.6	4.9	2.1	17.0
1970/71	4.1	1.7	5.4	5.8	2.4	19.4
1975/76	4.0	2.1	5.1	5.6	1.8	18.6
1976/77	3.6	2.1	4.7	5.1	2.0	17.5

Source: Ministry of Finance, *Budget Estimates* (various years).

Table R4.3 offers another view of the shifts in government expenditure. Despite the influence of the military in government, defense expenditures were under control until the 1970s, when they almost doubled their share of GNP. Both general services and social services have also risen as a share of GNP. These shifts have come at the expense of economic services, the share of which fell from 5.7 to 4.7 percent of GNP. Thus government has favored outlays that are not directly productive and cannot be expected to contribute to needed investments in agriculture, industry or economic infrastructure. However, the rise in expenditure in the social services, largely education and health, reflects the concern of the past two governments for increased equity in the distribution of benefits from development.

Monetary development

The Central Bank of Beracia (CBB) was created in 1959 with assistance from the International Monetary Fund. Prior to that, the monetary system was controlled by a combination of the Treasury, three commercial banks which were branches of large banks in the metropolitan country and several commodity boards. The Treasury, the commercial banks and the boards each held foreign reserves; the latter two held a small quantity of government debt; and currency was issued by the banks with the approval of the Treasury. Until the creation of the CBB, the money supply was backed almost completely by foreign reserves.

With the creation of the central bank, all foreign reserves were concentrated in the CBB, which also became solely responsible for currency. To give the bank effective control over the monetary system, the commercial banks were incorporated in Beracia and their lending policy subjected to CBB regulations, rather than solely to policies of the home office. Because the interest rate on government securities has been kept low by the Treasury, the commercial banks prefer not to hold them and the CBB has been the principal investor in government paper: (Some is also held by the National Provident Fund, the Insurance Company of Beracia and one or two other public financial institutions.)

In its stewardship over monetary development, the CBB has been fortunate in having two competent and respected public officials as its governors. After an initial period of reticence, the commercial banks, which had enjoyed virtual autonomy in Beracia, accepted the regulations promulgated by the CBB and generally adhere to these and to the informal guidelines laid down from time to time. Ironically, it has been the government-owned (and Treasury-controlled) National Commercial Bank (NCB) that has given the most trouble, sometimes exceeding CBB regulations in extending credit, especially when politically influential borrowers are involved.

The CBB has had less influence on the other major participant in money creation, the government. Although the successive governors have, by and large, been influential with the Treasury, the size of the government budget and its deficits are governed by a political logic that these officials have been able to contain at times, but never really to control. Hence the size of the deficit must be considered an independent variable in the system and other components of the money supply forced to accommodate to any desired outcome. This did not cause the CBB to lose control of the money supply through the 1960s, but was a contributing factor in the recent inflation.

The CBB has had a reasonably good record for monetary management, at least until recently. The money supply has been permitted to expand at a moderate rate, fostering the increased monetization typical of an economy at Beracia's stage of development and accommodating a rate of inflation that was considered acceptable by government leaders until 1971. Currency plus demand deposits (M_1) grew at 13.8 percent per year from 1960 to 1971 with inflation averaging 5.3 percent a year over that period (based on the implicit GDP deflator); the ratio of M_1 to GDP rose from 20.3 to 25.1 percent. If savings deposits are included in the money supply (M_2), growth was also 14.3 percent per year to 1971, with the share of GDP rising from 28.3 to 36.9 percent (See *Table R4.4*).

However, the picture has changed abruptly since 1971. By 1977, the rate of growth of M_1 had accelerated to 17.2 percent, and that of M_2 to 16.2 percent, while inflation had risen to 11.8 percent a year. Although the central bank has not been effective in restraining the money supply, the inflation cannot be blamed largely on the CBB; worldwide inflation, especially of oil prices, has had a severe effect on a country heavily dependent on imports. Government debt has also grown since 1971, more than tripling the CBB's mandatory holdings of government paper and contributing about 75 percent of the increase in central bank assets. Moreover, the outgoing military government was insistent that the CBB permit the commercial banks to increase their lending to stimulate investment in the face of a stagnating economy. The new Finance Minister has pledged to restore autonomy to the CBB as part of his program to get the money supply under control.

TABLE R4.4 Money supply (lepta million)

	1960	1965	1970	1971	1972	1973	1974	1975	1976	1977
Central bank assets										
Foreign exchange reserves	584	368	582	278	42	681	884	277	174	64
Government debt	636	1268	1215	2030	2 921	3 175	2 768	3 975	5 557	7 146
Loans to financial institutions	−130	639	1765	1576	2 068	2 131	2 358	2 796	3 167	3 327
Reserve base	1090	2275	3562	3884	5 031	5 987	6 010	7 048	8 898	10 537
Money supply										
Currency	815	1591	2778	2881	3 593	4 097	4 622	5 178	6 243	7 030
Demand deposits	608	1294	2596	3001	3 721	4 336	5 222	6 003	7 390	8 289
M_1	1423	2885	5374	5882	7 314	8 433	9 844	11 181	13 633	15 319
Savings deposits	551	1262	2567	2745	2 993	3 318	3 872	4 355	5 113	5 936
M_2	1974	4147	7941	8627	10 307	11 751	13 716	15 536	18 746	21 255

Financial markets

COMMERCIAL BANKS

To the three metropolitan-based banks that existed at independence have been added the National Commercial Bank (created in 1962) and two smaller, privately owned local banks. The three foreign banks had until the mid-1960s pursued conservative lending policies and at times had been forced by the monetary authorities to expand their loan portfolios to keep up with targeted expansion of the money supply. This tendency has been reversed with the creation of the newer banks. All of them, but especially the NCB, have pursued aggressive loan policies. The NCB has opened over 200 new branches since 1965 in an attempt to implement the government's policy of bringing commercial banking to all the people, especially in the rural areas. The older banks, trying to maintain their share of the market, have gradually become less conservative in their lending and expansion policies, so that now the problem of the CBB has been reversed to the more typical one of restraint over the banking system.

The interest rate structure of the commercial banks is regulated by the CBB, with advice from the Treasury. No interest is paid on demand deposits, but recently the competition for depositors has reduced charges considerably. The interest rates permissible on time and savings deposits were raised in steps, from 6 percent in 1970 to 9.0 percent in 1977 (*Table R4.5*). Loan rates to prime customers were raised from 10 to 14 percent, a move resisted by the Treasury but promoted intensively by the banking system in response to increased inflation. (Bankers were not so enthusiastic about the increase in deposit rates, but the Treasury insisted that the whole rate structure must be increased if any changes were to be made.)

TABLE R4.5 Nominal interest rates on selected instruments (selected years; percent per annum)

	1961	1965	1970	1972	1973	1976	1977
Domestic instruments							
Savings deposits	5.5	6.0	6.0	6.5	7.5	8.0	9.0
Commercial bank loans (prime customers)	9.5	10.0	10.0	11.0	12.0	12.5	14.0
Development bank loans	10.5	11.0	11.0	12.5	13.5	14.0	15.0
Foreign borrowing							
Commercial loans and trade credit (average)	8	8	10	12	12	12	11
Official lending (average for commitments)	n.a.	n.a	3.4	3.6	4.3	4.5	4.2
Memo GDP deflator	56.9	75.3	100.0	108.3	140.8	186.7	208.6
Capital goods deflator	70.9	81.7	100.0	112.5	144.5	177.3	185.6

In support of their requests for higher loan rates, bankers pointed to a growing backlog of applications for loans that they would like to fill if deposits could be increased more rapidly. Although bankers are loath to supply data on the subject, it is generally believed that they can reduce (but cannot eliminate) this backlog by adding significant loan charges and requiring that up to 20 percent of the face value of the loan be kept on deposit. One informed observer has estimated that these methods might increase borrowers' costs by 25 to 30 percent*. Loans have expanded from Lp 493 million in 1961 to Lp 1670 million in 1977, with a great deal of year-to-year fluctuation (*Table R4.6*).

There has been a fairly brisk increase in deposits since 1960: demand deposits have grown at 16.6 percent a year and savings deposits at a rate of 15 percent. However, this growth probably has less to do with the interest rates being offered than with the increased monetization of the economy and the concomitant expansion of the banking system. Much

* S. S. Edward. Development of the Banking System. In *The Economy of Beracia, 1975.* (Ed. by L. Kwatch).

TABLE R4.6 Source of investment finance (selected years; lepta million)

	1956	1961	1965	1970	1975	1976	1977
Foreign capital (all items net)							
Transfer payments	15	7	21	54	103	74	70
Direct investment	45	106	124	124	193	184	200
Commercial loans and trade credits	22	42	78	54	325	260	301
Official loans	43	257	369	424	994	857	732
Monetary sector	–38	19	17	–65	722	199	205
Investment income	–61	–64	–64	–56	–102	–113	–107
Total foreign sources (net)	26	367	545	535	2235	1461	1401
Domestic sources							
Commercial bank loans	n.a.	493	432	1030	1257	2109	1670
Development bank loans	n.a.	30	43	65	196	214	247
Corporate retained earnings (estimated)	n.a.	246	390	716	1410	1668	1902
Government savings	170	420	686	1109	1167	587	444
Other (equity investments; non-corporate sources; errors and omissions)	n.a.	779	851	1047	681	1763	2773
Total domestic sources	1322	1968	2402	3967	4711	6341	7036
Gross capital formation	1348	2335	2947	4502	6946	7802	8437

of the expansion of deposits has come from the newly opened branches, as agricultural cooperatives and small businesses in the small towns began to bank commercially for the first time. In their arguments against higher deposit rates, bankers included the observation that it would take a very much higher rate to induce savers to increase time deposits merely for the interest involved. Part of the success in increasing savings deposits has been due to reduced penalties for early withdrawal, so that for many depositors a time or savings account has all the benefits required from a demand deposit.

DEVELOPMENT BANKS

The government has responded in a modest way to fill the void created by commercial banks, whose policies prevent them from making long-term loans, other than for buildings secured by mortgage. Separate development banks have been created to make long-term loans to enterprises in mining, manufacturing, agriculture, housing and commerce. Although most of the capital has come from government, there is equity participation in the Natural Resources Development Bank and the Bank for Industrial Development from local banks and corporations. Loan volume for the development banks has grown from Lp 30m in 1961, when it represented 6 percent of commercial bank loans, to Lp 247m in 1977, 15 percent of commercial bank loans. Development banks are permitted to charge interest rates of 1–1.5 percent above the rates set for the commercial banks.

FOREIGN COMMERCIAL LOANS

Access to foreign bank lending is mainly (i) through foreign firms operating in Beracia or (ii) tied to imported equipment, with loans negotiated on behalf of the Beracian importer by the equipment supplier. The flow of finance from this source has been modest, reaching a peak of Lp 325m in 1975 (*Table R4.6*). The Central Bank keeps a record of all such borrowing and the rates paid. Its records show a rise from the average rate of 8 percent a year, charged in the 1960s, to about 12 percent in the mid-1970s (*Table R4.5*). However, these nominal rates mask additional costs to the borrower, the main one being the higher prices sometimes charged for equipment by suppliers who provide export credits. Spot checks by the CBB have shown higher equipment costs of from 5 to 35 percent, although it is not definite that the higher prices are caused entirely by tied financing.

FOREIGN DIRECT INVESTMENT

Beracia's rich mineral resources have always provided an attraction for foreign investors. Since independence, the government has continued to encourage foreign investors in mining, but only in joint ventures with government, and has increasingly restricted multinational partners to minority shares. However, foreign investors have also been welcomed in manufacturing, especially in the chemical and metal sectors. Consequently, there has been a steady flow of direct foreign investment to Beracia over the years, averaging around Lp 160m during the 1970s.

It is not possible to give precise estimates of the returns expected by foreign investors. A scan of the applications to the Investment Promotions Board (IPB) by these investors shows that some applicants for tax incentives expected to earn over 20 percent a year after taxes after allowing for the restrictions placed on profit repatriation by the CBB. A study by one economic adviser of existing firms with foreign participation indicates that the actual return to equity holders is generally lower than this, perhaps from 12 to 17 percent after taxes*. The same study showed, however, that smaller, locally owned firms frequently earn much higher rates of return, especially if certain expenses are corrected for obvious overstatements. (The corporate income tax is now 45 percent on profits, having been raised from 37.5 percent in 1960 and 40 percent in 1965).

FOREIGN AID

The government has had a good record of attracting and utilizing foreign aid. From 1970 to 1973, for example, net disbursements of

---

* S.J. Josephson (1974). Memorandum: Profit Levels in Industry. Unpublished internal memorandum of the Ministry of Finance

official loans totaled more than Lp 5bn, which was 10 percent of total gross capital formation during that period. Although most of the aid is for specific projects, during the 1971/72 balance-of-payments crisis, precipitated by a drought and the fall in copper prices, substantial amounts of program aid were made available. Beracia's donors have made assistance available under a wide variety of terms, from very concessional roles up to World Bank terms. The average interest rate on commitments has ranged from 3.4 to 4.5 percent in recent years.

There is some dispute among government officials about the ability of the government to attract more aid in order to increase public investment. The Prime Minister's Office and the Planning Commission have argued that better project formulation would attract more aid from existing donors. Treasury officials, however, have returned from IMF and World Bank meetings with a strong impression that World Bank and perhaps even bilateral aid to Beracia is probably limited because it is not among the very poorest countries, is relatively rich in natural resources and could perhaps attract more funds from private international capital markets. The Treasury has encouraged more private market borrowing and a greater domestic savings effort as sources of finance for expanded investment.

INFORMAL CAPITAL MARKETS

A glance at *Table R4.6* reveals that a large portion, often over one-third, of the finance for gross capital formation comes from sources not accounted for above, that is from non-corporate, own-financed investment and the informal capital market. Little is known about this market. Various studies of the rural economy have uncovered instances of lenders charging upwards of 50 percent a year for loans to farmers secured against the next harvest; in some cases, the loan is repaid by grain in amounts that imply substantially higher interest rates. Similarly, bankers have told of their own customers re-lending to small urban firms at 35 percent or more. In the latter case, it is thought that the commercial banks could, were they allowed to charge higher rates, capture a good deal of this market with acceptable risk at rates of perhaps 20 to 25 percent a year. Some Treasury (and, to a lesser extent, CBB) officials consider this pure usury, and quite contrary to allowing commercial banks to charge higher rates, have asked for legislation carrying severe penalties for lending at rates over the regulated bank rates.

Part III

Project Analysis

Project Analysis

Project analysis is a case-by-case method of selecting investments for their ability to contribute to a social welfare function. The selected projects are those that use scarce factors of production most efficiently and thus maximize the value of the objective function. In most applications of project analysis, the objective function includes only one goal, the growth of output. Resource scarcities are introduced by means of shadow prices, or opportunity costs, at which land, labor, capital and foreign exchange are valued. Shadow prices measure the marginal contribution that a resource makes to the welfare function. Non-growth goals, especially equitable income distribution, can also be included by applying appropriate shadow prices to certain income flows from the project. Under ideal but unrealizable conditions, projects selected under these rules would maximize a social welfare function. In practice, project analysis is not capable of optimum results, but can substantially improve the choice of investments and the productivity of resources, compared with the usual practice in most countries.

Part III introduces the concept of project appraisal and explores some controversial aspects of it. To repeat the caveat in the Introduction, the material here is not intended to substitute for a textbook on cost–benefit analysis. It will take the uninitiated student a certain distance in understanding project analysis, but to gain sufficient facility to analyze the cases, students should consult one or more of the texts listed in the bibliography. The student who is familiar with project analysis can work the cases without reading this introduction.

Elements of project appraisal

Project appraisal is based on the businessman's technique of measuring the profitability of an investment by discounting projected cash flows to see if these would provide an adequate return on the funds invested. 79

The two critical elements are cash flows and discounting. For the private firm, the cash flow measures all outlays for plant, machinery, inventories, raw materials, labor, etc. and all cash income from the sale of its output. Depreciation and other accounting costs that are not real cash outlays are not included. Future cash flows are discounted to reflect the fact that if the available funds were invested elsewhere, they would earn some return. Any future income from the investment must at least cover this alternative source of earnings to be worthwhile to the firm. The discount rate reflects the return that could be earned in the next best alternative investment and the discount process automatically accounts for the hypothetical payment of interest (at the discount rate) and repayment of principal on the invested funds. (Because of this, principal and interest are not included among cash flows; to do so would, in effect, be double-counting). To complete the picture, the businessman then adds all his discounted cash flows, negative (in years of investment and, perhaps, start-up) and positive (once production is underway). If the sum is positive, it signifies that the invested funds would earn more than in their best alternative use, from which the discount rate was selected; if negative, the investment is not as good as its alternative and should not be made. The appropriate discount rate is the weighted marginal cost of capital to the firm, that is the return that those who would invest additional capital in the firm—banks and other borrowers as well as shareholders—expect to earn on their investment. If the project cannot earn this expected return but is undertaken anyway, the firm would disappoint its investors, who could gain more by placing their funds elsewhere[1].

What is true for the firm is, with appropriate modifications, true for the nation. In the following discussions, we work with four assumptions, based on Harberger's (1972) collection of articles which set out his neoclassical, welfare economics approach to project analysis.

(1) Output maximization (growth) is the only goal relevant to project selection.
(2) Markets reflect both consumer utilities and producer marginal revenue products or opportunity costs.
(3) Government can use fiscal and monetary instruments to vary the savings rate within a range that would satisfy society's growth goals, so that projects need not be selected for their contribution to saving.
(4) Government can also use fiscal means to redistribute income.

The first assumption does not deny the existence of other national goals, but states that project selection is not an appropriate instrument with which to achieve them. The last assumption indicates that a more equitable income distribution could be attained instead by progressive taxes and subsidies. We will examine these assumptions in a later section.

A country maximizing growth of net output and a firm maximizing profits have similar investment aims: both want projects to produce as much output as possible for a given resource input and at the least to cover the cost of those resources. There are, however, critical differences that give social cost-benefit analysis a different character[2]. First, some cash outlays and revenues for the firm are not costs or benefits to society at all. Taxes, for example, are cash outflows to a firm but are merely *transfer payments* that stay within the country and represent no expenditure of real resources; subsidies are the converse case of a revenue to the firm but not to the country. Similarly, a trained worker who leaves the firm represents a loss to the firm of investment in training, but there is no loss to the nation if the worker takes up employment elsewhere in the economy. There are also real costs and benefits to the country that do not affect the firm's calculations. These *externalities*, such as the costs of pollution or the benefits of flood control from a hydroelectric dam, must be included in social cost-benefit analysis.

A second critical difference is that while the enterprise uses market prices to account for its outlays and revenues, these may be inappropriate indicators of the costs and benefits to society. To judge the value of a project to society, we need to know the *opportunity cost* of the resources used in the project and the benefits derived from it. The name 'opportunity cost' suggests alternative uses for any resource, such as labor, land, capital or foreign exchange. If, to take a contrived but simple example, 100 hectares of cotton land might be used for a new textile mill, the cost to society is the net value of cotton production that would be lost as a consequence. If the cotton were exported (or substituted for imports), the cost of forgone cotton, and thus the cost of the land, would be the net value of foreign exchange that could no longer be earned (or saved). This concept can be turned around. If a flood control project reclaims 100 hectares of land suitable for growing cotton, the benefit would be valued in terms of the additional cotton that can be produced net of input costs, whether for export or to substitute for imports. These are examples of the opportunity cost of land; suitably adjusted this is the basis for valuing all national costs and benefits of a project.

Another and more popular term for opportunity cost is *shadow price*. Much of the literature on project analysis is devoted to the theory and calculation of shadow prices to be used in social cost-benefit analysis. Because the procedure depends upon pivotal assumptions about goals and the nature of the economy, this facet of project appraisal has generated considerable controversy. For the time being, we have escaped controversy by employing the four simplifying assumptions. If growth is the goal and fiscal means can deal with savings and distribution, then the second assumption, that markets reflect the utilities of sovereign consumers and the costs to producers, is the key to calculating opportunity costs and shadow prices. These assumptions will be questioned in the last part of this chapter. Our object here is merely to indicate the nature of the shadow price estimate for three resources: labor, capital and foreign exchange[3].

Conceptually, the shadow wage is probably the easiest of the three to explain, because the connection to opportunity cost is intuitively clear. If a laborer is hired away from a textile mill to work in a new steel plant, then the loss to society would be the reduced output of textiles, net of reduced inputs, assuming the mill does not replace the worker. If the mill owner is rational, he would not have paid the worker more than the value of the additional output (marginal revenue product) produced by that worker, so the worker's wage represents a minimum estimate of the opportunity cost to society of his transfer from textiles to steel production. In the absence of further hiring by the textile firm, we would use the wage rate in textiles as the shadow wage. However if the textile mill replaces the worker, it would set in motion a chain of hiring and replacement that might go as far as a rural worker who migrated to the city to take up wage employment. The cost to society would not be the wage of the original textile worker who moved to the steel plant, but the marginal revenue product of the rural worker who migrated to the city. In that case, the rural wage, presumably equal to the marginal revenue product, is a better representation of the shadow price of labor. Another way of viewing this process is that, when the ultimate source of labor leaves the rural area, less of some crop, such as cotton, would then be produced and the cost to society is that reduction in cotton output net of the reduction in input costs. We use the rural wage to estimate the value of such a reduction, but could also use the value of the cotton and its inputs if we knew them. This calculation becomes complicated if we consider additional costs of migration, such as the possibility that more than one rural worker might seek work in the city for every additional job created by new projects (because the urban wage is so much higher and migrants are willing to take a chance on unemployment to get the large gain that such a wage would represent); or the external costs of crowding in the cities that receive the migrants. These considerations tend to move the shadow wage up from the rural wage towards the urban wage, even if the latter is controlled by government at some minimum level. Despite these nuances, the principle of calculating the shadow wage is clear[4, 5].

The principle is the same for the shadow price of capital, which under our assumption is the interest rate used to discount future cash flows, but the application is a bit more complex. There are two possible sources for the investment funds required to finance a proposed new investment: additional saving, including foreign saving, and diversion of funds from other investors who would undertake their own projects. In the case of domestic savers, the opportunity cost is the value they place on forgoing present consumption in order to save now and consume more later. This is measured by the interest rate they receive for their saving. These savers can vary from individuals who invest in savings banks to shareholders in large corporations to money-lenders who operate in the informal money markets, and the real rates of interest (net of inflation) that they receive can vary from zero or negative to 30 or even 50 percent a year. In the case of prospective investors who would give up their funds to finance the new project, the opportunity cost is the rate of return that these profit-seeking investments would have generated for the entire economy. We measure this forgone return indirectly by looking at the rates that would-be investors must pay for their capital and then allow for taxes on their earning (which raises the opportunity cost) and inflation (which lowers it). The treatment of foreign investors and lenders is similar, though it involves subtleties that, for present purposes, can be ignored. These estimates leave us with a set of widely varying opportunity costs for different classes of savers and investors. These are weighted according to the volume of the flows involved in each category and the relative likelihood that each would respond to an increased demand for funds (i.e. the elasticity of demand or supply with respect to interest rates); the weighted average is used as the shadow interest rate for discounting future flows. In real terms, the shadow rate is likely to be in the range of 10 to 15 percent a year for most LDCs[6].

The treatment of foreign exchange as a factor of production is based on the same considerations that led to the foreign exchange constraint in the two-gap model of growth: since imports of some goods are essential for growth and production, while export growth is limited by the nature of the commodities and their markets, any means of earning or saving foreign exchange contributes to the potential output of a country. The analysis of the shadow foreign exchange rate is analogous to that for the shadow discount rate. Consider a project that, on balance, will use foreign exchange (for example, a road construction project). If scarce foreign exchange is used by that project, what other potential users of foreign exchange might lose? Most obviously, other importers may have to forgo their allocations of foreign exchange, either because of a rise in the exchange rate or because, under controls, the government diverts exchange from them to the project. To place a social opportunity cost on that reduction in other users' imports, we assume that their wilingness to pay is based on the productivity of the imports to the importer. (This would hold for a producer good, such as machinery or fertilizer, and for a consumer good if we accept that the price represents consumers' marginal utility for the import.) Thus if the import is not obtained, there would be a reduction of output of consumer utility equal to the price paid by the importer. That price is composed of the foreign exchange payment, converted at the official exchange rate, plus any tariffs or other taxes paid, plus an allowance for any premium (rent) due to the scarcity of import licenses. Typically these importers' prices are considerably higher than the official exchange rate.

The calculation does not end with importers. If more foreign exchange is required to finance the road project, some of it may come from increased exports. In this case we wish to measure the opportunity cost of the resources that would be used to produce such exports. A convenient measure of this cost is the official exchange rate, less any taxes on exports, plus any subsidies to exports; i.e., it is a point on the undistorted supply curve for exporters. This cost is typically close to the official exchange rate. To obtain the shadow exchange rate, we take an average of the importers' and exporters' opportunity costs, again weighted by the volume of each, and the elasticity with respect to the exchange rate. Such calculations usually give values well above the official rate, in a range from 10 to 50 percent higher. This shadow rate would be applied, not only to foreign exchange costs, but also to foreign exchange benefits, because net earnings or savings of foreign exchange would permit an increase in imports or a decrease in exports[7].

Each shadow price is calculated under relative scarcity conditions that may change over time, so shadow prices may also be expected to change. This does not affect project analysis, since different prices can be applied each year in the future, as necessary. However, it is important that the project being analyzed does not itself affect shadow prices. It is assumed that any project has a marginal influence on factor markets, too small to affect prices noticeably. If that is not the case (as, for example, with a major oil discovery), then the external effects of changed prices on all other projects (e.g., the reduced cost of foreign exchange) must also be accounted for and charged to the project. At that point, project appraisal becomes a less appropriate technique than macroeconomic or inter-industry approaches.

The valuation of goods—whether used as inputs to the production process or produced for final use—is based on the same principles. If a good can be traded, either exported or imported, then its opportunity cost to the economy is the value of the foreign exchange that would be earned for its export (or paid for its import) multiplied times the shadow exchange rate. Thus cotton that might be exported, but is instead used in the local textile industry, is valued at the (fob) price it would fetch if exported; the textiles, which substitute for imported cloth, would be valued at the (cif) cost of the competing imported cloth (whether actually imported or not). If the good is not traded, such as electricity or transportation, then it would have either of two values, or a weighted average of them. To the extent that increased use of, for example, electricity by a new project is expected to come from increased supply (generating capacity), the opportunity cost of that power is the opportunity cost of the factor inputs that would be used to generate additional electricity. To the extent that supply is fixed and use by one project denies electricity to other users, then the opportunity cost is the marginal revenue product of the power in its alternative use. The analyst must exercise judgement in deciding which is the more likely outcome.

Selecting projects

The purpose of measuring a project's cash flow, applying shadow prices and then discounting the result is to derive a measure of the desirability of implementing the project from the national viewpoint, which can be called the social profitability. Three measures are popular. First, by discounting at the shadow interest rate and summing the result, we obtain the *net present value* (NPV) of the project's cash flow. If the NPV is positive, then the project would be profitable, that is the cash flow could repay the initial investment and, in addition, earn an annual return greater than the discount rate. If projects are taken one by one, then any project with a positive NPV is desirable from the national viewpoint (assuming the shadow prices, especially the discount rate, represent real factor scarcities). However, a preferable way to select projects is to array all possible projects and select from among them those that yield the highest possible net present values until the investment budget is exhausted. This form of capital budgeting has the desired result of giving the greatest possible increase in future output, suitably discounted, for a given investment budget.

Because other factors of production have been shadow priced, the scarcity value of these complementary inputs is also accounted for. Thus, the scarcity of foreign exchange has led us to add a premium to the official exchange rate. Any project that uses foreign exchange is penalized thereby and its NPV made lower by the premium, while any project earning foreign exchange receives an increment to its NPV. This is consistent with national goals, since exchange-earning projects help increase potential output from other projects and exchange-using projects reduce potential output. Similarly, if unskilled labor is shadow-priced at a discount because the wage is above the real opportunity cost, then projects using labor more intensively get a boost through reduced costs and higher NPV, consistent with government's intention of increasing employment. Note, however, that only *efficient* employment, that is, employment contributing to greater output, is encouraged by this method.

Planners do not often have a large range of potential projects from which to select. Rather, the typical decision is made on one project at a time, or at most two or three. In this situation, the rule of positive NPV will at least ensure that all projects selected are socially profitable. Two alternative indicators are often suggested and, under some conditions, can be used to give similar results. First, the *internal rate of return* (IRR) is the discount rate that makes the NPV equal zero. The higher the IRR, the more profitable is the project, in a sense understood by businessmen and intuitively clear to most political decision-makers. If the IRR is higher than the opportunity cost of capital (shadow discount rate), the project is socially desirable in the same sense that a positive NPV indicates profitability. However, the IRR suffers a major drawback: for projects that have negative cash flows for one or more years following positive flows, there will be two or more discount rates that make the NPV equal zero. In that case, there is no simple rate for project selection based on the IRR. Instead, the NPV method must be used. This problem may arise whenever a project requires replacement investment; when a phased investment lasts several years; or when disposal costs are high at the end of a project's life.

Second, the *benefit-cost ratio* (BCR) is perhaps the best known of the profitability measures. Its name describes its calculation. So long as all benefits and costs are discounted, shadow prices used, and projects taken one at a time, the BCR will give results consistent with the other two measures. However, the precise ratio may depend upon the way costs and benefits are netted out in the process and is therefore somewhat arbitrary, unlike the IRR, which gives a unique value for any cash flow (if it does not turn negative after the initial investment). The BCR can also be used to rank projects for capital budgeting. Although a trial-and-error process is still required, the BCR method has the attraction of placing the problem in terms of marginal costs and benefits[8].

Social profitability is not the only dimension of project desirability. Both the actual outcomes and our forecasts of them are subject to uncertainty, so that each expected value of the NPV (or IRR or BCR) has associated with it the risk that the value could be higher or lower. In order to make a decision on a project, we should know the probable variability of the projected outcome, since it may well be that decision-makers will choose lower expected returns if the risk of sub-standard results is less than for other, more profitable projects. One simple way of indicating the variability of an outcome is *sensitivity analysis*, in which probable alternative values of key variables, such as the world price of an export or the productivity of rain-fed agriculture, are used to calculate the possible change of the NPV or IRR. If, for example, a pessimistic value of a key variable still yields a positive NPV, then the risk of the project falling below the cut-off value may be low. If, however, the NPV is very sensitive to changes in key variables and can easily fall below zero, the project is risky.

A more sophisticated approach to measuring risk is *Monte Carlo simulation*. In this method, the likely probability distributions for key variables are fed into a computer programmed to calculate the NPV or IRR. The program then makes many different computations of the profitability measure, each time selecting the value of key variables randomly from the supplied distributions. The result is a series of NPVs (or IRRs) that yields a frequency distribution of the profitability of a project. The greater the variance of the NPV, the greater the risk that the project would fail to reach a minimum profitability[9]. Although both sensitivity analysis and simulation techniques can be used on any project, two cases in this collection are especially suitable to such treatment: Case 1, Expansion of the Torrence Copper Mine, and Case 2, Horio Rice Project.

If used systematically over several years, project selection should become more than a matter of choosing from a set of given alternatives: it should ultimately help to improve both the set of available investments and the policy environment in which planners operate. Investment appraisal can help to improve the formulation and design of projects if engineers are instructed to work with shadow prices in calculating costs and benefits. This should lead them to select technologies that are more appropriate, given factor scarcities, and make other design decisions that will tend to reduce social costs and increase social benefits. Thus, if shadow wages are below market wages, more labor-intensive technologies should be used; if the shadow exchange rate is high, project designs should begin to conserve imported materials; and if the discount rate reflects scarce capital, then capital-saving designs will be favored.

Investment appraisal can serve as an effective vehicle for discussing *macroeconomic price policies* with decision-makers, as the notion of opportunity cost becomes part of their thinking and particular values for shadow prices become accepted. Shadow prices that diverge from actual prices are a sign of disequilibrium in the economy and highlight areas in which policy changes could improve resource allocation significantly. If policy-makers accept that government investment selection should be guided by shadow prices, then they should be ready to agree that investment decisions by enterprises—public and private—ought to be guided by the same considerations. The only way to ensure that result is to move market prices towards the scarcity values indicated by shadow prices. Conveniently, the research that goes into shadow price determination covers much the same ground as that required to make sensible recommendations about macroeconomic policies affecting prices.

Assumptions and controversies

Perhaps the most intense controversy in project analysis today centers on the goal of *redistribution*. Output-oriented techniques use the Hicks compensation principle: more output is better, regardless of its distribution, so long as those who gain could compensate those who lose and still remain better off than before. Our assumption that fiscal processes can deal with redistribution is consistent with this principle, because it states that if more output is available as the result of a project, government has the means to redistribute it according to its equity goals. Most observers of developing countries (or of industrial countries, for that matter) would agree that redistribution is much more difficult than the assumption implies, that in fact compensation is seldom realized, even when the need for it is obvious. Some economists have moved from this observation to the conclusion that projects should be selected with distributional as well as output goals in mind. If governments cannot redistribute the gains from projects easily, then the projects themselves must attain the desired distribution. For example, if a particular group of rural poor is to benefit from development, then projects aimed directly at such groups should be selected, even if they achieve lower output (lower NPV or IRR) than alternatives that do not directly benefit the target group.

Two systems of project analysis deal systematically with distributional goals: Das Gupta, Marglin and Sen (UNIDO, 1972, Chapters 7 and 18) and Squire and van der Tak (1975, Chapters 6 and 10). Both propose that welfare weights be applied to flows of income, so that weights for the disadvantaged groups are greater than one and those for wealthier groups are below one. (So long as projects are being compared and not selected one by one, only the relative value of the weights is important.) The World Bank system uses utility functions to assign weights, which are necessarily arbitrary. UNIDO suggests that it is the realm of the decision-maker, not the planner, to choose such weights and proposes a method under which, in a dialogue between planners and politicians, the latter may be induced to reveal their preferences for a simple set of welfare weights. Under either method, projects that favor the target groups would receive a boost to their NPV and conversely for projects favoring other groups.

A serious problem with this method is that the welfare weights have an arbitrary element that can change the relative profitability of projects substantially. As Harberger (1978) has pointed out, relative weights well within the realm considered realistic by World Bank analysts can justify projects on distributional grounds that are very inferior on efficiency grounds to other projects. There is a danger that welfare weights will lull decision-makers into selecting projects that appear to be favorable, whereas they ought instead to address their attention to finding projects that are both redistributive and efficient (i.e. have NPVs greater than one without welfare weights). The World Bank does in fact advocate calculating the NPV or IRR both on pure efficiency grounds and with welfare weights, but it is not clear how decision-makers are supposed to choose if some projects score well without welfare weights and others score better only with those weights.

The use of welfare weights implies the need to identify income flows caused by the project, which creates measurement problems. It may not be difficult to estimate the immediate recipients of a project's cash flows. However, each project exists within a complex economy that causes secondary and tertiary redistributions of project income and these may easily outweigh the primary effect of a project. Thus the effects of a project must be traced through the economy before judgements can be made about its distributive impact. MacArthur (1978) demonstrates how this may be done, but his path-breaking article also illustrates the complexity of the calculations and the potential fragility of the econometric estimates. The 'tagging' of cash flows means that the precise source of investment funds must be identified and that projects may be distinguished on the basis of differing sources of funds. This is contrary to the usual assumptions that investible resources are fungible and all projects should bear the same cost of capital, regardless of the apparent immediate source of funds. (Of course, if alternative uses of the same investment funds are being compared, there should be no differentiation on the basis of investment finance.)

A third problem with welfare weights reverts to the underlying assumption. One would use welfare weights to skew the selection process only if the compensation principle is invalid. It would be invalid if the government's tax and expenditure power to redistribute were opposed by politically powerful groups in society that would lose from redistribution. Would redistribution via project selection avoid this opposition? If the wealthier, more powerful groups begin to see that resources are being diverted from projects favoring them, it seems logical to suppose they might use their power to thwart that reallocation process as well. Progressive income taxes are certainly a mobilizing signal to the wealthy, but would not a wealthy landowner be just as sensitive to, and oppose just as strongly, a road project designed to give access to small farmers and bypass his own lands? Welfare weights may indicate to planners which projects they would like to fight for on distributional grounds, but their use will not solve the problem of political opposition to redistribution that was the initial stimulus to the use of welfare weights.

A second controversy in shadow pricing questions the assumption that government can achieve any *saving* level required for its growth goals by manipulating monetary and fiscal policies. Two implications flow from this assumption. First, because other instruments are effective at increasing saving, project selection need not be concerned about saving but can be directed entirely at increasing output. Second, a methodological corollary of the first, the measure of output (the numeraire) in project appraisal can be total output, regardless of its disposition. This assumption and its implications have been under attack for over 20 years. The earliest critics were Galenson and Leibenstein (1955), who argued that because saving is scarce and precisely because governments find it difficult to use fiscal and monetary means to increase saving, project selection should favor investments that generate greater returns to capital, which are presumed to generate more saving than do wages. The implication is that growth is increased if capital-intensive projects are favored. Little and Mirrlees (1974, Chapter 14) incorporated this approach in their treatise on project analysis, suggesting that the shadow wage be raised above the marginal revenue product by a factor representing the relative scarcity of saving. Their prescription is based on the assumption that wages are consumed and returns to capital saved, but adjustments can be made in their formula to soften this extreme assumption. A premium on saving is one of the central tenets of the UNIDO (Chapter 14) approach also, but they accommodate it by deriving a shadow price of capital, distinct from the discount rate, that incorporates the marginal product of capital, the saving rate and the pure discount rate; it is typically greater than one. In that system, a project is favored (i) the less its investment is a diversion from savings (or other investments) and (ii) the more its future benefits are saved, rather than consumed.

A closely related controversy revolves around the discount process. Under the Harberger (1972, Chapter 4) approach described above, the discount rate and the opportunity cost of capital are the same, with the important caveat that both savers' (consumers') and investors' opportunity costs are averaged into the shadow rate. This procedure is justified by the assumption that capital markets reflect all we need to know about the productivity of capital and the preferences of consumers, whose utilities in turn ought to form the basis of social choice. UNIDO (1972, pp. 156–160) has argued that the assumption of consumer sovereignty reflected in capital markets cannot be justified, for two reasons. First, individuals investing over time cannot make the same kind of rational, experimental choices that are possible when they select goods for current consumption. Each passage of time occurs only once in a person's life: investing in education, for example, is different at 18 years than at 40 and the decision to enter college can be made only once. Moreover, there is inherently greater uncertainty about the outcome over time, so the interest rate revealed in the market will reflect perceived uncertainty as well as pure time preference. Finally, UNIDO argues, individual decisions about saving and investment may not reflect society's collective judgement about the value of future benefits, because individuals might be willing to sacrifice and save more for the future if they knew other individuals were doing the same. Because this sense of national purpose is at the heart of development, assuming away the external influence of altruism may be missing an important element of the investment decision.

In place of the opportunity cost of investment and saving, UNIDO discounts by a rate representing the pure time preference of policy-makers. To ensure that politically responsible officials make thoughtful decisions about the discount rate, UNIDO suggests that planners work with several discount rates and induce policy-makers, through a sequence of decisions on several projects, to reveal their preference for a discount rate. Once planners and policy-makers have achieved agreement on the rate, it can be used in judging all future projects. In order to reflect the productivity of capital, which is generally higher than the rate of pure time preference, UNIDO applies a separate shadow price to investment. The higher the productivity of capital and lower the discount rate, the higher the shadow price of investment and the greater the net cash flow must be to justify diverting capital to that project.

The choice between these two methods of discounting—by opportunity cost or by pure time preference—is not a settled issue in economics and each has articulate advocates. The choice hinges on several judgements that the analyst must make. First, to the extent he trusts markets to reflect relevant preferences, the analyst would choose the Harberger approach over UNIDO. The decision would go the other way if policy-makers are thought to have strong preferences that differ from those of the marketplace and are in a position to enforce these preferences (for example, in revolutionary socialist situations such as Soviet Russia in the 1920s, China in the 1950s or Cuba in the 1960s). Second, the planner must be able to engage policy-makers in a meaningful dialogue to discover their time preferences and not all politicians make this feasible. The alternative is for planners to set the discount rate, although it could still be one of pure time preference. Third, computational simplicity argues in favor of the opportunity cost approach. For reasons which will not be described here, the UNIDO combination of a pure rate of time preference and a shadow price of capital leads to some anomalous behavior of discounted cash flows and the potential for large shifts in the shadow price of capital, which may not even be defined for some values of its parameters.

These doctrinal disputes conceal more about consensus than they reveal about disagreement. Underlying the arguments is a basic approach, shared by all economists writing about investment appraisal, that its aim is to measure the contribution of scare resources, properly valued, to the attainment of agreed national goals. To a large extent, the refinement required by welfare weights and the disputes about precise methods of calculating shadow prices are much less important than the large improvements in resource allocation that can ensue if some — almost any—method of evaluation is systematically applied and its results acted upon. The misallocations of investment in most countries—developed and developing alike—would frequently have been made obvious by any efficiency measure[10].

Perhaps more important, the systematic use of some appraisal technique helps to make politicians aware of the economic costs and benefits of their decisions and adds an important dimension to the decision-making process. So the important issue for planners is not which of the methods to select, but simply to select one that is suitable for local conditions and that can serve as a mechanism through which planners and policy-makers can communicate.

Economists have increasingly tried to apply cost–benefit techniques to evaluate investment in *human capital*, including education, health and nutrition. A distinguishing feature of human capital is that its relation to market prices is much more tenuous than for physical capital. Investible funds are bought and sold and thus have easily recognized price–interest rates; the products of investment, goods and services, also have directly recognizable market prices. Even though, for the sake of social appraisals, we must adjust market prices to find opportunity cost, those adjustments are firmly anchored in readily observable data. Economists have been ingenious in discovering analogous ways to value human capital and have achieved some measure of success, notably in education. For the most part, education itself does not have a readily identifiable market price. However, both the individual and society incur costs in education (maintenance and forgone earnings for the student and the costs of running schools for the government) and the products of education, human skills are purchased in the labor market. The latter forms the basis of evaluating the benefits of education projects: discounted lifetime earnings of educated and less educated labor are compared and the difference is attributed to education. Then education projects can be analyzed just like factories, roads and dams, with resource outflows at the beginning (forgone earnings and the appropriate costs of the education system) and continuing resource benefits (the increased lifetime earnings of the educated). Although Case 7 is in the section on sectoral strategy, it incorporates project appraisal methods applied to education as an element in its analysis.

The controversy in appraising education investment centers on the meaning of differential earnings. Three fundamental objections arise. First, the education system may simply be receiving people with inherently superior skills, people who would earn higher salaries in the absence of education because of natural ability. Second, the children of educated, influential or wealthy parents probably have greater access to more and better education, but are also, because of their class status, likely to get better jobs and higher incomes. Then the correlation between education and income may not imply causality; both may be consequences of social status instead. Finally, the schools may be acting, not as a training or human capital-augmenting device, but rather as a screen to filter through those who are not only trainable, but who have other characteristics that production units value. Not least of these is the ability and willingness to perform a role within an organization and conform to that organization's standards. Although each of these possible interpretations of earnings differentials casts doubt on their meaning for cost–benefit analysis, it remains likely that some part of those differentials does represent a social return to education. The empirical issue is, how much[11]?

In the realms of health, nutrition and population policy, cost-benefit analysis is on even shakier footing. Costs and benefits of health programs can be classified in three ways. First, there are financial—and hence resource—costs of implementing control and curative programs, as well as some financial benefits if control or cure reduces the need for medical services that would otherwise be provided. Second, disease control will reduce morbidity (the fraction of a population that is ill), an obvious benefit, though some curative methods may actually increase morbidity temporarily if the treatment itself is disabling. Third, disease control is likely to reduce mortality (the death-rate) among the affected population.

Evaluation of the first class of benefits is straightforward, no different from the costs and benefits of a factory. However, there is real doubt about the measurement of reduced morbidity and mortality. To start with the former, the standard practice has been to define the benefit of reduced illness as the opportunity cost of lost days of labor. That is, a sick worker is either absent from work or is less productive. In either case, he produces less, a cost to society which is measured by the wage paid as a proxy for the worker's marginal revenue product. This is consistent with the standard treatment of the shadow wage. If the disease is prevented or cured, presumably the worker gains back those lost days or productivity, a benefit to society.

This measure of health benefits is open to several criticisms. First, there is an empirical problem: it is difficult to measure the precise effect of disease, as a study by Baldwin and Weisbrod (1974) makes clear. Second, by concentrating on the more easily measurable benefits to employed people, we miss important production benefits when the health of housewives and children is improved, because in developing countries they provide an important part of the rural labor force. Third, if the control or curative program is widespread, it will have many external effects, interacting with nutrition, fertility and labor markets, which may be relatively more important than the measurable ones. These externalities may occur in strictly economic projects also, but their importance may be relatively less and their identification and measurement relatively easier than in health. Fourth, production benefits exclude what could easily be the most highly regarded effect of health programs on the affected population: the consumption benefit of better health. People obviously like to feel better and will often go to great lengths to do so. Although in principle economists might put a market value on improved health, for example by measuring all the costs an individual incurs to get well, in practice there are many barriers to doing so. (Education is subject to the same problem: people also seek knowledge and training for its own sake, a consumption benefit not measured in human capital approaches.)

One test of the acceptability of the production-based measures of benefits is the likely effect on resource allocation. If our analyses depend on forgone output, that is, on a wage-based measure of benefits, then health programs aimed at able-bodied workers and especially at high-wage workers, will show the highest social returns. Health programs for children, mothers and the aged could not compete for investment and these groups would be neglected. It seems clear from the actual allocations that policy-makers would not accept this outcome, implying that they have different values or see important benefits that are not captured by the narrow measures economists have used[12].

When life-saving benefits of health investments are considered, the picture is even cloudier. Proposed measures of live-saving benefits have included the discounted lifetime value of forgone production; the discounted lifetime value of the saving lost to society; the value that voters or policy-makers place on programs intended to save lives; the premium that individuals pay to insure against the risk of death; the higher pay they will demand to undertake riskier occupations; and the compensation an individual would pay or receive to avoid or accept a known increased risk of death. Each has critical failings. The production based method has all the problems discussed above in relation to reduced morbidity. The saving principle is surely too narrow a measurement in a society that accepts some measure of consumer sovereignty and considers private consumption a social benefit. The revealed preferences of voters or policy-makers ignores individual choice and involves the circularity that policy-makers may need to have some objective measure of the value of life before making their own judgements about programs to save lives. The insurance principle measures the wrong thing, since insurance compensates surviving dependents rather than those risking death. Also, because premia depend on income, this approach values the lives of wealthy persons higher than those of poorer ones. The methods based on compensation for risk are better than other measures and may be valid when a project changes the risk of death somewhere in the range of risks covered by the insurance policies or wage premia that can be observed. But as the risk of death increases, willingness to accept risk diminishes. Also, this willingness varies enormously among individuals and groups. In developing countries, the limited experience with risk compensation may not apply to groups affected by the project: a wage premium paid to miners says little about the willingness of farmers to risk death[13].

The incompleteness or irrelevance of cost-benefit techniques in the human capital area, especially in health, has led some planners to adopt cost-effectiveness as a measure of desirability. In this concept, some common goal, such as disease prevented or lives saved, is accepted as numeraire or denominator and the cost of achieving this goal is the numerator: the lower the ratio, the better the project. Faced by the inherent inadequacies of cost-benefit techniques, this may be as good a method as any, but it has its own problems. Cost effectiveness is subject to the same drawbacks as other cost-benefit ratios, including ambiguities in the way the ratio is calculated and in the way projects should be selected according to their ratios. More fundamentally, however, because cost effectiveness provides no way to compare disparate benefits, such as lives saved and disease prevented, it says nothing about the selection among projects with different benefits. Its best use is in selecting from among various designs to achieve the same end: for example, to select the method of malaria control that will deliver benefits for the least resource cost. It is useless as a means of allocating an entire budget or in choosing among projects with different goals.

Notes

1 A good primer on investment appraisal for private enterprise is Bierman and Smidt (1975).
2 The term 'social' appraisal, though widely used, is misleading. It refers to project analysis for the nation (i.e. society) as a whole and follows the convention of welfare economics. However, it has the connotation of including social non-market considerations which project analysis cannot handle well, if at all. The World Bank has adopted a more precise terminology, distinguishing among private appraisal, economic appraisal (which measures economic costs and benefits to the nation) and social appraisal, which includes distributional aims, as discussed below. In this book we will use the traditional term, 'social' analysis, despite its shortcomings.
3 Roemer and Stern (1975), Chapter 3, provide an introduction to shadow price theory and measurement. For more complete treatment, see appropriate chapters in Harberger (1972), Little and Mirrless (1974), and UNIDO (1972).
4 Alternative measures of the shadow wage are presented in Harberger (1972), Chapter 7; Little and Mirrless (1974), Chapters 9 and 14; and UNIDO (1972), Chapters 8 and 15. An important concept, omitted here to keep the exposition simple, is that both employers' demand and laborers' supply schedules contribute to an estimate of the shadow price.
5 There is a once-popular notion that, with the high land–labor ratios common to many Asian countries and the high unemployment observed in most LDC cities, the shadow cost of labor must be zero or close to it. However, neither condition necessarily indicates a zero marginal product. Harberger (1972, pp. 158–161) cites evidence to show that, even in India, the rural marginal product of labor is positive and significant. Harris and Todaro (1970) show that, with allowance for migration, urban unemployment is consistent with a positive shadow wage. Finally, even if the marginal product of a worker were zero, he would be unlikely to work for a zero wage. In that case, the correct measure of the shadow wage is the non-zero value the worker places on his leisure, i.e. his supply price, and not zero.
6 This approach is based on Harberger (1972), Chapter 4.
7 See Bacha and Taylor (1971) for a full discussion of shadow exchange rates; a simplified approach to calculating them is in Roemer and Stern (1975), Chapter 3.
8 For a more complete discussion of these selection tools, see Roemer and Stern (1975), Chapter 2, which, however, incorrectly rules out BCR as a capital budgeting tool. (We are grateful to Robert Dorfman for pointing this out.)
9 This method is described in Pouliquen (1970).
10 See Schwartz and Berney (1977) for a collection of articles comparing and criticizing various approaches to project analysis.
11 On the education–human capital controversy, see Blaug's review article (1976).
12 Cost–benefit analysis of health programs is discussed by Dunlop (1975).
13 This discussion follows Mishan (1971).

References

BACHA, E. and TAYLOR, L. (1971). Foreign Exchange Shadow Prices: A Critical Review of Current Theories. *Quarterly Journal of Economics* **85**, 197–224

BALDWIN, R. E. and WEISBROD, B. A. (1974). Disease and Labor Productivity. *Economic Development and Cultural Change* **22,** 414–435

BEIRMAN, H., Jr. and SMIDT, S. (1975). *The Capital Budgeting Decision*, fourth edn. New York, The Macmillan Company

BLAUG, M. (1976). Human Capital Theory: A Slightly Jaundiced Survey. *Journal of Economic Literature* **14,** 827–855

DUNLOP, D. (1975). Benefit-Cost Analysis: A Review of its Applicability in Policy Analysis for Delivering Health Services. *Social Science and Medicine* **9,** 133–139

GALENSON, W. and LEIBENSTEIN, H. (1955). Investment Criteria, Productivity and Economic Development. *Quarterly Journal of Economics* **69,** 343–370

HARBERGER, A. C. (1972). *Project Evaluation.* Chicago, University of Chicago Press

HARBERGER, A. C. (1978). On the Use of Distributional Weights in Social Cost-Benefit Analysis. *Journal of Political Economy* **86–2,** Part 2, S87–S120

HARRIS, J. R. and TODARO, M. (1970). Migration, Unemployment and Development: A Two-Sector Analysis. *American Economic Review* **60–1,** 126–142

LITTLE, I. M. D. and MIRRLEES, J. A. (1974). *Project Appraisal and Planning for Developing Countries.* New York, Basic Books

MacARTHUR, J. D. (1978). Appraising the Distributional Aspects of Rural Development Projects: A Kenya Case Study. *World Development* **6–2,** 167–194

MISHAN, E. J. (1971). Evaluation of Life and Limb: A Theoretical Approach. *Journal of Political Economy* **79,** 687–705

POULIQUEN, L. Y. (1970). *Risk Analysis in Project Appraisal.* Baltimore, Johns Hopkins Press

ROEMER, M. and STERN, J. J. (1975). *The Appraisal of Development Projects.* New York, Praeger Special Studies

SCHWARTZ, H. and BERNEY, R. (eds.) (1977). *Social and Economic Dimensions of Project Evaluation.* Washington, D.C., Interamerican Development Bank

SQUIRE, L. and van der TAK, H. G. (1975). *Economic Analysis of Projects.* Baltimore, Johns Hopkins University Press

UNITED NATIONS INDUSTRIAL DEVELOPMENT ORGANIZATION (Partha Das Gupta, Stephen Marglin and Amartya Sen) (1972). *Guidelines for Project Evaluation.* New York, United Nations

Torrence Copper Mine

The Beracia Copper Company (BCC), a government-owned but independent corporation, operates three large mines and several small ones, together with smelters and refining plants. It mines about 80 percent of the copper exported from Beracia and processes 90 percent of it. The government restricts the export of unprocessed copper, so that small private miners must sell part of their output to BCC for smelting. BCC maintains capacity to smelt 200 000 tons per year into blister copper (99 percent pure copper) and to refine 180 000 tons into electrolytic copper bars (virtually 100 percent pure). The balance of mine output is exported as concentrates of about 30 percent copper. Virtually all exports are sold under long-term contract to international copper companies, some of which in turn provide management for the mines and processing facilities.

BCC's largest mine is a low-cost, open-pit mine at Torrence. It was taken over three years ago from the United Copper and Nickel Corporation (UCAN), an integrated American firm which began to develop the Torrence mine in 1959. The mine was opened in 1962. In 1977 it produced 70 000 tons of copper metal from ore with a copper content of from 3 to 4 percent. The mine has its own smelter and refinery, both of which operate close to capacity. The Beracia Railway Corporation operates a spur line to the mine and transports all the copper to the port of Limani. The Torrence Mine is managed as a separate company subsidiary to BCC. Management is under contract from UCAN, although a few Beracians have begun to fill engineering and management positions. However, under government prodding, the mine has Beracianized all supervisory positions in the mines and processing plants.

When the mine was originally developed, it was known there was a much smaller but potentially profitable copper deposit a few miles from the Torrence facility. It was a condition of the mining rights granted by the government that UCAN should develop the smaller mine as soon as possible. However, after development began in 1959, falling copper prices and rising costs dampened UCAN's enthusiasm for the adjacent mine and the processing facilities were constructed to handle only the output of the main mine. Despite constant prodding by government, UCAN never did develop the new mine and this was one of several issues which convinced the military government to take over Torrence–B in 1973. To ensure that decisions like this would not go by default in the newly nationalized company, the managing director is the investment manager for BCC. Development of the new mine, which is to be designated Torrence–B, has been a high priority since nationalization and development planning is complete. The Ministry of Mines has received, and referred to the Ministry of Planning, an investment program to open Torrence–B within three years. The details of the project are specified below.

OUTPUT

The mine is believed to contain at least 100 000 tons of recoverable copper metal in ore with a concentration of 3 percent. The intention is to exploit this over 10 years, with production at 10 000 tons per year. All output would be concentrated at the existing Torrence facilities, which would be expanded slightly for the purpose. However, there are no plans to expand the existing smelter or refinery, so the copper would be exported as an ore concentrate of 30 percent copper.

TABLE 1 Annual average of U.S. domestic producers' and London Metal Exchange copper prices, 1947–1977 (U.S. cents per pound)

Year	U.S. domestic producers	LME	Year	U.S. domestic producers	LME
1947	21.0	16.3	1962	30.6	29.3
1948	22.0	16.8	1963	30.6	30.2
1949	19.2	16.3	1964	32.0	44.0
1950	21.3	22.4	1965	35.0	58.5
1951	24.2	27.6	1966	36.2	69.4
1952	24.2	32.6	1967	38.2	51.5
1953	28.8	30.1	1968	41.1	56.2
1954	29.7	31.2	1969	47.5	66.6
1955	37.5	43.8	1970	57.7	64.2
1956	41.8	41.0	1971	51.4	49.1
1957	29.6	27.4	1972	51.3	48.6
1958	25.8	24.8	1973	59.4	80.9
1959	31.2	29.8	1974	77.0	93.1
1960	32.1	30.8	1975	64.5	55.9
1961	29.9	28.8	1976	69.6	63.6
			1977[a]	69.1	60.7

Note: [a]Through September.

Sources: R. F. Mikesell (1975). *Foreign Investment in Copper Mining*. Baltimore, The Johns Hopkins University Press, p. 60; International Monetary Fund (1977). *International Financial Statistics*, Washington, D.C.

REVENUES

The entire output would be exported under long-term contract to a Japanese company. BCC has obtained a tentative ten-year agreement to sell the entire mine output as a concentrate at an fob price equivalent to 50 percent of the London Metal Exchange (LME) price for refined copper bars, averaged over the previous three years. The price would thus be adjusted each year. *Table 1* presents a record of the relevant LME price for the past 30 years.

Price projections from one of the commodity forecasting services indicate that the LME price may be expected to rise by 6 percent in 1978, 10 percent in 1979 and 17 percent in 1980, all in constant 1977 prices. The same service projects a price of 103 cents per pound by 1985 (in 1977 dollars).

DEVELOPMENT COSTS

BCC estimates that it will take three years to purchase and install the necessary plant and equipment, to open the new mine and to expand the existing concentration plant. During the first two years, mining equipment worth U.S.$ 6.70m would be purchased and put in place. This includes a short rail line to transport ore to the concentration plant at Torrence. Concentration equipment worth U.S.$ 5.80m would be purchased and installed during the second and third years. Both types of equipment carry a duty of 10 percent. Other costs, spread more or less evenly over the three-year period, are: salaries of expatriate technicians and supervisors, Lp 2.40m; wages of construction workers, Lp 12.60m; imported materials, mostly fuels and explosives, U.S.$ 1.20m plus a duty of 15 percent; and local materials and services, Lp 5.40m. Although all facilities should be in place after three years, experience has shown that such schedules often lag behind by from six to twelve months. Moreover, although mine output is planned at full capacity for the first year of operations, there may be some shakedown problems that prevent output from reaching this level during the first year. Nevertheless, plans are being made on the basis of a three-year investment period and full production the following year.

OPERATING COSTS

Table 2 shows the annual costs of operating the mine and the additional costs of the expanded concentration plant. Under the new BCC policy, all salaried personnel for the new mine and expanded plant will be Beracian. Of those earning wages, 250 will be skilled workers earning Lp 1120 per month (plus the usual 25 percent in benefits and vacation time), who will by and large be trained and promoted from among the unskilled workers in the existing facilities. The balance will be unskilled

TABLE 2 Operating costs—mine and concentration plant

	Lp 1000 per year
Wages	8 820
Salaries	2 640
Imported materials (fuel, explosives, etc.)	7 820
Duty at 15 percent	1 170
Replacements and spare parts	2 700
Duty at 10 percent	270
Local goods and services	2 400
Other mining and concentration costs	500
Transportation to port and handling	1 150
Total annual costs	27 470

workers earning Lp 560 per month plus 25 percent, who will be hired from the surrounding farm area, where average income per worker, allowing for both subsistence production and idle days, is roughly Lp 210 per month over the entire year.

Transport costs reflect the average rates charged by Beracian Railways for output of Torrence Mine. However, consultants have estimated that the actual operating cost of carrying additional tonnage from Torrence would be 40 percent of the average cost*. The same study estimated that the import content of rail transport is about 65 percent.

To ensure a smooth flow of materials, inventories of imported goods (only) will be maintained at a level of three months' usage.

HOUSING

BCC typically builds houses for its workers at all its facilities at an average cost of Lp 24 000 per worker. This construction has been financed by loans from the Housing Bank at 7 percent over 20 years. Because worker housing is handled by a separate subsidiary of BCC, it is never considered part of the development or operating costs of mining. Workers are charged rent at the rate of 12 percent of their gross salaries, which is deducted from weekly wages.

FINANCE

BCC has been able to obtain loans through U.S. banks totaling $ 10m against equipment purchased in the U.S. These would be repayable in five equal annual installments from the year the mine is expected to begin production. Interest is at 8 percent on the outstanding balance.

---

*   E. Vickers (1974). Pricing Rail Transport Services in Beracia. *Beracia Development Journal* **10**, 115–140.

BCC has asked the government to cover the balance of any necessary investment by increasing its equity position. The corporation has been charged to earn at least 10 percent on its total assets before taxes and at least 15 percent on equity investment after taxes.

TAXES

Mining is heavily taxed in Beracia. In addition to import duties on both capital equipment and materials, which as a matter of principle are never waived for mining investments, there is a 15 percent duty levied on the fob price of exported copper. (The variable surcharge will not be levied on exports from the new mine.) And all mining companies, including state-owned firms, pay income tax at 45 percent of net profit. Depreciation, interest and other taxes are deductible expenses, but there is no depletion allowance.

Questions

1. Would the Beracia Copper Company make its required rate of return on the proposed development of Torrence–B?
2. Should government approve this investment and contribute the required equity funds?
3. What would be the effect on the social and private rate of return if
   (a) Production were delayed for a year, with no shift in development expenses, and outlays during the interim year were restricted to wages, salaries and capital charges?
   (b) Copper prices were to fall by 15 percent from the prices used in the analysis of question 1?

Further reading

BANKS, F. E. (1974). *The World Copper Market: An Economic Analysis.* Cambridge, Mass., Balinger

BROWN, M. S. and BUTLER, J. (1968). *The Production, Marketing and Consumption of Copper and Aluminum.* New York, Praeger

DELLAVALLE, P. (1975). Productivity and Employment in the Copper and Aluminum Industries. In *Technology and Employment in Industry* (ed. by A. S. Bhalla) pp. 275–308. Geneva, International Labour Office

FRY, J. and HARVEY, C. (1974). Copper and Zambia. In *Commodity Exports and African Economic Development* (ed. by S. M. Pearson and J. Cownie). Lexington, Mass., D.C. Heath

MIKESELL, R. F. (1975). *Foreign Investment in Copper Mining.* Baltimore, The Johns Hopkins University Press

SEIDMAN, A. (ed.) (1975). *Natural Resources and National Welfare: The Case of Copper.* New York, Praeger

UNITED NATIONS INDUSTRIAL DEVELOPMENT ORGANIZATION (1972). *Copper Production in Developing Countries.* New York, United Nations

UNITED STATES DEPARTMENT OF THE INTERIOR (1975 and 1976). *Minerals Yearbook, 1973* **1** and **3.** Washington, D.C., Government Printing Office

Horio Rice Project

Beracia's agricultural policies aim at raising productivity in the agricultural sector, increasing the production of food, industrial and export crops and improving the living condition of the rural population where most of the poor families, i.e. those below the poverty line, live. Development of the agricultural sector is viewed as a major tool in the attack on poverty.

At independence the modern agricultural sector was dominated by private large-scale farms, owned primarily by expatriates. In its first efforts to increase agricultural production, the government tried to group small-scale farmers into cooperatives, or *kerjasamas*, using such cooperatives as a means of introducing modern practices. The *kerjasama* approach has not been totally successful and the rice growing cooperative established in the Eastern Region has proved particularly unsuccessful. This cooperative, covering 1250 hectares, brought together previously landless farmers to work on government-owned land. The yield on the cooperative has been poor, despite the fact that the ecological conditions of the area are suitable for commercial rice production.

In 1969 the government created the State Farm Corporation (BSFC), charged with the dual function of taking over all large-scale private farms and absorbing those cooperatives which had failed to achieve reasonable levels of productivity. The present project is designed to help achieve these goals. The State Farm Corporation will take over the existing cooperative and buy 1500 hectares of land presently owned by large-scale private farmers. In addition it intends to bring an additional 500 hectares of less arable land under cultivation using low-lift pumps to supplement rainfall. The state farms will require loans to purchase equipment while the Beracia Industrial Development Corporation has agreed to open a new mill in the region to handle expanded production. The Public Works Department will provide feeder roads and extension workers are to be provided by the

Ministry of Agriculture. Although Beracia exports long grain rice to the Middle East, it continues to import short grain rice for local consumption. The project will produce short grain rice and thus will substitute for imported rice rather than add to exports.

PHASING

In its project document the Rice Development Unit of the State Farm Corporation has proposed the following schedule:

Year 1:   First 400 hectares of land now under rice cultivation by the Persatuan Kerjasama Pesawah Padi (Rice Growers' Cooperative) taken over by BSFC, together with 500 hectares taken over from large-scale private farms.

Year 2:   Remaining 850 hectares taken over from Persatuan Kerjasama Pesawah Padi together with 1000 hectares of land in private large-scale farms. First 250 hectares of irrigated land cleared and brought into cultivation.

Year 3:   Further 250 hectares of land suitable for irrigation, to be brought under cultivation.

The initial investment phase of the project thus lasts three years.

YIELDS

Farmers in the cooperative, using traditional means of cultivation, are averaging about 10 bags per hectare. The large scale private farms, using a newly developed seed (C3–P0) together with prescribed amounts of fertilizer, have raised their yield to about 40 bags per hectare. The BSFC is confident it can obtain similar yields on the land now managed by the cooperative. The additional land to be brought into cultivation is less suited for rice cultivation and hence requires supplemental irrigation. The BSFC still feels confident that with modern inputs this newly cleared land will yield about 20 bags per hectare. Note that one bag contains 80 kg of paddy, or unmilled rice, and yields 52 kg of milled rice; 35 percent of the weight is lost in milling.

Analysis of meteorological data demonstrates that the central region is subject to droughts once every five or six years and these droughts may be severe enough to destroy most of the crop. Since the low-lift pump irrigation depends on a reasonably high water level in the Horio River, a drought generally affects *all* the land under rice in this region. To allow for the effects of droughts, the BSFC, in its project report, suggests that for purposes of analysis the above-quoted yield figures be reduced by from 15 to 20 percent.

TRACTORS

The State Farms Corporation will need to buy tractors for plowing and harrowing. Although the large-scale farms are using a moderate-sized tractor, the BSFC proposes to use a heavier type of tractor for two reasons. First, the additional land to be placed under cultivation will require heavier farm machinery. Second, a loan for agricultural equipment from the government of Yugoslavia is available and the BSFC proposes to utilize this loan. While the tractors to be taken over from the large farmers still have from three to four years of productive life, the BSFC proposes to replace such equipment two years after they have been taken over in order to simplify maintenance and reduce spare parts inventory. New tractors used by the private sector cost Lp 66 500 each and the BSFC has agreed to reimburse the private farmers at a price of Lp 16 500 for each tractor appropriated.

Each tractor is expected to plow slightly more than 2 hectares a day during a 60-day planting season, or 125 hectares per year. In working out the purchase schedule, account has been taken of the delivery time to the project area. To tie in with the phasing of the project, the necessary tractors must be purchased about one year ahead of their use in the project area*.

The necessary purchase schedule is:

Year 0:   (beginning of project): Three tractors to cover 400 hectares to be placed under rice cultivation in year 1.
Year 1:   Seven tractors for the remaining 850 hectares taken over from the cooperative, 2 tractors for the new land to be brought into cultivation, plus 4 tractors taken over from private farms.
Year 2:   Two more tractors purchased for 250 hectares being cleared for planting in year 3, plus 4 tractors to replace those taken over from private farmers in year 1. In addition 8 tractors will be taken over from private farmers.
Year 3:   Eight tractors to replace those taken over from private farms in year 2†.

The project will thus acquire 26 tractors to cover the 3250 hectares planned to be under cultivation in year 3. The work life of a tractor is expected to be only five years, so that to maintain a stock of 26 tractors, three new tractors will have to be purchased in year 5, nine new tractors in year 6, five in year 7, nine in year 8, and so on. The type of tractor the BSFC proposes to use costs Lp 77 500 each, delivered to Horio, the capital of the Eastern Region. Consistent with the government's policy

---

*   The actual phasing of field activities has been considerably simplified for purposes of this case.
†   A summary of the physical phasing of the project is given in Appendix Table 1. In all the equipment phasing it is assumed that the physical relationships supplied are approximate so that, for example, it is possible for three tractors to work 400 hectares either because each tractor can, if necessary, cover slightly more than the prescribed 125 hectares/year or because the planting season is not exactly of 60-days' duration.

of promoting mechanization in agriculture, no import taxes will be levied on the tractors. The approximate operating cost of the tractors is given in *Table 1*.

TABLE 1 Operating cost of project tractor (Lp/ha)

| | Total cost | Of which | | |
		Foreign	Domestic	Taxes
Maintenance	4.05	2.95	1.10	–
Fuel	150.00	50.00	25.00	75.00
Labor	12.50	–	12.50	–
Total	166.55	52.95	38.60	75.00

Note: The estimates refer to the tractor type to be used by the BSFC. The smaller size tractor used by the private sector uses less fuel (Lp 135/ha) and private farmers pay tractor drivers Lp 8.00/ha or Lp 16/day.

COMBINES

The State Farm Corporation will also buy harvesting combines. It proposes to buy the combines from Yugoslavia (Zetan–MTZ150) at a cost of Lp 238 650 per combine. No import duty is levied on the combines. Each combine, which requires two men to operate, can cover 4 hectares per day over the 60-day harvest period, or 250 hectares per year. Efficient operation requires that the combines be available for the first harvest. In addition to the new combines, the BSFC will take over the combines now used on the private farms. The replacement value of such combines is Lp 219 250 and the BSFC, estimating that these combines have about two years of usable life left, has agreed to pay Lp 85 000 for each combine taken over from private farmers. Hence the following purchasing schedule must be adhered to:

Year 1:   2 new combines to harvest first 400 hectares switched to improve practices plus 2 'old' combines purchased from private farmers.

Year 2:   3 new combines for 850 hectares switched to improve practices, plus 1 new combine for first 250 hectares of newly cleared land, plus 4 'old' combines taken over from private farmers.

Year 3:   1 new combine for the second 250 hectares of newly cleared land and 2 combines to replace those taken over from private farmers.

Year 4:   4 new combines to replace those taken over from private farmers.

These purchases will give a total of 13 combines to harvest the project's 3250 hectares. The expected life of a combine is also estimated at five years. The operating cost for a combine is shown in *Table 2*.

TABLE 2 Operating costs of project combines (Lp/ha)

	Total cost	Of which		
		Foreign	Domestic	Taxes
Maintenance	6.05	4.45	1.60	–
Fuel	230.00	77.00	38.00	115.00
Labor	12.50	–	12.50	–
Total	248.55	81.45	52.10	115.00

Note: These estimates refer to the combine type to be used by the BSFC. The combines used by the private farmers use less fuel (Lp 210/ha) and private farmers pay combine drivers about Lp 9.00/ha. Offsetting these savings, however, the use of the smaller combines on the type of terrain to be covered would raise maintenance cost by some 10 percent.

LOW-LIFT PUMPS

The land to be cultivated with supplemental irrigation lies approximately 1.5 kilometers east of the Horio River, from which water is to be pumped. The BSFC will use 2 cusec pumps to deliver the water from the Horio River to the newly cleared land. Each pump will use a 7.5 hp diesel engine and can operate 18 hours/day, delivering 90 cubic meters/hour. Each pump will be used for 30 days. It is estimated that each pump can supply water sufficient for 40 hectares. Hence the BSFC would purchase six pumps in year 1, so that irrigation could begin on the first 250 hectares of land cleared and be ready for cultivation by year 2; and a further six pumps for the remaining 250 hectares of land to be cleared and cultivated. Each pump is estimated to cost Lp 88 000, including the engine and the expected operating life is seven years. The engine, costing Lp 65 200, is imported while the pumps are locally

TABLE 3 Operating cost of low-lift pump (Lp/ha)

	Total cost	Of which		
		Foreign	Domestic	Taxes
Fuel	180.00	60.00	30.00	90.00
Spare parts	23.35	16.10	7.25	–
Field maintenance[a]	11.55	1.45	9.80	0.30
Labor	15.00	–	15.00	–
Total	229.90	77.55	62.05	90.30

Note: [a]The domestic component includes Lp 6.50/ha of labour cost.

manufactured. The operating cost of a pump is shown in *Table 3*. The cost estimates assume that the irrigation water is distributed through PVC pipes, which are imported duty free at Lp 45.00 per meter. Effective irrigation of the new land requires approximately 2000 meters of PVC pipe per pump, or 50 meters per cleared hectare. PVC piping will last approximately 10 years.

CLEARING

The contract to clear the land to be newly planted in rice will be given to the Public Works Department (PWD). The charge is Lp 750/ha of which roughly 70 percent involves foreign exchange costs and 10 percent represents taxes. Land should be cleared the year before it is planted.

ON-FARM COSTS

Under the traditional practices used on the cooperative, all work such as ground preparation, seeding, and harvesting is done by hand. No fertilizer is used. *Table 4* shows the on-farm cost for a typical farmer using traditional practices.

TABLE 4 Average on-farm costs: traditional practices (Lp/ha)

	Cost
Hoeing (14 person-days/ha at Lp 6.95/day)	97.30
Seeds (57 kg/ha at Lp 0.45/kg)	25.65
Seeding (10 person-days/ha at Lp 6.95/day)	69.50
Weeding (10 person-days/ha at Lp 6.95/day)	69.50
Harvesting (39.5 person-days/ha at Lp 6.95/day)	274.53
Bags (10 bags/ha at Lp 5.25/bag, each bag lasts 3 years)	17.50
Sub-total	553.98
Contingency (at 10%)	55.40
Total	609.38
Say	610.00

The only significant foreign exchange cost in the items shown in *Table 4* refers to the imported jute used for the locally manufactured bags. The foreign exchange component is valued at 50 percent of the selling price of the bag and a 10 percent import duty is levied on raw jute.

The improved practices, used on the large-scale private farms, involve the use of high-yielding rice varieties and the application of substantial amounts of fertilizer in addition to the mechanization of land preparation and harvesting. The BSFC will adopt similar practices but use slightly heavier equipment and it is this cost data which is shown in *Table 5*. In addition the BSFC will use low-lift pumps to provide supplemental irrigation on the 500 hectares of newly cleared land.

The cost of fertilizer has fluctuated sharply over the past few years. For example the price of urea (fob Europe) was $ 48.30 per tonne in 1970, $ 316.00 per tonne in 1974 and $ 197.80 per tonne in 1975*. It was during the period of rising world prices and supply shortages, and based

* World Bank (June 1977). *Price Prospects for Major Primary Commodities*. Washington, D.C.

on forecasts of continued high prices, that the National Action Committee of the Government (NAC) authorized construction of a local fertilizer plant. However the supply shortages appear to have eased and the world price for fertilizer has dropped substantially. In 1977 the price of imported fertilizer†, ex-Limani, was $ 112 per tonne. There is a 20 percent duty on fertilizer. As the local factory can only meet a portion of the total demand, imports are permitted under license. The domestic price is some 35 percent above the world price, or approximately Lp 1314 per tonne, indicating that, in addition to the tariff and margins, imported fertilizer carries a scarcity premium. At the same time, however, the government subsidizes fertilizer in Beracia, both to encourage its use and to keep food prices in the urban centres low. After allowing for the 50 percent subsidy, the fertilizer price to the BSFC is Lp 657 per tonne or Lp 0.657 per kg.

TABLE 5 Average on-farm costs: improved practices (Lp/ha)

	Total cost	Foreign	Of which Domestic	Taxes
Plowing and harrowing by tractor (see *Table 1*)	166.55	52.95	38.60	75.00
Seeds: 78.5 kg/ha at Lp 0.95/kg	74.58	37.29	37.29	–
Fertilizer: at Lp 0.657/kg	164.25	147.82[a]	16.43	–
Seeding and fertilizing: 15 person-days/ha at Lp 20/day	300.00	–	300.00	–
Weeding: 30 person-days/ha at Lp 20/day	600.00	–	600.00	–
Combine harvesting (see *Table 2*)	248.55	81.45	52.10	115.00
Bags: 25 bags/ha at Lp 5.25/bag over 3 years	43.75	21.83	19.74	2.18
Sub-total	1597.68	341.34	1064.16	192.18
Plus 10% for contingency	159.77			
Total cost	1757.45			

Note: [a] Assumes that imports, rather than domestic production, would be the main source of additional fertilizer required by the project.

The State Farms will pay their workers an average of Lp 20 per day, the urban minimum wage, while the private farmers paid their labourers the legal minimum of Lp 16 per day for workers on large farms. The cost estimates, as prepared by the BSFC, are shown in *Table 5*.

EXTENSION SERVICE

Farmers presently cultivating land to be included in the project area receive free extension services which the Ministry of Agriculture

---

† This is a weighted average of the two types used in rice cultivation, with the weights being the proportions of the two different types of fertilizer recommended.

estimates cost Lp 17 000 per annum. A considerable increase in extension services will be required by the project. The Ministry estimates the total annual cost for these services at Lp 145 000 per annum from initiation of the project to year 4; thereafter the total annual cost will be Lp 95 000. The total cost of extension services includes office space and transportation; the latter item involves a small foreign exchange expenditure, but this may be considered negligible.

FEEDER ROADS

To accommodate the additional transport required to market the expanded output, the PWD will construct 20 kilometers of feeder roads in year 1 at a cost of Lp 87 000/km. The PWD, which is exempted from paying import duties, estimates that fuel, equipment and other imported items comprise 60 percent of the cost of construction. Maintenance of the roads will cost Lp 1200/km per year. The maintenance cost includes a 25 percent foreign exchange component.

TRANSPORTATION

The rice will be transported to the mill by truckers under the auspices of the State Transport Corporation. It will cost Lp 0.12 per kg to transport the paddy. Transport costs in Beracia include roughly 50 percent foreign exchange and 20 percent taxes. The new mill, to be constructed by the Beracia Industrial Development Corporation, will be centrally located in the project area, close to most farmers, so that the projected transport cost represents a saving of 50 percent over the existing situation.

MILLING

The Beracia Industrial Development Corporation will establish a new rice mill several kilometers outside Horio. The mill will be capable of processing all the expected output from the rice project. The capital outlay for this project is shown in *Table 6*.

The government has agreed to waive all taxes on the imported equipment and building materials. The mill is scheduled to be constructed and brought into operation in year 1. The BIDC will charge

TABLE 6 Capital outlay: rice mill (thousand Lp)

| | Total cost | Of which | |
		Foreign	Domestic
Milling equipment and vehicles	395.5	395.5	–
Building	492.2	197.0	295.2
Total	887.7	592.5	295.2

Lp 25.50 per bag to process the paddy. The cost estimates, shown in *Table 7*, assume operating costs to be completely variable. These costs are roughly comparable to those charged by existing mills.

TABLE 7 Paddy milling costs (Lp/bag)

	Total cost	Of which		
		Foreign	Domestic	Taxes
Operating costs	19.55	6.80	11.05	1.70
Depreciation	1.27	0.85	0.42	–
Interest, profits, taxes	4.68	–	2.98	1.70
Total	25.50	7.65	14.45	3.40

RICE MARKET AND PRICE

Although food grain production has grown by nearly 5 percent per annum over the period from 1956 to 1973, Beracia still imports substantial quantities of food grain which continue to represent some 10 percent of total imports. Rice represents a considerable portion of such imports. As the world market price for rice is forecast to increase over the medium and long term, government has adopted as a target the achievement of 80 percent of self-sufficiency in food grains.

Over the period from 1967 to 1972, Beracia paid an average† price of Lp 1477 ($ 170) per tonne for imported rice. Because only a small margin, 3–4 percent, of world production enters world trade, the international rice market is extremely 'thin' and hence subject to substantial fluctuations in price. For example, the average percentage deviation from a five-year moving average over the period from 1955 to 1976 was 13.9 percent for rice, higher than that found for such commodities as palm oil, coffee, tea, wheat, groundnut oil, soya beans, etc.* Thus while the average price paid by Beracia for rice rose to Lp 4630 ($ 533) per tonne in 1974, it fell to Lp 2172 ($ 250) per tonne in 1976. The current (1977) prevailing price is Lp 2285 ($ 263) per tonne. The BSFC suggests that a 'safe' price assumption to use is a cif price of Lp 2500 per tonne, in constant 1977 prices, ex-Limani, the major port. To convert this to an equivalent ex-mill price at Horio, a deduction must be made for transport costs between Limani and Horio. This conversion of the ex-Limani price to an ex-Horio price is shown in *Table 8*. Thus Lp 85.25 per bag of paddy represents the price equivalent to a local farmer of an imported bag of rice. Alternatively, assuming similar quantities, a farmer can receive Lp 85.25 per bag of paddy and compete with imported rice.

†   These prices are a weighted average of 'Thai 5 percent broken' and 'Thai 25 to 35 percent broken.'
*   World Bank. *Price Prospects for Major Primary Commodities*, p. 33

TABLE 8 Conversion of imported rice to an equivalent price for domestic rice and paddy

	Lp/kg of rice	Lp/bag of paddy
Import price, cif Limani	2.29	119.08
Plus duty at 5%	0.11	5.95
Less transport and handling charges	–0.09	–4.68
Equals price at mill near Horio	2.31	120.35
Less		
(a) mill charges		–25.50
(b) transport to mill[a]		–9.60
Equals price to farmer		85.25

Note: [a] About 50% foreign exchange and 20% taxes.

FINANCING

Under Section 17 of Law 748, governing the acquisition of private assets, the agency taking over the asset must 'fairly and without prejudice' evaluate the asset. The BSFC estimates that private farmers earn an annual income, before taxes, of about Lp 775 per hectare and suggests that the present value of the farm be calculated on the assumption that farms have a 'life' of 50 years and that the appropriate discount rate to use is 9 percent, the current maximum rate allowed for savings deposits. Under these assumptions the present value of a hectare of farm lands is Lp 8500 (approximately)*. The BSFC has recommended that each of the private farmers be paid this amount within two years of the acquisition of his land, the two-year time period being recommended to permit competing title claims to be settled.

TREASURY COMMENTS

The Treasury was asked to review the project and two substantial issues were raised in their brief. First, the Treasury noted that many of the private farm owners are not Beracian citizens. It is therefore reasonable

---

*   The formula used is

$$PVA = R \left[\frac{1 - (1+i)^{-n}}{i} \right]$$

where

PVA = present value of asset
R = annual rental value (Lp 500)
i = interest rate (9 percent)
n = life of asset (50 years)

Note that if the farm life (n) is taken as infinity, the above formula reduces to

$$PVA = \frac{R}{i}$$

to assume that after their farms have been acquired such non-nationals will want to remit their payments of Lp 8500/ha abroad. Even if this outflow could be phased over several years, the balance of payments effect of such a quantity of potential remittances would be undesirable. And if the payments were to be spent locally there would be a very substantial inflationary effect. The Treasury therefore proposes that the landowners be paid in non-negotiable, self-liquidating 20-year bonds, with an interest rate of 5 percent. This proposal would mean that private farmers receive Lp 686/ha for 20 years*. Treasury suggests an interest rate of 5 percent because that is the rate carried by the most recent government bonds issue.

Second, the Treasury notes that the latest World Bank mission to Beracia presented data on the likely future prices for rice and fertilizer (*Table 9*). The Treasury wishes to know whether the BSFC considered this information in its project planning.

TABLE 9 Price forecast (in constant 1977 dollars; 1977 = 100)

	1977	1978	1979	1980	1985	1990
Rice	100.0	105.8	115.3	123.2	140.9	146.2
Fertilizer (average)	100.0	106.8	112.1	118.9	149.8	156.3

Source: IBRD Mission Report, *The Future of the Beracian Economy* (confidential) 1977.

Questions

1. What return will the BSFC earn on this project?
2. What financing must the Beracia Agricultural Development Bank (BADB) provide to the BSFC? (Note: the BADB charges an interest rate of 6 percent annually beginning from the date of the loan.)
3. Are the compensation terms for the private farmers fair?
4. Should this project be included in the development budget on its economic merits?

* The formula used is

$$A = \frac{PVA\ (i)}{1 - (1 + i)^{-n}}$$

where A =   annual payments
            PVA =   present value of asset (Lp 5480/ha)
            i =   interest rate (5 percent)
            n =   years (20)

Note that this formula is the same as that given in the preceding footnote for R.

5. Is the expansion of the rice growing area using irrigation economically justified?
6. How would the differential price projections for rice and fertilizer affect the economic merits of the project?

Further reading

ANDERSON, R. L. and MAASS, A. (1974). *A Simulation of Irrigation Systems: The Effects of Water Supply and Operating Rules on Production and Income on Irrigated Farms.* Washington, U.S. Department of Agriculture, Technical Bulletin 1431

WICKHAM, T. H., BARKER, R. and ROSEGRANT, M. V. (1978). Complementarities among Irrigation, Fertilizer and Modern Rice Varieties. In International Rice Research Institute, *Economic Consequences of the New Rice Technology.* Los Banos, Philippines

GOTSCH, C. H., and FALCON, W. P. (1975). The Green Revolution and the Economics of Punjab Agriculture. *Food Research Institute Studies* **14–1**

INTERNATIONAL RICE RESEARCH INSTITUTE (1978). *Irrigation Policy and Management in Southeast Asia.* Los Banos, Philippines

REIDINGER, R. B. (October 1974). Institutional Rationing of Canal Water in Northern India: Conflict between Traditional Patterns and Modern Needs. *Economic Development and Cultural Change* **23–1**

Appendix

TABLE 1 Summary of the physical phasing of the project (first 15 years only)

Item								Years								
	0	1	2	3	4	5	6	7	8	9	10	11	12	13	14	15
Land (hundred hectares)																
Under cultivation by cooperatives	0	4	8.5													
Under cultivation by private farmers	0	5	10.0													
Cleared land for irrigation	0	0	2.5	2.5												
Total flow	0	9	21.0	2.5	0	0	0	0	0	0	0	0	0	0	0	0
Total stock	0	9	30.0	32.5	32.5	32.5	32.5	32.5	32.5	32.5	32.5	32.5	32.5	32.5	32.5	32.5
Tractors (units)																
New	3	9	6	8	0	3	9	6	8	0	3	9	6	8	0	3
Old	0	4	8	0	0	0	0	0	0	0	0	0	0	0	0	0
Total flow	3	13	14	8	0	3	9	6	8	0	3	9	6	8	0	3
Total stock	3	16	26	26	26	26	26	26	26	26	26	26	26	26	26	26
Combines (units)																
New	0	2	4	3	4	0	2	4	3	4	0	2	4	3	4	0
Old	0	2	4	0	0	0	0	0	0	0	0	0	0	0	0	0
Total flow	0	4	8	3	4	0	2	4	3	4	0	2	4	3	4	0
Total stock	0	4	12	13	13	13	13	13	13	13	13	13	13	13	13	13
Irrigation equipment																
Low-lift pumps (units)																
Total flow	0	6	6	0	0	0	0	0	6	6	0	0	0	0	0	0
Total stock	0	6	12	12	12	12	12	12	12	12	12	12	12	12	12	12
PVC pipes (thousand meters)																
Total flow	0	2	2	0	0	0	0	0	0	0	0	2	2	0	0	0
Total stock	0	2	4	4	4	4	4	4	4	4	4	4	4	4	4	4

Limani Cement Plant

Ministry of Industries
20 February 1978

Principle Secretary
Ministry of Planning

PROPOSED CEMENT PLANT AT LIMANI

My Minister has instructed me to inform you that he intends to propose to the Economic Committee of the Cabinet that the Government actively support a private investment in a 400 000-tonne cement plant, to be built and operated by Sadfi Brothers, Ltd., the owners of the existing plant near Kefala. I enclose, for your personal use, a copy of the internal minute on this proposal, as well as copies of the correspondence with Mr H. G. Sadfi, the Managing Director.

The Committe on Investment Incentives, which I chair, has already met and agreed to recommend to the Economic Committee of the Cabinet the following incentives for this project: (i) relief from duties on all equipment, vehicles and intermediate imports used in the manufacture and marketing of cement; (ii) an income tax holiday for seven years from the first year of production. At the request of the Incentives Committee, I am approaching the Managing Director of the Bank for Industrial Development and the Principal Secretary, Treasury, to see if the recent Danish grant can be passed on to Sadfi Brothers at a concessional interest rate of 11 percent, repayment over 10 years after a three-year grace period for both principal and interest.

Although the recommended concessions were not dependent on it, my Minister is very keen to see this project located in Aragua, rather than in Limani, as proposed by Sadfi. However, as you will see from the enclosed correspondence, the investors are reluctant to move the project there and may well require additional incentives, including an outright subsidy, to locate in Aragua.

Should you require further information, please do not hesitate to call me.

(Signed by)

Principal Secretary.

MINISTRY OF INDUSTRIES
INTERNAL MINUTE
ANALYSIS OF SADFI BROTHERS 400 000-TONNE CEMENT PLANT

General. Sadfi Brothers, Ltd, who operate the 300 000-tonne Kefala Cement Company plant, have proposed to construct a 400 000-tonne plant on the outskirts of Limani, adjacent to a limestone deposit. The company seeks government approval for the investment and to mine the limestone, which is on government-owned land; and also requests investment incentives as detailed below. Sadfi Brothers have submitted a full report to the Ministry in support of their proposal. It includes certification from an outside consultant on technical feasibility and a tender from an equipment supplier who also offers finance for the shipment. The information in this report is based on that proposal and conversations with Mr H. G. Sadfi, the Managing Director, and his associates.

Raw materials. The limestone deposits near Limani have been thoroughly explored by the Mines Bureau of the Ministry of Natural Resources. They are of adequate quality for the proposed plant and can be expected to last from 15 to 20 years. It is unlikely that additional deposits exist within the area, which has been extensively prospected. The deposit can evidently be mined at relatively low cost. Gypsum will be available from the same source as that serving the Kefala plant and at reasonably low cost. Water is plentiful at the site. Fuel can be supplied from the Limani refinery.

Consumption. Estimates of apparent consumption of cement in Beracia over the period from 1967 to 1978 are shown in the table. We assume that renewed economic growth will stimulate cement consumption to resume the growth evidenced from 1967 to 1974. Projecting that trend forward from 1978 we estimate an increase in consumption of about 30 percent to over 1.8m tonnes by 1982, more than enough to justify immediate investment in additional capacity of 400 000 tonnes. In the absence of additional production, we would be forced to import more cement to avoid stifling the recovery of investment, to which the Government has given a high priority.

TABLE 1 Apparent consumption of cement, 1967–1978 (1000 tonnes)

Year	Production	Imports	Exports	Apparent consumption
1967	545	240	50	735
1968	630	255	95	790
1969	860	210	110	960
1970	875	195	85	985
1971	790	135	35	890
1972	870	225	45	1050
1973	1110	150	70	1190
1974	1250	75	95	1230
1975	1200	65	100	1165
1976	1240	50	90	1200
1977	1250	40	60	1230
1978	1250	100	50	1300

As suggested in the Ministry manual on project appraisal, we checked this estimate of Beracia's consumption against that for countries with similar incomes. Using UN figures on production (United Nations *Yearbook*), an average country of Beracia's size and income in 1977 would consume only between 700 000 and 1 000 000 tonnes of cement. If Beracia's cement consumption should not resume its former growth and should instead begin to adopt the pattern of an average country, then the proposed plant would still be in a position to export to neighboring countries, as existing plants do now.

Price. The new plant would sell cement at the domestic control price ex factory at Limani, which is Lp 290 per tonne in 1978, but is revised upward annually to allow for higher cost of production. Because of high transport costs, fob export prices are much lower, averaging Lp 230 per tonne during 1977. (Because cement is considered an essential commodity, the bonus voucher has been reduced to 20 percent.) Imports now cost Lp 250 per tonne cif and bear a 15 percent duty, paid by most users, although not the government. These prices have risen at least as quickly as the general rate of inflation over the past few years.

The domestic price of Lp 290 per tonne applies to all cement sold ex factory in Kefala and would also apply to Limani. In order to reduce regional disparities, wholesale prices of cement are controlled throughout the country. The wholesale markup is 12 percent throughout the country. That markup is based on the ex factory price if the cement is sold within a 50-mile radius of Kefala. The base price increases by 10 percentage points for each 50-mile band beyond Kefala. (Thus, in Aragua, 340 miles away, the base price is Lp 290 + 6 × 10% × 290 = Lp 464 per tonne; the wholesale price is then 12 percent higher, or Lp 520 per tonne.) At this rate we expect that wholesalers can cover most of the transport cost. If a new plant were established in an outlying region, the control price would be revised to Lp 290 at the new production point and a new set of wholesale prices would be established for nearby regions, based on transportation from the new source.

Investment costs. Sadfi Brothers submitted bids on equipment for both mining and plant operations from two different sources. The low bid totaled Lp 175m for all machinery, vehicles and other equipment delivered to the plant site (assuming it is in Limani) and installed. Under the existing tariff schedule, Sadfi would be required to pay 12.5 percent duty on this amount. Construction of the plant and site installations would cost Lp 72m if undertaken by the same local firm that constructed Kefala Cement. Additional investment would include inventories of spare parts and maintenance materials equivalent to six months' production; packaging materials (4 months' worth); and fuel (1 month's worth). An inventory of one month's sales of cement would be maintained, but this would not require additional investment because it would be set aside from production in the first two years.

Depreciation. According to Sadfi Brothers, most of the equipment would be depreciated over 15 years. However, about Lp 20m of the mining equipment would be written off over 8 years and replaced. Buildings and site improvements must, under the income tax code, be depreciated over 30 or more years.

Annual operating costs. Based on their experience with Kefala Cement, Sadfi Brothers estimate that annual operating costs will be as follows:

Workers   500 at an average wage of Lp 990 per month plus 25 percent benefits (considered to be an essentially fixed cost).

Supervisors and technicians   20 Beracians at an average Lp 51 000 per year including benefits; 10 expatriates at an average Lp 190 000 per year. Latter to be phased down to 5 after third year of production and eliminated after fifth year.

Fuel   Lp 24.60 per tonne, all imported, duty-free.

Water and power   Lp 8.10 per tonne.

Maintenance materials and spare parts   Imported; total Lp 18.10 per tonne including 7.5 percent duty on cif value.

Packaging   Imported; costs Lp 16.20 per tonne including 20 percent duty on cif value.

Other manufacturing costs   These are largely fixed and total about Lp 6.5m.

There is a possibility of substituting for the imported bags, since Beracian Paper Products Limited now produces a cement bag which costs about 7 percent less than the duty-paid price of an imported bag.

Transportation. All cement is sold fob at the factory or port to wholesalers and final users; private truckers pick up the cement at the factory warehouse. For this reason, Sadfi's proposal contains no cost estimates for transportation. However, the factory is located near enough to the port so that there would be little difference in transport costs between the new factory's cement and imported cement which is picked up at the pier.

Implementation. Sadfi Brothers is prepared to go ahead as soon as the necessary license is issued and investor incentives are approved. Construction could start in 1979 and would take three years to complete. Construction costs would be spread roughly evenly over that peiod; half of the machinery would be imported during the first year of construction and the rest during the second year; inventories would be purchased during the third year of construction; final goods inventory would be accumulated from production during the first two years of production. Production would begin during the fourth year of the project (i.e. soon after construction was finished). From their experience with Kefala Cement, Sadfi expects to produce at 30 percent of capacity during the first year of production, 70 percent during the second year, and at full capacity by the third year.

Finance. Sadfi Brothers has arranged a supplier's credit to cover the machinery and equipment on the following terms: 20 percent paid in cash upon delivery; balance repayable at 10 percent over eight years after a one-year grace period for principal repayment from the date of the import of the last machinery. Sadfi has applied to the Bank for Industrial Development for a loan to cover construction costs. The BID is considering making such a loan from the proceeds of the Danish grant, which the Ministry of Finance has made available to the BID at the customary 9 percent rate of interest. BID would make this available to Sadfi at their statutory interest rate of 15.0 percent, with principal repayable over seven years starting the year after construction is completed. Sadfi also expects to be able to obtain overdraft facilities from the commercial banks up to Lp 10m to cover working capital at the prime bank rate of 14 percent. The balance of finance would be equity investment by Sadfi Brothers.

Incentives. Sadfi Brothers request the following concessions from the government to enable them to proceed with this investment:

(a) Duty relief on all machinery and spare parts for the life of the project;

(b) An income tax holiday for seven years from the start of production, after which they would pay the full rate of 45 percent on net profits; and

(c) Concessional lending rates from the BID, which could afford to lower its rate to 11 percent and still make a profit on the Danish grant which was passed on from the Treasury at 9 percent.

Analysis. This is a very attractive project. It will prevent imports of cement from rising during the early 1980s as demand continues to increase. Once the project reaches capacity output, it will save Lp 76m in foreign exchange each year. It will also contribute Lp 83m of value added to GDP each year while employing 500 workers for the life of the project. The profitability to the country can be indicated by the pay-back period, which is the sixth year of production, but only the fourth year from the start of full production. At full production, the ratio of annual cash flow to investment is 26 percent; deducting depreciation, the before-tax profit rate is 21 percent. These profitable results, together with the additional benefits of foreign exchange saving, value added and employment, make the project very attractive. However, because the loan terms offered to Sadfi are stringent, the private profitability after taxes is likely to be low and the concessions requested are therefore justified.

Alternative location. Ministry of Natural Resources informs us that there is a more extensive and richer deposit of limestone, with nearby gypsum deposits, near Aragua in Northern Region. It would be consistent with government policy to favor industrial projects in less developed regions if this project were moved to Aragua. Although there is little industry in the region, there has been some road and irrigation work in recent years, and there may be enough consumption of cement in nearby regions to justify the plant. In any case, it would be worthwhile to promote regional equity and to encourage new industries to locate in Aragua even if this meant that some of the cement would have to be transported back to the port and capital area. (The rail spur from Aragua to the main line could probably carry the additional traffic.)

Recommendation. Sadfi Brothers should be given a license to construct the proposed cement plant. Furthermore, the concessions they request should be granted, but only on the conditions that they relocate their project from Limani to Aragua and use domestically produced bags to package cement.

R. Miguel
16 December 1977

SADFI BROTHERS LIMIITED

Post Office Box 1402
Kefala, Beracia

10 February 1978

Principal Secretary
Ministry of Industries
Kefala

Dear Sir:

Thank you for your letter of 10 January explaining your Ministry's position on our Limani Cement Project. We are, of course, extremely grateful for the support your Ministry has shown for our project, which we agree to be in the interests of our country. It is particularly gratifying that the potential financial difficulties of a private investor making this beneficial investment have been recognized and that you are recommending incentives and concessional loan rates for our project.

I would, however, like to call your attention to certain facts that will explain the difficulties we would face in moving this project to Aragua, as your letter suggests. Upon receiving your letter, we conducted some research to determine the extent of the market in Northern Region. As you know, over half of the cement produced in Beracia is now consumed near the capital and along the coast and we see no trend to change that pattern. However, of course, as the entire market in Beracia grows, consumption in each region will grow as well and eventually it may become feasible to produce cement in each region to serve that region.

Aragua, as you know, is 350 miles from Limani. We estimate that, if the market should continue to grow at its present rate, by the time the proposed plant is at full capacity in the mid-1980s, it could sell about 25 percent of its output in Northern Region at a saving to the consumer close to the full cost of shipment from Limani, Lp 195 per tonne by rail. Another 25 percent could then be sold in surrounding regions at transport costs roughly equal to those now being incurred on cement shipped from the coast. However, the balance of output would have to be shipped most of the way to Limani or Kefala for sale, incurring additional transport costs of perhaps Lp 185 per tonne on average. By the mid-1990s, on the other hand, the market in Northern and surrounding regions should have grown sufficiently so that about half the output of the plant can be sold in Northern Region at the full transport savings and the rest can be sold in areas where Aragua cement would compete on equal terms with that from Limani.

You will appreciate that, although by the early 1990s a plant at Aragua could do quite well, it would have great difficulties selling half of its output for the first several years of operation. Buyers at the coast would strongly prefer to import cement rather than pay the higher transport costs from Aragua. This would almost certainly turn our project into an unprofitable one.

In addition, we anticipate higher costs in Aragua. It might cost some 5 percent more to ship our machinery to Northern Region and install it, and construction costs would be about 10 percent higher. In general, materials and utilities would also be 5 percent more expensive. We would have to pay supervisors and technicians an incentive of at least 15 percent over their salaries in Limani, but on the other hand we might be able to get good laborers for about 10 percent less. On balance, the additional costs would further reduce the attractiveness of a cement plant in Aragua.

For these reasons, we would not agree to move to Aragua under the terms you propose. We need the incentives requested simply to produce profitably in Limani. In order to move to Aragua, we would require further concessions, including some outright subsidy on our sales to the coast. In the absence of such subsidies, we anticipate that a plant in Aragua would not yield anything like the 17.5 percent we now earn on our investment (after taxes) in Kefala Cement and, indeed, may well make losses. These returns are a matter of public record and you can see that we could not jeopardize our investment position by undertaking a project so inferior to those we have already invested in.

On another matter raised in your letter, we are also reluctant to switch from imported cement bags to those produced by Beracian Paper Products, Ltd. We have experience with these bags in our Kefala plant and discovered that breakage is substantially higher. Our customers report that about 10 percent of the bags show some breakage in handling, compared with half that amount with the imported bags. Although not all the cement is lost in such breakages, about half of it probably is lost and, of course, additional costs are incurred in salvaging the rest of the cement from broken bags. It is true that we do not incur these losses, since we do not make good losses resulting from breakage once the cement has left our factory. However, if our competitors are not also required to use local bags, customers would have a preference for their cement and this would increase our difficulties in selling. Finally, as it is our understanding that the materials used in producing local bags are all imported, there is no saving to the economy in using these instead of imported bags.

Let me repeat my offer to discuss with you, or other appropriate officials of the Government, these or any aspects of the Limani Cement Project which may be of concern. Rest assured that in proposing this investment we have foremost in our minds the interests of our country.

Yours very truly,

H. G. Sadfi,
Managing Director.

MINISTRY OF PLANNING
GUIDELINES FOR PROJECT ANALYSIS

Foreign Exchange Content (for average project: use direct information on each
project in preference to these averages if available)
Construction: 45 percent
Utilities: 50 percent
Fuel
    Local refinery: 90 percent
    Imported: 100 percent
Transport
    Road: 60 percent
    Rail: 70 percent

Tax Content
Construction: 5 percent
Utilities: 5 percent
Fuel (local refinery): 2 percent
Transport
    Road: 25 percent
    Rail: negligible

Questions

1. Should the government encourage Sadfi Brothers to build this cement plant at Limani?
2. If so, should any or all of the following incentives be granted:
   (a) Duty relief?
   (b) A seven-year tax holiday; and/or
   (c) A loan at a concessional interest rate of 11 percent?
3. What are the economic costs of locating the plant in Aragua rather than Limani? How do these compare with the distributional benefits of higher incomes in Aragua?
4. Is Sadfi right that he would need subsidies to make it worthwhile to locate in Aragua? If so, how much and how might these be structured?

Further reading

DOYLE, L. A. (1965). *Inter-economy Comparisons, a Case Study: A Comparative Study of Industrial Development, Currency Devaluation and Inflation*. Berkeley, University of California Press

UNITED NATIONS INDUSTRIAL DEVELOPMENT ORGANIZATION (UNIDO) (1969). *Industrialization of Developing Countries: Problems and Prospects. Construction Industry*. Vienna

UNITED NATIONS INDUSTRIAL DEVELOPMENT ORGANIZATION (UNIDO) (1969). *Industrialization of Developing Countries: Problems and Prospects. Building Materials Industry*. Vienna

Filopenia–Limani Road Project

At present the industrial town of Filopenia, with a population of 480 000, is connected to the port of Limani by a 193 kilometer bituminous road and a 177 kilometer railway. The present road is narrow (4.6 meters wide), in poor condition and has frequent pavement failures in areas where use of irrigation has water-logged the embankment. It has several grades above 8 percent and three sharp curves where accidents are frequent. The road is used by slow-moving traffic, e.g., bicycles and farm vehicles; in order to pass such slow-moving vehicles, other traffic has to leave the paved surface and travel on the shoulder. The movement of vehicles from the paved road to the shoulder and back, together with the general increase in traffic, raises vehicle operating and road maintenance costs.

Two alternative proposals to deal with this problem are being considered by the Ministry of Planning. The first is the proposal put forward by the PWD, which calls for funds for widening the road from its present width to 6.0 meters, strengthening the water-logged embankments, widening some of the bridges and drainage structures, and making other minor improvements. An alternative proposal has been submitted by the Regional Planning Office (transport division) which argues that the present road be replaced by a shorter limited access highway. While the latter proposal is admittedly costlier, the Regional Planning Office argues that the rapid industrial growth taking place in Filopenia, and the concomitant increase in traffic between Filopenia and the port of Limani, makes it imperative that a modern, limited access highway be constructed. The savings in vehicle operating cost, the lower cost for goods destined for export markets, and the potential for opening up new agricultural areas will, it is argued, more than compensate for the additional cost of the new highway.

The Public Works Department argues that once the road is widened it will be able to handle an average daily traffic (*ADT*) load of 1700 vehicles, a traffic level that is not forecast until 1986. While the traffic

TABLE 1 Projected average daily traffic by type of vehicle
(road segment: Filopenia–Limani)

Year		Vehicle type		Total average
	Trucks	Buses	Cars	daily traffic
1974	320	80	150	550
1975	345	85	161	591
1976	373	90	172	635
1977	402	95	184	681
1978	435	101	197	733
1979	469	107	210	786
1980	525	116	231	872
1981	588	125	254	967
1982	659	135	280	1074
1983	738	145	307	1190
1984	827	157	338	1322
1985	943	173	379	1495
1986	1075	190	424	1689
1987	1225	209	475	1909
1988	1397	230	531	2158
1989	1592	253	596	2441
1990	1751	273	650	2674
1991	1926	295	708	2929
1992	2119	319	771	3209
1993	2331	344	842	3517
1994	2564	371	917	3852
1995	2820	401	1000	4221
1996	3046	425	1070	4541
1997	3289	451	1145	4885
1998	3552	478	1225	5255
1999	3837	506	1311	5654
2000	4144	537	1403	6084
		Summary growth rates (%)		
1974–80	8	6	7	8
1980–85	12	8	10	11
1985–90	14	10	12	12
1990–95	10	8	9	10
1995–2000	8	6	7	8

Source: Ministry of Transport, Government of Beracia (March 1974). *Survey of Road Transport Capacity* **XI**

forecast for existing traffic is subject to some margin of error, the data
shown in *Table 1* are in general accepted by the Regional Planning
Office as well. Hence both analyses use these projections as their
starting point. On the basis of past experience and recent inflation in
construction costs (about 15 percent over the two years from 1975 to
1977), the PWD estimates that widening 1000 kilometers of road would
cost Lp 30m for materials, primarily bitumen, and machinery and
require 28 500 person-years of unskilled labor and 1750 person-years of
skilled labor. It is estimated that some 80 percent of the material and
equipment cost is for imported materials. The widening project can be
completed in one year.

The PWD foresees two types of benefits for the project. First, the
widened road will allow traffic to move quickly and with less diversion

TABLE 2 Vehicle operating cost[a,b] (lepta per thousand km, 1975 prices)

ADT^c at	Cars		Trucks		Buses	
	600–900	1500–1800	600–900	1500–1800	600–900	1500–1800
Fuel	268.82	292.33	441.86	471.79	570.23	628.70
Oil	16.00	17.45	20.10	21.03	22.71	24.01
Tires[c]	18.57	25.30	136.48	144.03	377.69	434.97
Depreciation	130.35	165.57	230.66	245.63	312.03	360.08
Interest	84.99	110.05	97.67	106.73	102.31	120.56
Maintenance:						
Parts[d]	36.93	47.01	211.43	256.89	307.61	349.68
Skilled labor	0.43	0.51	2.01	2.17	2.22	2.49
Unskilled labor	3.91	4.55	15.07	15.32	26.44	31.64
Insurance	28.16	34.38	25.80	28.93	30.27	34.21
License fees	26.98	33.89	25.97	29.71	34.00	40.05
Occupants' time/						
drivers' wage	101.13	144.02	64.84	70.12	200.37	220.88
Total	716.27	875.06	1271.89	1392.35	1985.88	2247.27

Note: [a]For paved road with 4.75 meter width.
      [b]Exclusive of all import duties or taxes.
      [c]All vehicles on road.
      [d]Foreign exchange component: 75%.
      [e]Foreign exchange component: 50%.
Source: Ministry of Transport (August 1976). *Vehicle Operating Costs in Beracia* (A Preliminary Survey).

to the unpaved shoulder, thus lowering vehicle operating costs. *Table 2* shows the vehicle operating costs for trucks, buses and passenger vehicles at different *ADT* levels on the assumption that the road is not widened. (These estimates were done in 1975. Since then, vehicle operating costs may have risen by about 18 percent.) Should the road be improved, the vehicle operating costs would remain at their present

TABLE 3 Maintenance cost on paved road 1975 estimates (Lp/km/year)

ADT^a	Road width	
	$4.75\,m^b$	$6.0\,m^c$
500–599	1650	2400
600–699	1725	2400
700–799	1800	2400
800–899	1875	2400
900–999	2100	2400
1000–1099	2400	2400
1100–1199	2750	2525
1200–1299	3175	2650
1300+	3650	2780

Note: [a]ADT = average daily traffic.
      [b]Consisting of

Foreign exchange:	30%
Local raw materials:	45%
Unskilled labor:	22%
Skilled labor:	3%

      [c]Consisting of

Foreign exchange:	35%
Local raw materials:	40%
Unskilled labor:	20%
Skilled labor:	5%

level up to an average daily traffic flow of 1300 vehicles, which is taken as the full capacity level of the widened road. In addition, the PWD forecasts a saving in maintenance cost on the widened road, as shown in *Table 3*. While the improved roadbed implies a higher maintenance cost, if the road is not widened the maintenance costs on the existing road would rise over time, eventually exceeding that of the improved road. The PWD argues that widening the road is to be preferred to building a new road, and asks that funds for improving the Filopenia–Limani road be included in the next annual development plan.

The alternative proposal put forward by the provincial planning department involves construction of a new road. This road would cut the distance between Filopenia and Limani to 145 kilometers and would have a capacity for up to 8500 vehicles per day, a traffic level which is not expected to be achieved until the early part of the next century. The provincial planning department has obtained cost estimates for the new road from a study on construction costs in Beracia carried out by the consulting firm Barton E. Major (BEM) which is

TABLE 4 Road construction costs by level of technology, 1975 prices

	Type of technique		
	Capital-intensive	Intermediate	Labor-intensive
Labor (person-years/km)			
Unskilled	18.0	91.0	162.5
Skilled	3.5	4.9	6.3
Equipment operating costs[a] (Lp/km)			
Depreciation	45 500	28 100	22 400
Spares	17 065	10 565	8 395
Maintenance–labor	5 450	3 400	2 700
Tires	15 765	9 760	7 760
Fuel and oil	74 100	45 895	36 480
Materials[b]	35 715	35 715	35 715
Total	193 595	133 435	113 450
Construction period (years)	2.0	3.0	4.0

Notes: [a]Excluding duties and taxes.
[b]Import content: 80%
Source: B. E. Major (1970). *Choice of Technique in Road Construction: A Survey of Beracian Conditions* **III**. San Francisco

shown in *Table 4*. Since rural unemployment is still widespread during parts of the year in areas through which the road passes, the provincial planning department proposes to construct the road using a labor-intensive technique, the costs of which are shown in *Table 4*. This would delay the opening of the road. However, it is argued that the benefits of the additional employment created would outweigh the costs of additional construction time. The maintenance cost on the new road, as estimated by BEM, is given as a function of the average daily traffic levels. Thus,

$$M_T = \text{Lp}(820 + 1.95 \times ADT)/\text{km}$$

and

$$M_F = \text{Lp}(130 + 1.25 \times ADT)/\text{km}$$

where M_T is total maintenance cost and M_F is the foreign exchange component. The domestic component of maintenance costs $(M_T - M_F)$ consists of 2 percent skilled labor, 28 percent unskilled labor and 70 percent raw materials. These estimates were based on data collected in 1975.

The benefits for the new road would come from three sources. First, vehicle operating costs will be lowered compared with the operating costs on the old road. The reduced vehicle operating costs are shown in *Table 5*. Second, the new highway will attract new traffic (generated traffic) both because of the lower vehicle operating costs and because of the shortened distance. It is believed that 90 percent of the traffic using the existing road will switch to the new road because few vehicles make

TABLE 5 Vehicle operating costs[a] new road segment: Filopenia–Limani, 1975 (Lp/thousand km)

Item	Car	Truck	Bus
Fuel	225.76	377.38	484.94
Oil	14.52	16.60	17.93
Tires[b]	8.73	117.89	296.82
Depreciation	74.43	196.04	244.09
Interest	47.82	61.70	54.37
Maintenance			
Parts[c]	23.85	127.20	176.19
Skilled labor	0.27	1.34	1.46
Unskilled labor	2.19	10.43	17.26
Insurance	19.40	20.64	21.77
License fees	19.50	21.09	23.42
Occupant's time/driver's wages	56.86	40.80	126.00
Total	493.33	991.11	1464.25

Notes: [a]Excluding duties and indirect taxes.
  [b]Foreign exchange component: 75%.
  [c]Foreign exchange component: 50%.

intermediate stops between Filopenia and Limani. On the basis of studies carried out by the Center for Social and Economic Research at the University of Beracia*, generated traffic will add about 10 percent to the traffic diverted from the existing road in the first year, 15 percent in the second, and 20 percent in the third. Thereafter, the generated traffic is expected to grow at the same rate as diverted traffic. Based on survey data, approximately 55 percent of the generated traffic would be a result of the shorter distance on the new road and the remainder a result of the lower operating costs.

*   S. Mains (1975). The Demand for Road Services: Preliminary Results of a Survey in Filopenia. *Beracia Development Journal* **XIII,** 218–258

In addition it is estimated that some traffic will be diverted from the railways. Major difficulties in estimating the likely volume of traffic that will switch from rail to road arise from the fact that the comparative transport costs do not really measure the full distribution cost. Moreover, the railway tariff for high value commodities exceeds costs so that the railway could meet the road transport competition by lowering its own rates. Allowing for these uncertainties, it is estimated that when the new road is opened, diverted traffic from the railway will amount to 30 trucks and 5 buses per day. No allowance is made for passenger cars because it is assumed that for railway passengers bus transport is the only alternative. The traffic diverted from the railway is expected to grow at half the rates forecast for traffic diverted from the existing road, a forecast which recognizes the generally slower growth in rail traffic. The railway servicing the Limani–Filopenia segment has excess capacity in both freight and passenger areas. The PWD charges that there are no benefits from traffic diverted from the railway because, with excess rail capacity, the marginal cost of rail transport is zero. The provincial planning department, however, argues that long-run marginal railway costs are not zero and there is a real benefit from diverting traffic to the road. They claim that the freight and passenger cars not used could be diverted to other railway segments when there are equipment shortages.

The data on railway costs are difficult to evaluate. The provincial planning department has suggested that for freight traffic the benefit is Lp 0.17/kilometer for trucks and Lp 0.29/kilometer for buses. These estimates are based on present fares charged to commodity and passenger traffic. A recent study* suggested that if passenger and freight services were to be charged their full cost, then passenger fares would be decreased by some 50 percent and freight charges would have to increase by some 25 percent, although admittedly this would vary by segment of line and type of commodity. On the basis of the information provided, the provincial planning department suggests that a strong case can be made for allocating funds to the construction of the new road.

The chief of the transport section, Ministry of Planning, must present a list of projects for inclusion in the annual development plan. To do this properly he needs answers to the following.

---

* E. Vickers (1976). Pricing Rail Transport Services in Beracia. *Beracia Development Journal* **XIV**, 115–140

Questions

1. Should funds be allocated in the next annual plan for widening the road or should the new road be built?
2. If the road is to be widened, when is the optimal time for undertaking such a project?
3. If the road is not to be widened, when should a new road be constructed?
4. At the time a new road is to be constructed, which technique—the labor-intensive, the intermediate or the capital-intensive technique—should be used?
5. What would be the employment benefit of constructing the new road by the alternative technique?

Further reading

HARBERGER, A. (1974). Cost–Benefit Analysis of Transportation Projects. In *Project Evaluation*, pp. 248–279. Chicago, Markham Publishing Company

VAN DER TAK, H. G. and RAY, A. (1973). The Economic Benefits of Road Transport Projects. In *Benefit-Cost and Policy Analysis*, pp. 132–168. Chicago, Aldine Publishing Company

ADLER, H. A. (1965). Economic Evaluation of Transport Projects. In *Transport Investment and Economic Development* (ed. By G. Fromm) pp. 170–194. Washington, D.C., Brookings Institution

FROMM, G. (1965). The Design of the Transport Sector. In *Transport Investment and Economic Development*, (ed. by G. Fromm) pp. 89–107. Washington D.C., Brookings Institution

BROWN, R. T. The 'Railroad Decision' in Chile. In *Transport Investment and Economic Development* (ed. by G. Fromm) pp. 242–270. Washington, D.C., Brookings Institution

Control of Schistosomiasis at Kichele Farm

TO: Chief, Social Services Section;
Chief, Project Analysis Section.

FROM: Principal Secretary.

RE: Schistosomiasis control at BSFC Farm at Kichele.

Please see the attached correspondence from the Principal Secretaries of the Ministries of Agriculture and Health, respectively. We must decide whether to reallocate funds from other development budgets, most probably transportation, agriculture and industry, to fund this eradication program.

I have been impressed with the reports written recently by the Project Analysis Section on investments in rice farms and the copper industry. Would it be possible to apply that methodology or a similar one to decisions on the health program? Please attempt to do so and report to me on your results. This exercise may provide useful tools for analyzing the health investment budget in the future, so you should be explicit about your assumptions and should evaluate the usefulness of whatever method(s) you propose to analyze this project. If you can also provide some simple guideline to judge the usefulness of future health programs, such as the cost per life saved or per disease prevented, that would be especially helpful.

The Minister has on several occasions expressed an interest in knowing more about the impact of our health services. He feels there may be many profound social benefits to improved health that we do not now account for, but which would have a large effect on our development goals. In reviewing this case, it would be helpful if you could provide guidance for a brief to the Minister on the broad development aspects of health programs such as the one proposed.

8 December 1978

Ministry of Agriculture
Kefala

8 November 1978

Principal Secretary
Ministry of Planning
Kefala.

State Farms Corporation—Kichele Farm—Schistosomiasis Control

State Farm managers at Kichele are facing a serious health problem which was not foreseen in 1976 when the irrigated rice farm was planned and started. Snails have been breeding in the irrigation channels and the consequent outbreak of schistosomiasis has been severe among both workers and their families. The local health officer has estimated that 65 percent of the full-time workers have contracted schistosomiasis at some time during the farm's operation. The prevalence* among members of their families living on or very near the farm is not known, but is probably very nearly as high as for the workers.

The direct costs of schistosomiasis infection to BSFC are considerable. First, the corporation has undertaken to treat both the workers and their resident family members. Second, treatment disables workers for periods of from 2 to 7 days, depending on the treatment used. Third, we suspect that infected workers, even if treated, cannot work as hard or as long hours as uninfected workers, so that productivity is lower than it would be if schistosomiasis were eradicated. The Principal Secretary, Ministry of Health, has agreed to provide more specific estimates of these costs in the near future.

These productivity losses are very serious for a farm as productive as Kichele. This farm has costs per crop and yields per hectare for each crop very similar to those projected for the irrigated portions of the BSFC rice farm near Horio, which is being considered for investment now. Unlike the Horio farms, however, Kichele has access to water year round and has thus been able to produce two rice crops per year on its irrigated acres.

This is done with a workforce of 800, including 500 farm laborers and 300 irrigation workers, who work about 300 days per year each. The majority of these men work in close proximity to snail-infested water. However, schistosomiasis is endemic to the region surrounding the farm, from which new workers are drawn. Thus we find that the newly recruited workers, who replace about 10 percent of the workforce each year, have about the same prevalence of schistosomiasis as farm workers. We make housing available, either on the farm or nearby, for about half of our workforce and their families, a total of 1800 people.

We have approached the Ministry of Health to institute a program for the control of schistosomiasis at Kichele Farm. They have agreed with the need for and potential benefits from such a program, but are unable to provide for it in their budget, either this year or next. Of course, there has been no provision for it in the budget of the Ministry of Agriculture, nor can State Farms provide the funds, since they are charged by the Minister of Finance to operate as a commercially profitable organization. Under these circumstances, the Principal Secretary, Ministry of Health, joins with me in requesting a supplementary

---

*   *Prevalence* refers to the number of a population that is infected by a disease at any time; it is a stock measure. *Incidence* refers to the change in the number of cases, a flow measure.

TO: Principal Secretary

allocation to the development budget of the Ministry of Health of Lp 431 000 over three years to finance the provision of health officers, medicines and chemicals for the control of schistosomiasis at Kichele Farm. The Ministry of Health will provide detailed cost estimates directly to you.

(Signed)

Principal Secretary

MINISTRY OF HEALTH
KEFALA

26 November 1978

Principal Secretary
Ministry of Planning,
Kefala.

Schistosomiasis Control Programs—State Farms Corporation (Kichele)

This letter is in support of the request of the Ministry of Agriculture
(PS–Agric. to PS–Plan. of 8 November 1978) for a supplementary development
budget allocation to provide materials and services for the control of
schistosomiasis at the State Farm at Kichele. Such a program would entail three
years of intensive snail reduction, mass diagnosis of workers and their families
and treatment of diagnosed cases. Thereafter, there would be annual costs at a
lower level for snail control and for diagnosis and treatment of new workers and
their families. The recurrent annual costs of diagnosis and treatment can, after
three years, be subsumed under the recurrent budget of the Ministry of Health.

Investment Costs. Over the first three years, SFC workers would, under
guidance of the health officer in charge, treat irrigation waters with moluscicides;
our ministry would provide a technician to carry out a program of sampling
irrigation waters to measure the snail population. Three-year totals would be as
follows:

Chemicals (molluscicides)	181 100
Channel treatment by farm workers at Lp 20 per day	3 600
Sampling—wages of one technician	43 800
Transport	6 600
Capital equipment	4 100
Total	Lp 239 200

As snails are being reduced, health workers would conduct an intensive
campaign to detect and cure schistosomiasis in workers and their families, at the
following estimated total costs over three years:

Medical staff	
Resident doctor (one)	104 300
Medical auxiliaries (two)	11 600
Laboratory equipment	6 600
Transport	6 900
Treatment	
Drugs	22 000
Hospitalization	43 100
Total	Lp 194 500

Approximately 2700 work-days would be lost over the three years as a result of
hospitalization or illness resulting from the treatment of out-patients.

All chemicals and drugs would be imported and about half of the capital
equipment represents imported equipment, the rest being construction. Our

TO: Principal Secretary

costs assume that, as in the past, no duties would be charged on Ministry of Health imports. All costs are estimated at today's prices.

    Recurrent costs. Once the snail population has been reduced, it will be necessary to continue to apply molluscicide and to sample irrigation water, but at about half the annual rate that obtained during the reduction period. However, so long as the snail population is controlled by these methods, costs of diagnosis and treatment will be reduced substantially. New workers, estimated at about 10 percent of the workforce each year, and resident family members will have to be screened and those found infected must be treated, all at the following annual costs:

Medical staff (part-time)	12 000
Drugs	4 900
Hospital costs	2 300
Total	Lp 19 200

During this stage, only about 270 work-days should be lost because of treatment; those lost will be entirely attributable to new workers whose entry to Kichele farm work will thus be delayed. The screening and treatment costs can be covered by our recurrent budget for health without difficulty and should not therefore be considered a cost of the Kichele snail control program. We suggest that, after three years, State Farms assume the cost of continuing snail control.

    Cost savings. In the absence of the proposed health measures, we anticipate that schistosomiasis will continue to infect the workforce at Kichele at about the rate observed during the past few years. If this is correct, then annual costs of diagnosis and treatment in the absence of snail reduction and control would continue at the current low level:

Medical staff (part-time)	12 000
Drugs	3 000
Hospitalization	5 400
Total	Lp 20 400

    In addition, treatment would incapacitate workers for a total of about 330 days per year.

    Productivity Gains. Although there will certainly be some gain in productivity among workers once schistosomiasis has been controlled, the precise measurement of these gains is conjectural. We have not done any research on the subject in Beracia. However, our colleagues in East Africa have measured productivity gains resulting from schistosomiasis control on irrigated sugar estates and they report that uninfected workers seem to earn about 5 percent more than infected and untreated workers; as earnings are based on production per worker, this should be a good measure of productivity. Infected but success-fully cured workers do better than untreated workers, but not so well as uninfected workers; we might guess that the productivity gains from successful treatment of infected workers would be about half those for complete absence of the disease.

    Based on recent experience, we would project that, in the absence of a control program, the fraction of workers who have at some time contracted schistosomiasis would grow from the current 65 percent to about 90 percent in about three years and then level off. At current rates of detection and cure, at any time no more than a third of these individuals will have been cured; the rest will be harboring active cases of schistosomiasis. If we institute the reduction and

TO: Principal Secretary

control program proposed, we can expect to have prevented any increase in the prevalence of the disease from the current level and, after three years, to have cured about three-fourths of those currently infected. These forecasts account for the men recruited from surrounding areas to replace about 10 percent of the farm workers each year; recruits are expected to have about the same prevalence of the disease as the departing workers. We assume, of course, that State Farms will not be permitted to turn away applicants with schistosomiasis, but will instead be required to hire and treat them if they meet other requirements, as has been the practice in the past.

   Reduced mortality. If the East African experience with schistosomiasis is any guide to conditions in Beracia, we may also expect that eradication of the disease will reduce the death-rate among the male population by about 18 percent from ages 20 onwards. (This rate allows for those who would remain infected from previous contact.) I have asked our chief demographer to prepare estimates of the reduced mortality that might be expected from elimination of schistosomiasis in males and he has provided life tables to show this effect. A copy is enclosed. Our medical records show that workers at Kichele are fairly evenly distributed between ages 20 and 35, with very few workers either younger or older. Although our experience is limited, these workers appear to be employed on our farms for an average of about 10 years each and new workers tend to be in their early twenties.

   In view of these clear-cut benefits from a schistosomiasis reduction and control program at Kichele, we support the request of the Ministry of Agriculture for a supplementary development allocation of Lp 431 000 over the next three years to finance this program.

(Signed)

Principal Secretary.

TABLE 1 Life table for Beracian males

	Results from 1970 census		Table adjusted for elimination of schistosomiasis[a]	
Age (x)	Survivors at x	Life after x	Survivors at x	Life expectancy after x
0	10 000	50.2	10 000	52.8
1	8 812	56.0	8 812	58.9
5	8 355	54.9	8 355	58.0
10	8 173	51.1	8 173	54.3
15	8 084	49.1	8 084	49.9
20	7 972	44.8	7 972	45.5
25	7 837	40.5	7 862	41.1
30	7 693	36.2	7 719	36.9
35	7 507	32.0	7 541	32.7
40	7 256	28.1	7 302	28.7
45	6 937	24.2	6 995	24.8
50	6 406	21.0	6 503	21.5
55	5 834	17.8	5 938	18.3
60	4 972	15.5	5 129	15.8
65	4 208	12.9	4 347	13.2
70	3 088	11.6	3 291	11.6

Note: [a]Using estimates of Joel E. Cohen (1974) for Zanzibar—2/11 of deaths for each cohort (20 years old or more) caused by schistosomiasis.

Questions

1. What assumptions need to be made in order to appraise this health project using cost–benefit analysis?
2. Does this project pass the cost–benefit test for Beracia? How confident are you about this estimate? What are its most vulnerable assumptions?
3. What cost-effectiveness measures can be developed for this project? How useful might these be in health planning? in national planning, when allocations among sectors must be considered?
4. What costs and benefits of health projects are not captured by these measures? How do those omissions bias the results? If health resources were allocated strictly on the basis of those measures, would health goals be well served?

Further reading

BACKGROUND: HEALTH AND DEVELOPMENT

FELDSTEIN, M. (1970). Health Sector Planning in Developing Countries. *Economica* **37–146,** 139–163

MALENBAUM, W. (1970). Health and Productivity in Poor Areas. In *Empirical Studies in Health Economics* (ed. by H. E. Klarman), 31–53. Baltimore, Johns Hopkins

SORKIN, A. (1976). *Health Economics in Developing Countries*. Lexington, Mass., D. C. Heath

WORLD BANK (1975). *Health Sector Policy Paper*. Washington, D.C., pp. 1–47

METHODOLOGY: COST–BENEFIT VS. COST EFFECTIVENESS

COHN, E. (1972). Assessment of Malaria Eradication Costs and Benefits. *The American Journal of Tropical Medicine and Hygiene* **21–5,** 663–667

DUNLOP, D. (1975). Benefit–Cost Analysis: A Review of its Applicability in Policy Analysis for Delivering Health Services. *Social Science and Medicine* **9** 133–139

GROSS, R. N. (1970). Problems of Resource Allocation in Health. In *Public Expenditure and Policy Analysis* (ed. by R. H. Haveman and J. Margolis), Chicago, Markham

KLARMAN, H. E., *et al.* (1968). Cost Effectiveness Analysis Applied to the Treatment of Chronic Renal Disease. *Medical Care* **6–1,** 48–54

MISHAN, E. J. (1971). Evaluation of Life and Limb: A Theoretical Approach. *Journal of Political Economy* **79–4,** 687–705

RUCHLIN, H. and ROGERS, D. (1971). *Economics and Health Care*. Springfied, Ill., Charles C. Thomas

WEISBROD, B. A. (1971). Costs and Benefits of Medical Research: A Case Study of Poliomyelitis. *Journal of Political Economy* **79–3,** 527–542

CASE STUDIES: MALARIA AND SCHISTOSOMIASIS CONTROL

BALDWIN, R. E. and WEISBROD, B. A. (1974). Disease and Labor Productivity. *Economic Development and Cultural Change* **22–3,** 414–435

BARLOW, R. (1967). The Economic Effects of Malaria Eradication. *American Economic Review* **57–2,** 130–157

COHEN, J. (1974). Some Potential Economic Benefits of Eliminating Mortality Attributed to Schistosomiasis in Zanzibar. *Social Science and Medicine* **8–7,** 383–398

FENWICK, A. (1972). Costs and a Cost-Benefit Analysis: *Schistosoma Mansoni* Control Programme on an Irrigated Estate in Northern Tanzania. *Bulletin of the World Health Organization* **47,** 573–578

FENWICK, A. and FIGENSCHOU, B. H. (1972). Effect of *Schistosoma Mansoni* Infection on the Productivity of Cane Cutters on a Sugar Estate in Tanzania. *Bulletin of the World Health Organization* **47,** 567–572

PRESCOTT, N. N. (October, 1975). The Economic Dimension of Schistosomiasis: An Economist's Perspective. Mimeo. Magdalen College, Oxford University

Sectoral Planning

Sectoral Planning*

Part IV presents two cases calling for the application of planning models to key sectors of the economy: industry and education. In Part III we considered investment decisions by analyzing one project at a time. Here we recognize the importance of linkages among projects by dealing with several projects simultaneously. This requires a technique—input–output analysis, also called inter-industry analysis —that utilizes a limited amount of data on each of many potential projects and makes it possible to select a limited set of investments to achieve particular goals.

Part I suggested some important caveats about the value of formal, long-range, economic planning. In the spirit of that critique, the student should apply these economic tools to define the economic trade-offs involved and provide policy-makers with such information. There are no correct answers, simply ways of making the decision-makers better informed about the economic issues involved. The following sections introduce several useful analytic techniques: inter-industry analysis, effective protection, domestic resource cost and manpower planning.

Introduction to input–output analysis

The technique of input–output analysis is one of the basic tools of modern economics. Perhaps its most common use is in answering questions that concern macroeconomic planners. For example, if consumption were to be increased over a five-year period, how much of

* Students working on Case 6 will benefit from reading the first 27 pages of this introduction, unless they are already familiar with input–output analysis, effective protection and related techniques. Students working on Case 7 can confine their attention to the first and last sections of this introduction.   141

each commodity would have to be produced or imported? Not only do planners have to know what goods and services will be consumed, but also how much of other commodities must be available to produce these consumer goods. To answer such questions, planners need to know what goes into the production of each commodity, and they must have ways of manipulating such data to account for the production of all goods simultaneously. Input–output analysis does both.

A standard, simplified text that explains inter-industry analysis as a planning tool is Chenery and Clark (1959); a more complete and sophisticated treatment is Dorfman, Samuelson and Solow (1958); and a recent collection of articles of the state of the art in development planning is Blitzer, Clark and Taylor (1975). In this section we provide a brief introduction to input–output analysis sufficient to help the student through Case 6 on industrial strategy.

Input–output (or inter-industry) analysis employs a number of simplifying assumptions which permit solutions of a general equilibrium system of production. The supply and demand relationship for each commodity (or usually for each sector, which consists of a number of commodities) is shown on an input–output table such as the one here, which is also called a *flow matrix*.

Simplified input–output table (flow matrix) (values in $)

Outputs / Inputs	Sectors				Total intermediate use (5)	Final use (6)	Total use (7)
	Agriculture (1)	Basic industries (2)	Food processing (3)	Services (4)			
1. Agriculture	25	0	120	0	145	105	250
2. Basic industries	25	45	40	0	110	40	150
3. Food processing	0	0	80	0	80	320	400
4. Services	25	15	80	20	140	60	200
5. Total purchases	75	60	320	20			
6. Value added	175	90	80	180		525	
7. Total output	250	150	400	200			1000

Each sector is shown twice: as a supplier (row) and as a purchaser of inputs (column). In this simplified example, value added is not broken down between wage and non-wage income: intermediate purchases (deliveries) do not differentiate between competitive and non-competitive imports (i.e. commodities which must be imported because no local source of supply exists) and final demand is not broken down into its components (consumption, investment and exports). Nevertheless, this table is adequate to demonstrate the essential elements of input–output analysis. Note that the sum of value added (row 6) equals gross national product, which is the sum of all final expenditures in column 6; that is, all wages and other factor payments equal expenditures on final goods and services, the national income identity.

To make the flow matrix useful as a planning tool, it must be converted to a coefficients matrix which gives a production function for each commodity (or industry or sector). To do this, assume that the production function for each sector permits no substitution. Define gross output as X_j and intermediate inputs as X_{ij}. The general production function is defined as

$$X_j = f(X_{1j}; X_{2j}; \ldots X_{nj}) \tag{IV.1}$$

That is, to use the table, food processing (X_3) requires 120 units from agriculture (X_{1j}), 40 units from basic indistries (X_{2j}), etc. Because there is no substitution, we rewrite the production function in the form of minimum requirements for each input, i.e.,

$$X_j < \frac{X_{ij}}{a_{ij}} \tag{IV.1a}$$

Assuming efficiency, no more than the necessary amount of any input would be used, so that (1a) reduces to

$$X_{ij} = a_{ij} X_j \tag{IV.2}$$

where a_{ij} is the direct input coefficient of industry i into industry j. Thus a_{ij} measures the quantity of the output of industry i required by industry j per unit of total output. For example, 400 units of food processing (X_3) requires 40 units from basic industries (X_2), so $a_{23} = \frac{40}{400} = 0.10$.

Similar calculations for all the flows permit us to convert the flow matrix into a *coefficients matrix*, often called the A-matrix because its elements are designated a_{ij}. Note that the production functions for each commodity can be read down the columns: one unit of processed food (X_3) requires 0.30 units of agricultural commodities (X_1), 0.10 units of basic industries (X_2), etc.

Coefficients matrix

	A (1)	B (2)	F (3)	S (4)
1. A	0.10	0	0.30	0
2. B	0.10	0.30	0.10	0
3. F	0	0	0.20	0
4. S	0.10	0.10	0.20	0.10
5. TP	0.30	0.40	0.80	0.10
6. V	0.70	0.60	0.20	0.90
7. X_j	1.00	1.00	1.00	1.00

We can now ask, what output (production) levels $[X(A); X(B); X(F); X(S)]$ are needed to meet a set of final demands. Say that we project the following levels of final demand:

Sector	Projected final demand (FD)
Agriculture	$ 105
Basic industry	$ 40
Food processing	$ 320
Services	$ 60

These are the same levels we started with, but any other set would serve equally well. To solve for the output (production) levels required to meet this final bill of goods, we can set up four equations in four unknowns, based on the output rows of the coefficients matrix:

$$
\begin{aligned}
X(A) &= 0.10X(A) + 0X(B) + 0.30X(F) + 0X(S) + 105\\
X(B) &= 0.10X(A) + 0.30X(B) + 0.10X(F) + 0X(S) + 40\\
X(F) &= 0X(A) + 0X(B) + 0.20X(F) + 0X(S) + 320\\
X(S) &= 0.10X(A) + 0.10X(B) + 0.20X(F) + 0.10X(S) + 60
\end{aligned}
$$

or

$$
\begin{aligned}
0.9X(A) - 0X(B) - 0.30X(F) - 0X(S) &= 105\\
-0.10X(A) + 0.7X(B) - 0.10X(F) - 0X(S) &= 40\\
-0X(A) - 0X(B) + 0.8X(F) - 0X(S) &= 300\\
-0.10X(A) - 0.10X(B) - 0.20X(F) - 0.9X(S) &= 60
\end{aligned}
$$

It is now a simple (but tedious) matter to solve for the four unknowns. In matrix form we can write the first equation system as follows:

$$
\begin{array}{cccc}
X(A) & X(B) & X(F) & X(S)
\end{array}
$$
$$
\begin{bmatrix}
0.10 & 0 & 0.30 & 0\\
0.10 & 0.30 & 0.10 & 0\\
0 & 0 & 0.20 & 0\\
0.10 & 0.10 & 0.20 & 0.10
\end{bmatrix}
\begin{bmatrix}
X(A)\\X(B)\\X(F)\\X(S)
\end{bmatrix}
+
\begin{bmatrix}
105\\40\\320\\60
\end{bmatrix}
=
\begin{bmatrix}
X(A)\\X(B)\\X(F)\\X(S)
\end{bmatrix}
$$

or $\mathbf{AX + FD = X}$ where $\mathbf{A}$ is the coefficient matrix. This becomes $\mathbf{X - AX = FD}$ and the solution is $\mathbf{(I-A)X = FD}$ where $\mathbf{I}$ is the identity matrix (ones on the diagonal, zeros elsewhere):

$$
\begin{array}{cccc}
X(A) & X(B) & X(F) & X(S)
\end{array}
$$
$$
\underbrace{
\begin{bmatrix}
0.90 & -0 & -0.30 & -0\\
-0.10 & 0.70 & -0.10 & -0\\
-0 & -0 & 0.80 & -0\\
-0.10 & -0.10 & -0.20 & 0.90
\end{bmatrix}}_{\mathbf{(I-A)}}
\underbrace{\begin{bmatrix}
X(A)\\X(B)\\X(F)\\X(S)
\end{bmatrix}}_{\mathbf{X}}
=
\underbrace{\begin{bmatrix}
105\\40\\320\\60
\end{bmatrix}}_{\mathbf{FD}}
$$

To solve for $\mathbf{X}$ we obtain

$$\mathbf{X = (I-A)^{-1}\,FD,} \tag{IV.3}$$

where $\mathbf{(I-A)^{-1}}$ is the inverse (frequently called the *Leontief inverse*) obtained by a process of matrix inversion, an explanation and description of which can be found in any standard text on matrices. (Inverting a matrix to solve equation (IV.3) is analogous to dividing both sides of an algebraic equation by a common factor, i.e. $ax = y$ becomes $x = \dfrac{y}{a} = a^{-1}y$).

The inverse matrix is:

$$
\begin{array}{cccc}
X(A) & X(B) & X(F) & X(S) \\
\begin{bmatrix}
1.111 & 0 & 0.417 & 0 \\
0.159 & 1.429 & 0.238 & 0 \\
0 & 0 & 1.250 & 0 \\
0.141 & 0.159 & 0.351 & 1.111
\end{bmatrix}
\end{array}
$$

The coefficients of the inverse, r_{ij}, give the quantity of direct plus indirect inputs of commodity i needed to produce one unit of commodity j. Thus, for example, to produce one unit of $X(F)$, processed food, requires 0.417 units from the agricultural sector—0.30 units directly in the production of $X(F)$ (something we knew from the A-matrix) *plus* 0.117 units of $X(A)$ that are used by all other sectors that produce inputs, directly or indirectly, for sector F. The inverse matrix is the result of an infinite chain of inputs as sector F requires inputs from B which requires inputs from A which requires inputs from S which requires inputs from A and so on, *ad infinitum*. Note that all diagonal elements (r_{ii}) are greater than or equal to one because to produce $X(F)$ requires, not only one unit of $X(F)$, but additional units for the other sectors that supply F.

To solve for the output levels we multiply the inverse matrix by the final demand vector. Matrix multiplication involves multiplying each row element by each element in a column and summing the products. Thus,

$$
\begin{bmatrix}
1.111 & 0 & 0.417 & 0 \\
0.159 & 1.429 & 0.238 & 0 \\
0 & 0 & 1.250 & 0 \\
0.141 & 0.159 & 0.351 & 1.111
\end{bmatrix}
\times
\begin{bmatrix}
105 \\
40 \\
320 \\
60
\end{bmatrix}
=
\begin{bmatrix}
X(A) \\
X(B) \\
X(F) \\
X(S)
\end{bmatrix}
$$

is equal to:

$$
\begin{aligned}
1.111(105) &+ 0(40) + 0.417(320) + 0(60) = X(A) \\
0.159(105) &+ 1.429(40) + 0.238(320) + 0(60) = X(B) \\
0(105) &+ 0(40) + 1.250(320) + 0(60) = X(F) \\
0.141(105) &+ 0.159(40) + 0.351(320) + 1.111(60) = X(S)
\end{aligned}
$$

$$
\begin{aligned}
250 &= X(A) \\
150 &= X(B) \\
400 &= X(F) \\
200 &= X(S)
\end{aligned}
$$

These are, of course, the output levels we started with.

If we wish to solve for a different set of final demand, say

$$FD(A) = \$\ 115$$
$$FD(B) = \$\ \ 44$$
$$FD(E) = \$\ 350$$
$$FD(S) = \$\ \ 65$$

we would get

$$1.111(115)\ +\ \ \ \ \ 0(44)\ +\ 0.417(350)\ +\ \ \ \ \ \ 0(65)\ =\ X(A)$$
$$0.159(115)\ +\ 1.429(44)\ +\ 0.238(350)\ +\ \ \ \ \ \ 0(65)\ =\ X(B)$$
$$\ \ \ \ \ 0(115)\ +\ \ \ \ \ \ 0(44)\ +\ 1.250(350)\ +\ \ \ \ \ \ 0(65)\ =\ X(F)$$
$$0.141(115)\ +\ 0.159(44)\ +\ 0.351(350)\ +\ 1.111(65)\ =\ X(S)$$

and the required output levels would be:

$$274\ =\ X(A)$$
$$164\ =\ X(B)$$
$$438\ =\ X(F)$$
$$218\ =\ X(S)$$

Note that while final demand for agriculture increased by $ 10 (115–105), the total output (production) has had to increase by $ 24. The larger production increase is caused by the indirect deliveries made by agriculture to other sectors, all of which have increased their production levels as well.

By pre-multiplying the $(I-A)^{-1}$ matrix by a vector of import require-ments for each sector, m_j, we can obtain total (direct plus indirect) import needs. Or by pre-multiplying $(I-A)^{-1}$ by a vector of labor coefficients (l_j), we can obtain total employment effects. And so forth, for any factor of production. However, the general solution $(I-A)^{-1}$ is only valid as long as the initial assumptions about nonsubstitution among inputs remains true. If not, the **A** matrix changes and so does the general solution.

USES OF INTER-INDUSTRY ANALYSIS

In economic planning, there are two basic ways in which input–output analysis is employed. The first and more fundamental is to ensure that development plans are *consistent*. The simple example just given demonstrated this approach. Let us say that the macroeconomic planners have used aggregate models and political directives to deter-mine target growth rates for the economy. From that knowledge, it should be possible to estimate the breakdown of final demand into kinds of commodities and services, the data we assumed in the simplified model above. Then the input–output table can be put to work to determine the total quantity that each industry must produce to satisfy final demand and these results compared with existing and planned capacity. To the extent that capacity falls short of the direct plus indirect demands for goods and services, it is necessary either to plan investment to increase domestic capacity or to import the needed goods. This in turn implies resource constraints—on savings, investment implementation capacity, and foreign exchange earnings—which must be satisfied if the plan targets are to be met. Should the initial targets prove inconsistent with resource constraints, either targets must be reduced or additional measures taken to increase investment and import capacity.

Although this process of checking for plan consistency has been described as if it takes several steps to accomplish, in fact the use of the Leontief inverse and the vectors of coefficients for factor inputs enables planners to complete the process in one step with the help of a computer, which can make several iterations of the calculations at low cost. Such a consistency check can be done in detail for the economy as a whole, for individual sectors such as industry or agriculture, or for a single region of the country. Of course, the smaller the unit being analyzed, the more conditions must be specified in advance to make the model work. The consistency principle of input–output analysis has many applications in national and sectoral planning. One of the most common of these, *manpower planning*, is discussed below.

The second use of inter-industry analysis, *optimality planning*, is more sophisticated. Instead of establishing a set of national or sectoral targets in advance and testing their feasibility, a set of goals is defined and given priority weights, the result of which is called an objective function. Then the input–output model is operated to find the highest possible value of the objective function, within the limits set by the resource constraints. The most common technique for doing this is called *linear programming*, a computer-based method that searches for solutions consistent with the inter-industry model and the resource constraints, then selects from among these consistent outcomes the one that maximizes the objective function. A more complex technique, which has the advantage of permitting consideration of economies of scale and the phasing of complementarity investments, is mixed integer programming; it is, however, much more demanding in technical skills and computer time. The interested reader should consult the articles by Taylor and Westphal in Blitzer, Clark and Taylor (1975), which survey the state of the art in programming models and suggest their strengths and weaknesses.

Without going into the intricacies of the subject, four drawbacks to the use of inter-industry models should be mentioned. First, for very rudimentary economies, such as several in Africa and many island countries, there may not be enough flows between industries to justify the expense of estimating an input–output table and using it. Consistency checks can be made quite easily by competent economists with a good knowledge of the economy's structure.

Second, if the inter-industry model is to be useful for indicating specific investments over a five- or ten-year period, it must be a very detailed table, with columns and rows for each activity that might need expanding. For example, a row for textiles might be too aggregated for investment planning purposes. Instead, it might be necessary to differentiate among types of textiles and even to divide the industry into its processes, spinning, weaving and finishing. This obviously can vastly complicate the model and increase the difficulty and cost of operating it. It is more likely, then, that the model would be used only to indicate the broadly defined industries that require investment, with project identification and appraisal techniques used subsequently to identify precise investments.

Third, the fixed coefficients of an input–output table impose rigidities on development planning that can mislead decision-makers. In the face of apparently scarce resources such as saving and foreign exchange, the only adjustments possible within an intra-industry framework are to reduce gross output targets or to change the sectoral output mix, e.g. towards less capital- or input-using *products*. Technological substitution within sectors is typically not built into these models, so the important alternative of less capital- or import-intensive *processes* does not present itself. In principle, programming models could incorporate alternative processes, but this does complicate the models considerably and is not often done. (Non-linear techniques, still in their infancy, do handle alternative technologies well.)

Fourth, and perhaps most compelling, for economies undergoing rapid structural change an input–output table soon becomes out of date and useless for planning. The analyst cannot rely on a single coefficient matrix, but must update it as the structure changes. For example, if the country's first steel mill is being built during the planning period, the coefficients matrix must be adjusted to allow for the effect of steel on subsequent planning. This can frequently be done on the basis of project feasibility studies, but does increase the complexity of any exercise involving input–output techniques.

Despite these and other problems, the construction and use of input–output tables teaches planners and, through them, policy-makers a substantial amount about the economy they are dealing with. At the very least, it indicates the structure of the economy. If used well, it can indicate both the critical bottlenecks to continued expansion and the nature of the trade-offs among national goals that may be in conflict. As long as the technique is seen as a tool to aid policy analysis and not as an end in itself, planning agencies should be encouraged to consider the use of input–output techniques.

Although its nature can only be suggested here, one by-product of linear programming analysis has interesting implications for cost–benefit analysis. In planning, one usually defines the objective function as some goal of development, such as output growth, and tries to find the quantities of goods and services from each sector that will maximize that goal or goals. Now consider a given constraint in the linear program, such as the availability of foreign exchange to purchase imports. Once the value of the objective function is found, the programmer can increase the amount of foreign exchange by one unit, run the program again, and find a slightly higher value for the objective function. The difference between the first and second solution, i.e. the additional output made possible by the unit increase in foreign exchange, is precisely the opportunity cost of foreign exchange which we sought in Part III, because it tells us directly the incremental output gained (or lost) if we increase (or decrease) the quantity of foreign exchange. This is an alternative way of estimating shadow prices for any resource. The drawback of this method, however, is that linear programming models are not able to handle in detail the taxes, quotas and other distortions which must be considered in estimating shadow prices.

There is a second way that linear programming can be used to find shadow prices. The objective function can be defined as the factor cost of producing goods and services (rather than as value of output), in which case the aim is to minimize costs. The input–output core of the model is then adjusted to reflect, not quantities, but costs and prices of production (using the same input–output coefficients). The result is the *dual* of the original (or primal) program. Its solution gives prices, rather than quantities, and these are the same opportunity costs (shadow prices) described above, except that they can all be solved simultaneously.

Efficiency indicators

A second approach to sectoral planning, which shares much in common with input–output techniques but does not require the whole inter-industry paraphernalia, is to work with specific, narrowly defined industries, even down to the project level, then to accumulate favorable investments into a collection of projects which becomes the sector plan. The key to this approach is some measure of project desirability, such as the efficient use of resources to increase output, to increase employment or to redistribute income, etc. The goal that best lends itself to this treatment is efficient growth, so we shall work with the goal in this section and in the cases.

It will strike the reader that this volume has already devoted considerable attention to one such measure of efficient resource use, namely cost–benefit analysis, and it is the authors' bias that, if feasible, sector programs should be constructed from full-fledged project appraisals. The technique has already been explained in Part III: using resource flows and shadow prices for as many potential investments as possible, the analyst should compute internal rates of return or, preferably, net present values for each. These data could come from results for existing industries, from pre-feasibility studies and other consultants' reports, and from similar investments made in other countries. Once IRRs or NPVs have been calculated, projects should be selected to maximize the net present value accruing to a fixed amount of investment in the sector, which must be determined before-hand, presumably by the central planners. This method, like all the partial equilibrium indicators discussed in this section, cannot deal with inter-industry linkages, at least not as conveniently as input–output analysis. But it does provide a good first approximation to a productive investment strategy and, in the process, teaches the sectoral planners much about the existing and prospective industries in their sector.

An application of the cost–benefit method of sector planning is the use of rate-of-return analysis for education, discussed critically in Part III and illustrated in Case 7. This method makes an interesting contrast to the manpower planning approach. Whereas manpower planning assumes that the demand for any given skill is perfectly inelastic with respect to wages, i.e. any increase in output requires a fixed increase in certain skills, rate-of-return analysis makes the opposite assumption: because we assume that price differences between workers with different educations are maintained for a lifetime regardless of the numbers educated, the implication is that elasticities of demand must be perfectly elastic. The truth must lie somewhere between, though the use of both methods will at least set the boundaries.

The difficulty with cost–benefit analysis as a sectoral planning tool is that one seldom has sufficient data on the vast number of potential projects to find NPVs or IRRs for all of them. Two shortcuts have been proposed and used extensively: the effective rate of protection and the domestic resource cost. Both attempt to rank all potential investments according to some indicator of efficiency and then to select the best projects, just as if the internal rates of return were known. However, the approach to each is different.

THE EFFECTIVE RATE OF PROTECTION

The effective rate of protection (*ERP*) was first explored systematically by Harry Johnson (1965), applied extensively to developing countries by Balassa (1971a and b) among others, and has been fully explained in a text by Corden (1971). It begins with the observation that protective tariffs permit domestic producers to charge more for their output than would be permissible in world competition, so that the value added in domestic prices (V^d) can be higher than the value added evaluated at world (border) prices (V^w). The effective rate of protection is defined as the fraction by which domestic price value added exceeds world price value added, or

$$ERP = \frac{V^d}{V^w} - 1 \qquad (IV.4)$$

If *ERP* is positive, it implies that value added in domestic prices exceeds that in world prices and, at least by world standards, domestic manufacturers are spending too much on labor, capital and other value added items. The causes could be many—low productivity of labor and/or capital, wages too high, profits too high, ineffective management, etc.—but the implication is that the industry could produce the same output with less expenditure on resources. For industries substituting for imports behind protective tariffs, the *ERP* would probably be positive, while for export industries (and some efficient import substituters) it should be zero or negative. If the value added and domestic and world prices could be measured for all potential investments in a sector, then planners could choose those investments with the lowest *ERPs* until the investment constraint was exhausted.

Seldom, however, do planners have the data to calculate value added for each industry at domestic and world prices. Rather, most studies of effective protection use the nominal or actual effective tariff rates and some knowledge of the input–output structure, from which they infer the *ERP*. Assume (unrealistically perhaps) that planners know the border prices of output and the inputs for a given industry, as well as the tariff that applies to each. Value added at world prices is simply the cif price of competing imports less the cif value of inputs (neglecting domestic non-traded inputs, for which some assumption must be made). If producers take full advantage of protective tariffs, then their output price is the cif price of competing inputs (P^w) plus the applicable protective tariff (t_j); while, for each unit of output, their input costs are given by the cif input cost per unit of output (C^w) plus the applicable duty on inputs (t_i). Thus,

$$\frac{V^d}{V^w} = \frac{P^w(1 + t_j) - C^w(1 + t_i)}{P^w - C^w} \qquad (IV.5)$$

We can now divide both numerator and denominator through by P^w and, since $\frac{C^w}{P^w}$ gives the input coefficient, a_{ij}, in world trade, we have

$$\frac{V^d}{V^w} = \frac{1 + t_j - a_{ij}(1 + t_i)}{1 - a_{ij}} \qquad (IV.6)$$

Equation (IV.6) assumes only one input. Recognizing that there are likely to be several inputs and reverting back to the expression for ERP of equation (IV.4), we have

$$ERP_j = \frac{1 + t_j - \sum_i a_{ij}(1 + t_i)}{1 - \sum_i a_{ij}} - 1 = \frac{t_j - \sum_i a_{ij}(t_i)}{1 - \sum_i a_{ij}} \qquad (IV.7)$$

To bring out some implications of this approach, it might be helpful to use a simple numerical example. If the industry is textiles, cloth is the output and cotton is the only input, then say there is a uniform duty on inputs and outputs, $t_j = t_i = 20$ percent. If inputs represent 40 percent of output $(a_{ij} = 0.4)$, then from equation (IV.7), $ERP = \dfrac{(20 - 0.4 \times 20)}{(1-0.4)}$ = 20 percent; i.e., the effective rate is the same as the nominal rate. If, however, to protect the textile industry the tariff on competing cloth, t_j, is raised to 40 percent, then $ERP = \dfrac{(40 - 0.4 \times 20)}{(1-0.4)} = 53$ percent. In the first case, domestic value added could exceed world value added by 20 percent, but in the second case by as much as 53 percent, indicating a less efficient industry. Of course, the duties on inputs could be higher than those on outputs, as may well be true for export industries, in which case the effective protection would be lower than the nominal rate and could even be negative, indicating a very efficient industry, able to compete in world markets.

One of the practical difficulties in using equation (IV.7) to calculate the *ERP* is that it requires the use of input coefficients based on free trade, i.e. trade undistorted by protection. One way to approximate such coefficients is to use input–output data for countries that have very low duties. Another is to use the data for the country in question, but to adjust the input coefficients to allow for the presence of distorting tariffs. To do this, note that we observe not a_{ij}, but the domestic coefficient, b_{ij}, which is the ratio of costs to output value in domestic prices, or

$$b_{ij} \quad = \frac{C^d}{P^d} = \frac{C^w (1 + t_i)}{P^w (1 + t_j)} = a_{ij} \frac{(1 + t_i)}{(1 + t_j)} \tag{IV.8}$$

It is a fairly straightforward algebraic exercise (and one done in detail by Corden (1971) pp. 35–37) to substitute an expression for a_{ij} from equation (IV.8) into equation (IV.7) and derive an expression for the effective rate of protection using domestic price input coefficients:

$$ERP_j = \frac{\dfrac{t_j}{1 + t_i} - \displaystyle\sum_i \frac{b_{ij} (t_i)}{1 + t_i}}{\dfrac{1}{1 + t_j} - \displaystyle\sum_i \frac{b_{ij}}{1 + t_i}}$$

Note in this case, when we start with domestic coefficients, it is possible for very inefficient industries that the denominator of equation (IV.9) may be negative, typically giving a very high negative value for *ERP*. In this case the industry's value added at world prices is negative, i.e. it loses foreign exchange. This has to be distinguished from the case of negative *ERP* resulting from efficient industries whose input tariffs are higher than its own nominal protection: when a negative *ERP* indicates efficiency, the negative value is usually low and the cause is a negative numerator; when negativity is a result of inefficiency, the value is usually large and stems from a negative denominator.

Three characteristics of the *ERP* indicator are worth emphasizing. First, as with cost–benefit calculations, the *ERP* deals only with the industry itself and does not conveniently handle the effects of linkages to other industries. If the cotton textile industry is found to have a low *ERP* and is therefore to be promoted, but depends on a domestic cotton industry which is very inefficient, then the *ERP* for textiles alone may give a false signal, because together the two industries may be inefficient. Whether this is a drawback or not depends upon whether the promotion of one industry, such as textiles, necessarily implies the promotion of its linked industry, cotton growing. If the import of cotton is an option, then the *ERP* is a relevant indicator of efficiency.

Second, effective protection, unlike cost–benefit analysis, works with flows at one time period and cannot deal with the important differences between projects resulting from different time profiles. Discounting would clearly be advantageous, but typically is not feasible for many industries because the cash flow data are not readily available. Effective protection is a compromise that requires less data to get useful results.

Third, and more damaging, calculations of the *ERP* really only tell us how efficient an industry would be if domestic prices were determined precisely by tariffs. However, it is entirely possible that an industry might be efficient enough to produce at domestic prices below those permitted by protective duties, in which case the *ERP* might lead planners to reject an industry that could in fact be acceptable. The opposite is possible, also: if quota restrictions are used, domestic prices could be above the tariff-indicated level, so the *ERP* would indicate a more efficient industry than is the case. To avoid this drawback, it would be preferable to use actual prices to calculate value added, rather than to infer prices (and value added) from tariff structures, as is done in equations (IV.7) and (IV.9). Some studies have done this, but the necessary price data are not as generally available as tariff data.

DOMESTIC RESOURCE COST

The domestic resource cost (*DRC*) is a closely related concept of ranking potential investments, one developed by Bruno (1967) from his work on linear programming. Like effective protection measures, the *DRC* works with flows at one point in time and compares the value of domestic resources to foreign resources. But there are several differences in concept. As its name implies, the *DRC* measures the cost in terms of domestic resources expended to earn or save one unit of foreign exchange. For a single project, all domestic inputs, including value added items and non-traded goods and services, would be valued at domestic prices and constitute the numerator. The denominator would consist of the difference between the value of output at border prices (either an import substitute or a potential export) and the value of all potentially traded inputs, also at border prices, but denominated in foreign, not domestic currency. Thus,

$$DRC_j = \frac{\sum\limits_i w_i F_i}{P_j^w - C_j^w} = \frac{\sum\limits_i w_i F_i}{P_j^w - \sum\limits_i a_{ij} P_i^w} \qquad \text{(IV.10)}$$

where w_i is the price of each domestic input, F_i is the quantity of each domestic factor, including non-traded goods, P_j^w is the world (border) price of the output, P_i^w the same for inputs and a_{ij} is the Leontief coefficient. Since the numerator has the dimensions of local currency (lepta) and the denominator foreign exchange (dollars), the DRC has the same dimensions as an exchange rate. The lower the ratio, the lower the cost in domestic resources of earning or saving foreign exchange and the more efficient the project.

Several significant variations on the DRC are possible. First, it can be used, as cost–benefit analysis and effective protection, on a project alone, measuring only its direct contribution to saving or earning foreign exchange. However, as Bruno originally conceived it, the DRC can incorporate direct and indirect effects, that is, the coefficients can come from the Leontief inverse matrix. In that case, the DRC measures the effects throughout the economy of investing in a single industry. In the textile–cotton example, the DRC would measure the domestic resource cost of saving foreign exchange, considering cloth manufacture, cotton growing, fertilizer and tractor production for cotton farming, *ad infinitum*. Whether this is an appropriate way to rank projects depends on the circumstances: if textile production is likely to result in the expansion of all its supplyiing industries, then the linkages should be included in the DRC measure. But if the textile industry has the option of importing cotton instead, it would do so unless domestic production were competitive, in which case the DRC should refer to the textile industry alone.

Second, the domestic resources in the numerator of the DRC can be shadow-priced, so that the ratio gives the opportunity cost of a unit of foreign exchange for a given project in terms of the domestic resources needed to produce it. This, coupled with a third feature, provides a way to measure the shadow exchange rate. If all projects are ranked according to their DRCs, with domestic factors shadow-priced, then the planners simply select projects for investment with the lowest DRCs until the investment constraint is exhausted. The DRC of the last (or marginal) project to be selected then gives the marginal cost of foreign exchange, its shadow price. In the future, any project with a lower *DRC* should be implemented, but not any project with a higher one. Alternatively, if the shadow price of foreign exchange is known, then it becomes the cut-off value for choosing projects according to their domestic resource cost.

Variations on the *ERP* and *DRC* are possible. Except under strong assumptions, not likely to be met in reality, these project-specific measures of efficiency are unlikely to give identical rankings of investments. Despite the uneasiness this may cause, the discrepancies are probably not critical. The role of all these measures, including cost–benefit analysis, is really to screen out the really bad projects and point out the really good ones, and for this purpose these measures are usually consistent. Our data are seldom adequate to make the finer distinctions among projects in the middle of the range. Where different methods throw up substantially different results, it is a sign to the planner that further investigation is required and that the mechanical assumptions often used in sector-wide planning may not apply. Handy indicators are no substitute for detailed and critical investigation. In any case, once sector-wide techniques identify a list of possibly good projects, the next step should always be a thoroughgoing feasibility study and economic project analysis.

Education planning

The material discussed so far in this chapter is relevant to Case 6, Industrial Strategy. Two techniques of economic planning have, however, been adapted to planning investments in education, and these are applicable to Case 7. The application of cost–benefit analysis to education was explained briefly and criticized in Part III. Internal rates of return are calculated for each level of education, from primary through university, and for each kind of university degree, such as engineering, liberal arts, social sciences, law and medicine. Then, analogous to the use of project appraisal methods in other sectors, education investment would be allocated to those types of schooling with the highest rates of return. One assumption underlying rate-of-return analysis for education bears examination here. By using wage differentials observable in the economy as a predictor of the returns to future investment, it is implicitly assumed that the demand for educated labor is perfectly elastic. That is, no matter how many graduates are produced from one level of education, it is contemplated that the wage differentials between those graduates and others from lower levels of education will remain the same. The standard prescription for investment allocation would move all investment funds towards the level of education yielding the highest return. If this were done, however, the supply of graduates would rise sharply and, presumably, the wage would fall over time, violating the underlying assumption. A more general formulation could account for downward-sloping demands for educated labor. It would, of course, be more complex and require considerably more information.

The second technique, more widely used by education planners than the first, is manpower planning. It is closely akin to inter-industry analysis, in that it bases projections of future manpower needs on fixed relationships between future output and the inputs of labor skills needed to produce it. In this respect, manpower planning makes an opposite assumption to that of cost–benefit analysis. To maintain the rigid relationship between output and required skills, it is implicitly assumed that the demand for each type of skill is perfectly inelastic. Thus, if supply shifts, wages will shift also, but the same number of workers with such skills will be employed.

The essence of manpower planning can be encapsulated in the following equation, from Blaug (1972, p. 151), whose Chapter 5 forms the basis for much of the ensuing description:

$$\mathbf{E} = X \left(\frac{\mathbf{X_j}}{\mathbf{X}}\right) \left(\frac{\mathbf{L_j}}{\mathbf{X_j}}\right) \left(\frac{\mathbf{L_k}}{\mathbf{L_j}}\right) \left(\frac{\mathbf{E_i}}{\mathbf{L_k}}\right) \tag{IV.11}$$

where $\mathbf{E}$ is a vector of educational attainments necessary to produce gross output, X; $(\mathbf{X_j}/\mathbf{X})$ is a vector of sectoral output shares in gross output; $(\mathbf{L_j}/\mathbf{X_j})$ is a matrix (of diagonal elements only) of sectoral labor–output ratios; $(\mathbf{L_k}/\mathbf{L_j})$ is a matrix that breaks the labor force in each industry (L_j) into occupations (L_k); and $\mathbf{E_i}/\mathbf{L_k}$ is a matrix that gives the level(s) of education for each occupation.

Thus the steps in manpower planning are these.

(1) Project gross output (or value added, i.e. GNP) for some future target date.
(2) Use an inter-industry table or other data to break future output down into its sectoral components (agriculture, textiles, banking, etc.).
(3) Convert sectoral output into sectoral labor force by using sectoral average (or, preferably, marginal) labor–output ratios, the inverse of labor productivity.
(4) Divide each sector's labor force into its occupational or skill components (e.g. machinists, engineers, watchmen).
(5) Convert these skill components into educational attainments, i.e., the years and type of schooling required to perform each occupation.

The last step gives the stock of educated manpower that will be required to achieve the target output level. To translate educational requirements from step 5 into an investment plan for education, it is necessary to:

(6)   Assess the current stock of educated workers by type and years of schooling.
(7)   Allowing for attrition through retirement, death, disability, etc., project the stock of educated workers from the present labor force that will remain active in the target year.
(8)   The difference between 6 and 7 is the number of each level to be educated in the interim.
(9)   From current enrollments, teachers and plant, assess the likely numbers of graduates in each class in the absence of investment in education.
(10)   Plan expansion of the educational system to enable it to produce the increases in each category of graduate necessary to close the gap between steps (8) and (9).

Some of the problems with manpower planning are evident from our discussion of inter-industry techniques. Each of the labor force coefficients is, like any input–output coefficient, rigidly fixed, allowing no possibility of substitution. Moreover, these are based on historical, not likely future, relationships. This is particularly serious if the manpower plan is being designed for the long run, as seems essential because the gestation period for producing trained manpower through formal education is itself a long one. The labor–output ratio, taken from the input–output table, can vary considerably, either because new technologies emerge or because substitution can take place using existing technologies. The rigid division of each industry's labor force into its occupational components is equally suspect. Mechanics or draftsmen might be able to substitute for some engineers, for example, or mechanics for pipefitters; in many countries nurses perform tasks that are reserved for doctors in other countries. And changing technologies are also likely to shift the occupational mix, as when for example more advanced looms reduce the requirements for loom-tenders in a textile mill.

Perhaps the greatest leap of faith in manpower planning is the assumption that each occupation is characterized by fixed formal educational requirements; that is, engineers must be graduates of engineering schools and electricians of secondary or vocational schools. On the contrary, substitution is common. A very experienced maintenance mechanic, for example, could well perform some tasks done by engineers without further formal training. Many semi-skilled and skilled workers are actually trained on the job in any case, leaving to the formal educational system the basic tasks of teaching functional literacy and numeracy. The problems of associating differing educational attainments with wage differentials, discussed in Part III in the context of cost–benefit analysis, apply equally to the assumption of manpower planning that educational achievement and job classification are rigidly related.

Most manpower plans provide point or single-valued estimates of the requirements for each type of education. As with any long-term forecast, uncertainties are large and point estimates are not as useful as interval estimates which provide probable high and low values for each target variable. This is especially so in manpower planning, which works with differences between projections of eventual need and the likely supply, given no change in the educational system. Moderate errors in estimates of large numbers can lead to large errors in projected differences between such numbers. Planners may well want to trim their investment programs if there is a substantial possibility that the manpower requirements could be considerably less than the expected value.

How does the planner choose between the two methods, cost–benefit analysis and manpower planning? Given the inadequacies of each, he should probably use both if possible. In the process, each technique will provide information about the educational system and its outputs. Although neither method should be followed slavishly, each or both may provide some obvious signals, such as a high return to and need for more chemical engineers. When they do, the task of planners should be to provide these skills in the most efficient way, which may mean an expansion of engineering training or could mean upgrading workers already in industry. The key is to use the techniques to learn about the system, not as a crutch to substitute for informed decision-making about investment in education.

References

BALASSA, B. (1971a). Effective Protection: A Summary Appraisal. In *Effective Tariff Protection* (ed. by H. G. Grubel and H. G. Johnson). Geneva, GATT

BALASSA, B., et al. (1971b). *The Structure of Protection in Developing Countries*. Baltimore, Johns Hopkins University Press

BLAUG, M. (1972). *An Introduction to the Economics of Education*. Baltimore, Penguin Books

BLITZER, C. R., CLARK, P. B. and TAYLOR, L. (eds.) (1975). *Economy-wide Models and Development Planning*. London, Oxford University Press

BRUNO, M. (1967). The Optimal Selection of Export-Promoting and Import-Substituting Projects. In *Planning the External Sector: Techniques, Problems and Policies*. New York, United Nations

CHENERY, H. B., and CLARK, P. G. (1959). *Inter-industry Economics*. New York, Wiley

CORDEN, W. M. (1971). *The Theory of Protection*. London, Oxford University Press

DORFMAN, R., SAMUELSON, P. and SOLOW, R. M. (1958). *Linear Programming and Economic Analysis*. New York, McGraw-Hill

JOHNSON, H. G. (1965). The Theory of Tariff Structure with Special Reference to World Trade and Development. In *Trade and Development* (ed. by H. G. Johnson and P. B. Kenen). Geneva, Librairie Droz

Industrial Strategy

As part of the preparation of the Fifth Five-Year Plan, each ministry with economic responsibilities has been asked to produce a 10-year strategy for the sector(s) for which it is responsible. The Ministry of Planning is to review these ministry drafts and integrate them into the Fifth Plan.

Macroeconomic growth parameters

The Ministry of Planning has established a set of growth projections which are to guide the ministries in their sectoral planning. MinPlan estimates that the economy will regain its pre-1974 long-term growth rate (5.2 percent a year) over the next three years (1978–1980) and then should be able to grow at 5.5 percent a year over the next decade. This would be a dramatic improvement over recent performance, but well within the capabilities of the economy. As the recently improved measures for project formulation, analysis and implementation take effect, the ministry hopes to reduce the economy-wide incremental capital–output ratio (ICOR) from recent levels (4.1) to the level of the early 1960s of 3.7; investment must then average 20 percent of GDP. Furthermore, the ministry expects foreign capital from all sources to finance about 7 percent of investment, so that over the 10 years consumption should average 81 percent of GDP. Thus consumption would have to decline substantially from its 1977 share of 87 percent of GDP. If the target consumption share were achieved in the early 1980s and thereafter consumption maintained its share of GNP, then consumption would grow at only 4.8 percent a year over the period from 1977 to 1980. Correspondingly, investment must grow at an average 7.9 percent a year to equal 20 percent of GNP by 1990.

Using this investment growth rate, MinPlan has projected the total available investment over the 1977–1990 period, a 13-year total of **159**

Lp 196.1bn in 1977 prices*. This total has been allocated by sectors and the results presented to the ministries to serve as their guides in planning. Consistent with the government's policy of emphasizing rural development and basic needs, the allocation for manufacturing is 12 percent (Lp 23.5bn), an allocation less than manufacturing's share in previous five-year plans. However, MinPlan has stated its willingness to adjust these sectoral investment constraints if a reallocation would improve the Fifth Plan's ability to achieve national goals.

MinPlan has also projected the annual export growth rates by commodity as follows: copper, cotton and rice, rapid recovery, by 10 percent a year, to 1979, then 4 percent a year to 1990; timber and lumber, 4 percent over the whole 13-year period; other metals, 6 percent; other agricultural products, 6 percent; manufactures, 10 percent. These growth rates, projected from 1977 to 1990, together with the assumption that foreign capital will equal 7 percent of investment, would permit imports (of goods plus net services) to grow at only 4.9 percent over the period, thus decreasing the average ratio of imports to GDP. Of an incremental import capacity of Lp 6.45bn, MinPlan estimates that about 5 percent will be taken up by net service payments unrelated to goods imports and some 60 percent will be taken up by non-competitive imports, that is, by products for which the Beracian economy is unlikely to be able to substitute. Thus, by 1990 the ministry expects that the capacity to import competitive (substitutable) commodities will be about Lp 2.3bn higher than it was in 1977 (in 1977 prices).

Sectoral growth pattern

MinPlan has also made the first attempt to project sectoral demand growth, based on the recently completed input–output table for 1976. (The 1976 inter-industrial structure has been applied to 1977 national income totals, so that 1977 becomes the base year.) These projections start with consumer goods and estimate the increments for each sector that would be consistent with (i) the 4.8 percent growth rate of consumption and (ii) sectoral demand elasticities that have been taken from various studies in Beracia and other countries. Second, final demand for investment goods is estimated by assuming that all investment goods, including inventories, grow proportionately to total investment in 1977. Third, export commodity growth is based on the projected rates mentioned above. Finally, the possibility of import

* This total could be estimated by projecting investment for each of the 13 years and adding the results; or by integrating the following:

$$I_{total} = \int_0^{13} I_o (1 + 0.079)^t dt$$

with I_o taken as the 1977 value, 8836 million lepta.

substitution is introduced in this first round by assuming that manufacturing (sectors 6–27 only) might substitute completely for all 1977 competitive imports (estimated from the 1976 input–output structure).

Table 1 shows the resulting increment in final demand over the 1977–1990 period. In addition, the table shows the increase in total

TABLE 1 Maximum potential growth in final demand, total output and value added, 1977–1990[a]

		Final demand (Lp million)					
	Consump-tion	Invest-ment	Exports	Import substitution	Total	Total output	Value added
1. Agriculture, food	7 788	227	831	–	8 846	12 200	9 587
2. Agriculture, non-food	446	50	944	–	1 440	2 420	1 909
3. Livestock	2 491	52	–	–	2 543	3 253	2 324
4. Fishing and forestry	612	28	292	–	932	1 301	493
5. Mining	188	63	373	–	624	2 631	1 299
6. Food processing	2 294	63	215	52	2 624	4 050	626
7. Beverages	1 634	24	–	–	1 658	1 804	642
8. Tobacco	385	7	–	–	392	414	146
9. Textiles	1 018	31	449	134	1 632	2 778	677
10. Clothing	1 058	15	–	60	1 133	1 155	545
11. Leather	9	6	294	–	309	518	78
12. Footwear	524	7	118	73	722	729	246
13. Wood products	35	17	385	17	454	1 259	291
14. Furniture	533	7	–	–	540	631	231
15. Paper and products	–	9	74	43	126	939	203
16. Printing	507	9	–	–	516	733	227
17. Rubber products	179	7	–	43	229	613	236
18. Chemical products	1 097	37	165	130	1 429	3 364	862
19. Petroleum refining	529	31	–	86	646	2 743	888
20. Non-metallic minerals	48	17	–	–	65	1 833	770
21. Ferrous metals	–	4	–	345	349	2 094	472
22. Non-ferrous metals	–	68	1 821	64	1 953	2 511	240
23. Metal products	262	142	147	220	771	1 623	414
24. Non-electrical machinery	52	705	–	375	1 132	2 181	873
25. Electrical machinery	341	626	–	384	1 351	1 811	584
26. Transport equipment	358	1 722	–	173	2 253	2 979	824
27. Other manufacturing	245	281	–	35	561	942	315
28. Construction	–	7 768	144	–	7 912	8 304	3 974
29. Electricity, water, gas	481	–	77	–	558	1 197	878
30. Wholesale and retail trade	6 730	–	–	–	6 730	12 108	7 389
31. Banking and insurance	835	–	–	–	835	2 521	1 467
32. Transport, communication	3 758	–	–	–	3 758	7 707	3 357
33. Education and health	4 899	–	–	–	4 899	4 900	3 556
34. Housing	2 627	–	–	–	2 627	2 627	1 931
35. Other services	1 761	–	–	–	1 761	5 190	3 021
Total	43 724	12 023	6 329	2 234	64 310	104 063	51 575

Note: [a]All quantities are *increments* over the 13-year period in constant 1977 prices.

output, found by multiplying the inverse input–output matrix, $(\mathbf{I}-\mathbf{A})^{-1}$, by incremental final demand; and the incremental value added, found by multiplying the incremental total output vector by the value added coefficients from the 1976 input–output table. This gives a set of maximum possible increases in output. Presumably projected investment will not be sufficient to permit the economy to produce all these goods, and it will be up to the various ministries to make their choices based on sectoral priorities as they are derived from national goals.

Industry program

The Ministry of Industry (MinInd) is responsible for manufacturing, represented by sectors 6 through 27 in the national input–output table. Its tasks include planning for those sectors; project analysis and recommendations to MinPlan; licensing of manufacturing investments; recommendations to the Cabinet on investment incentives in manufacturing; and recommendations to the Ministry of Commerce on controlled prices for manufactured goods produced in Beracia. In fulfilling these responsibilities, the ministry has been guided by the following national goals as applied to industry:

(1)   Maximum growth of output for the resources committed to manufacturing;

(2)   Employment growth sufficient to absorb about one-third of the migrants per year from the rural areas in addition to one-third of the natural increase in the urban population;

(3)   Increasing self-reliance within the manufacturing sector, in the sense that imports of manufactured goods should be reduced to the minimum consistent with other goals;

(4)   Industry, like other modern economic activities, must be distributed as widely around the country as possible, again consistent with other goals;

(5)   In distributing manufacturing geographically, due consideration should be given to the major national goal of equalizing incomes between rural and urban residents; and

(6)   Industry shall lead the rest of the economy in modernization, especially in modernization of its capital stock.

It has been MinInd's position that goals (1) and (6) should be dominant and that goal (2), employment growth, would follow naturally. The ministry's lower priority on the other goals has been a source of contention with MinPlan.

In response to MinPlan's directive that each ministry should produce the preliminary plan for its sectors, MinInd has chosen to select investments on the basis of capital–value added ratios, maximizing the increase in value added possible with the investment allocation given by MinPlan. To ensure that goal (6) (modernization) is also accommodated, only the most modern technologies have been considered. To select investments, MinInd has compiled investment–value added ratios from past experience and from consultants' and investors' prospectuses on potential new industries. These are summarized by sector in *Table 2*, together with ratios for employment

TABLE 2 Characteristics of manufacturing sectors

	Investment–value added ratio (1)	Employment–value added ratio[a] (2)	Value added per plant[b] (3)
6. Food processing	3.05 (2.0)[c]	40.6 (63)	3.5 (1.1)
7. Beverages	3.40	4.1	420
8. Tobacco	2.65	13.1	31.0
9. Textiles	3.60 (2.0)	25.0 (44)	116 (104)
10. Clothing	0.85	41.3	6.7 (0.7)
11. Leather	4.05	30.0	22.0
12. Footwear	1.60	46.3	61
13. Wood products	2.35 (2.10)	19.4 (27)	5.4 (0.8)
14. Furniture	1.95	25.0	6.1
15. Paper and products	3.60	18.1	123
16. Printing	0.90	12.5	16.0
17. Rubber products	2.25	4.2	150
18. Chemical products	3.10	3.9	250
19. Petroleum refining	4.60	3.1	340
20. Non-metallic minerals	4.55	7.1	106
21. Ferrous metals	5.15 (5.90)	13.1 (13.7)	1770 (590)
22. Non-ferrous metals	4.05	15.6	590
23. Metal products	2.30	31.3	32
24. Non-electrical machinery	1.90	8.1	84
25. Electrical machinery	1.95	9.4	126
26. Transport equipment	2.75	6.5	170
27. Other manufacturing	2.00	20.6	17

Notes: [a]The units are person-years per lepta million (constant 1977 prices).
[b]Lepta million (constant 1977 prices).
[c]Figures in parentheses represent alternative technologies.

and the average size of plant in each sector. (Characteristics for less modern technologies have been given in parentheses for some sectors.) As a first try, ministry planners have taken MinPlan's projections of maximum potential final demand and output and converted these into required investment, potential employment creation and potential number of new plants for industry over the 1977–1990 period (*Table 3*). From this list of production possibilities for large-scale manufacturing*, the industry planners have selected a set of investments that fits within the investment constraint of Lp 23.5bn and yields the maximum incremental value added, according to the parmeters of the national input–output table.

* Not enough is known of the small-scale, informal sector to include it in these plans.

TABLE 3 Production possibilities in manufacturing, 1977–1990[a]

	Potential value added[b] (Lp million)	Required investment[c] (Lp million)	Potential employment[c] (thousands)	Potential number of plants[d]
6. Food processing	626	1 909 (1 252)[e]	25.4 (39.4)	178 (569)
7. Beverages	642	2 183	2.6	2
8. Tobacco	146	416	1.9	5
9. Textiles	677	2 437 (1 354)	16.9 (29.8)	6 (7)
10. Clothing	545	463	22.5	81 (813)
11. Leather	78	316	2.3	4
12. Footwear	246	394	11.4	4
13. Wood products	291	684 (611)	5.6 (7.9)	54 (364)
14. Furniture	231	450	5.8	38
15. Paper and products	203	731	3.7	2
16. Printing	227	204	2.8	14
17. Rubber products	236	531	1.0	2
18. Chemical products	862	2 672	3.4	3
19. Petroleum refining	888	4 085	2.8	3
20. Non-metallic minerals	770	3 504	5.5	7
21. Ferrous metals[f]	472	2 785	6.2	1
22. Non-ferrous metals	240	972	3.7	1
23. Metal products	414	952	13.0	13
24. Non-electrical machinery	873	1 659	7.1	10
25. Electrical machinery	584	1 139	5.5	5
26. Transport equipment	824	2 266	5.4	5
27. Other manufacturers	315	630	6.5	19
Total	10 390	31 028 (29 569)	161 (190)	457 (1 891)

Notes: [a]All values are increments over the 1977–1990 period.
[b]From *Table 1*.
[c]These two columns obtained by multiplying the corresponding columns in *Table 2* by the potential value in this table.
[d]This column obtained by dividing the potential value added in this table by column (3) in *Table 2*.
[e]Figures in parentheses represent alternative technologies.
[f]Uses alternative small-scale plant.

The resulting investment plan is summarized in *Table 4*. It shows that, with an investment of Lp 23.5bn, all potential large-scale manufacturing investment, except that in petroleum and ferrous metals, can be included; for the marginal industry, non-metallic minerals, 71 percent of potential investment can be included within the constraint. The proposed program would create an additional Lp 8.81bn of value added in 1977 prices, create 150 400 new jobs; and result in the construction of 451 modern industrial facilities. The growth rate in large-scale manufacturing over the 13-year period would be 6.9 percent a year, a rate greater than the economy as a whole. Employment in manufacturing would grow by over 5 percent a year (based on 1976 employment data), a considerable improvement over the 2.6 percent rate for 1967–1976. (However, no allowance has been made for productivity increases from 1977 onwards.)

MinInd has sent *Table 4* to MinPlan as its first proposal for the national plan. It has also prepared a brief report on the state of industry in Beracia, reproduced here as Appendix A.

The industry sector officer in MinPlan has received the MinInd submission and been instructed to answer the following.

TABLE 4 Proposed manufacturing investment program, 1977–1990 (by Ministry of Industry)

	Investment (Lp million)	Incremental value added (Lp million)	Incremental employment (thousands)	Incremental number of plants
6. Food processing	1 909	626	25.4	178
7. Beverages	2 183	642	2.6	2
8. Tobacco	416	146	1.9	5
9. Textiles	2 437	677	16.9	6
10. Clothing	463	545	22.5	81
11. Leather	316	78	2.3	4
12. Footwear	394	246	11.4	4
13. Wood products	684	291	5.6	54
14. Furniture	450	231	5.8	38
15. Paper and products	731	203	3.7	2
16. Printing	204	227	2.8	14
17. Rubber products	531	236	1.0	2
18. Chemical products	2 672	862	3.4	3
19. Petroleum refining	–	–	–	–
20. Non-metallic minerals	2 492	548	3.9	5
21. Ferrous metals	–	–	–	–
22. Non-ferrous metals	972	240	3.7	1
23. Metal products	952	414	13.0	13
24. Non-electrical machinery	1 659	873	7.1	10
25. Electrical machinery	1 139	584	5.5	5
26. Transport equipment	2 266	824	5.4	5
27. Other manufacturing	630	315	6.5	19
Total	23 500	8 808	150.4	451

Questions

1. Would the investment plan fulfill national goals to the maximum extent possible?
2. If not, what alternative investment plans for manufacturing would improve goal·achievement?
3. What are the trade-offs among the goals to be served by manufacturing development?
4. How should MinInd be instructed to evaluate alternative investment plans in the future?

Appendix A   The state of industry in Beracia

The purpose of this brief is to provide some background to readers of the Ministry of Industry projections for manufacturing development to 1990. Although the manufacturing sector has been developing vigorously since independence, its share of GDP is still low: 14 percent for all manufacturing in 1977 and 12 percent for the modern, large-scale sector (firms of 20 or more employees). It employed 170 000 workers in 1976, 13 percent of the wage labor force, and its employees earn above-average wages: Lp 11 300 per year in 1976, 14 prcent above the national average for wage-earners. Although real wages in manufacturing rose by 18 percent from 1970 to 1973, they have fallen slightly since as high inflation surpassed wage increases. This may be a source of stronger union pressure for higher wage settlements over the next two or three years.

In terms of both output and employment, food processing is the largest branch of manufacturing, followed by beverages (though not for employment), textiles and clothing (*Table A.1*). Although some imports of these products continue to be permitted, domestic industry meets most of local demand, as is true for the leather and footwear industries. The wood products industry is oriented primarily towards export, especially of sawnwood and some board products, although it also

TABLE A.1 Large-scale manufacturing: output, value added and employment

Industry	Value of gross output—1977 (Lp million)	Value added—1977 (Lp million)	Employment—1976 (thousands)
6. Food processing	4 817	745	39.0
7. Beverages	2 025	721	3.6
8. Tobacco	576	203	2.7
9. Textiles	1 952	476	17.2
10. Clothing	1 090	514	26.1
11. Leather products	225	34	1.3
12. Footwear	514	174	12.8
13. Wood products	1 675	387	9.5
14. Furniture	611	223	8.4
15. Paper and products	224	48	1.1
16. Printing	680	211	3.2
17. Rubber products	359	138	0.7
18. Chemical products	1 525	391	2.0
19. Petroleum refining	1 424	435	1.7
20. Non-metallic mineral products	874	367	3.7
21. Ferrous metals	386	87	1.3
22. Non-ferrous metals	2 691	257	4.1
23. Metal products	377	96	3.4
24. Non-electrical machinery	181	72	0.7
25. Electrical machinery	393	127	1.3
26. Transport equipment	1 475	408	3.3
27. Other manufacturing	623	208	6.2
Total	24 697	6 322	153.3

supplies part of the domestic market. The paper industry, in contrast to those mentioned so far, is scarcely developed, being mainly a finishing and assembly operation. Development of capacity to produce pulp and paper is a priority for the next plan; softwood plantations have already been established.

The chemical industry is unevenly developed. The bulk of its output comes from the fertilizer industry, which is probably more fully developed than that for most countries of Beracia's income level and meets from 80 to 90 percent of domestic demand. Otherwise, the sector consists largely of paints, detergents and soap, pharmaceuticals and plastic products. Some small-scale industrial chemical production has been started, but a modern basic chemicals industry remains a target for the next plan. Similarly, the petroleum sector is dominated by the refinery. No petrochemicals are produced, although there have been pre-feasibility studies of a PVC plant to supply the local plastics industry.

TABLE A.2 Duties and premia on competing imports

	Nominal duty[b] (%)	Average license premium[b] (%)	Share under bonus voucher[a,b] (%)
1. Agriculture, food	5	5	0
2. Agriculture, non-food	20	20	0
3. Livestock	25	25	0
4. Fishing and forestry	15	30	0
5. Mining	15	10	0
6. Food processing	25	45	0
7. Beverages	180	45	0
8. Tobacco	150	45	0
9. Textiles	50	25	0
10. Clothing	120	–	100
11. Leather	30	30	0
12. Footwear	120	–	100
13. Wood products	100	–	100
14. Furniture	200	45	0
15. Paper and products	20	25	0
16. Printing	0	0	0
17. Rubber products	25	20	0
18. Chemical products	20	45	0
19. Petroleum products	0	55	0
20. Non-metallic minerals	15	20	0
21. Ferrous metals	15	30	0
22. Non-ferrous metals	10	0	0
23. Metal products	15–25	20	0
24. Non-electrical machinery	12.5	40	10
25. Electrical machinery	12.5	40	10
26. Transport equipment	75	–	100
27. Other manufacturing	25	30	0

Notes: [a]For this share, the license premium does not apply.
         [b]Percent of cif values.

TABLE A.3 Comparison between domestic and foreign
prices for selected commodities, 1977

	Domestic price premium[a] (%)
Rice polished	−5
Wheat	10
Flour	25
Sugar, refined	35
Beef, tinned	80
Fish, tinned	60
Soya beans	10
Soya bean oil	30
Cotton	−10
Jute fiber	40
Tobacco	45
Hides and skins	10
Rubber	40
Soft drinks	70
Beer	130
Liquor	190
Cigarettes	175
Cotton, grey cloth	35
Cotton fabrics, finished	65
Women's cotton dresses	100
Denim pants	85
Men's shirts[b]	120
Leather and products	60
Footwear[b]	90
Sawnwood	15
Plywood	25
Furniture[b]	275
Paper products	50
Tires	50
Chemical fertilizer	35
Pharmaceuticals	75
Plastic products	70
Motor spirit (gasoline)	50
Fuel oil	45
Rolled steel products	50
Metal products[b]	30–50
Machinery[b]	40–55
Trucks and buses[b]	60

Notes: [a]Percentage by which the domestic wholesale price exceeds the cif price of
closely competing imports.
    [b]Comparability between imports and domestic product cannot be assessed for
these products.

In minerals, the cement industry has been expanded to keep pace
with demand and additional capacity is planned for the early 1980s. No
basic iron and steel capacity exists, although one small rolling mill turns
out construction materials from imported billets. The copper industry,
which smelts and refines most of the copper mined here, is of course well
developed. The metal products and machinery industries are in their
infancy, concentrating on hardware, simple processing equipment,
small motors and the like. Finally, transport equipment mostly involves
the assembly of trucks and buses, although some rudimentary
automobile assembly may be included in the figures.

Tables A.2 and *A.3* provide some approximate data on the tariff protection afforded these industries and the prices they charge. Except for export industries and one or two food processing industries, Beracian manufacturing requires high protection and, as the price data indicate, takes advantage of it. Food processing (other than tinned products) and textiles manage to produce at prices only moderately above import prices, but the beverage and clothing industries appear to have serious cost problems and are forced to produce at double or more the import price. Most producer goods branches perform reasonably well, considering the stage of Beracian development, with prices from 30 to 70 percent above those of competing imports (net of duties). However, only the simplest production lines have been attempted and it seems likely that further development of the chemical, metals and machinery industries will require greater protection than is now the case.

Appendix B Inter-industry tables, 1976*

TABLE B.1 Beracia domestic coefficients matrix

	1 Agriculture, food	2 Agriculture, non-food	3 Livestock	4 Fishing and forestry	5 Mining	6 Food processing	7 Beverages	8 Tobacco	9 Textiles	10 Clothing	11 Leather
1 Agriculture, food	0.1047	0.0000	0.3939	0.0754	0.0000	0.3184	0.0161	0.0000	0.0000	0.0000	0.0000
2 Agriculture, non-food	0.0000	0.1024	0.0000	0.0000	0.0000	0.0012	0.0012	0.0332	0.2461	0.0000	0.0000
3 Livestock	0.0000	0.0000	0.0000	0.0031	0.0000	0.0405	0.0270	0.0000	0.0155	0.0007	0.2159
4 Fishing and forestry	0.0054	0.0046	0.0000	0.0016	0.0000	0.0673	0.0405	0.0000	0.0000	0.0000	0.0019
5 Mining	0.0022	0.0022	0.0000	0.0059	0.0358	0.0000	0.0000	0.0000	0.0000	0.0000	0.0000
6 Food processing	0.0000	0.0000	0.1845	0.0000	0.0000	0.1086	0.0742	0.0000	0.0010	0.0000	0.0663
7 Beverages	0.0000	0.0000	0.0003	0.0089	0.0000	0.0002	0.0754	0.0005	0.0000	0.0000	0.0000
8 Tobacco	0.0000	0.0000	0.0000	0.0000	0.0000	0.0000	0.0000	0.0525	0.0000	0.0000	0.0000
9 Textiles	0.0000	0.0000	0.0000	0.0000	0.0010	0.0117	0.0000	0.0000	0.1655	0.2981	0.0111
10 Clothing	0.0000	0.0000	0.0000	0.0000	0.0000	0.0000	0.0000	0.0000	0.0000	0.0000	0.0144
11 Leather	0.0000	0.0000	0.0000	0.0000	0.0000	0.0000	0.0000	0.0000	0.0000	0.0038	0.0000
12 Footwear	0.0000	0.0000	0.0000	0.0000	0.0000	0.0000	0.0000	0.0000	0.0000	0.0000	0.0000
13 Food products	0.0010	0.0000	0.0000	0.0265	0.0076	0.0000	0.0024	0.0000	0.0003	0.0000	0.0019
14 Furniture	0.0000	0.0000	0.0000	0.0000	0.0000	0.0000	0.0000	0.0000	0.0000	0.0000	0.0000
15 Paper and products	0.0000	0.0000	0.0000	0.0000	0.0003	0.0159	0.0179	0.0225	0.0010	0.0036	0.0029
16 Printing	0.0000	0.0000	0.0000	0.0000	0.0000	0.0019	0.0027	0.0041	0.0004	0.0000	0.0000
17 Rubber products	0.0000	0.0000	0.0000	0.0003	0.0050	0.0007	0.0010	0.0002	0.0023	0.0000	0.0017
18 Chemical products	0.0216	0.0229	0.0000	0.0170	0.0305	0.0293	0.0030	0.0027	0.0502	0.0009	0.0925
19 Petroleum refining	0.0000	0.0000	0.0019	0.0157	0.0165	0.0070	0.0073	0.0004	0.0061	0.0008	0.0064
20 Non-metallic minerals	0.0000	0.0000	0.0000	0.0000	0.0041	0.0019	0.0209	0.0000	0.0000	0.0000	0.0014
21 Ferrous metals	0.0000	0.0000	0.0000	0.0000	0.0041	0.0000	0.0000	0.0000	0.0024	0.0000	0.0018

* In these tables, coefficients include all inputs that are either produced domestically or could be; i.e. competing imports are included. Non-competing imports are treated as a factor of production and shown in the factor inputs section (rows 38 and 39) of Table B.1.

	1 Agriculture, food	2 Agriculture, non-food	3 Livestock	4 Fishing and forestry	5 Mining	6 Food processing	7 Beverages	8 Tobacco	9 Textiles	10 Clothing	11 Leather
22 Non-ferrous metals	0.0000	0.0000	0.0000	0.0000	0.0000	0.0000	0.0000	0.0000	0.0000	0.0000	0.0002
23 Metal products	0.0000	0.0000	0.0000	0.0090	0.0210	0.0238	0.0163	0.0005	0.0040	0.0007	0.0103
24 Non-electrical machinery	0.0000	0.0000	0.0000	0.0087	0.0525	0.0076	0.0083	0.0025	0.0137	0.0011	0.0096
25 Electrical machinery	0.0000	0.0000	0.0000	0.0023	0.0119	0.0002	0.0000	0.0000	0.0000	0.0000	0.0000
26 Transport equipment	0.0000	0.0000	0.0000	0.0039	0.0035	0.0005	0.0008	0.0000	0.0002	0.0000	0.0002
27 Other manufacturing	0.0000	0.0000	0.0000	0.0046	0.0000	0.0012	0.0008	0.0000	0.0015	0.0096	0.0109
28 Construction	0.0000	0.0000	0.0000	0.0000	0.0044	0.0000	0.0000	0.0000	0.0000	0.0000	0.0000
29 Electricity, gas, water	0.0000	0.0000	0.0000	0.0000	0.0005	0.0059	0.0030	0.0007	0.0095	0.0011	0.0076
30 Wholesale and retail trade	0.0088	0.0086	0.0128	0.0234	0.0360	0.0673	0.0525	0.1537	0.0935	0.0744	0.1908
31 Banking and insurance	0.0000	0.0000	0.0000	0.0074	0.0078	0.0045	0.0053	0.0053	0.0070	0.0037	0.0055
32 Transport and communication	0.0000	0.0000	0.0000	0.0000	0.0383	0.0172	0.0395	0.0392	0.0271	0.0524	0.0167
33 Education and health	0.0000	0.0000	0.0000	0.0000	0.0000	0.0000	0.0000	0.0000	0.0000	0.0000	0.0000
34 Housing	0.0000	0.0000	0.0000	0.0000	0.0000	0.0000	0.0000	0.0000	0.0000	0.0000	0.0000
35 Other services	0.1437	0.1407	0.5934	0.0091	0.0517	0.0452	0.0785	0.0509	0.0355	0.0160	0.0266
36 Intermediate total	0.0000	0.0000	0.0000	0.2228	0.3325	0.7780	0.4946	0.3689	0.6828	0.4669	0.6966
37											
38 Intermediate non-competitive imports	0.0125	0.0124	0.0000	0.0000	0.0000	0.0000	0.0000	0.0000	0.0000	0.0000	0.0000
39 Final non-competitive imports	0.0000	0.0000	0.0000	0.0102	0.0000	0.0526	0.0065	0.0203	0.0205	0.0104	0.1193
40 Value added	0.7858	0.7887	0.3791	0.7143	0.4939	0.1546	0.3558	0.3528	0.2437	0.4719	0.1503
41 Indirect taxes	0.0580	0.0582	0.0275	0.0527	0.1736	0.0148	0.1431	0.2580	0.0530	0.0508	0.0338
42	0.0000	0.0000	0.0000	0.0000	0.0000	0.0000	0.0000	0.0000	0.0000	0.0000	0.0000
43 Total	1.0000	1.0000	1.0000	1.0000	1.0000	1.0000	1.0000	1.0000	1.0000	1.0000	1.0000

	12 Footwear	13 Wood products	14 Furniture	15 Paper and products	16 Printing	17 Rubber products	18 Chemical products	19 Petroleum refining	20 Non-metallic minerals	21 Ferrous metals	22 Non-ferrous metals	23 Metal products
1 Agriculture, food	0.0000	0.0000	0.0000	0.0000	0.0000	0.0000	0.0001	0.0000	0.0000	0.0000	0.0000	0.0000
2 Agriculture, non-food	0.0000	0.0000	0.0000	0.0000	0.0000	0.0000	0.0075	0.0000	0.0000	0.0000	0.0000	0.0000
3 Livestock	0.0006	0.0000	0.0003	0.0000	0.0000	0.0000	0.0000	0.0000	0.0000	0.0000	0.0000	0.0000
4 Fishing and forestry	0.0085	0.0508	0.0000	0.1072	0.0000	0.0864	0.0154	0.0000	0.0000	0.0000	0.0000	0.0000
5 Mining	0.0000	0.0006	0.0000	0.0014	0.0000	0.0000	0.0051	0.0000	0.0921	0.0000	0.6438	0.0078
6 Food processing	0.0000	0.0032	0.0000	0.0056	0.0000	0.0000	0.0173	0.0000	0.0000	0.0000	0.0000	0.0000
7 Beverages	0.0000	0.0000	0.0000	0.0003	0.0000	0.0000	0.0025	0.0000	0.0000	0.0000	0.0000	0.0000
8 Tobacco	0.0000	0.0000	0.0000	0.0000	0.0000	0.0000	0.0000	0.0000	0.0000	0.0000	0.0000	0.0000
9 Textiles	0.0294	0.0000	0.0395	0.0005	0.0009	0.0476	0.0429	0.0000	0.0005	0.0000	0.0000	0.0002
10 Clothing	0.0000	0.0000	0.0000	0.0000	0.0000	0.0000	0.0000	0.0000	0.0000	0.0000	0.0000	0.0000
11 Leather	0.2594	0.0000	0.0000	0.0000	0.0000	0.0006	0.0000	0.0000	0.0000	0.0000	0.0000	0.0000
12 Footwear	0.0079	0.0000	0.0000	0.0063	0.0000	0.0000	0.0000	0.0000	0.0000	0.0000	0.0000	0.0000
13 Wood products	0.0000	0.2188	0.0860	0.0000	0.0000	0.0000	0.0000	0.0000	0.0003	0.0003	0.0000	0.0072
14 Furniture	0.0000	0.0000	0.0070	0.0000	0.0000	0.0001	0.0000	0.0000	0.0000	0.0000	0.0000	0.0000
15 Paper and products	0.0177	0.0005	0.0004	0.2620	0.1992	0.0006	0.0138	0.0002	0.0395	0.0000	0.0000	0.0076
16 Printing	0.0000	0.0000	0.0000	0.0004	0.0053	0.0000	0.0029	0.0000	0.0000	0.0000	0.0000	0.0001
17 Rubber products	0.0208	0.0026	0.0007	0.0027	0.0006	0.0147	0.0010	0.0006	0.0023	0.0015	0.0014	0.0021
18 Chemical products	0.0265	0.0071	0.0528	0.0432	0.0263	0.0182	0.1262	0.0123	0.0101	0.0017	0.0003	0.0206
19 Petroleum refining	0.0010	0.0155	0.0013	0.0053	0.0013	0.0085	0.0143	0.0796	0.0805	0.1331	0.0310	0.0078
20 Non-metallic minerals	0.0024	0.0015	0.0057	0.0000	0.0000	0.0004	0.0179	0.0000	0.0528	0.0067	0.0003	0.0021
21 Ferrous metals	0.0002	0.0012	0.0746	0.0000	0.0005	0.0000	0.0000	0.0000	0.0029	0.1875	0.0021	0.1956
22 Non-ferrous metals	0.0000	0.0009	0.0035	0.0000	0.0087	0.0000	0.0048	0.0000	0.0004	0.0082	0.0726	0.0567

	12 Footwear	13 Wood products	14 Furniture	15 Paper and products	16 Printing	17 Rubber products	18 Chemical products	19 Petroleum refining	20 Non-metallic minerals	21 Ferrous metals	22 Non-ferrous metals	23 Metal products
23 Metal products	0.0048	0.0092	0.0382	0.0080	0.0023	0.0052	0.0139	0.0091	0.0054	0.0252	0.0082	0.0280
24 Non-electrical machinery	0.0085	0.0185	0.0076	0.0311	0.0079	0.0128	0.0108	0.0041	0.0166	0.0166	0.0099	0.0098
25 Electrical machinery	0.0000	0.0000	0.0004	0.0000	0.0000	0.0000	0.0000	0.0000	0.0003	0.0000	0.0000	0.0036
26 Transport equipment	0.0000	0.0012	0.0008	0.0005	0.0002	0.0002	0.0004	0.0000	0.0010	0.0004	0.0000	0.0003
27 Other manufacturing	0.0087	0.0005	0.0349	0.0003	0.0006	0.0009	0.0059	0.0000	0.0013	0.0000	0.0000	0.0025
28 Construction	0.0000	0.0000	0.0000	0.0000	0.0000	0.0000	0.0000	0.0000	0.0000	0.0000	0.0000	0.0000
29 Electricity, gas, water	0.0060	0.0044	0.0068	0.0215	0.0037	0.0114	0.0150	0.0036	0.0255	0.0257	0.0102	0.0069
30 Wholesale and retail trade	0.0830	0.2745	0.1337	0.1037	0.0940	0.1111	0.1215	0.0139	0.0542	0.0390	0.0426	0.1295
31 Banking and insurance	0.0049	0.0079	0.0118	0.0038	0.0115	0.0037	0.0066	0.0030	0.0092	0.0019	0.0047	0.0064
32 Transport and communication	0.0375	0.0257	0.0406	0.0240	0.0344	0.0428	0.0285	0.0360	0.0467	0.0250	0.0206	0.0283
33 Education and health	0.0000	0.0000	0.0000	0.0000	0.0000	0.0000	0.0000	0.0000	0.0000	0.0000	0.0000	0.0000
34 Housing	0.0000	0.0000	0.0000	0.0000	0.0000	0.0000	0.0000	0.0000	0.0000	0.0000	0.0000	0.0000
35 Other services	0.0294	0.0401	0.0223	0.0144	0.0600	0.0296	0.0855	0.0341	0.0329	0.1352	0.0358	0.0272
36 Intermediate total	0.5572	0.6847	0.5689	0.6422	0.4574	0.3948	0.5598	0.1965	0.4745	0.6080	0.8835	0.5503
37												
38 Intermediate non-competitive imports	0.0260	0.0435	0.0057	0.1041	0.2098	0.1890	0.1441	0.4464	0.0498	0.1245	0.0014	0.1448
39 Final non-competitive imports	0.0000	0.0000	0.0000	0.0000	0.0000	0.0000	0.0000	0.0000	0.0000	0.0000	0.0000	0.0000
40 Value added	0.3378	0.2309	0.3657	0.2157	0.3100	0.3849	0.2563	0.3236	0.4199	0.2254	0.0954	0.2549
41 Indirect taxes	0.0790	0.0409	0.0597	0.0380	0.0227	0.0313	0.0398	0.0335	0.0558	0.0420	0.0197	0.0500
42	0.0000	0.0000	0.0000	0.0000	0.0000	0.0000	0.0000	0.0000	0.0000	0.0000	0.0000	0.0000
43 Total	1.0000	1.0000	1.0000	1.0000	1.0000	1.0000	1.0000	1.0000	1.0000	1.0000	1.0000	1.0000

	24 Non-electrical machinery	25 Electrical machinery	26 Transport equipment	27 Other manufacturing	28 Construction	29 Electricity, gas, water	30 Wholesale and retail trade	31 Banking and insurance	32 Transportation and communications	33 Education and health	34 Housing	35 Other services
1 Agriculture, food	0.0000	0.0000	0.0000	0.0000	0.0000	0.0000	0.0000	0.0000	0.0000	0.0000	0.0000	0.0000
2 Agriculture, non-food	0.0000	0.0000	0.0000	0.0025	0.0000	0.0000	0.0000	0.0000	0.0000	0.0000	0.0000	0.0000
3 Livestock	0.0000	0.0000	0.0000	0.0000	0.0000	0.0000	0.0000	0.0000	0.0000	0.0000	0.0000	0.0000
4 Fishing and forestry	0.0000	0.0000	0.0000	0.0010	0.0000	0.0000	0.0000	0.0000	0.0000	0.0000	0.0000	0.0000
5 Mining	0.0009	0.0022	0.0002	0.0000	0.0062	0.0000	0.0000	0.0000	0.0000	0.0000	0.0000	0.0000
6 Food processing	0.0000	0.0002	0.0000	0.0017	0.0000	0.0000	0.0000	0.0000	0.0020	0.0248	0.0000	0.0673
7 Beverages	0.0000	0.0000	0.0000	0.0000	0.0000	0.0000	0.0000	0.0000	0.0000	0.0000	0.0000	0.0000
8 Tobacco	0.0000	0.0000	0.0000	0.0000	0.0000	0.0000	0.0000	0.0000	0.0000	0.0000	0.0000	0.0000
9 Textiles	0.0002	0.0006	0.0032	0.0240	0.0000	0.0011	0.0000	0.0000	0.0000	0.0000	0.0000	0.0000
10 Clothing	0.0000	0.0006	0.0000	0.0000	0.0000	0.0002	0.0000	0.0000	0.0001	0.0041	0.0000	0.0000
11 Leather	0.0000	0.0000	0.0005	0.0012	0.0000	0.0005	0.0000	0.0000	0.0000	0.0000	0.0000	0.0000
12 Footwear	0.0020	0.0000	0.0000	0.0011	0.0000	0.0000	0.0000	0.0000	0.0000	0.0000	0.0000	0.0000
13 Wood products	0.0010	0.0004	0.0075	0.0019	0.0358	0.0013	0.0000	0.0000	0.0008	0.0000	0.0000	0.0000
14 Furniture	0.0081	0.0380	0.0000	0.0000	0.0000	0.0000	0.0000	0.0000	0.0000	0.0000	0.0000	0.0000
15 Paper and products	0.0013	0.0079	0.0002	0.0126	0.0004	0.0012	0.0049	0.0251	0.0000	0.0005	0.0000	0.0123
16 Printing	0.0003	0.0009	0.0000	0.0072	0.0000	0.0004	0.0017	0.0000	0.0112	0.0015	0.0000	0.0000
17 Rubber products	0.0063	0.0046	0.0143	0.0014	0.0000	0.0004	0.0000	0.0000	0.0313	0.0000	0.0000	0.0000
18 Chemical products	0.0173	0.0142	0.0197	0.0893	0.0073	0.0071	0.0000	0.0000	0.0000	0.0494	0.0000	0.0000
19 Petroleum refining	0.0040	0.0028	0.0356	0.0041	0.0067	0.0229	0.0036	0.0000	0.1063	0.0034	0.0000	0.0000
20 Non-metallic minerals	0.0086	0.0005	0.0087	0.0024	0.1736	0.0122	0.0000	0.0000	0.0002	0.0002	0.0000	0.0074
21 Ferrous metals	0.0775	0.0135	0.0279	0.0029	0.0816	0.0000	0.0000	0.0000	0.0000	0.0000	0.0000	0.0044
22 Non-ferrous metals	0.0238	0.0529	0.0038	0.0600	0.0000	0.0148	0.0000	0.0000	0.0003	0.0008	0.0000	0.0000

	24 Non-electrical machinery	25 Electrical machinery	26 Transport equipment	27 Other manufacturing	28 Construction	29 Electricity, gas, water	30 Wholesale and retail trade	31 Banking and insurance	32 Transportation and communications	33 Education and health	34 Housing	35 Other services
23 Metal products	0.0465	0.0071	0.0151	0.0074	0.0212	0.0174	0.0000	0.0037	0.0000	0.0000	0.0000	0.0000
24 Non-electrical machinery	0.0697	0.0056	0.0391	0.0087	0.0000	0.0026	0.0000	0.0000	0.0352	0.0000	0.0000	0.0000
25 Electrical machinery	0.0177	0.0633	0.0077	0.0059	0.0000	0.0228	0.0000	0.0000	0.0256	0.0016	0.0000	0.0000
26 Transport equipment	0.0072	0.0000	0.0015	0.0002	0.0000	0.0019	0.0000	0.0000	0.0862	0.0011	0.0000	0.0000
27 Other manufacturing	0.0022	0.0053	0.0031	0.0212	0.0094	0.0015	0.0043	0.0000	0.0063	0.0038	0.0000	0.0076
28 Construction	0.0000	0.0000	0.0000	0.0000	0.0000	0.0013	0.0081	0.0000	0.0031	0.0026	0.0931	0.0000
29 Electricity, gas, water	0.0054	0.0031	0.0185	0.0072	0.0000	0.0043	0.0031	0.0078	0.0155	0.0039	0.0006	0.0101
30 Wholesale and retail trade	0.1028	0.1444	0.1312	0.1148	0.0759	0.0257	0.0236	0.0110	0.0474	0.0156	0.0000	0.0223
31 Banking and insurance	0.0047	0.0060	0.0036	0.0094	0.0000	0.0095	0.0299	0.1791	0.0369	0.0051	0.0125	0.0517
32 Transportation and communication	0.0445	0.0358	0.0307	0.0371	0.0532	0.0130	0.1549	0.0234	0.0289	0.0020	0.0000	0.0086
33 Education and health	0.0000	0.0000	0.0000	0.0000	0.0000	0.0000	0.0000	0.0000	0.0002	0.0000	0.0000	0.0000
34 Housing	0.0000	0.0000	0.0000	0.0000	0.0000	0.0000	0.0000	0.0000	0.0000	0.0000	0.0000	0.0000
35 Other services	0.0221	0.0453	0.0430	0.0562	0.0000	0.0102	0.0323	0.0505	0.0388	0.0073	0.0103	0.1085
36 Intermediate total	0.4741	0.4552	0.4151	0.4814	0.4713	0.1723	0.2664	0.3006	0.4763	0.1275	0.1165	0.3002
37												
38 Intermediate non-competitive imports	0.0598	0.1724	0.2513	0.1301	0.0000	0.0000	0.0000	0.0000	0.0000	0.0000	0.0000	0.0000
39 Final non-competitive imports	0.0000	0.0000	0.0000	0.0000	0.0000	0.0000	0.0000	0.0000	0.0000	0.0000	0.0000	0.0000
40 Value added	0.4004	0.3225	0.2767	0.3340	0.4785	0.7337	0.6102	0.5818	0.4356	0.7257	0.7349	0.5821
41 Indirect taxes	0.0657	0.0499	0.0569	0.0545	0.0502	0.0940	0.1234	0.1176	0.0881	0.1468	0.1486	0.1177
42												
43 Total	1.0000	1.0000	1.0000	1.0000	1.0000	1.0000	1.0000	1.0000	1.0000	1.0000	1.0000	1.0000

TABLE B.2 Beracia inverse coefficients matrix

	1 Agriculture, food	2 Agriculture, non-food	3 Livestock	4 Fishing and forestry	5 Mining	6 Food processing	7 Beverages	8 Tobacco	9 Textiles	10 Clothing	11 Leather
1 Agriculture, food	1.1179	0.0009	0.5203	0.0883	0.0030	0.4327	0.0770	0.0028	0.0133	0.0059	0.1464
2 Agriculture, non-food	0.0007	1.1148	0.0017	0.0036	0.0015	0.0075	0.0026	0.0394	0.3306	0.0988	0.0074
3 Livestock	0.0001	0.0001	1.0086	0.0006	0.0004	0.0465	0.0336	0.0003	0.0192	0.0074	0.2247
4 Fishing and forestry	0.0068	0.0058	0.0182	1.0067	0.0029	0.0838	0.0562	0.0050	0.0049	0.0027	0.0155
5 Mining	0.0030	0.0030	0.0020	0.0035	1.0418	0.0044	0.0049	0.0009	0.0032	0.0019	0.0044
6 Food processing	0.0010	0.0010	0.2107	0.0091	0.0073	1.1393	0.1069	0.0064	0.0125	0.0068	0.1300
7 Beverages	0.0001	0.0001	0.0004	0.0001	0.0001	0.0004	1.0816	0.0006	0.0002	0.0001	0.0004
8 Tobacco	0.0000	0.0000	0.0000	0.0000	0.0000	0.0000	0.0000	1.0554	0.0002	0.0000	0.0000
9 Textiles	0.0016	0.0016	0.0044	0.0124	0.0042	0.0201	0.0033	0.0008	1.2032	0.3595	0.0225
10 Clothing	0.0000	0.0000	0.0000	0.0000	0.0000	0.0000	0.0000	0.0000	0.0000	1.0000	0.0000
11 Leather	0.0000	0.0000	0.0000	0.0000	0.0002	0.0000	0.0000	0.0000	0.0001	0.0039	1.0147
12 Footwear	0.0000	0.0000	0.0000	0.0000	0.0000	0.0000	0.0000	0.0000	0.0000	0.0000	0.0000
13 Wood products	0.0017	0.0003	0.0015	0.0346	0.0112	0.0042	0.0061	0.0008	0.0011	0.0007	0.0039
14 Furniture	0.0000	0.0000	0.0000	0.0002	0.0012	0.0002	0.0003	0.0002	0.0003	0.0002	0.0003
15 Paper and products	0.0008	0.0009	0.0059	0.0019	0.0047	0.0294	0.0344	0.0368	0.0066	0.0087	0.0134
16 Printing	0.0002	0.0002	0.0008	0.0007	0.0016	0.0036	0.0048	0.0061	0.0024	0.0021	0.0026
17 Rubber products	0.0002	0.0002	0.0007	0.0011	0.0082	0.0028	0.0039	0.0029	0.0053	0.0040	0.0046

	1 Agriculture, food	2 Agriculture, non-food	3 Livestock	4 Fishing and forestry	5 Mining	6 Food processing	7 Beverages	8 Tobacco	9 Textiles	10 Clothing	11 Leather
18 Chemical products	0.0282	0.0297	0.0237	0.0250	0.0410	0.0559	0.0150	0.0077	0.0811	0.0279	0.1217
19 Petroleum refining	0.0014	0.0013	0.0047	0.0214	0.0328	0.0206	0.0246	0.0119	0.0205	0.0166	0.0230
20 Non-metallic minerals	0.0006	0.0007	0.0012	0.0010	0.0077	0.0044	0.0256	0.0011	0.0027	0.0014	0.0054
21 Ferrous metals	0.0003	0.0003	0.0019	0.0044	0.0194	0.0095	0.0079	0.0017	0.0083	0.0038	0.0091
22 Non-ferrous metals	0.0003	0.0003	0.0008	0.0018	0.0050	0.0033	0.0027	0.0009	0.0024	0.0019	0.0039
23 Metal products	0.0007	0.0007	0.0062	0.0115	0.0281	0.0316	0.0238	0.0021	0.0087	0.0043	0.0182
24 Non-electrical machinery	0.0009	0.0008	0.0033	0.0121	0.0639	0.0152	0.0169	0.0078	0.0225	0.0115	0.0180
25 Electrical machinery	0.0002	0.0002	0.0006	0.0033	0.0165	0.0025	0.0028	0.0024	0.0027	0.0031	0.0029
26 Transport equipment	0.0004	0.0004	0.0013	0.0052	0.0097	0.0051	0.0073	0.0067	0.0060	0.0080	0.0066
27 Other manufacturing	0.0003	0.0003	0.0009	0.0055	0.0021	0.0038	0.0034	0.0021	0.0041	0.0122	0.0146
28 Construction	0.0002	0.0002	0.0004	0.0004	0.0054	0.0011	0.0010	0.0017	0.0014	0.0014	0.0023
29 Electricity, gas, water	0.0007	0.0007	0.0025	0.0020	0.0053	0.0114	0.0091	0.0048	0.0161	0.0083	0.0147
30 Wholesale and retail trade	0.0154	0.0149	0.0405	0.0468	0.0715	0.1122	0.0923	0.1821	0.1432	0.1296	0.2471
31 Banking and insurance	0.0014	0.0014	0.0049	0.0139	0.0222	0.0197	0.0233	0.0223	0.0243	0.0203	0.0263
32 Transportation and communication	0.0038	0.0038	0.0124	0.0128	0.0634	0.0462	0.0688	0.0761	0.0640	0.0897	0.0695
33 Education and health	0.0000	0.0000	0.0000	0.0000	0.0000	0.0000	0.0000	0.0000	0.0000	0.0000	0.0000
34 Housing	0.0000	0.0000	0.0000	0.0000	0.0000	0.0000	0.0000	0.0000	0.0000	0.0000	0.0000
35 Other services	0.0042	0.0043	0.0170	0.0216	0.0811	0.0779	0.1172	0.0755	0.0704	0.0489	0.0693

	12 Footwear	13 Wood products	14 Furniture	15 Paper and products	16 Printing	17 Rubber products	18 Chemical products	19 Petroleum refining	20 Non-metallic minerals	21 Ferrous metals	22 Non-ferrous metals	23 Metal products
1 Agriculture, food	0.0421	0.0104	0.0045	0.0184	0.0065	0.0102	0.0154	0.0017	0.0030	0.0063	0.0037	0.0035
2 Agriculture, non-food	0.0131	0.0008	0.0153	0.0026	0.0017	0.0169	0.0264	0.0005	0.0010	0.0004	0.0012	0.0010
3 Livestock	0.0602	0.0006	0.0015	0.0008	0.0005	0.0013	0.0024	0.0002	0.0003	0.0007	0.0005	0.0004
4 Fishing and forestry	0.0188	0.0679	0.0088	0.1500	0.0317	0.0899	0.0241	0.0010	0.0079	0.0024	0.0028	0.0038
5 Mining	0.0034	0.0043	0.0098	0.0059	0.0087	0.0020	0.0149	0.0012	0.1037	0.0116	0.7245	0.0546
6 Food processing	0.0394	0.0124	0.0086	0.0153	0.0102	0.0058	0.0340	0.0042	0.0061	0.0163	0.0092	0.0083
7 Beverages	0.0002	0.0000	0.0002	0.0007	0.0002	0.0001	0.0031	0.0000	0.0001	0.0000	0.0001	0.0001
8 Tobacco	0.0000	0.0000	0.0000	0.0000	0.0000	0.0000	0.0000	0.0000	0.0000	0.0000	0.0000	0.0000
9 Textiles	0.0453	0.0024	0.0532	0.0071	0.0046	0.0608	0.0608	0.0011	0.0027	0.0012	0.0033	0.0027
10 Clothing	0.0000	0.0000	0.0000	0.0000	0.0000	0.0000	0.0000	0.0000	0.0000	0.0000	0.0000	0.0000
11 Leather	0.2654	0.0001	0.0001	0.0001	0.0001	0.0007	0.0001	0.0000	0.0001	0.0001	0.0001	0.0001
12 Footwear	1.0080	0.0000	0.0000	0.0000	0.0000	0.0000	0.0000	0.0000	0.0000	0.0000	0.0000	0.0000
13 Wood products	0.0021	1.2831	0.1123	0.0168	0.0038	0.0037	0.0018	0.0003	0.0027	0.0014	0.0081	0.0109
14 Furniture	0.0003	0.0004	1.0074	0.0006	0.0003	0.0003	0.0003	0.0001	0.0005	0.0004	0.0010	0.0005
15 Paper and products	0.0312	0.0069	0.0076	1.3602	0.2760	0.0043	0.0292	0.0022	0.0599	0.0062	0.0051	0.0155
16 Printing	0.0023	0.0029	0.0029	0.0026	1.0075	0.0017	0.0055	0.0009	0.0019	0.0015	0.0020	0.0021
17 Rubber products	0.0250	0.0073	0.0050	0.0069	0.0042	1.0178	0.0043	0.0024	0.0063	0.0044	0.0086	0.0059
18 Chemical products	0.0696	0.0159	0.0735	0.0750	0.0474	0.0295	1.1560	0.0166	0.0231	0.0092	0.0307	0.0311

	12 Footwear	13 Wood products	14 Furniture	15 Paper and products	16 Printing	17 Rubber products	18 Chemical products	19 Petroleum refining	20 Non-metallic minerals	21 Ferrous metals	22 Non-ferrous metals	23 Metal products
19 Petroleum refining	0.0187	0.0405	0.0360	0.0252	0.0167	0.0234	0.0346	1.0939	0.1088	0.1923	0.0658	0.0617
20 Non-metallic minerals	0.0056	0.0041	0.0099	0.0032	0.0022	0.0021	0.0237	0.0009	1.0582	0.0111	0.0065	0.0064
21 Ferrous metals	0.0065	0.0098	0.1071	0.0102	0.0054	0.0048	0.0080	0.0037	0.0111	1.2430	0.0205	0.2540
22 Non-ferrous metals	0.0032	0.0041	0.0118	0.0041	0.0115	0.0020	0.0092	0.0013	0.0034	0.0151	1.0832	0.0678
23 Metal products	0.0126	0.0164	0.0477	0.0184	0.0082	0.0091	0.0211	0.0114	0.0130	0.0374	0.0305	1.0406
24 Non-electrical machinery	0.0197	0.0322	0.0205	0.0526	0.0230	0.0200	0.0211	0.0075	0.0318	0.0277	0.0581	0.0244
25 Electrical machinery	0.0033	0.0041	0.0045	0.0044	0.0031	0.0032	0.0035	0.0017	0.0054	0.0034	0.0131	0.0078
26 Transport equipment	0.0075	0.0111	0.0095	0.0081	0.0071	0.0072	0.0073	0.0042	0.0088	0.0060	0.0100	0.0076
27 Other manufacturing	0.0146	0.0044	0.0390	0.0036	0.0032	0.0033	0.0098	0.0010	0.0033	0.0027	0.0025	0.0051
28 Construction	0.0017	0.0035	0.0021	0.0018	0.0015	0.0014	0.0018	0.0004	0.0015	0.0009	0.0043	0.0019
29 Electricity, gas, water	0.0144	0.0113	0.0167	0.0343	0.0141	0.0157	0.0237	0.0061	0.0325	0.0377	0.0169	0.0192
30 Wholesale and retail trade	0.1765	0.3852	0.2151	0.1827	0.1490	0.1414	0.1763	0.0260	0.0907	0.0769	0.1064	0.1771
31 Banking and insurance	0.0248	0.0384	0.0358	0.0229	0.0315	0.0188	0.0301	0.0107	0.0258	0.0238	0.0293	0.0270
32 Transportation and communication	0.0827	0.1036	0.0951	0.0730	0.0734	0.0744	0.0737	0.0474	0.0807	0.0596	0.0804	0.0772
33 Education and health	0.0000	0.0000	0.0000	0.0000	0.0000	0.0000	0.0000	0.0000	0.0000	0.0000	0.0000	0.0000
34 Housing	0.0000	0.0000	0.0000	0.0000	0.0000	0.0000	0.0000	0.0000	0.0000	0.0000	0.0000	0.0000
35 Other services	0.0696	0.0879	0.0788	0.0503	0.0927	0.0536	0.1351	0.0492	0.0659	0.2094	0.1087	0.0966

	24 Non-electrical machinery	25 Electrical machinery	26 Transport equipment	27 Other manufacturing	28 Construction	29 Electricity, gas, water	30 Wholesale and retail trade	31 Banking and insurance	32 Transportation and communication	33 Education and health	34 Housing	35 Other services
1 Agriculture, food	0.0029	0.0032	0.0030	0.0057	0.0020	0.0010	0.0019	0.0024	0.0035	0.0119	0.0006	0.0332
2 Agriculture, non-food	0.0012	0.0017	0.0021	0.0137	0.0007	0.0007	0.0003	0.0001	0.0011	0.0020	0.0001	0.0008
3 Livestock	0.0008	0.0004	0.0005	0.0014	0.0002	0.0002	0.0002	0.0003	0.0004	0.0013	0.0001	0.0036
4 Fishing and forestry	0.028	0.0037	0.0035	0.0072	0.0048	0.0011	0.0020	0.0017	0.0047	0.0036	0.0006	0.0087
5 Mining	0.0261	0.0456	0.0076	0.0478	0.0276	0.0145	0.0013	0.0009	0.0042	0.0019	0.0026	0.0016
6 Food processing	0.0064	0.0075	0.0068	0.0126	0.0043	0.0022	0.0046	0.0060	0.0082	0.0309	0.0014	0.0870
7 Beverages	0.0001	0.0001	0.0001	0.0003	0.0000	0.0000	0.0000	0.0000	0.0000	0.0002	0.0000	0.0000
8 Tobacco	0.0000	0.0000	0.0000	0.0000	0.0000	0.0000	0.0000	0.0000	0.0000	0.0000	0.0000	0.0000
9 Textiles	0.0032	0.0053	0.0067	0.0361	0.0018	0.0023	0.0009	0.0004	0.0035	0.0052	0.0002	0.0021
10 Clothing	0.0000	0.0007	0.0000	0.0000	0.0000	0.0002	0.0000	0.0000	0.0001	0.0041	0.0000	0.0000
11 Leather	0.0022	0.0001	0.0006	0.0016	0.0001	0.0005	0.0000	0.0000	0.0002	0.0000	0.0000	0.0000
12 Footwear	0.0000	0.0000	0.0000	0.0011	0.0000	0.0000	0.0000	0.0000	0.0000	0.0000	0.0000	0.0000
13 Wood products	0.0038	0.0062	0.0105	0.0039	0.0471	0.0024	0.0010	0.0003	0.0028	0.0004	0.0044	0.0007
14 Furniture	0.0098	0.0411	0.0009	0.0006	0.0003	0.0010	0.0003	0.0001	0.0016	0.0001	0.0000	0.0001
15 Paper and products	0.0071	0.0162	0.0051	0.0261	0.0136	0.0042	0.0097	0.0103	0.0068	0.0039	0.0016	0.0225
16 Printing	0.0023	0.0031	0.0018	0.0098	0.0019	0.0013	0.0051	0.0314	0.0137	0.0022	0.0006	0.0025
17 Rubber products	0.0107	0.0084	0.0176	0.0050	0.0043	0.0017	0.0059	0.0013	0.0358	0.0006	0.0004	0.0010
18 Chemical products	0.0282	0.0257	0.0282	0.1132	0.0166	0.0114	0.0030	0.0024	0.0092	0.0595	0.0017	0.0069

	24 Non-electrical machinery	25 Electrical Machinery	26 Transport equipment	27 Other manufacturing	28 Construction	29 Electricity, gas, water	30 Wholesale and retail trade	31 Banking and insurance	32 Transportation and communication	33 Education and health	34 Housing	35 Other services
19 Petroleum refining	0.0385	0.0230	0.0584	0.0239	0.0543	0.0324	0.0263	0.0061	0.1309	0.0074	0.0053	0.0144
20 Non-metallic minerals	0.0126	0.0029	0.0117	0.0064	0.1855	0.0139	0.0024	0.0007	0.0032	0.0020	0.0174	0.0060
21 Ferrous metals	0.1199	0.0274	0.0450	0.0102	0.1102	0.0065	0.0028	0.0018	0.0105	0.0012	0.0103	0.0014
22 Non-ferrous metals	0.0347	0.0638	0.0087	0.0693	0.0046	0.0193	0.0014	0.0011	0.0053	0.0020	0.0005	0.0013
23 Metal products	0.0583	0.0140	0.0216	0.0140	0.0290	0.0201	0.0019	0.0056	0.0071	0.0023	0.0028	0.0036
24 Non-electrical machinery	1.0852	0.0156	0.0484	0.0202	0.0134	0.0064	0.0082	0.0025	0.0468	0.0021	0.0013	0.0031
25 Electrical machinery	0.0240	1.0711	0.0120	0.0101	0.0038	0.0257	0.0052	0.0014	0.0314	0.0023	0.0004	0.0012
26 Transport equipment	0.0157	0.0075	1.0081	0.0076	0.0088	0.0044	0.0150	0.0033	0.0921	0.0022	0.0009	0.0021
27 Other manufacturing	0.0052	0.0096	0.0055	1.0247	0.0117	3.0025	0.0064	0.0011	0.0087	0.0048	0.0012	0.0094
28 Construction	0.0016	0.0020	0.0016	0.0018	1.0014	0.0018	0.0090	0.0003	0.0041	0.0029	0.0933	0.0004
29 Electricity, gas, water	0.0142	0.0094	0.0244	0.0149	0.0117	1.0068	0.0079	0.0117	0.0219	0.0060	0.0020	0.0142
30 Wholesale and retail trade	0.1528	0.1915	0.1666	0.1646	0.1272	0.0431	1.0439	0.0249	0.0909	0.0310	0.0126	0.0420
31 Banking and insurance	0.0226	0.0263	0.0206	0.0309	0.0160	0.0171	0.0498	1.2264	0.0581	0.0102	0.0176	0.0754
32 Transportation and communication	0.0880	0.0821	0.0704	0.0801	0.0958	0.0269	0.1723	0.0368	1.0620	0.0116	0.0096	0.0230
33 Education and health	0.0000	0.0000	0.0000	0.0000	0.0000	0.0000	2.0000	0.0000	0.0002	1.0000	0.0000	0.0000
34 Housing	0.0000	0.0000	0.0000	0.0000	0.0000	0.0000	0.0000	0.0000	0.0000	0.0000	1.0000	0.0000
35 Other services	0.0691	0.0838	0.0769	0.1006	0.0443	0.0237	0.0529	0.0762	0.0721	0.0197	0.0168	1.1366

Further reading

CHENERY, H. B. and TAYLOR, L. (1968). Development Patterns: Among Countries and Over Time. *Review of Economics and Statistics* **50**, 391–416

HELFGOTT, R. B. and SCHIAVO-CAMPO, S. (1970). An Introduction to Industrial Planning. *Industrialization and Productivity*, No. 16, 5–34

HIRSCHMAN, A. O. (1958). *The Strategy of Economic Development*. New Haven, Yale University Press

HIRSCHMAN, A. O. (1968). The Political Economy of Import Substitution. *Quarterly Journal of Economics* **82,** 1–32

LITTLE, I. M. D., SCITOVSKY, T. and SCOTT, M. (1970). *Industry and Trade in Some Developing Countries*. London, Oxford University Press

ROEMER, M. TIDRICK, G. M. and WILLIAMS, D. (1976). The Range of Strategic Choice in Tanzanian Industry. *Journal of Development Economics* **3,** 257–275

SACHS, I., and LASKI, K. (1970). Industrial Development Strategy. *Industrialization and Productivity*, No. 16, 35–48

STERN, J. J. (June 1977). The Employment Impact of Industrial Investment: A Preliminary Report. World Bank Staff Working Paper No. 255

UNITED NATIONS INDUSTRIAL DEVELOPMENT ORGANIZATION (various dates to 1975). *Summaries of Industrial Development Plans* **1–4,** Vienna

Other relevant works include BRUTON (1970), INTERNATIONAL LABOR OFFICE (1972), MORAWETZ (1974), PREBISCH (1963), RANIS (1973) and THOMAS (1974), listed as references to Part I, and BALASSA (1971a and b), BLITZER, CLARK and TAYLOR (1975), BRUNO (1967), CHENERY and CLARK (1959), DORFMAN, SAMUELSON and SOLOW (1958) and JOHNSON (1965), listed as references to Part IV.

Education Planning

OFFICE OF THE PRIME MINISTER

TO: Chief, Education Division
FROM: Economic Advisor to the Prime Minister
RE: Education Development Projects

    The Government's Economic Policy statement of last July concluded that 'it is regrettable that the educational system has not produced the type of skills that could make educated labor contribute proportionately to the real development of this country.' More recently the PM asked that we review the educational system to make it more responsive to the developmental needs of the country. In addition, we must avail ourselves of the opportunity offered by the recent visit of the World Bank Mission, which indicated that they would be favorably inclined to support a request for the financing of education sector projects. This requires however that such proposals be based on the most up-to-date techniques of manpower and cost–benefit analysis. Since your division has not responded to the PM's request, I have taken it upon myself to begin the task of setting our educational house in order. Let me briefly review the problems of the education sector and suggest areas for analysis. My staff has compiled a set of highly relevant data which, I trust, should be sufficient to permit you to undertake the required study.

    In 1965 the Government introduced fee-free, compulsory primary education*. This has been the cornerstone of our education policy and we now expect to extend this to lower secondary education by next year. Student enrollment rates are shown in *Table 1*.

    The education system continues to be maintained at great cost. Almost 100 000 teachers are on the public payroll, over two-thirds of them at the primary level and another one-quarter in secondary education (*Table 2*). Teachers' salaries are above average for Beracian wage earners, which contributes to the

---

*In the Beracian educational system, primary school consists of grades 1 through 6, which are equivalent to elementary school grades in the United States. Students then enter secondary school, of which forms I through V are approximately equivalent to junior and senior high school in the United States, while form VI is considered roughly equal to the freshman year in college.

TABLE 1 Public (state) school enrollment, 1975

| Level | Ages | Enrollment (thousands) | | | Enrollment rates (%) | |
		Male	Female	Total	Male	Female
Primary, grades 1–3	6–9[a]	890	747	1637	88.5	76.6
Primary, grades 4–6	9[a]–12	680	487	1167	71.7	60.8
Secondary, forms I–III	13–15	353	210	563	50.8	31.4
Secondary, forms IV–VI[b]	16–19	58.5	18.0	76.5	8.6[c]	5.8[c]
Teacher training	16–19	12.5	27.2	39.7		
Technical and vocational	15–20	4.6	1.3	5.9	–	–
University	20+	7.9	3.5	11.4	–	–
Total		2007	1494	3501		

Notes: [a]Allows for repeaters; in calculating enrollment rates, the 9-year-old cohort is arbitrarily divided evenly between Primary, grades 1–3 and 4–6.
    [b]Excludes teacher training.
    [c]Includes teacher training.
Source: Ministry of Education. *Annual Report on the Education System, 1977.*

TABLE 2 Public (state) school teachers, 1975

Level	Number
Primary, grades 1–6	68 610
Secondary, forms I–VI	26 500
Teacher training	1 980
Technical and vocational	390
University	2 080
Total	99 560

Source: Ministry of Education. *Annual Report on the Education System, 1977.*

TABLE 3 Education budget, 1975/76

| Level | Expenditure (Lp million) | | | Distribution (%) | |
	Capital	Recurrent	Total	Students	Expenditure
Primary, grades 1–6	94.0	1135.5	1229.5	80.1	73.8
Lower secondary, forms I–III	34.7	217.0	251.7	16.1	15.0
Upper secondary, forms IV–VI	18.2	46.4	64.6	2.2	3.9
Teacher training	10.4	29.0	39.4	1.1	2.4
Technical and vocational	10.1	12.5	22.6	0.2	1.4
University	19.3	39.2	58.5	0.3	3.5
Total	186.7	1479.6	1666.3	100.0	100.0

Source: Ministry of Education (1978). *Report on Expenditures, 1975/76.*

high budget for the education system (*Table 3*). Total education expenses account for 3.5 percent of GDP, compared with 4 percent for all developing countries and 5 percent for the industrial countries.

As is typical in all educational systems, the cost per student in Beracia rises with the level of education (*Table 4*): government spends over 400 percent more on a vocational trainee as on a primary student and 750 percent more on a university student. In the United States the index of cost for university education

TABLE 4 Average yearly cost per student by level of education, 1975/76 (Lp/year)

Level	In-school cost[a]	Index	Student-borne cost
Primary, grades 1–6	404	1.00	286
Secondary, forms I–III	385	0.95	322
Secondary, forms IV–VI	607	1.50	375
Teacher training	730	1.81	250
Technical and vocational	2118	5.24	447
University	3439	8.51	1964
Engineering	8380	20.74	2845
Medicine	9510	23.54	3473
Agriculture	4090	10.12	1813
Other	2414	5.98	1769

Note: [a]Recurrent only.
Source: Ministry of Education. *Annual Report on the Education System, 1977.*

is only double that for primary. Clearly our per student costs are too high, especially for higher education. In part the problem is too few students at the higher levels. In addition the wastage rate (i.e., students who begin their education but then drop out) is high. For the primary level this is about 30 percent; for forms I and III, about 25 percent; for forms IV and V about 8 percent and 4 percent for form VI. Assuming that a student who drops out completes, on average, half of the grades at the relevant level, the percentage increase in the cost due to dropping out is $\dfrac{[1-(F/2)]}{(1-F)}$, where F is the failure (drop-out) rate.

In two other ways, it would seem our educational system is inefficient. First, consider the length of time it takes to get a degree. Starting at age 6, a good student spends six years in primary school, three years in lower secondary plus two to three years in Forms IV and V. (Many students, however, repeat one or more grades, especially in primary school, thus lengthening the process.) For university aspirants, this is followed by a one-year required sixth form, which for

TABLE 5 Age income regressions by education level for employed persons, 1971

Education level	Constant[a] (Lp)	Age[b]	Age-squared	Number of observations	R^2
Unschooled	1734.30 (300.86)	3.98 (1.95)	−0.05 (0.03)	173	0.32
Primary (6 years)	2530.75 (3238.14)	35.65 (4.95)	−0.36 (0.06)	204	0.92
Secondary (9 years)	1913.30 (204.46)	155.80 (39.63)	−1.62 (0.68)	156	0.97
Secondary	1780.10 (634.39)	350.43 (94.61)	−3.45 (1.20)	135	0.80
Technical or vocational (12 years)	1774.93 (1462.22)	420.86 (126.20)	−4.60 (2.18)	140	0.68
University (16 years)	1607.24 (2069.47)	697.57 (285.20)	−5.47 (3.47)	116	0.54

Notes: [a]Standard error of estimate in parenthesis.
    [b]No observations below age 15 for unschooled through secondary, 9 years; below 20 for 12 years; and below 25 for university.
Source: Schafft, N. (1975). The Returns to Education in Beracia. *Beracia Development Journal* **XIII,** 72–89

most students involves a further two years' work, so that the majority of students who enter university are 20 years or older. The first university degree usually takes from three to four years and in some fields more. Clearly this lengthy process keeps our most productive people out of the development effort too long.

Second, consider our employment situation. Because many members of the labor force, even those with education, cannot find jobs, a cost for which there is no corresponding benefit is incurred to educate such persons. Data relating to this aspect of the educated manpower situation is given in Appendix *Tables A.1-3*.

Shocking as this situation is, education appears to be desirable to the individual because there is considerable support in the nation for the government's policy to extend free education. A recent analysis, which I found most impressive, showed the earnings which people with different levels of schooling could obtain. This is reproduced in *Table 5*. The equations relate the annual earnings, in lepta, to the age of the worker, assuming that an unschooled worker joins the labor force at age 15. The second age term (age-squared) ensures that the annual income declines after a certain age, in line with actual observations, presumably reflecting declining productivity with increasing age. In Beracia, very few workers remain in the wage labor force beyond age 60, except those in highly skilled and managerial positions. While the samples are small, the coefficients are for the most part significant and the regression coefficients (R^2) are fairly high. I would imagine that these data will bear out my strong belief that (i) extending free schooling through year 9 is very desirable and (ii) that higher education is a financially rewarding experience, aside from its educational benefit. From this analysis it should be possible to develop guidelines for the allocation of government resources.

Equally important, and related, is the need for the educational system to provide those skills called for by our development goals. It should be possible, on such a basis, to set fairly precise targets on the *additional* skilled manpower we so urgently need. Again, I attach the relevant data in Appendix *Tables A.4, A.5* and *A.6*, which show the increases in output, as projected by our Perspective Planning section, together with data on the sectoral labor–output ratios, the skill composition of employment and university enrollments by skill. We have moreover a very serious deficit in the number of skilled persons required. To give but two pieces of evidence: in the U.S. there is one doctor for each 650 members of the population. In Beracia, one doctor must serve some 5000 people. In terms of scientists and engineers, we have only 0.75 per 10 000 of population while countries with a per capita income of about $ 1000 have 25 per 10 000 persons! Clearly then our development needs will also call for a rapid increase in trained manpower and an expansion of the education system.

I would request that you and your staff submit to me an analysis of the issues raised, addressing yourselves specifically to the following:

Questions

1. If cost–benefit measures were used as a guide, how should Beracia allocate its investment among levels of education?
2. Which levels and sectors of education would be expanded if manpower planning were used as a guide?
3. What assumptions underlie each of those planning techniques and how can we choose between them?

4.   What are the budgetary implications of expanding education along the lines suggested by either cost–benefit analysis or manpower planning?

Appendix

TABLE A.1 Estimated population by age and sex: Beracia, mid-1970 (thousands)

Age	Females	Males	Total
0–4	1 415.4	1 366.2	2 781.6
5	274.5	265.8	540.3
6	253.5	247.6	501.1
7	255.4	245.6	501.0
8	248.7	242.2	490.9
9	258.1	248.1	506.2
10	251.2	243.1	494.3
11	229.5	220.5	450.0
12	224.2	217.2	441.4
13	216.4	208.0	424.4
14	206.7	192.1	398.8
15	189.6	188.8	378.4
16	185.0	171.2	356.2
17	181.8	182.9	364.7
18	171.0	156.2	327.2
19	185.1	176.2	361.3
20	163.2	147.0	310.2
21	117.4	114.4	231.8
22	127.7	122.8	250.5
23	136.4	126.1	262.5
24	120.8	116.1	236.9
25–29	588.9	599.1	1 188.0
30–34	458.2	492.9	951.1
35–39	395.5	432.8	828.3
40–44	340.1	348.5	688.6
45–49	332.8	321.7	654.5
50–54	303.5	265.8	569.3
55–59	302.4	256.6	559.0
60–64	216.0	153.9	369.9
65+	331.0	294.5	625.5
Total	8 680.0	8 363.9	17 043.9

Source: Bureau of Statistics (March 1974). *Estimates of Population for Beracia: 1970,* Research Report No. 14.

TABLE A.2 Beracia: labor force participation rates, 1969 (percent)

Age group	Male	Female	Total
15–19	0.680	0.468	0.576
20–24	0.922	0.461	0.698
25–29	0.974	0.403	0.686
30–39	0.974	0.439	0.696
40–49	0.963	0.462	0.713
50–59	0.866	0.378	0.640
60–64	0.699	0.255	0.514
Total	0.878	0.433	0.659

Note: Includes wage earners, proprietors and resident heads of farm households.
Source: Schafft, N. (1974). The Demographic Transition in Beracia. *Beracia Development Journal* **XII**, 18–32

TABLE A.3 Estimated unemployment rates in Beracia by age, sex and education (percent)

Education	Sex	Age				All ages
		15–19	20–29	30–39	40+	
Unschooled	M	8.8	6.1	3.4	3.2	4.5
	F	12.1	6.7	5.0	3.9	5.8
	T	10.7	6.4	4.3	3.5	5.2
Primary (completed 3 years or more)	M	16.9	6.4	2.6	2.5	5.8
	F	19.7	15.0	6.8	4.0	14.1
	T	17.8	8.5	3.1	3.0	7.3
Nine years	M	24.3	10.3	4.2	6.5	10.3
	F	55.1	24.2	18.8	20.0	34.9
	T	32.1	13.1	5.5	7.0	14.0
Twelve years	M	–	25.6	2.4	4.0	13.3
	F	–	25.4	7.0	7.0	25.1
	T	–	25.5	3.0	4.5	15.4
University	M	–	3.1	0.4	–	n.a.
	F	–	4.4	–	–	n.a.
	T	–	3.2	0.4	–	n.a.

Source: ILO Survey conducted for Government of Beracia (unpublished).

TABLE A.4 Perspective plan targets

Sector	Maximum projected increments of value added 1977–1990 (Lp million, 1977 prices)	Employment/value added ratio (person-years/Lp million, 1977 prices)
1 Agriculture, food	9587	n.a.
2 Agriculture, non-food	1909	n.a.
3 Livestock	2324	n.a.
4 Fishing and forestry	493	n.a.
5 Mining	1299	n.a.
6 Food processing etc.	626	40.6
7 Beverages	642	4.1
8 Tobacco	146	13.1
9 Textiles	677	25.0
10 Clothing	545	41.3
11 Leather	78	30.0
12 Footwear	246	46.3
13 Wood products	291	19.4
14 Furniture	231	25.0
15 Paper and products	203	18.1
16 Printing	227	12.5
17 Rubber products	236	4.2
18 Chemical products	862	3.9
19 Petroleum refining etc.	888	3.1
20 Non-metallic minerals	770	7.1
21 Ferrous metals	472	13.1
22 Non-ferrous metals	240	15.6
23 Metal products	414	31.3
24 Non-electrical machinery	873	8.1
25 Electrical machinery	584	9.4
26 Transport equipment	824	6.5
27 Other manufacturing	315	20.6
28 Construction	3974	4.6
29 Electricity, gas, water	878	4.0
30 Wholesale and retail trade	7389	17.2
31 Banking and insurance	1467	3.8
32 Transport, communication	3357	20.9
33 Education and health	3556	18.5
34 Housing	1931	n.a.
35 Other services	3021	n.a.

Source: Ministry of Planning, Beracia, Perspective Planning Section.

TABLE A.5 Estimated labor force requirements by educational level and sector (per unit of labor)

Educational level	Agriculture forestry, fishing	Mining	Food and beverages	Textiles clothing, footwear	Wood products	Paper and products	Chemical products
University graduates—liberal arts, social sciences, etc.	0.0034	0.0340	0.0282	0.0211	0.0109	0.0203	0.0324
Engineering, science, etc.	0.0002	0.0296	0.0119	0.0021	0.0010	0.0068	0.0410
Medicine, dentistry, etc.	–	0.0010	–	–	–	–	–
Agriculture, veterinary (4 years)	0.0104	–	–	–	–	0.0216	–
Teacher training	–	–	–	–	–	–	–
Technical/vocational	0.0012	0.0117	0.0038	0.0021	0.0060	0.0027	0.0358
Technical/artisans	0.0395	0.1796	0.1201	0.1500	0.2222	0.1959	0.1485
Commercial	0.0062	0.0526	0.1051	0.0628	0.0506	0.0392	0.1348
Secondary, forms IV–VI	0.0140	0.0230	0.0410	0.0330	0.0090	0.0080	0.0390
Secondary, forms I–III	0.0802	0.0464	0.0688	0.0640	0.0188	0.0189	0.0802
Agriculture	0.0390	–	–	–	–	0.0689	–
Nursing	–	0.0030	–	–	–	–	–
Primary, 4–6 years	0.6370	0.5540	0.5711	0.6148	0.6279	0.5771	0.4678
Primary, 0–3 years	0.1689	0.0651	0.0500	0.0501	0.0536	0.0405	0.0204
Total	1.0000	1.0000	1.0000	1.0000	1.0000	1.0000	1.0000

TABLE A.5 (*continued*)

Educational level	Non-metallic minerals	Basic metals	Machinery	Other industries	Construction	Electricity, gas, water	Commerce
University graduates—liberal arts, social sciences, etc.	0.0181	0.0070	0.0062	0.0174	0.0180	0.1101	0.0316
Engineering, science, etc.	0.0207	0.0270	0.0279	0.0186	0.0380	0.1463	0.0225
Medicine, dentistry, etc.	–	0.0005	–	–	–	0.0010	–
Agriculture, veterinary (4 years)	–	–	–	–	–	–	–
Teacher training	–	–	–	–	–	–	–
Technical/vocational	0.0160	0.0160	0.0151	0.0046	0.0080	0.0727	0.0033
Technical/artisans	0.1262	0.3099	0.3252	0.1832	0.2310	0.2311	0.0235
Commercial	0.0745	0.0990	0.0930	0.0953	0.0320	0.1110	0.1862
Secondary, forms IV–VI	0.0150	0.0490	0.0300	0.0220	0.0035	0.0160	0.0479
Secondary, forms I–III	0.0238	0.0961	0.0501	0.0422	0.0080	0.0323	0.1314
Agriculture	–	–	–	–	–	–	–
Nursing	–	0.0005	–	–	–	0.0020	–
Primary 4–6 years	0.6065	0.3914	0.4224	0.5596	0.5305	0.2685	0.4658
Primary 0–3 years	0.0992	–	0.0301	0.0571	0.1310	0.0090	0.0878
Total	1.0000	1.0000	1.0000	1.0000	1.0000	1.0000	1.0000

TABLE A.5 (*continued*)

Educational level	Banking and insurance	Transport, communication	Education	Health	Other services	Domestic services
University graduates—liberal arts, social sciences, etc.	0.2893	0.0394	0.0444	0.0337	0.0134	0.0020
Engineering, science, etc.	0.1525	0.0197	0.0735	0.0152	0.0030	–
Medicine, dentistry, etc.	–	–	0.0014	0.1760	–	–
Agriculture, veterinary (4 years)	–	–	0.0018	–	–	–
Teacher training	–	–	0.7103	–	0.0081	–
Technical/vocational	0.0425	0.0135	0.0174	0.0400	0.0005	–
Technical/artisans	0.0645	0.0805	0.0220	0.0400	0.0842	–
Commercial	0.2201	0.1374	0.0700	0.0699	0.0827	0.0078
Secondary, forms IV–VI	0.0470	0.0290	–	0.0250	0.0300	0.0025
Secondary, forms I–III	0.0895	0.0644	–	0.0502	0.0572	0.0055
Agriculture	–	0.0012	–	–	–	–
Nursing	–	–	0.0032	0.2757	–	–
Primary, 4–6 years	0.0947	0.5728	0.0560	0.2120	0.6263	0.4115
Primary, 0–3 years	–	0.0421	–	0.0623	0.0946	0.5707
Total	1.0000	1.0000	1.0000	1.0000	1.0000	1.0000

TABLE A.6 University enrollment by field, 1974

	Students	Faculty
Humanities, arts, social sciences, law	6 010	370
Education	2 890	240
Natural science, engineering	1 190	540
Medicine	490	600
Agriculture	370	290
Total	10 950	2 040

Source: University of Beracia. *Report of the Chancellor, 1976.*

Further reading

ADELMAN, I. (1966). A Linear Programming Model of Education Planning: A Case Study of Argentina. In *The Theory and Design of Economic Development* (ed. by I. Adelman and E. Thorbecke), pp. 385–417. Baltimore, The Johns Hopkins University Press

BECKER, G. S. (1975). *Human Capital*, 2nd edn. New York, Columbia University Press

BLAUG, M. (1972). *An Introduction to the Economics of Education*. Baltimore, Penguin Books

BLAUG, M. (ed.) (1968 and 1969). *Economics of Education*, Vol. 1 and 2. Baltimore, Penguin Books

BLAUG, M. (1976). *The Economics of Education: An Annotated Bibliography*, 3rd edn. Oxford, Pergamon Press

BLAUG, M. (1973). *Education and the Employment Problem in Developing Countries*. Geneva, International Labour Organization

BOWLES, S. (1971). Efficient Allocation of Resources in Education. In *Studies in Development Planning* (ed. by H. B. Chenery) pp. 247–269. Cambridge, Harvard University Press

BOWLES, S. and GINTIS, H. (May 1975). The Problem with Human Capital Theory: A Marxian Critique. *American Economic Review* **65–2**, 74–82

DAVIS, R. G. (1966). *Planning Human Resource Development*. Chicago, Rand McNally

DOUGHERTY, C.R.S. (1971). Optimal Allocating of Investment in Education. In *Studies in Development Planning* (ed. by H. B. Chenery), Cambridge, Harvard University Press

HARBERGER, A. C. (1975). On Allocation Resources to Education. In *Investment in Education: National Strategy Options for Developing Countries*. Washington, D.C., World Bank

MINCER, J. (1974). *Schooling, Experience and Earnings*. New York, Columbia University Press for National Bureau of Economic Research

PSACHAROPOULOS, G. (1975). *Earnings and Education in OECD Countries*. Paris, OECD

PSACHAROPOULOS, G. and HINCHLIFFE, K. (1973). *Returns to Education: An International Comparison*. Amsterdam, Elsevier Scientific

Part V

Macroeconomic Planning

Macroeconomic Planning*

Any country that has undertaken even rudimentary national planning has employed some version of the aggregate, macroeconomic projections model that is one of the enduring legacies of the Keynesian revolution in economics. The most common uses of these models has been to determine feasible growth rates for national development plans, or alternatively, to estimate requirements for national saving and foreign aid, given target income growth rates. Short-run versions of Keynesian models are used by industrial and developing countries alike to determine how fiscal and monetary policies should be shaped to maintain employment and control inflation. Decisions on exchange rate and other payments policies depend on macroeconomic projects as well.

This chapter contains three cases that involve macroeconomic forecasting to some degree. Case 8 is centered exclusively on forecasting, while Cases 9 (Balance-of-payments Crisis) and 10 (Fiscal Planning and Reform) focus on other issues, but include macroeconomic forecasting as key inputs to analysis. Taken together, these three emphasize the interrelatedness of macroeconomic policy analysis. Whereas national income projections are essential to forecasting the balance of payments and the government deficit, the reverse is equally true. Moreover, measures taken to correct a foreign exchange deficit have important implications for the government budget, which in turn influences both national income and foreign trade. Ideally, these and other issues would be analyzed simultaneously in one large, moderately disaggregated, macroeconomic planning model. That is done by some models, notably the Brookings model of the United States economy. It is more common, however, to approach each policy issue separately, sometimes under the pressure of an impending crisis, and to reach

---

* Each section of this introduction is keyed to one of the cases, so that students need not read the entire chapter before starting to work on a particular case.

mutually consistent policies in each area by a process of iteration, however informal and sporadic. The cases have been designed in that spirit.

Several different techniques, covering a broad spectrum of economic theory, are useful in analyzing these macroeconomic cases. Part V reviews some of them, beginning with macroeconomic forecasting and continuing with balance-of-payments issues, approaches to fiscal policy analysis and analysis of income distribution policies. As before, these discussions are meant to be indicative, not comprehensive, and to suggest further reading.

Macroeconomic forecasting models

The simplest and most widely used macroeconomic model in development is the Harrod–Domar model, an extension of Keynes's aggregate demand approach. In its most frequently used form, the model combines an aggregate saving function.

$$S = sY, \tag{V.1}$$

with a production function in which capital is the only scarce factor,

$$\Delta Y = v\Delta K = vI, \tag{V.2}$$

and the national accounting identity,

$$I = Y - C + F = S + F. \tag{V.3}$$

In these equations, S is national saving, Y is a measure of national output, say gross national product, K is the capital stock, I is investment, C is consumption and F is foreign saving (including foreign aid), equivalent to the excess of imports over exports. The parameter, s, is the marginal (and in this simple formulation, also the average) saving rate, while v is the ratio of incremental output to incremental capital, the inverse of the familiar incremental capital–output ratio (ICOR). If we let F equal a fraction, f, of Y, then by substituting equation (V.1) into (V.3) and the result into (V.2), we get

$$\Delta Y = v(s + f)Y, \text{ or}$$

$$g(Y) = \frac{\Delta Y}{Y} = v(s + f). \tag{V.4}$$

That is, the growth rate of output, $g(Y)$, depends only upon the incremental capital–output ratio, $\frac{1}{V}$, and the saving rate, national plus foreign[1].

The typical use of this model in national development plans has focused on the last equation. The ICOR would be estimated by totaling investment over several years from the national accounts, then comparing it with the increase in GNP over those years. The incremental saving rate would be estimated over the same period and some estimate made of the amount of foreign savings (including aid), F, likely to flow in during the five-year plan. From these parameters, the feasible growth rate would be calculated. For example, if the ICOR were 3.0, saving rate were 15 percent and foreign investment were expected to total 3 percent of GNP, then a growth rate of 6 percent a year could be achieved. Alternatively, a government might set a target rate of growth and determine the values of the parameters necessary to achieve it. Such calculations led to concentration on the efficiency of investment (which would raise v), the rate of saving and the level of foreign aid as policy variables that are critical to growth. Although the Harrod–Domar formulation grossly oversimplifies the requirements of growth, it nevertheless has caused governments to become concerned with these three important parameters. While the limited nature of the relationship is now widely recognized, it remains a useful shorthand. More important, relations like it remain at the core of even quite complex models of growth.

More complex macroeconomic projection models add Keynesian aggregate demand equations and some representation of the foreign trade sector. A still fairly simple version of these projection models would start with a more realistic formulation of the Harrod–Domar production function, equation (V.2), such as

$$\Delta Y_t = v\Delta K_{t-1} = v(I_{t-1} - \delta K_{t-1}) \tag{V.5}$$

In this formulation, the change in output depends upon increases in capital stock in place the year before. It also allows explicitly for depreciation of the capital stock, at the rate δ per year. Then, to make this equation fit the rest of the model, we convert equation (V.5) from incremental to total product:

$$Y_t = Y_{t-1} + v(I_{t-1} - \delta K_{t-1}) \tag{V.6}$$

Equation (V.6) is the supply side of the model, determining the level of output. To it we can add five equations that determine aggregate demand:

$$I_t = S_t + F_t \tag{V.7}$$

$$S_t = sY_t \tag{V.8}$$

$$F_t = M_t - E_t \tag{V.9}$$

$$M_t = mY_t \tag{V.10}$$

$$C_t = Y_t - I_t + F_t \tag{V.11}$$

The new variables in these equations are imports (M), exports (E), and consumption (C); m is the marginal (and average) propensity to import. The system of six equations, (V.6–11), has six dependent (endogenous) variables $(Y, I, S, F, M$ and $C)$ and four exogenous variables which must be determined from outside the model $(Y_{t-1}, I_{t-1}, K_{t-1}$ and $E_t)$.

To use this model, it is necessary first to estimate the parameters and lagged variables in equations (V.6), (V.8) and (V.10). The saving and import rates and the ICOR can be estimated in the manner suggested above, while lagged investment and GNP can be taken as the latest data available in the national accounts. The capital stock and depreciation rate present different problems. Few countries have data on the capital stock, though most do estimate depreciation for the national accounts. If investment and depreciation data are available for, say, 10 years or more, an acceptable approximation may be to cumulate for as many years as possible and to let the capital stock equal cumulated gross investment less cumulated depreciation. The rate of depreciation follows from this estimate. Alternatively, Harberger (1972) has suggested the possibility of estimating capital stock from the relationship:

$$I = (g(K) + \delta)K \qquad (V.12)$$

where I is gross investment, $g(K)$ is the growth rate of the capital stock and δ is the depreciation rate. In steady state, $g(Y) = g(K)$. Hence as a crude approximation, we can estimate the capital stock at the beginning of the year by assuming a reasonable rate of depreciation, using the growth rate (observed over three or so years of stable growth) and inserting the level of gross investment into equation (V.12). This could be done for several years to get an approximation of the capital stock at the beginning of that period. By cumulating net investment from that time to the present, a rough estimate can be made of the present capital stock.

Long-term projections, such as those done for five-year plans, require that the model be run sequentially. Once the parameters and initial conditions for the lagged variables have been set, the model can be run for several years; in any current year, the lagged variables are those generated by the model run of the previous year. However, values of the current exogenous variables, E_t and I_t, must be supplied for each year of the run. For short-term projections, supply equation (V.6) may not be considered relevant, especially if there is excess capacity in the economy. Then equations (V.7–11) can be rearranged to determine output as follows:

$$Y_t = C_t + I_t + E_t - M_t \qquad (V.13)$$

$$C_t = Y_t - S_t = (1-s)\, Y_t \qquad (V.14)$$

$$M_t = mY_t \qquad (V.15)$$

In this attenuated model, investment becomes an exogenous variable, so the system determines Y, C and M; foreign capital inflow is assumed to adjust to the net trade flow.

A simple change in specification of variables converts the long-run version of the model into a version of the well-known two-gap model. If, instead of letting the foreign capital inflow, F, be determined within the set of equations (V.6–11), we predetermine F to equal some expected inflow of aid and investment, then there are still six equations, but only five unknowns, and the model is overdetermined. Equations (V.7) and (V.9) become inequalities or constraints on the system:

$$\bar{I}_t \leq S_t + F_t \qquad\qquad\qquad\qquad\qquad\text{(V.7a)}$$

$$\bar{M}_t \leq E_t + F_t \qquad\qquad\qquad\qquad\qquad\text{(V.9a)}$$

This model is run by specifying a target growth rate for GNP, as is typically done for national development plans. Then equation (V.6) can be used to specify the required investment over time $\bar{I}$, while equation (V.10) yields the imports, $\bar{M}$, necessary to meet the growth target. Equation (V.7a) then represents a savings gap, in the sense that foreign capital is seen as filling the gap between required investment and projected national saving [from equation (V.8)]. Similarly, equation (V.9a) represents a foreign exchange gap because F makes up any deficit between required imports and exogenously projected exports. Two seminal articles on two-gap models are by McKinnon (1964) and Chenery and Strout (1966).

Two-gap models have been widely used to project requirements for foreign aid. Once a target growth rate has been agreed between a donor and recipient, and the model has generated the implications for investment and imports, the two gaps provide estimates of the aid required to validate the growth target. Aid must fill the larger of the two gaps, which then becomes an equality. Although the other gap remains an inequality *ex ante*, the variables within it must eventually adjust to yield an *ex post* equality, since both gaps are simply identities from the national income accounts. Thus, for example, if the foreign exchange gap is the larger and is just filled by foreign aid and investment, then the economy would generate less than its potential national saving. In a sense, foreign saving would substitute for part of national saving. Similarly, if the saving gap were larger, the economy might import more than it needed to bring equation (V.9a) into equality. If foreign aid were insufficient to fill the larger gap, then the target growth rate could not be achieved.

The two-gap model has the interesting implication that foreign exchange becomes a factor of production, in the sense that it is required to produce national output and a shortfall in foreign exchange means less production. This feature is a result of the rigidities of the model: the fixed requirement for investment, implied by the fixed coefficients production function; the requirements for imports; and the exogenously determined growth of exports, generally assumed to be too slow to sustain the target growth rate. These rigidities are suspect as descriptions of real economies. Labor can be substituted for capital to increase production over the long run, either through use of different technologies or by shifting emphasis to more labor-intensive sectors. Import demand may be reduced as a fraction of output and export growth may be enhanced by a number of foreign exchange policies, as suggested by Case 9.

Each of these models would benefit from disaggregation. A minimally useful model ought to

(1)   break imports into categories, such as those presented in Report 2 for Beracia, and relate the demand for these to relevant variables of income or output;
(2)   disaggregate exports into analytically appropriate categories, such as mining, agricultural and manufacturing products;
(3)   introduce government into the aggregate demand equations by dividing consumption and investment into their private and public components;
(4)   divide savings into component categories, such as government, household and corporate saving or, consistent with Kaldor's consumption function, into saving by wage earners and capitalists;
(5)   relate private consumption to disposable income, thus introducing fiscal policy into consumer demand;
(6)   introduce investment in inventories; and
(7)   include balances for money and for international payments.

A more fundamental disaggregation would use an economy-wide inter-industry model of the type discussed in Chapter 4. Actually, the macroeconomic model is grafted onto the input–output model. This fairly advanced application of models to planning is, however, beyond the scope and purpose of this casebook[2].

Balance-of-payments adjustments

Imbalance in foreign trade and payments plagues all countries from time to time. The developing countries, however, are typically confronted by structural problems that have roots in the development process and make it particularly difficult to correct balance-of-payments deficits. The genesis of this situation lies in the comparative advantage of less developed, tropical countries, whose most profitable exports have been mineral products, such as copper, bauxite and phosphates; agricultural raw materials, such as cotton and rubber; and tropical foodstuffs such as coffee, cocoa, tea and rice. Many of these

products, especially agricultural products, generally face low income
elasticities of demand, and thus the volume imported by the industrial
world grows more slowly than its national income.

One response to slowly growing traditional exports has been import
substitution, principally the encouragement of consumer goods
industries to replace imports of processed foods, textile, clothing, footwear, paper products and certain chemical-based products. This
strategy has been successful in slowing the growth of import demand for
a time in some countries, but the end result has been dependence on
imports of industrial raw materials, semi-finished goods and capital
equipment. In several cases, where agriculture has been neglected,
developing countries also require imported foodstuffs. (Bruton, 1970,
catalogues the effects of import substitution strategies on development.)
Because both industrial production and investment then depend upon
imported inputs, rapid income growth requires rapid growth of imports
and the foreign exchange to pay for them. Traditional exports cannot
keep pace.

One possible escape from this bind is non-traditional exports, either
new cash crops or manufactures. Although industrial world protectionism is becoming an important retarding influence on export
diversification, the main enemy of non-traditional export growth until
now has been the policies of the developing countries themselves. Most
significant of these are the maintenance by LDCs of overvalued
exchange rates, historically to discourage production of primary
exports that face price-inelastic world demand, and the complementary
structure of protective tariffs and import quotas, erected to promote
import-substituting industries. The net result has been twofold. First,
import substituting firms have been so well protected from foreign
competition, that they produce at high cost and are in no position to
export in competitive world markets. Second, price incentives—
including the overvalued exchange rate and relatively high domestic
prices for goods sold domestically—work uniformly against exports of
any kind.

The outcomes are exacerbated by conditions and policies that
contribute to domestic price inflation and further reduce the international competitiveness of agriculture and industry. In this
inflationary world, no country is immune from escalating prices, a
substantial portion of which may be caused by the rising cost of
essential imports. However, so long as a country's prices rise by no more
than those of its trading partners, its relative costs and thus its competitiveness does not change. A problem arises when domestic inflation is
more rapid than in world markets. In developing countries, four factors
tend to raise domestic price inflation above world levels. First, supply
elasticities, especially for agricultural goods, are often low, so that
output does not respond rapidly to increases in income and demand.
Inputs such as seed, fertilizer and water may not be readily available to

most farmers; storage facilities may be inadequate to maintain stocks; and the transport system may not be able to handle increased marketings even if available. These and other structural causes are themselves symptoms of underdevelopment. Second, if wage rates are determined at least partly by a political process, as happens when unions negotiate with government and when minimum wages are established, then it often becomes difficult to resist wage demands in excess of productivity increases. Third, the habit of high and negotiable protection, which seduces enterprise managers away from competitive instincts, also reduces their resistance to wage and other cost increases. Instead of protecting profits by raising productivity and reducing costs, managers may focus on political relief, such as subsidies, quotas or increased protection. Firms not fully utilizing protection may simply raise prices and expect to find consumers willing to pay in inflationary markets. Finally, governments may and usually do add to inflationary pressures by succumbing to the many claims for additional expenditure; demands from the military for more hardware, from civil servants, including teachers, for pay increases; and from various sources for increased investments in development projects. Unwilling or unable to raise tax revenues, governments find it easier to increase their deficits and rely on their central banks to issue more money instead.

The result is clear: import demand outstrips the country's capacity to earn foreign exchange, creating chronic deficits in the balance of payments on current account (exports less imports of goods and services). Long-term foreign investment and official aid help to fill this gap in payments. In fact, to the extent that a country is attractive to foreign investors and welcomes them, it must run a deficit on current account—import more than it exports—in order to transform foreign capital into foreign goods and services. However, most countries prefer to lessen their dependence on foreign capital as they develop, and in any case foreigners may not be prepared to fill the current account deficit completely. Thus some basic adjustment is needed to generate structural change in the economy, which in turn will reduce the demand for imports and increase the supply of new exports. Most often, crises bring about such changes. Thus the failure of a major export crop or a decline in the world price of an export commodity may require immediate corrective measures. To be effective, however, these must take into account the long-run, structural shifts which alone will eliminate the chronic tendency towards deficits. The balance of this section discusses the three approaches to policy measures that have been used in adjusting foreign trade and payments: the elasticities, absorption and monetary approaches.

ELASTICITIES APPROACH

One means of estimating the effects of devaluation deals with the response of supply and demand to shifts in the relative prices between traded goods and those not traded in world markets. The exchange rate largely etermines the price between importables and exportables, on the one hand, and home goods, such as construction, utilities, transportation and most services, on the other. A devaluation of the exchange rate (raising the local currency price of dollars or other foreign currency) has several simultaneous effects in the home market:

(1) Exporters receive more local currency for each dollar's worth of sales, raising the returns to factors in those industries and encouraging production for export.
(2) Import-competing producers, who now face higher-priced competition because the exchange rate has raised the cost of competing imports, may be encouraged to displace more imports.
(3) Importers must pay higher local prices per dollar of goods imported, hence will demand fewer imports.
(4) Domestic consumers of exportable products will also have to pay more for them in local currency, since they command higher local currency prices on world markets; this will cut down their consumption of such goods, releasing larger supplies for export.

All these effects of devaluation depend on the price elasticities of various demands and supplies, hence the name of the approach. There is a large literature on the elasticity conditions—called the Marshall–Lerner conditions—under which a devaluation will improve the balance of current account. (See any of several standard texts on international economics, including Kindleberger, 1973, Chapter 19, and Södersten, 1970, Chapter 16.) For our purposes, it is sufficient to note some salient features of this kind of analysis and then to focus on a pragmatic way of estimating the response of trade flows to devaluation.

In judging whether the elasticities are sufficient to improve the balance on current account, it is important to remember that we are working with *excess* supply and demand curves. The supply of a commodity available for export depends not only on the production of that commodity but also on its consumption at home. As devaluation raises the local price of an exportable, its supply increases *and* its local demand decreases. Both effects increase the quantity available for export. The price elasticity of export supply is the *sum* of the two price elasticities (of commodity supply and demand), both taken as positive and each weighted by the respective ratio of quantity (supplied or demanded) to the quantity exported. Even if both elasticities are low, their weighted sum can be large. This will be especially true for exportable commodities for which a large share of production is consumed at home; staple foods such as rice and maize are good examples. Similarly, the home country's demand for imports is the excess of its demand for the importable commodity less its domestically produced supply of that commodity. Again, the elasticity of import demand is a weighted sum of the two component elasticities and thus larger than either.

For non-traditional exports and for imports, we assume that de-valuation has no effect on foreign markets. In effect, the foreign price elasticity of supply of imports and of demand for exports are both perfectly elastic for the developing country in question. For traditional exports, however, the supply from even quite small countries can affect world prices. In these cases, foreign demand elasticity must be brought into the picture, because an increase in quantity supplied will cause a fall in world price and hence a non-proportional rise or fall in export revenues, measured in dollars (or any foreign currency). The latter point is important: our concern in measuring the effect of a devaluation is in the response of dollar export revenues and import costs. If world prices are not affected, then revenue changes will be proportional to quantity changes. For traditional exports, however, this is unlikely to be the case.

A devaluation will evoke a more favorable response from imports and exports, the greater the relevant elasticities. For non-traditional exports, a 10 percent devaluation causes a 10 percent rise in the domestic price, because world prices are assumed constant. Then the quantity of these commodities exported, and thus the revenue earned, will rise 10 percent if the elasticity of supply is one, and 20 percent if the elasticity is two. The same calculation applies to import demand and its price elasticity, because the world price of import supply is also fixed. For traditional exports that face a downward sloping demand, any shift of supply will lower the world price in dollars. If the world demand with respect to the country's exports is inelastic (elasticity below one), then revenues will fall with devaluation; if elastic, they will rise[3]. The higher that elasticity, the better the conditions for an improved balance on current account.

Are the elasticities likely to be large enough? There has been a long debate on this point, with participants divided into elasticity optimists and pessimists. Some features of developing countries—highly protected manufacturing, scarce capital and skilled labor, lack of entrepreneurs, little experience with foreign markets, inability to produce several necessary imports, an undiversified economy—argue for low elasticities and unsuccessful devaluations. However, experience in several countries has shown that responses to relative price changes can be substantial in both industry and agriculture. The excess demand and supply nature of the schedules also points to high elasticities. Further, although price changes may have little effect in the short run, over a few years, as people adjust to the new prices, the elasticities are likely to increase. It may also be that large devaluations will evoke proportionately larger responses than small ones, as producers and consumers have 'inert areas' over which relatively small changes do not affect decisions. Finally, econometric estimates by Khan (1974) have yielded sufficiently high estimates of demand elasticities for several countries to justify cautious optimism.

The task of the policy analyst is to estimate relevant elasticities for meaningful categories of imports and exports and then, for any proposed degree of currency devaluation, to apply these elasticities to the expected price changes. The result equals the percentage increase in quantity demanded or supplied. For example, if the price elasticity of import demand is −0.7 and a devaluation raises its effective price by 20 percent, then the quantity imported will fall by 14 percent. Applying estimated quantity changes to each category of trade, the resulting change in the current account balance can be calculated to indicate whether the proposed level of devaluation is likely to be successful. The first step in forecasting is to identify useful categories of trade. The kinds of disaggregation discussed above and used in the Beracia reports are probably minimal: imports into foods, luxury and semi-luxury consumer goods, fuels, intermediate producer goods, raw materials and capital equipment; exports into each of the major traditional commodities and, perhaps, separate categories for non-traditional exports of agricultural products and manufactures.

The second step is to identify a relevant price for each category of trade. Our concern is with the rate at which a dollar's worth of foreign currency converts into local currency for each item, a measurement we have already used in estimating the shadow exchange rate. For imports, the relevant quantities are the official exchange rate, tariffs, subsidies, if any, and any quota premium; for exports, the elements are the same, with the exception of the quota premium. In addition, since domestic and foreign inflation can affect the real value of exchange, we have to add elements for the foreign and domestic price levels. If world prices rise more than domestic costs, domestic producers become more competitive in world markets, just as with a devaluation. If, on the other hand, domestic prices rise more than world prices, domestic producers are less competitive in foreign markets, as with a revaluation of the currency.

The price indicator that encompasses these elements is the effective exchange rate (EER), which differs for each category of trade. Thus, for exports, the indicator is

$$EER_x = R_o (1 - t_x) (1 + s_x) \frac{P_w}{P_d} \tag{V.16}$$

where R_o is the official exchange rate, t_x is the average duty on exports (or on the particular category of exports), s_x is the average subsidy on exports or the particular category, P_w is an index of world prices relevant to exports or a category of exports and P_d an index of domestic prices relevant to the costs of production for export. A similar formula applies to imports:

$$EER_m = R_o (1 + t_m) (1 - s_m) (1 + q) \frac{P_w}{P_d} \tag{V.17}$$

where q is the quota premium and the other variables have analagous definitions. Note that the domestic and foreign price indexes need not be the same for each category. For a specific export commodity, P_w should be an index of the world market price for that item; *International Financial Statistics* (IFS), published monthly by the International Monetary Fund (IMF), compiles time series on prices of major commodities in world trade. For other exports and for imports, some general indicator of price movements in international trade would be sufficient; such indicators are also published in IFS. For domestic prices, some indicator of changes in the cost of production is desirable. In practice, a wholesale price index of GNP deflator is convenient and usually adequate.

The effective exchange rate indicates what should have been obvious, that devaluation of the official exchange rate is not the entire story. Anything that affects the rate at which importers and exporters convert foreign into domestic currency will affect their competitiveness and potential profitability. Thus if a devaluation is accompanied by a reduction in import duties, part of the effect of devaluation will be cancelled. Alternatively, a subsidy may substitute for devaluation in promoting non-traditional exports. Moreover, if, because of low foreign demand elasticities, it is considered unwise to stimulate production of traditional exports, then these producers can be shielded from the impact of devaluation by increasing export duties so that $(1 + t_x)$ rises proportionately to the devaluation.

Two elements of the effective exchange rate have implications that should be emphasized. First, if devaluation is part of a package that includes liberalization of import controls, quota premiums will eventually be reduced and imports may actually rise, not fall. This requires that the devaluation is able to stimulate enough export growth to finance the added imports. The aim of devaluation in this case is not an improvement of the current account, which has presumably been kept in acceptable balance through controls over imports. Rather, it is to eliminate the controls and move towards a market-determined foreign exchange regime. (An excellent series of case studies, summarized by Bhagwati (1978) and Krueger (1978), documents the experiences of several countries with devaluation-liberalization packages.)

The second implication is that even if the exchange rate, tariffs, subsidies and controls are managed to achieve an effective devaluation, continuing domestic inflation in excess of world inflation will erode the impact of devaluation. For a country with chronic inflation, it will be necessary to continue devaluing so that domestic producers' initial advantage is maintained. South Korea, Brazil and Colombia have managed their exchange regimes in just this way. We will return to this subject in discussing monetary policy.

To measure elasticities of import demand and export supply, it will be advantageous to estimate the respective demand and supply functions econometrically. It is convenient to work with log-linear equations, because these yield coefficients that are estimates of elasticities. For any category of import demand.

$$\text{Log } (M/P_m) = c_1 + c_2\text{Log } Y + c_3\text{Log } EER + c_4'\text{Log } (M/P_m)_{-1} \text{ (V.18)}$$

where M is the dollar expenditure on the class of imports, P_m is an index of the price of this category of import, Y is real GNP, EER is the relevant effective exchange rate and $(M/P_m)_{-1}$ is the quantity of imports for the previous period. Dollar expenditure on imports is deflated to approximate the quantity of imports, which is what the elasticity measurement calls for. Thus, projections using the resulting elasticities will be in constant prices of the base year from which projections are made. The coefficient, c_2, is the income elasticity of demand for one period (say a year), while c_3 gives the price elasticity with respect to current changes in the effective exchange rate for one period and should be negative. Coefficient c_4 is an adjustment term, which recognizes that elasticities may change over time. The long-run price elasticity is $\dfrac{c_3}{1-c_4}$. Equation (V.18) without the lagged term will give a direct estimate of the long-run elasticity (c_3), but assumes, probably unrealistically, that all adjustments take place in one period (see Khan, 1974).

The export supply equation would be completely analogous, with deflated export values, E/P_e, substituting for M/P_m and the relevant effective rates inserted. For each traditional export commodity, the effect of any increase in supply (estimated from price elasticities) on world market prices must be estimated. For many major commodities, world demand elasticities have frequently been estimated by the World Bank and others; the relevant literature should be consulted. (In countries that are major exporters of these commodities, such estimates are generally known to planners.) Remember, though, that for any one country the price elasticity of demand is greater than that for the entire market. The formula is to divide the world market elasticity by the market share of the country in question.

So far the discussion has dealt with the trade account of the balance of payments, which accounts for some 70 percent of total payments for the third world as a whole. Of the other major items in the current account, payments of interest on foreign debt is a fixed quantity and not responsive to changes in the exchange rate. It is more difficult to predict the behavior of profit remittances and private transfers. These may behave much like short-term capital movements, which are discussed below.

Some *capital flows* may be influenced by exchange rate devaluation. Long-term loans from foreign banks and others are likely to be denominated in foreign currency, so that both principal and interest payments would be fixed in, say, dollars. These lenders are interested in interest income at low risk. The only way that devaluation is likely to affect their decision to invest is if a successful devaluation leads to an improved payments situation and thus reduces the risk of default. This effect, probably slight in most cases, would be very hard to quantify.

Direct (equity) investment by foreign corporations and individuals responds to market opportunities that may well be influenced by devaluation and accompaning stabilization measures (see next section). To the extent that devaluation succeeds in its goal of making production for import substitution and export more profitable, it may attract new foreign investors. They will also respond to an improved payments situation, because it is likely to reduce the stringency of or need for exchange control and make repatriation of dividends much easier than otherwise. These incentives will be effective only over the long run, however. One devaluation does not guarantee the kind of environment that foreign investors like. Foreign investment is more likely to respond once a government has demonstrated its willingness to maintain the new levels of the effective exchange rate by controlling inflation and/or devaluing as necessary.

The most immediate response to a devaluation is likely to come from short-term capital flows. These include a variety of instruments, such as bank deposits held overseas by nationals or corporations doing business in the country, short-term trade credits, payments due to a country's exporters or due from its importers, short-term bank loans, and so forth. As a country's payments situation worsens and devaluation becomes a possibility, anyone who has the capability of getting capital out of the country for a short period may try to do so. For example, an exporter may ask his customer overseas to delay payment in the hope that his domestic currency will be devalued and he can convert foreign currency later at a higher (devalued) rate in local currency. Or a domestic firm may delay seeking a short-term loan from a foreign bank until it can convert into local currency at the devalued rate. More blatantly, those who can move funds out of the country at the old rate will do so, hoping to return them after devaluation and make a speculative profit. In fact, this tendency to move or keep funds out of the country as devaluation becomes a possibility will contribute to the need to devalue, as the outflow of short-term capital adds to the payments deficit. After devaluation, the reverse flow occurs as speculators realize their profits by repatriating capital. This tends to strengthen the currency, which may appreciate if it has been allowed to float for a time.

Estimating these reflows of speculative capital is problematic at best. One approach would be to assume that a large fraction of the unusual outflow prior to devaluation will return in the months following it. However, since speculators' expectations may be difficult to assess, the safest course would be not to count on these short-term movements. In any case, to the extent that devaluation is intended to cure a long-term structural problem in the country's trade, such short-term capital movements should not be permitted to affect decisions on the exchange rate.

ABSORPTION APPROACH

The elasticities approach results in an estimate of the shift in the current account balance for a proposed devaluation. Suppose, for example, that a proposed devaluation is expected to eliminate a deficit and bring the current account into balance. For example, if exports of goods and services, E, was less than imports of goods and services, M, suppose that after devaluation the two are forecast to be equal. If this consequence of an elasticities projection were handed to a macroeconomist for comment, she or he would suggest that not all factors have been considered. Rather, she or he would argue that to generate such an improvement in the balance of payments, it will be necessary to increase national income more than expenditures on consumption and invest-ment. If national income is not expected to rise, it will be necessary to reduce expenditures.

This view of the problem, called the absorption approach for reasons that will become clear, is based entirely on the national income identity,

$$Y = C_p + C_g + I_p + I_g + E - M, \qquad (V.19)$$

where the symbols are the same as introduced previously in this chapter and the subscripts refer to private and government expendi-tures. Now if we designate the current account balance as $B = E - M$ and call all the expenditure items, 'absorption', designated A, then

$$Y = A + B \qquad (V.20)$$

and changes in national product are given by

$$\Delta Y = \Delta A + \Delta B. \qquad (V.21)$$

Assume an elasticities analysis indicates that devaluation will improve the balance of payments, so $\Delta B > 0$. Then

$$\Delta A = \Delta Y - \Delta B < \Delta Y. \qquad (V.22)$$

That is, whatever the change in GNP, absorption must increase by less. If GNP does not increase, absorption must decrease. Unless consumption and investment are restrained to the levels indicated by equation (V.22), the expected improvement in the balance of payments will not materialize. That is, the elasticity conditions are necessary for an improvement in the payments balance, but not sufficient.

Recognition of the absorption problem set off an examination in the literature of the possible behavioral characteristics of an economy that might reduce absorption as a consequence of devaluation. The various mechanisms are reviewed by Kindleberger (1973, pp. 374–378) and Södersten (1970, pp. 285–291). For a developing country, the most promising of these mechanisms is probably the increase in efficiency and output which may result as factors of production move towards activities in which the country enjoys comparative advantage. However, the policy analyst is well advised not to depend entirely on these forces, which are likely to be weak. Rather, she or he should prepare policy alternatives that will restrain aggregate demand for consumption and investment sufficiently to validate the projected balance-of-payments improvement. The potential targets for reduced or restrained absorption can be identified by going back to equation (V.19), which can be rearranged as

$$Y - C_p - C_g = I_p + I_g + B,$$

from which we get

$$S_p + S_g = I_p + I_g + B,$$

or

$$\Delta S_p + \Delta S_g = \Delta I_p + \Delta I_g + \Delta B, \tag{V.23}$$

with S_p and S_g being private and government savings, respectively. The greater the improvement in payments, the greater the increase in private and government savings and/or the less the increase in investment.

The need to contain absorption suggests all the fiscal and monetary tools normally used to control aggregate demand: restrained growth of the money supply to raise interest rates, thus increasing incentives to save and reducing incentives to invest; increased taxes to restrain consumption and increase government revenues; controls on government spending—both consumption and investment—to turn higher revenues into higher government saving; and an incomes policy to restrain wage and salary increases. These policies should not result in a net deflation of the economy. They are necessary merely to counter the expansionary effect of the improvement in the balance of payments. Income and employment need not fall, but the source of each will be switched from domestic activities into trade-related ones. Note also that the need for contractionary policies may not be great at first. If elasticities are low in the short run, say for the first few months to a year, then the improvement in the current account will not be great. In fact, there could even be a net deflationary effect, measured in local currency, because low import demand elasticity and a higher domestic price for imports may raise this expenditure leakage considerably for a short time, until importers are able to adjust to the higher prices (Cooper, 1971). Over time, however, as the elasticities increase and the payments situation begins to improve, fiscal and monetary controls on the economy will be essential.

To be sure that expenditure is consistent with the desired improvement in the balance on current account, the analyst will have to make aggregate demand projections of the type discussed above. These should, among other things, account for the projected shifts in import demand and export supply that are forecast by the elasticities approach; and the effects of devaluation on government revenues from duties on imports and exports, which rise with devaluation. Note that expenditure forecasts are in local currency, so that projections are affected by devaluation in two ways: (i) quantities may be changed (e.g., imports fall), while (ii) local currency prices are raised (e.g., import costs rise), so expenditure on imports may either rise or fall. If the model's projections show an excessive rise in absorption in current prices, government will have to intervene to reduce absorption.

MONETARY POLICY

Manifestations of monetary concerns have alreeady appeared in our discussions of the elasticities and absorption approaches. The price stimulus of a devaluation depends in part on the government's ability to maintain the new relationship between domestic and foreign prices in the face of domestic inflation. This can be accomplished either through continuing devaluation or by restraining domestic price increases, which is a task for monetary policy. Similarly, the absorption problem requires restraint of aggregate demand, in which monetary policy can also play a role by raising interest rates, thus encouraging saving and discouraging investment.

A simple model, based entirely on identities, relates the balance-of-payments problem to money creation. Designating the money supply (currency, demand and time deposits) as MS, then any change in the supply can be attributed to changes in net foreign assets (NFA) or net domestic credit (NDC):

$$\Delta MS = \Delta NFA + \Delta NDC. \tag{V.24}$$

The annual change in net foreign assets is given by:

$$\Delta NFA = E - M + F, \tag{V.25}$$

where $E - M = B$, the balance on current account used in the absorption approach, and $F =$ the balance on capital account, the 'foreign savings' of our discussion of the Harrod–Domar model. Thus the change in net foreign assets is the same as the change in international reserves, the 'bottom line' of the balance of payments.

The change in net domestic credit can be divided into its public and private components:

$$\Delta NDC = (GBD - GEB - GBP) + BLP, \tag{V.26}$$

where GBD is the government's budgetary deficit, including current and capital expenditures and all revenues; GEB is government's external borrowing (including official transfers), which finances part of that deficit; *GBP* is government's borrowing from the public, non-banking sector; and *BLP* is commercial bank net lending to the public. The items in parenthesis give net domestic credit creation due to the government. Finally, let the domestic price level depend upon changes in the money supply:

$$g(P_d) = f(g[MS]) \tag{V.27}$$

where the symbol, g, indicates a growth rate. This brings us back to the elasticities approach, because equation (V.27) provides the domestic price level needed to calculate effective exchange rates [equations (V.16) and (V.17)].

Assume now, as before, that a proposed devaluation is expected to improve the balance on current account, a result of an elasticities analysis. Further assume that the capital account is expected either to be neutral, or, perhaps because of speculative capital inflows, to further improve the payments balance, so that $\Delta NFA > 0$. The latter result depends, however, on maintaining the change in the effective exchange rate by controlling domestic price inflation. The relationship expressed in equation (V.27), which is a version of the quantity theory of money demand, indicates that a low target inflation rate means limiting increases in the money supply.

The target money supply growth, combined with the projected improvement in the balance of payments, implies a controlled increase in net domestic credit [equation (V.24)]. Equation (V.26) then shows which policy variables may be influenced to restrain domestic credit creation. Commercial bank lending to the public may be restrained through a variety of devices, including reserve requirements, rediscount rates and direct controls. The efficacy of these measures will depend upon the development of the banking system and the discipline that the central bank is able to maintain over the commercial banks. A more direct and certain method of money supply restraint is to reduce the government's deficit by controlling its expenditures, also one of the more powerful instruments for restraining absorption. With increases in revenues caused by the devaluation's effect on trade tax revenues, the problem may not be one of reducing expenditures, but of resisting pressures to increase them in the face of higher domestic prices for traded goods. Because government's external borrowing has already been determined in the analysis of the balance of payments, it can be considered fixed for this exercise. Government could in principle borrow more from the public to control the money supply, but may find this difficult because credit stringency will cause potential bondholders to shift investible funds into other assets, or into consumption.

In summary, once the elasticity projections show a potential improvement, all signs point to government budgetary policy as the key variable, both to restrain aggregate demand and to control the money supply. Other policy measures will certainly help and may be necessary, but control of the budget is probably a necessary condition for success in devaluation.

POLITICAL ECONOMY

Devaluation should never be attempted without a full assessment of the political issues involved. Exchange rate changes have far-reaching implications. Many other prices in an economy depend on it and the incomes of many people are affected by it. If the exchange rate is devalued, the resulting price and income shifts will set up political forces that may be strong enough to force government into actions that counteract devaluation, such as granting wage increases or raising government expenditures. These forces can, and often do, force out the finance minister or even overturn the government, through parliamentary action in a few cases or military action in others.

The politics of devaluation differ for each country. However, as a first step in analyzing them it is necessary to establish who will gain and who will lose from devaluation, and here some generalizations are possible. Gainers include manufacturing firms whose domestic prices depend on the rate at which local currency exchanges for foreign currency: those competing with imports and those actually or potentially producing for export. A few manufacturers may not be able to raise their prices with devaluation and these would be losers. They would include firms, such as breweries, producing goods whose import is banned by government; those, such as cement plants, who enjoy considerable natural protection from transport costs and already charge below the import-competing price; and those whose prices are controlled and are not expected to rise with devaluation. Construction, utility and transport companies, which provide services that cannot be imported or exported but which must import equipment and fuel, will also lose from devaluation. One kind of service will gain, however: the tourist industry, whose potentially lower dollar prices may attract more customers from overseas.

Farmers producing cash crops that are either imported or exported will gain from devaluation, unless government attempts to control the prices they receive. The position of wage earners will depend upon the industry they are in and, more critically, on how government deals with wage changes in its attempt to control expenditure increases. It is generally the case that real wages must fall, both to reduce demand for imports and to restrain inflationary pressures following devaluation. Thus those already having jobs will suffer real income losses. Urban consumers, who include the middle class and most wage-earners, are also likely to be losers, since devaluation will increase the prices of goods they consume. This group includes four with considerable political power: trade unions, civil servants, students and the military.

Over time, as exporters and import competitors increase their output, incomes of miners, farmers, workers and capitalists will rise. If the country has a comparative advantage in labor-intensive manufacturing and agriculture, employment should increase, so those not having wage employment before devaluation will gain from it. If, in addition, smallholders participate in cash crop production, as is true in many African countries, then the overall effects on income distribution could be egalitarian, or neutral at worst. However, these benefits of devaluation, which depend on restructuring towards exporting and efficient import substitution, can only be fully realized over a period of several years. In the interim, government must maintain the new incentive structure brought on by devaluation and its accompanying measures. This means that those losing from devaluation cannot be permitted to regain their relative positions. Since they are likely to be politically more potent than the potential gainers, and since the gains will take time to accrue while the losses will be immediately apparent, a successful devaluation is a politically risky business, not to be undertaken by shaky governments.

A final note on timing. Typically, governments devalue at times of crisis, when they have no alternatives. Politicians understand the dangers and try to avoid prescribing bitter medicine. Yet, precisely because of the political risks, it is unwise to wait for a crisis to devalue. Far better to begin the painful process of structural change in times of prosperity, when incomes are rising and the issue is not whether incomes are maintained or fall, but whether they rise substantially or only modestly. The one exception may be war or other externally imposed crises, when nationalism is at a peak and the public may be willing to sacrifice for the country's good. These are, fortunately, rare times and they may not last long. If they arise, however, they present an opportunity that a determined government can turn to advantage.

Planning fiscal reform

Fiscal policy—the management of government's expenditures and the design of its tax structure—has traditionally been assigned three basic aims. First, government should tax and spend to promote the greatest potential future consumption with the least possible expenditure of resources, both current and future, consistent with society's valuation of future *versus* current consumption. This is really a dual goal, implying the need to generate sufficient investible resources for desired growth and the need to use all resources as efficiently as possible. Second, taxes should be levied and expenditures directed in ways that promote an equitable distribution of income and wealth in society. At the very least, fiscal mechanisms should reduce the worst disparities in income and should attempt to provide equal treatment to those in similar circumstances. Third, fiscal policy should work to stabilize economic activity by reducing cyclical unemployment and restraining inflation. In developing countries, taxes also have an important role to play in insulating the domestic economy from swings in export prices and other external shocks.

GROWTH AND EFFICIENCY

Fiscal policy and development planning are tightly linked in numerous ways, many of them implicit in the discussions in this book. In fact, the first development plans of many countries were, to a great extent, fiscal plans with some macroeconomic analysis grafted on. Even today, when macroeconomic forecasting is at the root of national planning, the bulk of most development plans refers to government expenditure.

The Harrod–Domar relationship between investment, savings and growth, which is the foundation of much macroeconomic development planning, provides the most basic link with fiscal policy. Recall the Harrod–Domar result, that growth depends upon the share of saving in national income. This fundamental relationship survives in even the most complex models of development. Government influences the saving rate, first, because it is one of the principal sources of saving in the economy and, second, because its tax structure affects the ability and desire of private households and firms to save. Government saving is defined as the excess of its tax revenues, T, over its consumption expenditure, C_g. Thus national saving can be broken into its private and public components,

$$S = Y - C_p - C_g = S_h + S_c + (T - C_g), \tag{V.28}$$

where the subscripts, h and c, refer to private households and corporations, respectively.

Government's contribution to national saving can be substantial. For developing countries as a group, public saving contributed about one-fifth of gross investment in 1963, while for some countries (e.g. Turkey, Tunisia, Singapore and Uruguay) the share was much higher (World Bank, 1977, pp. 424–430). Thus if the government aims to increase growth, it must itself contribute to this aim by increasing its own saving. This in turn implies both increased taxes and restraints on government consumption expenditures, such as civil servants' salaries and defense expenditures. Outlays on investment, such as road construction or irrigation schemes, do not, of course, reduce public saving. We shall return to this point later.

One of the prevailing post-war prescriptions for accelerated development, epitomized by Nicholas Kaldor (see Bird and Oldham, 1975), urged governments to increase their tax revenues. This would be done largely by shifting from *indirect taxes* on commodities (tariffs, sales and excise duties) to *direct taxes* on both personal and corporate income. In doing so, both the tax base—the income subject to taxation—and the tax rates would be increased. It has been widely noted that developing countries collect in taxes a much smaller share of gross national product than industrial countries. Chenery and Syrquin (1975, pp. 110–111) provide cross-country regression results demonstrating that, on average, countries with per capita incomes (in 1964 dollars) below $ 500 have tax ratios below 22 percent, while wealthier countries have ratios above 27 percent.

Average tax ratios can only be used to make static comparisons. *Marginal tax rates* $\frac{\Delta T}{\Delta Y}$ or the *income elasticity of tax revenue* $\frac{\Delta T}{T} \div \frac{\Delta Y}{Y}$, the marginal over the average tax ratio) can show the extent to which taxes have risen with income. If the marginal rate is above the average (i.e., if the elasticity is greater than one), then the average tax ratio can be expected to rise as income grows. In a study of 27 developing countries, using data from 1953–1955 to 1966–1968, Chelliah (see Bird and Oldham, 1975) shows that several developing countries with low tax ratios in the early period, notably India, Korea and Chile, had quite high elasticities, ranging from 1.9 for Chile to 2.4 for India, and thus rising tax ratios. This is one indicator of *tax effort*, the extent to which a country's tax system is able to generate more investible resources over time. Chelliah shows that for his sample of LDCs, the average elasticity of excise and sales taxes is highest (2.4), followed by the elasticity of income taxes (1.7). Taxes on international trade have somewhat lower elasticities on average (1.4). Thus a country wishing to increase its tax yield would shift from taxes on imports and exports to those on domestic trade and incomes.

The notion of tax effort can be refined, however. Since tax ratios are noted to rise with income, tax effort can be defined as the extent to which a country generates taxes *in excess* of the average for its income class. Further, since the shares of mining and of exports in national income also affect tax capacity, the tax ratio can be regressed on these variables as well as on per capita income, to get a standard against which to measure tax effort. Doing this, Chelliah finds that India, Morocco, Chile and Tunisia, with relatively high tax elasticities, also have high tax ratios relative to the standard for countries of their respective income, mining and export classes. However, other countries with high elasticities—Korea, Honduras and Paraguay—have only average or below-average tax ratios for their standards; while Kenya, Taiwan and Ceylon, with low elasticities, nevertheless show above-average tax effort on this basis.

Not all economists agree that increased tax yield is the path to accelerated economic growth. Stanley Please (see Bird and Oldman, 1975) has argued that higher revenues may serve to ease restraints on government consumption and thus not lead to greater public saving.

The largest element of government consumption is the payment of civil servants' and teachers' salaries. Because civil servants tend to be one of the most effective pressure groups in most developing countries, control over government expenditure is politically difficult and cannot be taken for granted.

Even if government is able to channel additional revenues into public saving, it is unlikely that national saving would rise by the full amount of added government saving. Tax revenue is raised at the expense of private income and will reduce both private consumption and private saving. This can be demonstrated easily for a proportional tax on private income, Y_p, at the rate, t (and assuming no transfers). If consumption depends upon disposable income, $(Y - T)$, then

$$C_p = (1 - s)\ (Y_p - T) = (1 - s)\ (1 - t)\,Y_p. \tag{V.29}$$

Since private saving is the residual between income and consumption plus taxes,

$$S_p = Y_p - C_p - T = Y_p - (1 - s)\ (1 - t)\,Y_p - t\,Y_p = s\ (1 - t)\,Y_p. \tag{V.30}$$

Thus if the tax rate, t, is increased, both private consumption and saving are decreased. However, the tax yield, $T = t\,Y_p$, must exceed the decrease in private saving, $st\,Y_p$, by a considerable margin because saving rates are typically below one-third of private income.

Government can, by judicious selection of the taxes it levies, reduce this loss of private saving. Any tax that afects consumption more than saving will, by increasing the relative rewards to saving, limit the effect on private saving. For example, an excise or sales tax on luxury consumer goods is likely to affect private saving less than a levy of similar yield on income, although both will reduce private saving to some extent. Taxes on interest income and profits, which have the virtue of high elasticities and, probably, some redistribution in favor of lower income groups, also have the liability of reducing the rewards for additional private saving. In raising revenues, as in all fiscal policy, government's task is to strike a balance among sometimes competing goals.

In its role as saver, government influences the saving parameter of the Harrod–Domar relationship. In its role as investor, government affects the capital–output ratio that determines the efficiency with which saving is converted into growth. Government can use its tax resources to make four types of investment. It can create physical overhead capital; invest in human capital; finance public enterprises; and finance private investment through banks, development finance companies and other intermediaries.

Physical overheads include roads, railroads and other investments in transportation; dams for flood control, irrigation and power; distribution systems for water and electricity; and telephone and other communication systems. These are large, lumpy investments with long gestation periods. Returns are typically realized over long periods, beyond the investment horizons of most private enterprises. For some types of social overheads, many of the benefits are external economies, such as the flood control or recreation potential created by a power dam, which cannot easily be captured by limiting access and charging fees to users. Largely for this reason, the social marginal product of overhead capital is greater than the private marginal product. It was for such overhead projects, especially relating to water resources, that social cost–benefit analysis was developed and still makes its greatest contribution. Vast sums are involved in overhead projects. By ensuring that those implemented meet the social cost–benefit criteria described in Part III, government guards against the inefficient use of its capital and contributes to a lower overall capital–output ratio, hence to greater growth.

Not all of government's investments are in its capital or development budget. Expenditures on social overheads, especially education and health, are considered part of the recurrent budget and thus reduce the accounting measurement of government saving. The accounting distinction between capital and recurrent expenditures is simple enough: physical capital, such as roads, hospitals and schools, are considered part of investment; expenditures on consumable goods, such as medicines, and services, such as salaries of doctors and teachers, are part of government consumption. To the extent that these current outlays create greater human capacity for production, however, they should be considered part of investment, just as the salary of an engineer is charged to investment by the firm hiring him to design a new plant. However, as discussed in Part III, not all of expenditure on education and health can be shown to lead to greater productive capacity. The distinction between investment and consumption will inevitably be fuzzy, and in such circumstances the simpler accountant's definition is likely to prevail.

Governments of all ideological hues, especially those in the third world, are increasingly turning to publicly owned enterprises to produce goods and services that can be, and traditionally have been, produced by the private sector. This is an old story for utilities, railroads and other so-called 'natural monopolies'. But the trend extends to manufacturing, agriculture, banking and other sectors. Many reasons for this trend have been advanced, the most general being that government wishes these enterprises to achieve social goals that private owners are unlikely to serve as effectively. However, attention to such social goals—employment, provision of cheap services to target groups, regional development—often comes at the expense of efficient operation of the enterprise. This is a complex subject, outside the scope of this casebook, but one of growing importance in development. The point is that, with government's equity investment in its own firms growing as a share of its development outlays, economists need to pay more attention to the theory of public enterprises and to government as an equity investor.

The fourth way in which government invests in development is to channel part of its saving through financial intermediaries to the private sector. This may be done because government considers itself a more effective saver than investor, that is, it can raise more tax revenue than it has productive projects to spend them on. Alternatively, government may be using its tax capacity to channel investments into sectors that the private sector might not otherwise develop. It may also consider that the provision of some government loan capital will stimulate private saving by increasing the yield on equity investments in private enterprises.

The last possibility leads to another mechanism that developing country governments have used extensively to promote private investment: tax relief. Rather than channel its saving to private investors, governments forgo potential revenues—and thus reduce potential future government saving—in order to raise the return on private investment and stimulate more of it. If the investment would have been made anyway, the tax relief is redundant and revenues are really lost. If the relief stimulates saving and investment that would not otherwise have taken place, then no revenue is forgone because none would have been forthcoming without the investment.

Investment incentives through tax relief have taken several forms. A common one in the industrial countries is the investment tax credit, under which a fraction of investment can either be written off against profits in calculating taxes, or else can be taken as a credit, dollar-for-dollar, against income (i.e. profit) taxes due. A closely related incentive, accelerated depreciation, does not reduce taxes, but delays their payment and thus increases the investor's internal rate of return to equity. Developing countries have tended to employ tax holidays, especially to attract foreign investors. Under this incentive, no tax need be paid on profits for a specified period. In order to counteract the incentive to use capital that is imparted by these tax relief schemes, some governments have made incentives dependent on the amount of labor employed. Others have provided tax credits, based on export earnings, to compensate in part for the discouraging effects of overvalued exchange rates. Finally, relief from duties on imported inputs have characterized the promotional schemes of many countries.

It is difficult to judge whether these incentives really induce additional investment, domestic or foreign, or are generally redundant. On the one hand, calculations using commercial project appraisal can demonstrate that some incentives, such as tax holidays and import duty relief, can have a substantial effect on the internal rate of return to equity. On the other hand, surveys of investors have generally shown that tax incentives are far down the list of conditions important to investment decisions (Lent, in Bird and Oldman, 1975).

DISTRIBUTIONAL EQUITY

It has been an underlying tenet of neoclassical welfare economics that resources could be allocated efficiently, whatever the distributional consequences, and that equity goals should be achieved by transfers—taxes and subsidies—through the fiscal system. In the ideal case, these transfers could not themselves alter incentives to work, save, use efficient techniques, and so forth. Although no one suggests that the ideal is achievable, there remains a consensus among policy-makers in most countries that the fiscal system should bear a burden for reducing economic disparities, even at the cost of some efficiency. In Part III, we discussed the implications of equity goals for project selection. This section focuses on the role of taxes and expenditures more generally in achieving a more equitable distribution of income.

Economic science is not equipped to say what an equitable distribution of income and wealth ought to be, nor can it prescribe how tax burdens and expenditure benefits ought to be shared. The best economics can do is to suggest how taxes might be imposed and expenditures made to achieve alternative redistributive goals with a minimum of disincentives to production. (See, for example, Musgrave and Musgrave, 1976, Chapter 16.) For this task the underlying concept is that of *incidence*. Although the concept has three alternative definitions (see Musgrave and Musgrave, 1976, pp. 379–380), it will be adequate for our purposes to slight these distinctions and deal only with *budget incidence*, the average effect on family income of both taxes and expenditures. If, for example, a family with an annual income of $ 10 000 pays, directly or indirectly, taxes of $ 2750 a year, then its tax incidence is 27.5 percent. If it also receives the benefits of transfers and government expenditures, directly or indirectly, of $ 2500 a year, then its expenditure incidence is 25 percent and its *net incidence*, the difference between the two, is −2.5 percent. If net incidence is higher (and positive) for low-income families than for high-income families, the fiscal system is redistributing in favor of the poor and is considered *progressive*; if net incidence declines (goes from negative to positive net benefits as income rises), the system is *regressive*.

In describing incidence, it was necessary to hedge and speak in terms of 'direct or indirect' burden and benefit. The direct or statutory burden of a tax can be misleading as a measure of incidence if the taxed unit, such as a manufacturing corporation, has the ability to *shift* its tax burden to other units, as by raising the price of its output to consumers. Potential shifting is a complex empirical question which depends upon the nature of the tax and of the markets for goods and factors. The partial shifting of an excise or sales tax from producers to consumers is a familiar problem to all students who have taken even one course in microeconomics: more is shifted to the consumer, the less elastic is demand relative to supply. Similar issues arise with other taxes. For example, the corporate income tax may be shifted partially from share-holders to consumers (that is, to households) if corporations with some monopoly power attempt to restore profits by raising prices; or particularly to labor if corporate owners are able to react by moving investment from a taxed sector to one paying lower taxes. Property taxes can also be shifted in similar ways. The outcome of tax shifting is a rather vexed empirical topic, one beyond the scope of this discussion. Its relevance is that studies of tax and expenditure incidence typically must employ heroic assumptions about the shifting of taxes, and these can significantly influence the results. Hence our knowledge of fiscal incidence is subject to a rather wide margin of error.

Incidence studies depend upon knowledge of consumption patterns and income sources, according to the income level or class of the family. Household budget surveys and national income accounts data can be used—'manipulated' may be a more appropriate word—for this purpose, as discussed in the next section and illustrated in Case 11. In tax incidence studies, assumptions are first made about shifting of various taxes to consumers of particular commodities or suppliers of particular factors of production. Then these shifted taxes are allocated to households in each income class based on the expenditure pattern and income sources of each income group. The incidence of government expenditure is handled in the same way.

Despite the margin of error introduced by required assumptions about shifting of taxes and expenditures, some general conclusions emerge from studies of incidence in developing countries. These have been summarized by McLure (1977). Citing studies for several Latin American countries, Greece, India, Kenya, Pakistan, Philippines and West Malaysia, McLure concludes that the poor tend to bear a considerable tax burden, amounting to 10 percent or more of income, but that taxes also tend to be progressive overall, especially at the very top of the income scale. However, despite overall progressivity, the tax system 'does not appear to contribute appreciably to the reduction of inequality in the distribution of income' in several countries, including Argentina, Guatemala, Kenya and the Philippines.

Details from studies of two very different countries—Colombia by McLure (see Musgrave and Gillis, 1971) and Tanzania by Huang (1976)—are consistent with McLure's general observations. They also yield similar results on the professivity of each type of tax. Income taxes in both countries are designed to be progressive and appear to be so in practice, although to a greater extent in Tanzania than Colombia. Taxes on corporate income, despite assumptions that these are half shifted to consumers, nevertheless show progressivity, more so in Colombia than Tanzania. Taxes on goods, however, show a different pattern. With the exception of the progressive import duty in Tanzania, the general sales, excise and import taxes in both countries are progressive from the lowest to the middle income groups, but become regressive from then on. But taxes on alcohol, beer and tobacco are markedly regressive across all income classes in both countries. Taken as a whole, the tax system in Colombia is somewhat erratic, but slightly regressive, for the lower five income brackets, and progressive for the upper brackets; overall it is progressive. The result is dominated by the regressive sumptuary taxes on alcohol and tobacco at the lower end and the progressive taxes on income in the upper ranges. In Tanzania the tax system is quite progressive, largely because the income tax is, uncharacteristically, of dominant importance and because Huang included in-kind consumption, which is not taxed.

In reforming tax systems to achieve greater progressivity, two considerations should be borne in mind. First, there are severe limitations on the more intensive use of the most progressive of taxes, the individual income tax. Income taxes account for much less than half of total revenue in most developing countries. Any attempt to increase their contribution to progressivity by raising rates for higher income brackets may well meet with administrative difficulties, especially tax evasion. An alternative might be greater resort to property taxes, especially on urban and large rural holdings, as a means of taxing high-bracket income more effectively. Second, there may be scope in some countries for making commodity taxes more progressive than they are, by exempting commodities, such as food and clothing, with low income elasticities for which the poor expend a higher proportion of income than the rich (Ahluwalia, 1974, pp. 83–85). Note, however, the conflict between the sometimes extreme regressivity of taxes on beer and cigarettes and the desire by many governments to discourage, and hence to penalize, their consumption by means of taxation.

On the expenditure side, McLure's (1977) review of incidence studies includes only seven Latin American countries and West Malaysia. The results, with one exception, show high progressivity, as the poor receive benefits amounting to 50 percent or more of their income from private sources. Consequently the net budget incidence of the eight countries for which expenditure incidence was measured is strongly progressive, with the 'incomes of the poorest families commonly increased by 30 percent or more, [while] the most affluent families lose as much as 3 to 10 percent [or more] of income in the fiscal process.' McLure is very skeptical of incidence comparisons among countries, largely because of the assumptions necessary to make estimates. However, the general impression of a progressive fiscal structure seems valid.

STABILIZATION

Earlier we spoke of the elasticity of the tax system as a measure of its ability to increase revenues over the long run as incomes rise. This same concept has another application in terms of economic stability. The more elastic the tax structure, the more revenues rise automatically with upswings in money income—whether resulting from rises in output or from inflation—and the more such upswings are dampened by the leakage of private incomes into government revenue. Similarly, in downswings, as incomes fall and tax revenues automatically follow, greater elasticity means a greater reduction in this leakage, hence dampening the downswing and limiting unemployment. This stabilization of aggregate demand has been an important aim of fiscal policy in the industrial world. Despite the inability of fiscal stabilizers alone to control inflation in recent years, their use has unquestionably improved the ability of governments to guide their economies and automatic stabilizers remain an important legacy of the Keynesian revolution.

This stabilizing role of the tax system is applicable to both industrial and developing countries. Its importance is probably not as great in the third world, however, because foreign trade, rather than domestic demand, is likely to be the principal cause of destabilizing shocks. If export prices rise, for example, fiscal stabilizers will certainly dampen the effect on disposable income and aggregate demand, and thus reduce the inflationary impact. However, more can be achieved by attacking the problem at its source, applying a variable tax to major export commodities. Then exporters' incomes will not rise by the full amount of the price increase and the initial impetus to demand expansion is restrained. Many countries apply variable export duties on commodities like copper, rubber and palm oil. In extreme cases, as with cocoa in Ghana, the price to producers is fixed in domestic currency, so that none of the price swing is passed on to the producer.

If export production rises, the stabilizing effect of the variable tax is much reduced. At constant prices, revenues increase only proportionally, a case of unit elasticity. If, however, the country commands enough of the market to cause world prices to fall, the elasticity could fall below one and the tax would be destabilizing (that is, revenues rise less than income). In that case, a greater burden falls on the general stabilizing properties of the total tax and expenditure system.

Where import controls have been imposed and tend to be relaxed in times of buoyant export earnings, the revenue yield to government and its stabilizing effect are reinforced because additional imports bring additional tariff revenue. Controls used this way are, however, destabilizing to domestic producer incomes. They cause swings in the supplies of imported inputs, which in turn causes swings in output and employment in domestic manufacturing. Also, if the imported supply of consumer goods varies with export earnings, competing domestic manufacturers may be forced to vary their production on that account.

Perhaps the real problem of fiscal stabilization lies not in the automatic features of the tax system, but rather in government's reaction to increased revenues. Stabilization depends on the net effect of increased taxes on government's deficit. If higher revenues are taken as a signal to increase expenditures, much or all of the stabilization effect could be cancelled. Government deficits are, to a considerable extent, funded by the central bank through money creation. Stabilization depends upon a reduction in the growth of the money supply under inflationary pressure and its increase during recession. If government is unable to resist the pressures for higher expenditures, especially during booms, the central bank is unlikely to be able to carry the burden for stabilization alone. In short, government must not only increase its saving over time to promote growth, but it must also permit its saving to vary counter-cyclically to promote stabilization.

Finally, these swings in government's budgetary balance must, in the absence of import controls, be matched by swings in external reserves. If variations in domestic income are dampened by fiscal action, then the demand for imports will vary less than export earnings. Hence reserves will fluctuate. Here, again, it may require a strong government to resist the pressures to spend reserves as they accumulate (along with budgetary surpluses) during export booms. But those reserves will be required during export slumps in order to stabilize incomes and imports.

Income distribution

DISTRIBUTION IN ECONOMIC THEORY

By the 1970s, many development economists had begun to agree with Chenery (1974), that 'more than a decade of rapid growth in underdeveloped countries has been of little or no benefit to perhaps a third of their population.' It was not that distributional concerns were neglected in early development plans, since almost all of them contained fulsome statements about raising the living standards for the mass of people, increasing employment opportunities for the unemployed, and providing better housing, health and social amenities for the poor. But these benefits were to be achieved as a natural consequence of rapid growth and not through deliberate policies. In the final analysis it appeared that rapid growth had often failed to 'trickle down' to improve the welfare levels of the very poor.

Discussions of income distribution usually concentrate on two basic divisions: the functional and the personal (or size) distribution. *Functional distribution* is the division of income between labor and property. Often these categories are subdivided, with labor income split between wages, salaries and executive compensation; while property income is frequently divided into income from rents, interest and dividends. A third category, income from unincorporated enterprises, must also be divided between labor and property income, a division which must usually rely on some ingenious statistical device in the absence of firm data. *Personal (or size) distribution* is the division of income among individuals or families according to the level of income earned[4].

Functional distributions are usually explained in terms of marginal productivity theory, which suggests that factors of production receive incomes corresponding to the market value of their contribution to production. While marginal productivity theory has an appealing normative flavor, it is based on a highly abstract concept of the market place and is unable to explain the role of education and its relationship to income, the persistence of discrimination and the level of profits earned by entrepreneurs or capitalists. Despite the mathematical elegance of marginal productivity theory, it is at best an incomplete explanation of the functional distribution of income.

Economists have enjoyed even less success in prescribing a desirable size distribution of income, the concept more relevant to concerns about interpersonal welfare (Atkinson, 1970). To derive egalitarian conclusions about the distribution of income, modern welfare economists have had to employ questionable assumptions about measurable utility and interpersonal comparisons[5]. Despite the lack of a theoretical foundation, economists recognize the need to take account of income distribution in development. One basis for this outlook is the realization that individuals behave as if the welfare of the poor does matter and societies reflect such concern, at least to some extent, in their legal and economic framework. There is a measure of genuine altruism in most societies. While the concern for income distribution is a reflection of this, it should be noted that such altruism is typically focused on the provision of some minimum income or consumption level rather than on an optimal distribution of income. Without a satisfactory theory relating distribution to growth, it is inevitable that the possibility of a trade-off between growth and equity will be a contentious issue[6].

MEASURING INEQUALITY

The degree of inequality in the size distribution of incomes can be expressed in a number of summary statistics, each of which suffers from some shortcoming. The coefficient of variation is defined as the standard deviation of the income distribution divided by its mean. It is not much used because it fails to account for the skewness of the distribution, has no finite upper bound and is influenced by extreme values. Three widely used measures meet some or all of these short-comings: the Pareto coefficient, the Gini coefficient and the Theil index[7].

The Pareto distribution, which usually fits the upper end of the income distribution, is defined as:

$$N = AY^{-b} \tag{V.31}$$

or

$$\log N = A - b \log Y_I \tag{V.31a}$$

where Y is the level of income, above the mode, and N the proportion of income receivers with incomes equal to or greater than Y. The value of A is dependent on the units of measurement used and has no economic significance. The value of b, the *Pareto coefficient*, is independent of the choice of units and is a measure of income distribution, being larger in absolute value for more unequal distributions and smaller for more equal ones. Values around 2.0 are found for many developing countries and values around 1.5 are more common for developed countries. While the Pareto function describes only the upper part of the income distribution, it is used frequently. Income tax data, which in developing countries generally only cover the upper part of the distribution, are frequently available to compute b. In the absence of more complete data on income distribution, it is often the best measure of inequality one can derive.

A more complete measure of income concentration begins with the cumulative distribution of income received by all individuals or households. These data yield a *Lorenz curve*, which is plotted on a graph showing the cumulative percentage of income receivers on the horizontal axis and the cumulative percentage of total income received

TABLE 1 Hypothetical income distribution data

Percent of population	Cumulative percentages	Percent of income	Cumulative percentages
0–10	10	0.9	0.9
10–20	20	3.7	4.6
20–30	30	5.1	9.7
30–40	40	6.3	16.0
40–50	50	7.7	23.7
50–60	60	9.0	32.7
60–70	70	10.6	43.3
70–80	80	12.8	56.1
80–90	90	16.0	72.1
90–100	100	27.9	100.0

on the vertical axis. A hypothetical income distribution is shown in the table above and used to derive the Lorenz curve in the figure opposite. The 45° line indicates perfect equality: along it, x percent of the total population received x percent of total income. At the opposite extreme, if all income goes to one person, the curve degenerates to the horizontal and vertical axes. The larger the area between the line of equality and the Lorenz curve—the 'area of concentration' in the figure—the greater the degree of inequality.

The *Gini coefficient*, G, is a measure of this degree of income inequality. It is defined as the ratio of the area of concentration (A) to the total area under the line of equality ($A + B$). In the absence of negative incomes, the Gini coefficient has limits of zero, indicating perfect equality, and one, if all income goes to one person.

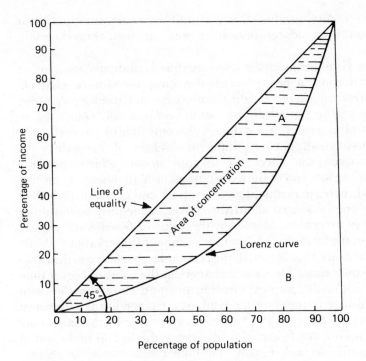

Hypothetical Lorenz curve

Two alternative formulae for deriving the Gini coefficient (G) are considered here, although a number of methods for deriving a value for G are extant[8]. Suppose there are n individuals (households) with income y_i $(i = 1, 2, 3, \ldots n)$ labeled in ascending order,

$$y_1 \leqslant y_2 \leqslant y_3 \leqslant \ldots \leqslant y_n$$

Let F_i be the cumulative population share corresponding to the ith individual, and Y_i the cumulative income share with $F_0 = Y_0 = 0$. Then we can define the Gini coefficient as

$$G_1 = 1 - \sum_{i=0}^{n-1} (F_{i+1} - F_i)(Y_{i+1} + Y_i) \tag{V.32}$$

or, alternatively, as

$$G_2 = \sum_{i=1}^{n-1} (F_i Y_{i+1} - F_{i+1} + Y_i) \tag{V.33}$$

For the data shown in the table the value of G is 0.3818.

The Gini has a number of useful properties. Its value is independent of mean income, so that if everyone's income is increased by the same proportion, the value of G remains unchanged. Moreover, the measured inequality is reduced, as it should be, by any transfer from a richer person to a poorer person as long as their ranks remain unchanged.

While the Gini coefficient is often used as a summary measure of income distribution, it has several faults. First, the Gini is relatively insensitive to change in income distribution. Second, its observed range of variation within countries over time seems small, compared to possible sampling errors in the data on income. Third the coefficient does not distinguish between different *locations* of inequality; for example between the effects of unemployment, which increases inequality at the low end of the distribution, or high monopoly profits, which would increase inequality at the upper end of the distribution. Presumably one's concern about the degree of inequity would differ between these two cases. Moreover, the value of G will vary slightly depending on the formula used and the number of observations. While such differences are usually small, they can be large relative to the likely change in G over time. Thus small changes in the value of G over time could result from either improvements in income distribution, the use of different formulae to measure the Gini, or a change in the number of observations used to derive the coefficient. For example, the data in the table yields a Gini coefficient of 0.3818 using the first formula and of 0.3762 using the second. Finally, the Gini coefficient is not readily decomposable into inequality measures for sub-groups of the population. As will be seen in Case 11, such decomposition can be useful in analyzing the contribution of various sub-groups, such as urban and rural dwellers, to overall inequality.

The *Theil index*, T, has all the desirable properties of the Gini coefficient and is also decomposable. It is defined as

$$T = \sum_{i=1}^{n} \left(\frac{y_i}{Y}\right) \log\left[\left(\frac{y_i}{Y}\right) n\right]$$

where $Y = \sum^{n} y_i$ = total income.

When there is perfect equality, $T = 0$; with perfect inequality, $T = 1$.

Like the Gini coefficient, the Theil index, T, is relatively insensitive to small changes at low income levels. Although it is useful in describing distribution data, the Theil index cannot be derived from any known probability distribution.

Whatever the limitations of inequality indicators, the data on the income distribution create more problems. The primary sources are surveys providing data on incomes and, in some cases, on consumption and other socio-economic characteristics of the units (individuals or households) sampled. Reliable data of this kind are scarce[9]. First, income is inherently difficult to measure. Properly defined, it should include transfers, non-wage income and income-in-kind, and include only permanent income stripped of its transitory components. Extensive questionnaires and lengthy interviews are necessary to collect such data. Yet in practice questions on income are often added as afterthoughts to surveys dealing with other matters. Second, appropriate price indices to convert changes in money incomes to real values are often lacking. There is some evidence to suggest that the price deflators relevant for different groups move at different rates; this would be true in economies marked by highly segmented markets, as when urban dwellers consume many imported goods, while rural households consume a narrow range of local commodities. Under such conditions, unless suitable deflators are available, it is not possible to assess changes over time with any confidence. Third, data obtained from surveys are frequently inconsistent with national accounts. Anand (1980) notes that discrepancies of 25 percent between national accounts estimates of personal income and those derived from survey data are common in most developing countries. Fourth, data are least satisfactory for low and high income households, the two portions of the distribution critical to measures of income inequality. The upper income groups receive a large portion of their income from non-wage sources which are difficult to trace and have an incentive to understate their incomes to avoid either taxes or social embarrassment. The poor often receive income in kind, the valuation of which poses many difficulties. Finally, there is no internationally accepted system for collecting and reporting data on the distribution of income, so international comparisons are suspect. In discussions of income inequality, the judgments of informed observers may often be more valid than comparisons based on supposedly scientific data.

THE KUZNETS HYPOTHESIS

Despite the poor quality of data, economists and other policy analysts have tried to formulate generalizations about changes in income distribution and poverty levels during the process of development. Kuznets (1955) conjectured that income inequality would first worsen as development began and eventually improve. If one were to plot the shares of the lowest income groups (e.g. the lowest 20 percent) against GNP per capita, the share would first decline, reach a low point, and then rise again, resulting in a U-shaped or 'Kuznets' curve. This hypothesis was tested by Kuznets (1963) who did find evidence that the early periods of growth were characterized by a period of increasing inequality in the size distribution of total income.

The simplest method for estimating a Kuznets curve from cross-country data is to specify that the income shares of different percentile groups are related to the level of per capita GNP, all measured in constant prices, by a quadratic relationship in the form:

$$S_i = a_i + b_i \log Y + c_i (\log Y)^2 + u_i \tag{V.35}$$

where S_i is the income share of the ith percentile group; Y is the level of GNP per capita; and u_i is a random error term. Considerable effort has gone into attempts to verify the existence of the Kuznets curve. Because few countries have sufficiently long time-series data on income distribution, nearly all efforts are based on cross-country data[10]. It is important to remember, however, that Kuznets's original formulation of the hypothesis involved time-series and not cross-section data. Perhaps the most careful analysis to date has been that of Ahluwahlia (1976), whose cross-country regressions support the U-curve hypothesis.

What can be learned from these cross-country studies? First, the socialist countries have the highest income equality, in large part because income from ownership capital does not accrue to the individual. Second, the developed countries are evenly split between those characterized by moderately uneven and relatively even income distributions. Finally, most of the underdeveloped countries show markedly greater inequality than the developed countries. According to Ahluwahlia (in Chenery *et al.*, 1974), about half of the underdeveloped countries fall in the high inequality range with another third displaying moderate inequality. The income share for the lowest two quintiles (a quintile is one-fifth of a population) in all developing countries averages about 13 percent of total income, but with considerable variation about the mean. For the industrialized countries the average income share of the lowest two quintiles is close to 18 percent.

Historical studies have two advantages over cross-section data. First, they can bring to bear a variety of source materials and other evidence on the assessment of survey data, thus establishing a more complete picture of development. Second, they can present a disaggregated view of changes in income distribution and poverty. Studies available for Brazil, Mexico, Malaysia, Korea, Sri Lanka, Indonesia, Taiwan and Kenya tend to confirm the downward portion of the 'Kuznets curve.' Among those economies that have exhibited sufficient growth to allow for a change in the level of development, inequality apparently increased in Brazil, Mexico, Malaysia, Indonesia and Kenya. The evidence for Colombia and the Philippines suggests no deterioration, but in both cases income distribution was already highly unequal, even before growth began. Taiwan and Korea stand apart. Taiwan has achieved both rapid growth and improvements in the distribution, while Korea has grown rapidly without worsening a relatively equal income distribution, although even the Korean findings have recently been challenged.

Even if the relative position of the poor may worsen as a country moves down the Kuznets curve, they probably do not suffer a decline in absolute real income or consumption levels, as some have alleged. Ahluwahlia's cross-country study (1976) finds little support for absolute impoverishment, despite strong evidence of worsening relative income. Note that all of this analysis is based on data covering broad

TABLE 2 Income distribution and growth

| | Economic state | |
	Before	After
Population		
Rural	80	60
Urban	20	40
Total	100	100
Wage rates ($)		
Rural	100	100
Urban	200	200
Income ($)		
Rural	8 000	6 000
Urban	4 000	8 000
Total	12 000	14 000
Per capita	120	140
Gini coefficient	0.1	0.2

income groups—the poorest 20 or 40 percent—and may well hide specific sub-groups for which real income has declined. And none of this denies that over short periods of rapid growth some absolute impoverishment may occur, even if the longer-term prospects are brighter.

There are hypotheses but no rigorous theory about the causes of the observed changes in equity. Kuznets argued that development typically involves accelerated growth in the high income, non-agricultural sectors, which slowly absorb population from agriculture. It is easy to show that such population shifts alone will worsen income distribution. Consider an economy with 80 persons employed in agriculture at $ 100 a year and 20 persons working in the industrial (and related urban) sector at an annual wage of $ 200. After some development (but assuming no population growth) has taken place, 20 people have shifted from agriculture to industry, as is shown in the table above. Per capita income was $ 120 before growth and has risen to $ 140, entirely because of the population shift to the higher income sector. Lorenz curves for the two stages are shown in the figure on page 234. Note that the area of concentration has increased and the Gini coefficient has doubled, from 0.1 to 0.2. This effect is reinforced by the greater weight now given to the modern industrial sector, which has a less equal internal income distribution than does the rural, agricultural sector.

This example illustrates another important feature often encountered in country data. Total income per capita has increased *and* 40 percent of the population is now better off. Thus, while income distribution has worsened, many of the poor are in better circumstances and no one is absolutely worse off. By Paretian rules, this is an improvement in welfare, despite a less equal distribution.

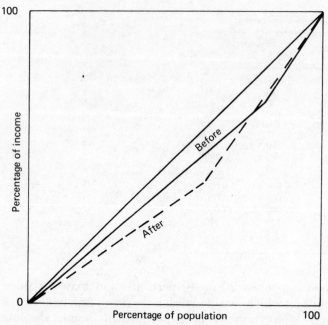

Lorenz curves with growth. Source: Table 2

Over time, the loss of rural labor will help raise agricultural labor productivity and serve to reduce intersectoral inequalities. Similarly, within the urban sector incomes will become more equal as labor skills improve and become more widely dispersed. These processes will ameliorate the original worsening of the income distribution. One obvious corollary is that employment opportunities in the modern sector must expand rapidly enough to absorb the available urban labor force. Policies which increase the demand for labor will raise real wages across the spectrum of the labor market even if, as many believe, the increase in total employment is small. Unfortunately, too often development policies, even those that are supposed to reduce poverty, tend to retard employment growth and frustrate the very objective they are meant to achieve. (See Part I for a fuller discussion of employment policies.)

Unequal distributions of wealth and access to capital produce even greater concentration in incomes (Ahluwahlia, in Chenery *et al.*, 1974). An important asset affecting income distribution is agricultural land, which is maldistributed in many developing countries. The problem of rural poverty is inseparably linked to the availability of land and to the capital needed to operate and improve it. Land reform often does not work because it is not effectively implemented or because inadequate provision is made to supply new smallholders with the capital, technology and modern inputs needed to raise incomes.

A number of dynamic forces tend to reinforce the concentration of incomes. First, differences in savings rates by income classes perpetuate the unequal distribution of wealth. From various country studies it appears that the lowest income groups save little while the bulk of household savings come from the top 10 to 15 percent of the income distribution. Second, there is evidence, less conclusive than that on savings, that the rate of population growth is faster among the poor than for society as a whole. If so there is a tendency toward greater dilution of capital owned by these groups and, in the case of the agricultural poor, increasing land fragmentation. Finally there is the question of access to capital, financial and human. Market fragmentation, institutional constraints and reliance on non-market allocation mechanisms all tend to work against the ability of the poor to raise finance, while poor education and few skills prevent them from being absorbed in an expanding modern sector. Education for the poor, especially improvements in literacy, can be important policy tools for reducing income differentials (Ahluwahlia, 1976, and in Chenery *et al.*, 1974).

Kuznets's original hypothesis suggested that eventually the 'trickle down' theory does work as development moves a country towards the upward slope of the U-curve. But it has been argued by some (Bacha, 1977) that the Kuznets curve has shifted so that developing countries today face a much steeper and longer downward slope and that the upward slope may never be reached. First, it is argued, the industrial countries experienced major political transformations following the two world wars, which greatly increased the degree of popular participation in the political process, established the state as a major agent for social welfare, and led to eventual reductions in inequality. The developing countries have not had similar socio-political transformations. Second, the Latin American dependency school holds that capitalist growth in the periphery requires inequality to generate demand patterns, based on import substitution and oriented towards foreign technology, which sustain the modern sector. With growth concentrated in this high technology sector, few employment opportunities are created and inequality is perpetuated. A similar phenomenon occurs where development is based on resource exploitation. In such economies a narrowly based, high-income, mining sector introduces a cleavage in technology and life-styles into a low-income traditional economy, exerting a profound effect upon income distribution which may persist over a long period. In all such cases there is a congruence of interests among the multinational corporations, domestic capitalists, government officials, labor unions and others to maintain the status quo. For radical analysts the basic conclusion is unequivocal: any sharp reduction in inequality requires far-reaching structural changes in the production structure, a process of change that may need to be violent and probably requires a determined reformist military government or a revolution.

GROWTH AND EQUITY

Rapid growth, as traditionally measured by increases in the gross national product, can be consistent with a worsening of the income distribution. GNP growth is a weighted average of the growth in its component shares. Because gross national product is equal to national income, the components of GNP could be either the sectors of production or income groups. Consider the data in the table below on GNP by income recipients.

TABLE 3 GNP by income recipients

| Population shares (%) | Gross national product | | Growth rate (%) |
	Year 0	Year 1	
20	50.0	55.00	10.0
20	25.0	26.88	7.5
20	15.0	15.75	5.0
20	7.0	7.21	3.0
20	3.0	3.09	3.0
100	100.0	107.93	7.93

In the base year the lowest 20 percent of the population receive some 3 percent of the national product; the upper quintile receive half. The economy as a whole grew at nearly 8 percent, a high rate of growth. This growth rate is equal to the rate of growth in income (or product) for each quintile weighted by each quintile's share in GNP in the base-year:

$$G_y = s_1 g_1 + s_2 g_2 + s_3 g_3 + s_4 g_4 + s_5 g_5 \qquad (V.36)$$

where G_Y is the growth rate in total GNP, s_i are the base-year income shares and g_i are the growth rates for the income of each of the population groups. In fact in the above example, and in many countries where the actual income distribution pattern is not too different, over 85 percent of the growth rate observed is determined by the growth rate of income for the top 40 percent of the income distribution. As a result of this pattern of growth, by year 1 the income share of the top 20 percent has risen to 51 percent, while the share of the lowest quintile has fallen to 2.9 percent.

Because GNP growth may mask a worsening of the income distribution, alternative measures, which would presumably yield a more accurate measure of welfare changes, have been proposed. Ahluwahlia (Chenery et al., 1974) suggests either weighting the growth rates for various income groups by their population share or using 'poverty' or welfare weights. If population, rather than income, shares are used, the GNP growth rate in the above example is only 5.7 percent. If we use 'poverty' weights, and arbitrarily assume these weights are inversely proportional to the base-year income weights, the poverty-weighted GNP growth rate is 3.9 percent[11].

Using population shares implies that society treats all increments of income equally, regardless of the recipient; use of poverty weights implies that society assigns a higher value to incomes going to the poor. If the poverty-weighted GNP growth rate is less than the traditionally measured GNP growth rate, growth will have worsened income distribution, and conversely. For example, Sri Lanka experienced an annual growth rate of only 5.0 percent over the period 1963–1970 as traditionally measured, but the growth rate was 7.2 percent by a poverty weights measure. Growth was apparently concentrated on the incomes of the poor. By contrast, in Brazil, where traditionally measured GNP grew at 6.9 percent per annum from 1960 to 1970, the poverty-weighted growth was only 5.4 percent and income distribution worsened (Chenery, *et al.*, 1974).

Although poverty-weighted GNP growth rates measure improvements in both total welfare and equity, they are not likely to become widely used. Economists have not been able to specify the welfare function needed to derive such weights, so those used have been largely arbitrary. Hence any objective evaluation of economic performance is lost and, because poverty weights might differ among countries, international comparisons would be meaningless. In any case, welfare-weighted GNPs are unnecessary. If income data are available by income groups for more than one year, the change in income distribution can be measured directly, using the Gini or Theil coefficients, and a separate indicator of poverty-weighted income growth is redundant.

A different measure of welfare enjoying some popularity is the Physical Quality of Life Index (*PQLI*). This index combines data on infant mortality, life expectancy at age 1, and literacy, and is supposed to meet the need for a non-income-based measure of physical well-being. Thus, for Sri Lanka, where income distribution improved in the 1960s, the *PQLI* rose from 65 in the 1950s to 80.1 in the 1970s. Proponents argue that, although data on the three social indicators combined in the *PQLI* are still of uneven quality, they are more readily available than data on income distribution. Moreover, these indicators measure development results rather than inputs. And being relatively unethnocentric and objective, they provide a reasonable standard for performance comparison. Life expectancy and infant mortality are surrogate measures for the availability of clean water, the well-being of mothers, the level of nutrition and the general environmental characteristics outside the home. Literacy not only indicates well-being, but is a measure of a skill important to development. The extent to which poor groups are literate helps determine the extent to which they are able to share the benefits of growth.

While the *PQLI* adds to our knowledge of how economic growth affects welfare, it is difficult to argue that it is superior to increases in income as measured by GNP. While there are a number of countries, such as Sri Lanka, which score high on the *PQLI* scale but low in terms of per capita income growth, there is a strong correlation between the *PQLI* and income per capita. As nations become wealthier, larger allocations are made to education, health, housing and other social services. Such increases may not be as rapid as the increase in total resources, nor is it inevitable that the poor receive the bulk of the benefits, but an improvement in the *PQLI* would almost inevitably result from improvements in economic well-being. Hence it is not clear how much additional information is captured by the *PQLI*. Moreover, the variables that make up the index reflect a narrow definition of well-being. If literacy is defined as being able to pass a simple reading test, does it tell much about the ability of a farmer to gain access to new technology? A transistor radio may be of greater value to a subsistence farmer, economically, intellectually and culturally, than the knowledge of a few written words. Similarly, the measure of health—infant mortality and life expectancy—may not measure happiness. To create a healthy population is only one goal of development. The provision of jobs, of cultural outlets, and of security are all part of well-being. The inadequacy of per capita GNP as a measure of total welfare cannot be denied, but it is not clear that the *PQLI* deals any more satisfactorily with the multifaceted nature of development.

Will redistributive policies reduce the rate of growth? In the absence of any theoretical framework relating growth and distribution, no definitive answer is possible. It has been argued that, because higher income groups provide the bulk of savings and the lack of savings is a major constraint on growth, an unequal income distribution is needed to generate required domestic savings. The reality is more complex. A number of experiments have been performed with input–output models. These show that if the initial income distribution is replaced by a more equal one, the savings rate will fall. But because the consumption basket of the lower income groups tends to be less capital- and import-intensive, the fall in savings and exports would be at least partly offset by a fall in the capital–output ratio and in import demand (Cline, 1972). However, the very aggregate nature of these input–output models masks the serious problem of how specific production technologies can be rapidly adopted to produce a different output. A country whose automobile assembly plants produce Mercedes-Benz cannot rapidly shift that plant to the production of agricultural tractors suited to small-scale farmers.

Land reform, a policy often carried out in the name of equity, may reduce growth if the agricultural sector is characterized by economies of scale, as would be the case for large-scale irrigation systems and plantation crops. Even without scale economies, there will probably be a short-run drop in output until the new landowners gain access to the inputs of capital, fertilizer and suitable mechanical implements, and learn how to use them productively.

Nationalization, a measure more often aimed at reducing the role of non-nationals than at redistributing income, may do little to promote, and may actually set back, a more equal distribution of incomes. In the absence of complementary policies, the main beneficiaries are likely to be, not the poor, but the bureaucrats and organized workers who run the enterprise after takeover. And if the climate of uncertainty created by nationalization reduces investment levels, future growth is also compromised. Nevertheless, there will be welfare gains if the nationalized firms generate a surplus which is appropriated by the treasury and used to finance poverty redressal projects, or if the nationalized firm produces mass consumption goods (or inputs used extensively in their production), the pricing of which was formerly influenced by a significant degree of monopoly[12]. The general conclusion to be drawn is that nationalization alone provides no panacea.

While it is difficult to be specific about the interactions between redistribution and growth, it is clear that the nature of the trade-off depends on the degree of equity aimed for. Even radical economists would agree that moves to establish an absolutely egalitarian distribution of income would severely reduce savings, retard innovation and reduce growth for some time. However, it seems extremely unlikely that the present gap between the rich and poor found in many developing countries is essential to growth. There probably is some trade-off between growth and equity, and it is a pressing task of development economics to measure it. Meantime, it is becoming widely acknowledged that a reduction in inequality is both desirable and necessary to achieve a sustained improvement in the welfare of the poor.

DISTRIBUTION POLICIES

Without a satisfactory theoretical framework, economists can only prescribe distribution policies with caution, based on partial analysis. And without reliable time-series data on distribution, we cannot even test the efficiency of alternative policies. Since all economic policies affect income distribution, the task of analysis is formidable. We focus here on those measures specifically designed to redress poverty and others which have strong distributional implications. Broadly speaking, income redistribution policies fall into three categories: those directly confronting the distribution of assets and wealth; those aimed at improving the economy's capacity to absorb the poor; and interventionist policies that try to alleviate the effects of poverty without attacking its root cause.

Two redistribution policies have already been mentioned: land reform and nationalization. Even assuming these measures are carried through, and not frustrated by the controlling elites, neither provides a guarantee that income distribution will become more equitable. Complementary measures must be taken to assure that the new owners can effectively use their newly acquired assets. Another policy tool is the increasing reliance on public enterprises which, though not primarily aimed at income redistribution, are sometimes charged with improving equity by providing jobs, increasing competition and capturing the 'commanding heights' of the economy. Analysis of the effect of public enterprises on income distribution is fairly simple. If the public enterprise operates more efficiently, reduces monopoly elements or undertakes risky, but economically sound, ventures which the private sector could not undertake, equity may be served. But in many cases public enterprises operate inefficiently behind special government protection and do not obviously promote income redistribution.

Worker management of firms will give labor control over profits as well as wages and presumably reduce worker alienation. Meade (1972) develops the equilibrium conditions for such a firm. He concludes that the profit-maximizing, labor-managed firm will reduce opportunities for new employment, but increase the returns to those already employed. This is so because the firm now aims at maximizing its surplus—price less current non-labor inputs—per worker rather than profits. A new worker will be hired only if his or her marginal revenue product exceeds wages *plus* profits per worker, a more stringent condition than that marginal revenue product exceeds wages alone. Free entry of firms would, however, lead to the same employment as under capitalist management. This analysis also holds for certain forms of cooperative which are a variant of the worker-operated firm. When labor and management objectives become merged, the result is usually higher wages for those employed at the cost of new jobs in that sector or firm. Whether this improves income distribution depends on whether sufficient employment opportunities exist elsewhere to absorb all the members of the labor force.

Because the distribution of human capital is an important determinant of income distribution, better access to education is said to improve equity, at least over the long run. However, statistical tests of this hypothesis often reject it. Note that even 'free' education is rarely costless and that the hidden costs are usually regressive, and borne more heavily by the poor. These hidden costs include the loss of the productive services of children attending school and the need to purchase paper and pencils, and even additional clothing (see Case 7). If education is to redistribute income effectively, the poor may need financial help to take advantage of such opportunities.

Policies that improve the efficiency and growth of the economy often improve income distributiion (see Part I). In labor-surplus economies, measures to create employment will improve equity as most unemployed are poor. Appropriate tax measures can help reduce the after-tax income of the rich, while many growth-promoting government development expenditures—especially those for rural infrastructure, public health and education—can provide services used predominantly by the poor. Improvements in financial markets usually increase access for small borrowers, who are excluded by the restrictive practices associated with controlled interest rates. Most direct interventions in the marketplace—minimum wage legislation, protectionist trade policies, credit restrictions, price supports, etc.—work against the poor, who have limited information, few extra-legal connections, no collateral and hence limited access to the restricted markets. Other elements of an economic package to improve income distribution might include rural public works, rural industries, expanded food production, promotion of labor-intensive manufactured exports and small-scale urban industries.

While many policy measures are available to improve income distribution, historically the size distribution of income appears to be stable even in the face of massive policy interventions. Changes in the Gini coefficient of more than five percentage points would seem to require the simultaneous application of a number of different policies, which together can induce massive structural change. Even these co-ordinated policies work slowly on income distribution[13].

An alternative approach is to alleviate poverty in the short run through direct intervention. This approach focuses on specific poverty groups and assumes that there is some objectively defined minimum level of income which everyone should attain, with government help if necessary. The first step is to define a 'poverty line', so that the economic and social characteristics of the poor can be clearly identified. This is a far from simple task, requiring a decision on whether absolute or relative poverty levels should be used, how to incorporate economies of scale in consumption, and what allowance to make for non-essential expenditures. Once the necessary data have been obtained, it should be possible to design specific programs and policies aimed at redressing poverty, and monitor their progress over time. But this is not a simple task and may well require a reorientation of the priorities and practices of statistical and planning offices.

The basic needs approach explicitly recognizes that improved welfare of the poor depends crucially on the provision of essential service—health, potable water, housing, sewerage facilities, education, etc.—which must be provided through the public sector (see Part I). Programs to provide such goods to the poor can vary from food stamps or subsidies to school lunch programs to nutrition fortification measures; from the construction of low-cost housing to rent supplements. The ultimate goal of all such measures is the same: to reduce the immediate effects of poverty and, by creating a better housed, fed and educated population, to allow the poor, or perhaps their children, to participate more effectively in economic development. While basic needs and other programs to redress poverty have been implemented in a number of countries, their effectiveness in improving the income distribution and permanently reducing poverty, especially if unaccompanied by other policy measures, remains to be demonstrated (see Srinivasan, 1977).

Notes

1   A full description of the model is in Jones (1976), Chapter 3.
2   For illustrations and a more complete discussion of the use of macroeconomic models, see Taylor (1979).
3   Demand elasticities are negative, of course. Here we work with the absolute value of the elasticity for convenience.
4   Other distributions are of course possible, e.g. by occupation, geographic region, race or ethnic group, sex, and by nation states. We shall have little to say about these distributions here.
5   Two excellent introductions to the theory, facts and myths of income distribution are found in Jan Pen, *Income Distribution* (1971) and Martin Bronfenbrenner, *Income Distribution Theory* (1971).
6   Cline (1975) and Lal (1976) review the debate on this issue.
7   A large number of alternative measures are available, each of which falls short of a statistical ideal. See, for example, Pen (1971) and Shail Jain (1975).
8   This section draws heavily on Annex A of Sudhir Anand (1980).
9   Data on income distribution for a fairly large number of countries can be found in Shail Jain (1975); F. Paukert (1973); Adelman and Morris (1973); Chenery *et al.* (1974) and Ahluwahlia (1976). The quality of this data is often very poor, as the sources cited admit.
10 One of the earliest attempts was that of Adelman and Morris (1973) using 1960 income deciles for 44 countries.
11 This concept of poverty weights is akin to the weights sugested by some for use in social project analysis. See Part III.
12 Even if the pre-nationalized firm had no monopoly power, the nationalized firm might still charge a lower price for basic necessities *and* if the losses were made up by taxes on the rich, real income distribution would be imporved. See Bell in Chenery *et al.*, 1974.
13 cf. Adelman, Hopkins, Robinson, Rodgers and Wery (1979).

References

MACROECONOMIC FORECASTING MODELS

CHENERY, H. and STROUT, A. M. (1966). Foreign Assistance and Economic Development. *American Economic Review* **56,** 679–733
HARBERGER, A. C. (1972). *Project Evaluation: Collected Papers.* Chicago, University of Chicago Press
JONES, H. G. (1976). *An Introduction to Modern Theories of Economic Growth.* New York, McGraw-Hill
McKINNON, R. I. (1964). Foreign Exchange Constraints in Economic Development, *Economic Journal* **74,** 388–409
TAYLOR, L. (1979). *Macro Models for Developing Countries* (Economic Handbook Series). New York, McGraw-Hill

BALANCE-OF-PAYMENTS ADJUSTMENTS

BHAGWATI, J. N. (1978). *Foreign Trade Regimes and Economic Development: Anatomy and Consequences of Exchange Control Regimes.* Cambridge, Mass., Ballinger
BRUTON, H. S. (1970). The Import-Substitution Strategy of Economic Development. *The Pakistan Development Review* **10,** 123–146
COOPER, R. N. (1971). An Assessment of Currency Devaluation in the Developing Countries. In *Government and Economic Development* (Ed. by G. Ranis), pp. 472–512. New Haven, Yale University Press

KHAN, M. S. (1974). Import and Export Demand in Developing Countries. *IMF Staff Papers* **21–3,** 678–693
KINDLEBERGER, C. P. (1973). *International Economics.* Homewood, Illinois, Richard D. Irwin, Chapters 19–22 and Appendix G
KRUEGER, A. O. (1978). *Foreign Trade Regimes and Economic Development: Liberalization Attempts and Consequences.* Cambridge, Mass., Ballinger
SODERSTEN, B. (1970). *International Economics.* New York, Macmillan

PLANNING FISCAL REFORM

AHLUWALIA, M. S. (1974). The Scope for Policy Intervention. In *Redistribution with Growth* (Ed. by H. Chenery *et al.*), pp. 73–90. London, Oxford University Press
BIRD, R. M. and OLDMAN, O. (1975). *Readings on Taxation in Developing Countries.* Baltimore, Johns Hopkins University Press
CHENERY, H. and SYRQUIN, M. (1975). *Patterns of Development 1950–1970.* Baltimore, Johns Hopkins University Press
HUANG, Y. (March 1976). Distribution of the Tax Burden in Tanzania. *Economic Journal* **86,** 73–86
McLURE, C. E. Jr. (June 2–4 1977). Fiscal Economics and the Distribution of Income in Developing Countries. Paper presented at the conference Distribution, Poverty and Development, Bogota, Colombia
MUSGRAVE, R. A. and MUSGRAVE, P. B. (1976). *Public Finance in Theory and Practice.* New York, McGraw-Hill
MUSGRAVE, R. A. and GILLIS, S. M. (1971). *Fiscal Reform for Colombia.* Cambridge, Mass., International Tax Program, Harvard Law School
WORLD BANK (1977). *World Tables 1976.* Washington, D.C.

INCOME DISTRIBUTION

ADELMAN, I and MORRIS, C. T. (1973). *Economic Growth and Social Equity in Developing Countries.* Stanford, California, Stanford University Press
ADELMAN, I., HOPKINS, M. J. D., ROBINSON, S., RODGERS, G. B. and WERY, R. (1979). A Comparison of Two Models for Income Distribution Planning. *Journal of Policy Modeling* **1,** 37–82
AHLUWAHLIA, M. (1976). Inequality, Poverty and Development. *Journal of Development Economics* **III,** 307–342
ANAND, S. (1980). *Inequality and Poverty in Malaysia: Measurement and Decomposition.*
ATKINSON, A. B. (1970). On the Measurement of Inequality. *Journal of Economic Theory* **2,** 244–263
BACHA, E. L. (1977). The Kuznets Curve and Beyond: Growth and Changes in Inequalities. Harvard Institute for International Development Discussion Paper No. 29
BRONFENBRENNER, M. (1971). *Income Distribution.* Chicago, Aldine-Atherton
CHENERY, H. B., *et al.* (1974). Redistribution with Growth. London, Oxford University Press
CLINE, W. R. (1972). *Potential Effects of Income Redistribution on Economic Growth: Latin American Cases.* New York, Praeger
CLINE, W. R. (1975). Distribution and Development: A Survey of Literature. *Journal of Development Economics* **1,** 359–400
JAIN, S. (1975). *The Size Distribution of Income: A Compilation of Data.* Baltimore, Johns Hopkins University Press
KUZNETS, S. (1955). Economic Growth and Income Inequality. *American Economic Review* **45,** 1–28
KUZNETS, S. (1963). Quantitative Aspects of the Economic Growth of Nations: Part VIII—Distribution of Income by Size. *Economic Development and Cultural Change* **XI,** Part II

LAL, D. (1976). Distribution and Development: A Review Article. *World Development* **4,** 725–738

MEADE, J. E. (1972). The Theory of Labor-Manager Firms and of Profit Sharing. *Economic Journal* **82,** Supplement 402–428

PAUKERT, F. (1973). Income Distribution at Different Levels of Development: A Survey of the Evidence. *International Labour Review*

PEN, J. (1971). *Income Distribution*. Harmondsworth, Middlesex, England, Penguin

SRINIVASAN, T. N. (1977). Development, Poverty and Basic Human Needs: Some Issues. *Food Research Institute* **XVI,** 11–28

Macroeconomic Forecasts for 1978 and 1979

In March of each year, the Ministry of Finance, joining together with the economic staff of the Central Bank and the Macroeconomic Planning Unit of the Ministry of Economic Planning (MEP), form the Inter-Ministerial Planning Group (IMPG), which has the task of preparing a set of macroeconomic projections. These projections, which all government ministries and agencies accept for planning purposes, will be published in the *Economic Survey* that accompanies the budget for fiscal year 1978/79.

No systematic methodology for making these projections has been developed. In past years the procedure was to build up an estimate of gross domestic product from various economic indicators, such as the expected level of copper prices and likely yields in agriculture. Against this supply-based forecast, an estimate would be made of aggregate demand—the likely level of investment, exports, public and private consumption—and a consensus would be reached through a process of discrete adjustments. This year the chief of the MEP, Ms Stringla, proposes that a simple macroeconomic model be estimated and used. She feels that, despite its simplicity, the model will add rigor to an exercise which has so far lacked it. The model put forward consists of four structural equations and one identity, as follows:

$$GDP = f(k, INV)$$
$$IMP = f(GDP)$$
$$PC = f(GDP, PC_{t-1})$$
$$GC = f(GC_{t-1}; t)$$
$$GDP = PC + GC + INV + IS + EXP - IMP$$

where

GDP = gross domestic product at market prices;
INV = investment (fixed);
PC = private consumption;

245

GC = government consumption;
IS = changes (investment) in stocks;
EXP = exports of goods and non-factor services;
k = incremental capital–output ratio; and
t = time.

Ms Stringla, who has just returned from a year's study leave, argues that this approach will take advantage of the more powerful econometric tools now available to planners. Because it only requires that two exogenous variables (investment and changes in stocks) be estimated, the model requires less data than the supply-oriented approach*.

In line with the Planning Minister's general outlook, Ms Stringla argues that government investment must be stepped up if the economy is to be raised out of its doldrums. Government capital formation, which averaged 33 percent of total fixed investment over the period from 1956 to 1970, is now running at a rate close to 25 percent of total investment and, perhaps most important, has shown a decline in real terms over the past three years. Thus the Planning Ministry suggests that government fixed investment be allowed to grow by 8 percent in 1978 and by 10 percent in 1980, both in real terms. Private investment, sensitive to the poor economic performance since 1974, could be expected to grow by perhaps 4 percent in 1978 and 7 percent in 1979. This information, Ms Stringla suggests, is sufficient to project total investment. The other exogenous variable, changes in stocks has always been treated as a residual and Ms Stringla notes that in any event there are no rigorous theories of stock formation, especially at an aggregate level.

She therefore suggests that after three years of declining stocks, one can assume that over the next two years there will be some stock accumulation and suggests that real stock changes be set at an increase of Lp 145m in 1978 and Lp 180m in 1979.

The representative from the Ministry of Finance, Mr Chochmo, argues that there is little basis to believe the Stringla model will produce reasonable results and suggests that the traditional approach to estimating gross domestic product be followed. He then outlines the data at hand for estimating GDP by producing sectors. To project the agriculture sector, Mr Chochmo uses the information shown in *Table 1*, which brings together data on the structure of value added in that sector and on the physical level of production.

For the mining and quarrying sector the main indicators are the production levels for copper, other metals and quarrying. The relevant data are shown in *Table 2*.

For the manufacturing sector, the Ministry of Finance representative argued that there is evidence of an upturn in activity. The industrial

---

* The model is adopted from an MA thesis. See Q. R. Stringla (1977). An Econometric Macro-Model for a Data-Scarce Economy: the Case of Beracia. Unpublished MA dissertation, University Merbahaya

TABLE 1 Value added production index for agriculture (1975=100)

		Production index			
		Actual		Forecast	
Commodity	Weight	1976	1977	1978	1979
Cotton	30.1	101.2	105.4	114.0	124.0
Timber	19.3	104.8	109.6	115.6	123.1
Rice (unmilled)	16.5	104.5	109.0	124.8	140.7
Livestock	8.7	106.6	111.5	118.3	122.4
Fish	7.3	102.0	101.8	103.0	105.0
Other grains	6.1	103.5	106.8	112.5	116.8
Miscellaneous	4.5	105.7	108.8	116.1	119.7
Pepper	2.3	98.1	101.2	106.2	110.3
Pineapple	2.2	85.3	106.2	129.8	130.0
Coconut	1.9	97.1	98.6	100.0	101.4
Tea	1.1	96.0	92.5	88.5	85.0
Total	100.0	102.7	107.2	115.3	123.4

Source: Value added weights and growth rates for 1975–1976: Department of Statistics; 1977–1979 data from various agencies: Ministry of Agriculture; Department of Fisheries; and Tea Board.

TABLE 2 Value added production index for the mining and quarrying sector (1975=100)

		Production index			
		Actual		Projected	
Commodity	Weight	1976	1977	1978	1979
Copper	80.7	99.1	102.3	107.9	114.6
Tin	5.3	127.7	124.0	130.0	135.0
Iron ore	4.1	101.3	102.8	104.2	107.5
Other metals	3.7	105.6	107.6	109.1	112.5
Quarrying	6.2	107.4	102.5	105.4	110.0
	100.0	101.5	103.7	108.8	115.0

Source: Value added weights and growth rates for 1975–1976: Department of Statistics; projections based on data from Ministry of Natural Resources.

production index for the last half of 1977 showed a dramatic improvement over its level recorded during the first half of the year, increasing by 6.4 percent over the level of a year earlier. He argues that this information, plus the continuing strong demand for import licenses, indicates a growth in large-scale manufacturing of 7.5 percent in 1978 and 8.5 percent in 1979. Small-scale indistries, an area about which relatively little is known, will continue to be extrapolated at an annual rate of 2.6 percent, following long tradition.

For the construction sector, Mr Chochmo projected an acceleration in construction activity, principally because the Finance Minister would present an 'activist budget with sharply higher development expenditures.' Construction is a major component of development expenditures.

Turning to the other sectors, Mr Chochmo noted that 'statistical relationships' used in the past seemed to work well and he saw no reason to abandon this tested methodology. Thus for the wholesale and retail trade sector he suggested the following econometric form:

$$\ln VA(WRT) = a + b \ln VA(AG + Mn + Mg)$$
where $VA(WRT)$ = value added in the wholesale and retail trade sector; and
$$VA(Ag + Mn + Mg) = \text{the sum of value added in agriculture, mining and manufacturing}$$

For the transport, storage and communication sector the functional form suggested is:

$$\ln VA(TSC) = a + b \ln VA(Ag + Mn + Mg + WRT + Cn)$$
where $VA(TSC)$ = value added in transport, storage and communications;

and $VA(Ag + Mn + Mg + WRT + Cn)$ = the sum of value added in agriculture, mining, manufacturing, wholesale–retail trade and construction.

Electricity, gas, water, sanitary services and all other services, Mr Chochmo suggested, should be assumed to comprise a constant proportion of the value added in all other sectors.

After some debate on which methodology to use, the representative from the National Bank, Mr Kwacha, took the floor. He pointed out that advances and loans to the manufacturing sector had risen by 15.7 percent in 1977 and this, he argued, confirms the expected sharp upturn in manufacturing activity. Similarly, advances to the construction sector had also shown a substantial increase in 1977, rising by 11.4 percent. Admittedly, new licenses for manufacturing plants did not show an upturn in 1977. Data from the Ministry of Industry shows that new manufacturing permits increased by only 5 percent in 1977 over 1976 and data for the first few weeks of 1978 showed only another marginal increase.

Mr Kwacha then suggested that it would be useful to prepare the macroeconomic projections using both methodologies. In this way he suggested that one projection would provide a cross-check on the other and in the final analysis a reconciliation of the two approaches was needed. He suggested that the following points be addressed in reports to be tabled at the next meeting:

Questions

1. To what extent does the Stringla model produce acceptable results?
2. What modifications to the model should be incorporated immediately and which modifications, while desirable, must await development of better statistics and additional time to carry out research?

3. What statistical problems have been encountered in estimating the model?
4. How do the results of the two approaches compare and how can the differences be reconciled?
5. What alternative methodology might be implemented in the future to ensure better consistency between the supply and demand projections?

Further reading

BEHRMAN, J., and HANSON, J. A. (1979). *Short-term Macroeconomic Policy in Latin America*. Cambridge, Mass., National Bureau of Economic Research

FRANK, C. R., Jr., KIM, K. S. and WESTPHAL, L. E. (1975). *Foreign Trade Regimes and Economic Development: South Korea*. New York, National Bureau of Economic Research, Chapters 8 and 9

GHATAK, S. (1978). *Development Economics*. London, Longman

Balance-of-Payments Crisis

INTERNAL MEMORANDUM
NATIONAL BANK OF BERACIA   January 21, 1978

To: Balance-of-payments Advisory Committee.

From: Auric Dackhtilo, Governor.

   The attached memorandum from the Finance Minister will be presented to
the Economic Advisory Committee of the Cabinet at its next regular meeting.
The Prime Minister has asked me to comment on the Finance Minister's
proposal before that meeting. This gives us an opportunity to prepare our own
policy proposal—both short- and long-term—to address Beracia's balance-of-
payments crisis. In formulating such a policy proposal, you should consider the
following:

(1)   How realistic is the balance-of-payments projection prepared by the
      Ministry of Finance? In particular, are export supply and import demand
      likely to be as responsive to the Ministry's policy package as they forecast?
      (The attached forecasts for world prices of key commodities may be helpful
      in making these judgements.) Since we have not been able to complete our
      proposed study of price elasticities in Beracian trade, it will be necessary to
      back up any alternate projections of our own with elasticity measurements
      from other countries. I understand that the IMF staff has done these from
      time to time.
(2)   Does the policy package suggested by the Minister seem likely to achieve its
      promised results? If not, what alternative set of policies should we propose
      to the Cabinet?
(3)   What are the aggregate demand implications of the Minister's proposals,
      including his budget projections? Does it seem likely that the suggested
      policies will generate sufficient additional saving to yield the improved
      balance on current account that the Ministry projects?
(4)   What are the implications for monetary policy of any set of policies that you
      recommend and of those suggested by the Minister?
(5)   Finally, the Prime Minister is especially concerned with the effect of any
      foreign exchange policies on the poorest 60 percent of the country's families.
      Can you assess that effect and make suggestions to ameliorate any hard-
      ships caused by the policies we recommend?

CENTRAL BANK OF BERACIA

Prices of Selected Traded Commodities

Commodity	1970	1974	1975	1976	1977 (Jan–June)	1978	1979	1980	1985
Copper bars, (LME, $/tonne)	64.1	93.4	56.1	63.5	63.5	69.0	76.2	89.9	96.1
Cotton (Mexican, at Liverpool, c/lb)	30.7	66.2	55.9	79.3	81.7	71.4	70.2	68.0	69.0
Logs (Lauan, Manila, $/m³)	43.0	82.0	67.5	92.0	107.0	114.8	116.8	123.8	134.2
Rice (Bangkok, $/tonne)	144.0	542.0	363.1	254.5	258.4	292.1	329.6	373.2	373.2
Wheat (Canadian No. 1, $/tonne)	63.2	208.7	181.3	149.1	119.4	127.6	142.5	166.3	171.3
Maize (U.S. No. 2, Gulfports, $/tonne)	58.4	132.0	119.6	112.4	115.0	115.6	120.6	128.8	129.1
Steel (Germany, $/tonne)	124.9	250.0	300.8	329.5	314.6	—	—	—	—
Petroleum (Saudi Arabian light crude 34°, $/barrel)	1.30	9.80	10.70	11.50	12.10	12.10	12.70	13.30	13.90
Urea (Europe, $/tonne)	48.3	315.8	198.0	112.0	119.0	124.7	129.8	136.5	169.7
Import prices (non-oil LDCs, 1970 = 100)	100	191	187	199	n.a.	—	—	—	—

CABINET MEMORANDUM
Balance-of-payments Policies and Projections

1.   The severe and seemingly chronic deficit in our balance of payments was a major issue in the recent election. The Prime Minister and I agree that the election provided our Coalition Government with a mandate to attack that problem and, if necessary, to use radical measures to solve it. Preliminary estimates of the balance of external payments for calendar 1977, prepared for me by the National Bank of Beracia, indicate that the deficit on current account was $ 167m (Lp 1450m), compared with Lp 1514m in 1976 and Lp 2254m in 1975. Despite a further drawing of $ 11m from the IMF this year (on top of the major drawing of $ 46m under the special oil facility in 1976), the Central Bank lost another $ 13m of reserves in 1977. Nothing in our prospects for 1978 indicates a substantial improvement. The prices of some of our export commodities may be expected to rise on world markets, but the stagnation in exportable production is expected to continue in the absence of a stronger stimulus. Moreover, I am fearful that import controls, which have been effective for the past several years, may soon begin to lose effectiveness as importers become better able to circumvent regulations established by the Ministry of Trade. Thus, unless some drastic steps are taken, we can expect to see a major erosion of reserves in 1978.

2.   Certain principles should guide our approach to the balance-of-payments problem. First, any short-run solution must contain the seeds of long-run structural improvement consistent with renewed growth of the economy. Second, policies must be consistent with our reliance on the private sector to increase investment, especially in industry and agriculture, and to remain the major instrument of production for export and for import replacement. Third, dependence on controls must be reduced, both because they are beginning to fail and because they are inconsistent with our reliance on the private sector for a large share of investment. Fourth, the foreign exchange regime should be simplified as much as possible, reducing the need for bureaucratic intervention in the market for foreign exchange and for traded commodities.

3.   Consistent with these principles, I propose the following measures:
   a.   Devaluation of the currency by 25 percent against the dollar, from Lp 8.69 per dollar to Lp 10.86 per dollar; this can be accomplished over a short period by a managed floating of the exchange rate.
   b.   Elimination of all import controls over the next 12–18 months.
   c.   Institution of a stand-by surcharge of up to 30 percent on all imports, to be imposed by the Minister of Finance at his discretion if the situation warrants it.
   d.   Elimination of the bonus voucher scheme.
   e.   Controls over goverment expenditure, which will be permitted to grow by only 5 percent in 1978/79.

The combination of devaluation and the stand-by surcharge should be sufficient to control import demand once controls are relaxed. The end to controls would end the effectiveness of the bonus voucher scheme, but the devaluation should adequately compensate exporters and maintain the incentive to export. Controls over government expenditure should guarantee that government will not add inflationary pressure to the economy.

4.   Tables 1 to 3 indicate the improvements I anticipate from these policy measures. Devaluation should have a positive effect on the volume of commodity

SECRET

exports and these, combined with favorable price trends, may be expected to yield a 12 percent growth of the dollar value of exports this year and further 14 percent increase in 1979 (Table 1). The devaluation should restrain demand for consumer good imports and I project no growth over the next few years. However, the stimulus to domestic production will mean an increase in the imports of all producer goods, so that the dollar value of imports is expected to grow by 7 percent in 1978 and 8 percent the following year. Should the devaluation not be sufficient to obtain these results, I would impose the standby surcharge to augment it.

5.   The impact on the balance of payments would be felt only marginally in 1978, but substantially in 1979. The current account deficit may be expected to fall from $167m last year to $143m this year and to $109m in 1979. I have been conservative in projecting foreign capital inflows. It will take time for foreign investors to revise their expectations about the Beracian economy and, indeed, they may be rather wary of investing immediately after devaluation. Hence I project a decline in direct investment and commercial loans this year, but a recovery in 1979. Nor have we projected any sharp rise in short-term capital, although a devaluation and related controls may well attract some speculative trends back to Beracia. I have been told by our aid donors not to expect a major increase in the rate of commitments. In any case, since most of our aid is related to projects, it seems unlikely that foreign aid disbursements can increase much from current levels. Over the next two years, I would attempt to postpone any repayments to the IMF, which would enable us to accumulate a net increase in reserves of $16m. That would increase reserves from $42m now to $58m in two years, still equivalent to less than one month's imports at projected 1979 levels. Clearly, our reserve position will remain precarious for some time. Should our projections be too optimistic, it may be possible to borrow more from the IMF.

6.   To ensure that the balance on current account improves as projected, it will be important to restrain domestic demand. Government must contribute to that goal by reducing the growth of its own expenditures and I propose to institute strict controls over increases in all budgetary items for the coming fiscal year. Although expenditures on debt service and certain other transfers cannot be easily reduced, it should be possible to impose a limit of 5 percent on the growth of all other expenditures and my projections for 1978/79 assume that will be accomplished (Table 4). That, combined with the increase in revenue from economic growth, inflation and devaluation, should be sufficient to reduce the government deficit from Lp 1419m in the current fiscal year to Lp 478m in 1978/79. However, should we discover that the reduction in expenditure growth is not feasible, it will be necessary to recommend higher tax rates when the next budget is presented to Parliament. The cooperation of all ministers in controlling expenditures is necessary to avoid a tax increase next year.

7.   The Cabinet is invited to agree that the policy measures outlined in paragraph 3 should be implemented and to empower the Minister of Finance to take the necessary steps.

K. I. Nujdge,
Minister for Finance,
January 14, 1978.

TABLE 1 Commodity exports—projections to 1979 (devaluation of 25 percent) (values in million 1977 U.S. dollars)

Commodity	1977 (actual)		1978		1979	
	Volume (thousand tonnes)	Value	Volume	Value	Volume	Value
Copper	215.4	244	225	280	240	318
Cotton	72.3	126	80	136	90	158
Rice	412.8	71	480	83	560	96
Timber	730.8	87	760	91	800	99
Other metals	—	38	—	41	—	45
Other agriculture	—	38	—	40	—	43
Manufactures	—	87	—	104	—	127
		691		775		886

TABLE 3 Balance of payments—projections to 1979 (devaluation of 25 percent) (million U.S. dollars)

	1977 (actual)		1978		1979	
	Cr	Dr	Cr	Dr	Cr	Dr
Goods						
Exports (fob)	691		776		881	
Imports (fob)		753		805		870
Merchandise balance		62		29	11	
Services						
Freight and insurance	8	73	8	78	9	85
Investment income	8	61	6	65	6	68
Other services	37	67	40	69	43	72
Balance on services		148		158		167
Balance on goods and services		210		187		156
Transfers (net)						
Private	36		37		40	
Government	7		7		7	
Balance on current account		167		143		109
Long-term capital (net)						
Official loans	84		81		81	
Corporate investment	23		17		23	
Commercial credits	17		12		17	
Basic balance		43		33	12	
Private financial capital (net)						
Commercial banks	16		16		20	
Other	1		1		1	
Errors and omissions	2		—		—	
Overall balance		24		16	33	
Central bank reserves (net)						
Gold and foreign exchange	13		16			32
IMF	11		—		—	
Net change in reserves	24		16			32

TABLE 2 Commodity imports—projections to 1979 (devaluation of 25 percent)

Commodity class	Value in million 1977 U.S. dollars cif		
	1977 (actual)	1978	1979
Consumer goods			
Food grains	70	69	69
Other essentials	18	17	20
Semi-luxuries	10	8	7
Luxuries	9	7	5
	107	101	101
Raw materials/intermediate goods			
Capital good inputs	99	108	120
Consumer good inputs	156	168	182
Fuels	179	192	208
	434	468	510
Capital goods	285	314	344
Total	826	883	955

TABLE 4 Government accounts—projections to 1978/79 (current prices, assuming 25 percent devaluation) (lepta million)

	1976/77 (actual)	1977/78 (estimated)	1978/79 (projected)[a]
Expenditures			
Goods and services	6 227	6 730	7 060
Debt service, transfers[b,c]	1 135	1 349	1 448
Gross capital formation	2 032	2 200	2 350
Subsidies	152	160	170
Total	9 546	10 439	11 028
Revenues			
Import duties[b]	1 200	1 370	1 690
Export duties[b]	643	770	1 010
Sales tax[b]	3 028	3 430	3 950
Direct tax			
Mining	399	400	450
Other	2 157	2 480	2 850
Other revenues	530	570	600
Total	7 957	9 020	10 550
Deficit	1 589	1 419	478

Notes: [a]Assumes no change in tax rates.
[b]Allows for effect of 25% devaluation for last five months of 1977/78 and all of 1978/79.
[c]Based on estimated servicing of official foreign loans as follows (in million dollars):

	1977	1978	1979
Debt outstanding	950	1031	1112
Interest due	24	26	28
Principal due	32	34	37
Total debt service	56	60	65

Questions

1. How realistic is the balance-of-payments projection prepared by the Ministry of Finance? In particular, are export supply and import demand likely to be as responsive to the Ministry's policy package as they forecast? (The attached forecasts for world prices of key commodities may be helpful in making these judgements). Since we have not been able to complete our proposed study of price elasticities in Beracian trade, it will be necessary to back up any alternate projections of our own with elasticity measurements from other countries. I understand that the IMF staff has done these from time to time.

2. Does the policy package suggested by the Minister seem likely to achieve its promised results? If not, what alternative set of policies should we propose to the Cabinet?

3. What are the aggregate demand implications of the Minister's proposals, including its budget projections? Does it seem likely that the suggested policies will generate sufficient additional saving to yield the improved balance on current account that the Ministry projects?

4. What are the implications for monetary policy of any set of policies that you recommend and of those suggested by the Minister?

5. Finally, the Prime Minister is especially concerned with the effect of any foreign exchange policies on the poorest 60 percent of the country's families. Can you assess that effect and make suggestions to ameliorate any hardships caused by the policies we recommend?

Further reading

EXTERNAL SECTOR POLICIES: THEORETICAL ISSUES

BHAGWATI, J. N. and KRUEGER, A. O. (1973). Exchange Control, Liberalization and Economic Development. *American Economic Review Papers and Proceedings* **63**, 419–427

DIAZ-ALEJANDRO, C. F. (1965). *Exchange Rate Devaluation in a Semi-Industrialized Country: The Experience of Argentina, 1955–1961.* Cambridge, Mass., The MIT Press, Chapters 1 and 2

KINDLEBERGER, C. P. (1968). Disequilibrium System of Foreign Trade and Developing Countries. In *Economics of Trade and Development* (Ed. by J. E. Theberge). New York, John Wiley

KREININ, M. E. (1971). *International Economics: A Policy Approach.* New York, Harcourt Brace, Chapter 5

MEADE, J. E. (1951). *The Balance of Payments.* London, Oxford University Press, Chapters 11 and 12

MEIER, G. M. (1968). *The International Economics of Development.* New York, Harper and Row, Chapter 4

OFFICER, L. H. (1976). The Purchasing Power Parity Theory of Exchange Rates: A Review Article. *IMF Staff Papers* **23–1,** 1–60

SCHYDLOWSKY, D. M. (1971). Short-run Policy in Semi-Industrialized Economies. *Economic Development and Cultural Change* **19,** 391–413, and Comment and Reply. *Economic Development and Cultural Change* **22,** 345–348 (1974)

PROBLEMS OF MEASUREMENT AND POLICY

GOLDSTEIN, M. and KHAN, M. (1976). Large versus Small Price Changes and the Demand for Imports. *IMF Staff Papers* **23–1,** 200–225

HOUTHAKKER, H. S. and MAGEE, S. P. (1969). Income and Price Elasticities in World Trade. *Review of Economics and Statistics* **51,** 111–125

HUFBAUER, G. C. (1971). West Pakistan Exports: Effective Taxation, Policy Promotion and Sectoral Discrimination. *Development Policy II: The Pakistan Experience* (Ed. by W. P. Falcon and G. F. Papanek) 56–114. Cambridge, Mass., Harvard University Press

INTERNATIONAL BANK FOR RECONSTRUCTION AND DEVELOPMENT (1979). *Commodity Price Trends*

KAFKA, A. (1956). The Brazilian Exchange Auction System. *The Review of Economics and Statistics* **35,** 308–322

EXTERNAL SECTOR POLICIES: COUNTRY EXPERIENCE[1]

DIAZ-ALEJANDRO, C. F. (1975). *Foreign Trade Regimes and Economic Development: Colombia.* New York, National Bureau of Economic Research

FRANK, C. R. Jr., KIM, K. S. and WESTPHAL, L. E. *Foreign Trade Regimes and Economic Development: South Korea.* New York, NBER

KRUEGER, A. O. *Foreign Trade Regimes and Economic Development: Turkey.* New York, NBER

LEITH, J. C. (1974). *Foreign Trade Regimes and Economic Development: Ghana.* New York, NBER

For other relevant works, see the bibliography to Part V.

---

[1] Recently a series of country studies on exchange control have become available. As the studies all follow the same analytic framework—prepared by the project co-directors J. N. Bhagwati and Anne O. Krueger—it is possible to compare the impact of similar policies in different country settings. The sample of readings below all refer to the evolution of the control regime and liberalization policies. Other studies in the series are of Israel, Egypt, the Philippines, India and Chile.

Fiscal Planning and Reform

FIRST DRAFT

CONFIDENTIAL

To: Principal Secretary

From: The Minister
Re: Fiscal Reform   February 20, 1978

I have read with interest the report prepared by our new foreign adviser, Mr Stephen. Although his analysis seems correct to me in many respects, I note that he has spent only a short time in Beracia and is not yet fully acquainted with the special aspects of our economy that make this country different from any other. Moreover, his report is, evidently at your request, purely analytical; he stops short of any specific policy recommendations. (In this respect, I must say, he is a most unusual foreign adviser!)

Nevertheless, Mr Stephen's observations should be taken seriously. I suggest, therefore, that you form a small inter-departmental task force to consider Stephen's report, verify his analysis and prepare a set of recommendations for me to consider. Given the urgency of our fiscal problem and the impending budget hearings for the coming fiscal year, this work should be completed within one month.

In proposing reforms of our fiscal system, the following goals should be considered by the task force:

(1)   The deficit must be eliminated within three years, as I have pledged to the Cabinet.

(2)   Tax proposals must be consistent with our intention to resume pre-1974 growth performance, specifically by providing incentives to save, to invest efficiently, to increase employment and to diversify exports.

(3)   The Government has pledged to improve the incomes of the poorest 60 percent of the population at a rate at least as fast as the rest of the population and the tax system is to contribute to this goal.

(4)   The instabilities that have plagued our economy—mainly caused by unstable world prices for our exports and recurring droughts—should be ameliorated by, among other things, a compensatory tax structure. Similarly, the tax structure should provide automatic stabilizers to help restrain inflation to our target rate, 6 percent a year.

In the process of completing this assignment, the task force should also have in mind Mr Stephen's recommendation on additional data compilation. What further statistics would be useful to us in such studies?

REPORT TO THE MINISTRY OF FINANCE

ANALYSIS OF THE FISCAL SITUATION IN BERACIA

Giles M. Stephen
Consultant
January 1978

Introduction

This report results from a request by the Principal Secretary that I 'analyze the fiscal situation, with respect to both revenues and expenditures, in order to provide the Ministry with background data on which to base future fiscal policies' (memo of December 2, 1977, from Principal Secretary, Ministry of Finance). Policy recommendations were not solicited and none has been provided, although suggestions have been transmitted informally in conversation with the Principal Secretary.

In preparing this report, I had access to all the data compiled by the Ministry of Finance, including the Department of Inland Revenue, Department of Customs and Excise, and the Budget Division, but did not obtain access to individual tax returns, as the laws of Beracia prohibit this. Although the data available have been meticulously compiled, much data of potential interest, though undoubtedly available from tax returns and other original documents, are not being compiled by the Ministry. The one recommendation I feel at liberty to make is that the Ministry hire two consultants, a tax economist and a data-processing specialist, to review the data available in tax returns and other original documents; suggest a series of data compilations that would be useful in analyzing fiscal policy issues; and design a system for processing the data from original documents. It should be noted that, according to Ministry interpretations of the existing tax law, special legislation may be required to permit these consultants to have access to the original documents for purposes of their study.

Fiscal Performance since Independence

The broad outlines of Beracia's fiscal performance since Independence have been delineated in the Economic Report for 1976 and various internal memoranda of the new Government. Consolidated government expenditure, which peaked at over 19 percent of GDP (at current market prices), in fiscal year 1970/71 (hereinafter referred to as F1971), fell to 17.5 percent of GDP in F1977. However, not all categories have moved together and therein lies the most important feature of government expenditure. The entire decline in the expenditure share of GDP was due to the curbing of government investment during the economic crisis that has persisted from 1974 to the present: since F1974, gross public capital formation has grown only 10 percent in nominal terms (and has actually fallen in nominal terms since F1975), which of course represents a substantial decline in real terms. If the Government is to stimulate the economy to recover to its pre-1974 growth performance, it will have to increase its own investment substantially.

While public investment has been stagnant or declining, government consumption has been growing rapidly. Over the entire period since independence, consumption by central and local government (largely wages of government employees) has grown 1 percent more rapidly than GDP in current prices (i.e. while GDP in current prices has grown at 11.8 percent a year, government expenditures have grown by 13 percent); since 1971, growth in government consumption accelerated to 16 percent a year, about the same as

GDP growth. Although it would be too much to say that government consumption expenditure is out of control, it is clear that the degree of control is insufficient. Indeed, government has contributed to inflation itself as it has tried to ameliorate unemployment by hiring more workers and to ameliorate the effect of inflation on the cost of living by raising government wages. (Government's own wage policy may well have contributed to the rapid increase in wages elsewhere in the economy.)

Consolidated government revenue has almost kept pace with expenditure. Actually, during the decade after independence, revenue increased as a share of GDP from 14 to 17 percent and the deficit virtually disappeared. However, during the 1970s the revenue share has fallen substantially—to 14.6 percent in F1977—and he deficit has reappeared, although it is only slightly greater a share of GDP than in the year following independence. As will be detailed below, the recent slide in revenue performance can be attributed largely to the sluggish performance of import and export duties.

Based on international standards, Beracia's revenue performance has been good until recently. Using regressions provided by Chenery and Syrquin (Patterns of Economic Development, 1950–1970, London, Oxford University Press, 1975), I estimated that a country of Beracia's characteristics should have had revenue equivalent to about 16 percent of GDP in the mid-1960s, but about 17 percent by the early 1970s. Beracia exceeded the standard slightly during the 1960s, but has fallen substantially below it during the past several years. Thus the tax effort is now deficient, not only by Beracia's own historical standards, but by international ones as well.

Indirect Taxes

Taxes levied on commodities and services have always yielded over 60 percent of revenue in Beracia, which is typical of other LDCs. The contribution of indirect taxes, which peaked at about 70 percent of consolidated government revenue in the mid-1960s, has again fallen to its post-independence level of just over 60 percent in F1977.

Taxes on trade

Import duties which tripled in the decade from F1961 to F1971 but have been sluggish since, only increasing by 27 percent in the six years since F1971. This decline in relative importance, from 23 to 15 percent of revenues, can be blamed entirely on the balance-of-payments crisis brought on by the pincers of oil price increases and copper price decreases. Beracia's import controls, used to protect international reserves, have had a negative effect on government revenues. It has been precisely those luxury and semi-luxury goods, which bear the highest duty rates, that have been cut back most.

Export duties have followed a similar pattern, their contribution to revenues falling from 10 to 8 percent in the past six years. This is, of course, a reflection of the heavy dependence on copper exports for revenue. Not only does the 15 percent duty rate yield a widely fluctuating revenue as the world price changes, but the 25 percent surcharge on all revenue in excess of $ 900 a tonne accentuates the instability in copper tax yields.

The structure of import and export duties is detailed in the background paper, 'Trade and Payments in Beracia, 1956–1977' and need not be repeated here. One summary judgement is, however, in order. Export earnings and import expenditures fluctuate together and taxes on trade, as now structured, therefore follow cyclical patterns. So long as the Treasury depends upon trade for a fourth to a third of its revenues, non-trade taxes will bear an overwhelming burden for stabilizing revenues.

Sales and excise taxes

Sales and excise taxes have always played a major role in Beracia's fiscal regime. From independence, when they contributed 28 percent to total revenue, sales and excise taxes have grown steadily in importance until they reached a peak contribution of 40 percent in F1976. Over the entire period, the elasticity of sales and excise revenue to GDP has been 1.3, reflecting both their heavy incidence on goods with high income elasticities and an upward shift of the rate structure. However, that performance masks a substantial worsening during the 1970s. Although the share of sales and excise taxes rose slightly as a share of total revenues, comparing F1977 with F1971, during this period the growth in this source of revenues was 22 percent less than that of GDP in current prices. This low elasticity of a major revenue source helps explain the decline in the revenue share of GDP during the past few years. It can be partially explained by the severe recession in Beracia, which has most likely caused the consumption of taxed commodities and services to fall more drastically than real GDP. The structure of sales and excise taxes during F1971 and F1976 is summarized in Table 3. Excise taxes are levied on six narrowly defined products and, in Beracia, are collected from producers. The rates shown are levied on before-tax prices (e.g., the ex-factory price). The values of consumption, estimated from records of the Customs and Excise Department, are based on the tax-included prices paid by consumers. Note that the effective collection rates differ substantially from the nominal tax rates.

The most important of the excises are the taxes on beer and other alcoholic beverages, tobacco products and petroleum fuels. As far as I have been able to determine, there have been no studies of the demand elasticities for alcoholic beverages and tobacco in Beracia and hence no attempts to measure the revenue-maximizing tax rate on these commodities. It is widely known, however, that local brews, which escape taxation, are strong competitors for beer among rural (and many urban) consumers. This would indicate a high price elasticity of demand for beer, in which case the excise rate of 250 percent could be well beyond the revenue-maximizing levels. The problem with cigarettes is different, although the conclusion is the same. Neighboring countries levy much lower taxes on tobacco products, so there is a strong incentive to smuggle cigarettes into Beracia. In fact, it has been alleged that in border towns the per capita sales of local cigarettes are a small fraction of that in the center of the country. It may well be that a reduction in the tax rate would raise sales of locally manufactured cigarettes sufficiently to yield higher revenues.

The excise rate on petroleum fuels was reduced substantially after the petroleum price increase. It now stands at 35 percent for 'industrial' users, including farmers and the transportation industry, but at 50 percent on private users, defined as households and private motor vehicles. The effective distinction is, however, made on the basis of product. Thus kerosene, consumed primarily by households, and motor spirits bear the higher rate, while diesel fuels and all other products bear the lower rate. A commercial operator of vehicles who pays the higher tax is entitled to deduct the difference from his income tax, but this offset has little effect for the mass of small operators, such as taxi companies, who seldom pay income taxes.

The most controversial excise taxes are on processed foods, especially on milled grain, cooking oils and sugar. Several aspects ameliorate the seriousness of what would otherwise be a quite regressive tax. First, the rates, which were reduced in 1975/76, are low, at least in comparison with other excise taxes or with the sales tax. Second, only the output of incorporated producers is taxed, so that small-scale mills or oil presses escape. This, in turn, means that rural consumers generally do not bear the tax, although of course the rural price may be somewhat higher as a consequence of the 'protection' received by small producers by the tax on incorporated producers. The revenue from these taxes accounts for about 3 percent of total revenue, a contribution that could be made up by slight changes in other taxes, should government decide to eliminate food excises.

Sales taxes are levied at two rates, 20 and 30 percent. Clothing and textile products are now taxed at the lower rate, as are tickets to theaters and other entertainment, while restaurant meals bear the higher rate. Consumer durables, a broad category which includes furniture and light fixtures as well as appliances, are taxed at 30 percent. Automobiles bear the 30 percent rate, but commercial vehicles are taxed only at 20 percent. In terms of generating maximum revenue, several of these rates bear reconsideration, especially that on textiles and clothing. Most shopkeepers in Kefala to whom I talked felt rather strongly that sales are being reduced by the high taxes on clothing and textiles. They complain especially because market women who sell these products in the rural areas do not pay the tax.

Direct Taxes
Business income taxes
Ever since the colonial government converted a sliding tax on copper revenues into a larger corporate profits tax, the tax on mining profits has been an important revenue source for the government. It is applied at the same rate as the corporate profits tax, 45 percent. Revenues from this tax grew fairly steadily until F1970, as copper revenues rose. However, the price swings of the 1970s had their effect on mining profits and tax revenue from this source has been unstable. The share of the mining profit tax in total direct tax revenues has varied from 22 percent in F1972, to a high of 38 percent in F1974, then back to a low of 17 percent in F1977 (Table 4).

The non-mining corporate profits tax has been a more reliable generator of income, its share of direct tax revenues varying between 40 and 45 percent. However, the administration of this tax seems to have deteriorated since independence. Although the rate of 45 percent has not been changed, the share of corporate profits tax revenue in GDP (market prices) fell from 2.4 percent in F1957 to a low of 1.4 percent in F1973. Since then it has recovered to 1.7 percent. The decline through the early 1970s can be blamed on two factors. First, the standards of administration have fallen as colonial civil servants in the Inland Revenue Department were replaced by local administrators, not all of whom have been adequately trained in tax administration and accountancy. Second, the overly liberal use of tax holidays, accelerated depreciation and similar invest-ment incentives have seriously eroded the tax base*. The improvement of the past few years does not necessarily indicate a reversal of these conditions. Much of it can be explained by accelerated inflation, which creates inventory profits and otherwise increases profits, especially for firms with large fixed depreciation and interest payments.

Personal Income Tax
All personal income, whether from wages, salaries, interest, dividends, profits or rents, is subject to tax in Beracia. The simplified rate structure, adopted in 1961, is shown in Table 5. The first Lp 3000 of annual income is exempt for any individual and an additional Lp 1500 of exempt income is allowed for each dependent up to three, so that the highest exemption is Lp 7500 for families of four or more. Table 5 shows the average tax rates at the top of each income range, assuming a family of four. Under the simplified tax code, no other deductions from income are allowed, except that owners of unincorporated businesses are permitted to calculate profits in the same manner as corporations do for the corporate income tax before adding profits to their taxable income.

* A recent study, based on tax returns filed in Fiscal 1974, showed that total reported corporate (non-mining) profits were Lp 1750m. If fully taxed at 45 percent, these profits would have yielded revenue of Lp 788m, compared with the actual yield of Lp 572m. The shortfall can be taken as a measure of the erosion due to tax concessions to stimulate investment.

Enforcement of the personal income tax, like that of the corporate income tax, has become more lax over the years. Thus, despite the steeply progressive marginal tax rates and rising per capita income, the income tax has represented a declining fraction of GDP: at independence, the personal income tax yielded revenue equivalent to about 1 percent of GDP at market prices, but by F1971, the ratio had declined to 0.7 percent. Since then, the ratio has risen to 0.8 percent, mainly because of the effect of accelerated inflation on the progressive rate structure.

Several factors may be responsible for the declining importance of the income tax. First, the departure from Beracia of expatriate businessmen, professionals and farmers substantially decreased the number of high-income individuals on the tax rolls. At the same time, Beracian authorities have not been successful in identifying the growing number of Beracian businessmen and professionals with high incomes. Second, even those businessmen and professionals who do report some income typically have under-reported their income. Tax authorities have not been skilled in detecting this evasion, nor have they been encouraged by the political authorities to tighten their enforcement. Third, a major loophole has been used increasingly by employers: since income in kind, such as housing or transportation, is not included in the tax base, employers have been providing these items for managers and, to a growing extent, for other employees. Government's proclivity to provide subsidized housing for its employees has the same effect. A rise in rents, which are not deductible, and offsetting increase in salaries would result in higher tax collections from government employees*. Fourth, the 1965 Act that exempted farmers who are Beracian citizens from all income taxes has prevented government from tapping this growing source of income. Many farmers also engage in non-farm activity which, by convention, has been considered farm income by the tax authorities. A recent survey indicated that in some districts as much as one-third of all farm family income is derived from non-farm activities.

As a consequence of these developments, the income tax base consists largely of wage and salary earners whose taxes are withheld by their employers. The growth of taxes from this source has been more than offset by the erosion of the tax base for the reasons given. Since taxes withheld now comprise a major share of revenue, it seems unlikely that the decline of the income tax will continue, even if inflation were to abate. With broader coverage and stricter enforcement, it should have been possible to increase income tax revenues in, say, F1977, at least to the post-independence ratio to national income. However, the political consequences of stricter enforcement would have to be faced.

Social Security Tax

The one tax with an unblemished record of steady growth has been the social security tax, levied on employers at the rate of 7.5 percent of all salaries and wages paid. Not only have average wages and employment been increasing (see Tables R2.3–R2.5), but the coverage of the social security tax has been broadened over the years. Whereas social security tax revenues represented approximately 3.3 percent of wages paid in 1967, the yield grew to about 3.8 percent in F1976. The major change has been a gradual expansion into the service industries, which had

---

* It has been estimated that governments at all levels provide housing for civil servants whose salaries total roughly Lp 3000m a year in 1977 prices. Rental is charged at 7.5 percent of salaries, although a fair market value would probably imply rents at twice that rate. The affected civil servants earn incomes in the range of Lp 10 000 to Lp 60 000 per year. If salaries were increased to compensate for the rise in rents, the resulting income tax yield could be significant.

not been taxed at independence. However, in all sectors only the largest employers pay the tax; small businesses seldom do. Family workers are legally exempt.

The simplicity of the tax and the visibility of the tax base has made this an easy tax to enforce. Since social security revenues now form almost one-fourth of direct tax revenues, expanded coverage or higher rates could have a significant impact on government revenues. However, it must also be recognized that this is a tax on employment and may well discourage job creation, with adverse consequences for income distribution.

Local Government Finance

Local governments, primarily at the provincial level, have accounted for a growing share of government expenditure: from 12 percent of consolidated government expenditure in F1957, the local government share rose steadily to 16 percent in F1977. It has increased its share of both consumption and investment outlays, but its investment performance has been more notable: local government's share of public investment has doubled, from 5 to 10.5 percent, since independence. To a considerable extent this reflects the central government's emphasis on urban infrastructure investments, many of which are made under local government auspices.

Legally, local governments cannot run deficits. However, this is largely a legal fiction, since about 80 percent of local government revenues are transfers from the central government and these are often made on an emergency basis during the fiscal year to avoid deficits. In order to finance growing local government expenditure, the central government has had to transfer an increasing portion of consolidated government revenue to local units: the share has risen from 11 percent at independence to 15 percent in F1977. Thus the ability of the government to balance its budget is inextricably tied to the control of local government expenditure.

The only major revenue source for local governments is the property tax, levied on commercial and residential properties. Although they finance only about 20 percent of local government expenditures, property tax revenues have grown at about the same rate as GDP since the mid-1960s, a better performance than for most centrally administered taxes. This growth can be explained largely by the legal requirement that banks report all loans secured by property to local authorities, which then are able to tax the property. Properties, both residential and commercial, that do not involve bank mortgages tend to escape the property tax. Thus enforcement has been efficient as far as it goes, but not ambitious. It should be possible to double the revenue yield easily by extending the tax to other properties, but tnis would require additional administrative expenditure.

Questions

1. Is it likely that, under the present tax and revenue structure, the deficit will be eliminated over the next three fiscal years? If not, what tax reforms do you recommend to achieve this goal?

2. What reforms of the tax structure would you recommend to increase savings, improve the efficiency of investment, increase employment and diversify exports? Are these changes consistent with those required to balance the budget?

3. What expenditure and tax reforms would be particularly effective in raising the income share of the poorest 60 percent of the population?
4. Does the tax structure provide automatic stabilization in the face of fluctuating export prices and recurring drought? How might this feature be improved?
5. What additional data would be useful in analyzing questions such as these?

TABLE 1 Central government expenditures (Lepta million)

Fiscal year	Goods and services	Debt service and transfers	Gross capital formation	Subsidies	Total
1956/57	434.9	183.4	327.3	6.3	951.9
1957/58	433.3	216.1	378.6	7.1	1035.1
1958/59	498.5	232.3	421.5	7.6	1159.9
1959/60	508.8	259.0	449.1	8.3	1225.2
1960/61	535.7	262.7	459.0	10.8	1268.2
1961/62	547.0	285.3	500.9	13.4	1346.6
1962/63	642.3	350.7	532.1	15.1	1540.2
1963/64	788.1	410.2	620.0	16.8	1835.1
1964/65	930.0	477.3	721.8	19.9	2149.0
1965/66	1054.3	532.1	700.0	22.7	2309.1
1966/67	1149.2	617.2	803.6	25.8	2595.8
1967/68	1344.3	705.8	993.9	29.8	3073.8
1968/69	1501.7	824.4	1147.4	40.0	3513.5
1969/70	1758.6	979.4	1200.3	50.9	3989.2
1970/71	1992.0	1182.8	1331.6	62.0	4568.4
1971/72	2413.4	1245.0	1393.0	79.6	5131.0
1972/73	2728.8	1364.3	1398.8	101.3	5593.2
1973/74	2993.7	1581.6	1672.1	150.5	6397.9
1974/75	3614.9	1810.8	1886.5	163.6	7475.8
1975/76	4309.9	2133.8	1938.2	142.0	8523.9
1976/77	4919.6	2352.3	1817.7	151.8	9241.4

Source: Ministry of Finance.

TABLE 2 Central government revenues

Fiscal years	Taxes on trade	Sales and excise taxes	Direct taxes		Other revenues	Total
			Mining	Others		
1956/57	283.1	231.3	61.5	215.7	5.7	797.3
1957/58	302.7	264.3	66.5	246.1	6.8	886.4
1958/59	354.4	303.0	78.6	282.5	9.0	1027.5
1959/60	367.8	326.7	84.3	266.9	10.3	1056.0
1960/61	424.6	348.7	95.8	291.6	13.0	1173.7
1961/62	420.8	407.6	100.5	327.4	15.4	1271.7
1962/63	473.4	473.2	103.4	366.9	15.2	1432.1
1963/64	577.3	558.4	118.0	403.1	13.9	1670.7
1964/65	670.3	701.0	139.8	453.5	14.0	1978.6
1965/66	790.5	790.2	213.9	523.2	16.9	2334.7
1966/67	926.0	927.9	253.5	571.7	18.9	2698.0
1967/68	1076.6	1093.3	277.5	604.9	25.0	3077.3
1968/69	1224.5	1239.5	360.4	627.1	32.3	3483.8
1969/70	1372.2	1449.0	431.9	663.4	42.1	3958.6
1970/71	1384.7	1532.6	336.2	724.5	55.0	4033.0
1971/72	1283.8	1686.3	283.6	964.9	73.7	4292.3
1972/73	1572.7	1945.8	573.3	913.4	87.5	5092.7
1973/74	2071.9	2348.2	719.5	1168.8	99.9	6408.3
1974/75	2077.8	2753.2	575.7	1380.2	210.4	6997.3
1975/76	1825.1	2925.2	389.8	1604.9	376.7	7121.7
1976/77	1843.4	3027.7	398.8	1882.4	499.8	7652.1

Source: Ministry of Finance.

TABLE 3 Sales and excise tax revenues, 1970/71 and 1975/76

Taxable commodity	Value of final consumption[a] (Lp million)		Tax rate[b] (%)		Revenue (Lp million)	
Excise taxes	1970/71	1975/76	1970/71	1975/76	1970/71	1975/76
Milled grain	1876	2680	10.0	7.5	157.1	127.7
Oils and fats	403	615	15.0	12.5	44.0	55.9
Sugar and sweets	350	554	15.0	12.5	35.2	50.4
Alcoholic beverages	480	1038	200.0	250.0	309.5	726.1
Tobacco products	440	870	200.0	250.0	285.0	613.5
Fuels	610	2380[c]	80–100	35–50	286.5	675.4
Sales tax						
Clothing and textiles	1690	3577	30	20	348.3	504.2
Meals in restaurants	201	572	30	30	44.2	123.6
Entertainment	95	231	20	20	15.4	30.1
Consumer durables	20	50	30	30	5.3	11.5
Vehicles	19	29	20–30	20–30	2.1	6.8
Total					1532.6	2925.2

Notes: [a]Value of consumption at market prices (i.e. *including* taxes).
[b]Nominal rate levied on manufacturer's ex-factory price (for excise taxes) or on retailer's sale.
[c]Includes some intermediate uses.
Source: Ministry of Finance.

TABLE 4 Direct tax revenues of central government

Fiscal year	Business income tax		Personal income tax	Social security tax	Total
	Mining	Other			
1956/57	61.5	129.4	58.9	27.4	277.2
1957/58	66.5	150.7	64.6	30.8	312.6
1958/59	78.6	180.0	66.7	35.8	361.1
1959/60	84.3	154.2	72.0	40.7	351.2
1960/61	95.8	166.2	76.6	43.8	382.4
1961/62	100.5	184.9	90.4	52.1	427.9
1962/63	103.4	206.7	100.1	60.1	470.3
1963/64	118.0	218.3	110.9	73.9	521.1
1964/65	139.8	243.7	122.8	87.0	593.3
1965/66	213.9	282.5	132.0	103.7	732.1
1966/67	253.5	317.8	138.2	115.7	825.2
1967/68	277.5	322.0	152.8	130.1	882.4
1968/69	360.4	319.1	162.0	146.0	987.5
1969/70	431.9	330.0	171.7	161.7	1095.3
1970/71	336.2	362.3	172.0	180.2	1050.7
1971/72	283.6	567.2	181.4	216.3	1248.5
1972/73	573.3	427.0	225.7	260.7	1486.7
1973/74	719.5	571.6	285.4	311.8	1888.3
1974/75	575.7	675.3	331.6	373.3	1955.9
1975/76	389.8	770.4	385.2	452.4	1997.8
1976/77	398.8	913.4	437.5	531.5	2281.2

Source: Ministry of Finance.

TABLE 5 Income tax rates, family of four

Income range (Lp/yr)	Marginal tax rate	Average rate at top of range
0–7 500	0	0
7 501–15 000	10	5
15 001–25 000	20	11
25 001–40 000	30	18
40 001–60 000	40	25
60 001–80 000	50	32
80 001–100 000	60	37
100 001+	70	

Source: Ministry of Finance (1961). *The Income Tax Code*.

TABLE 6 Local government accounts (Lepta million)

Fiscal year	Expenditure			Revenue		
	Goods and services	Gross capital formation	Total	Local taxes and fees	Net transfers from central government	Total
1956/57	102.0	16.5	118.5	26.7	91.8	118.5
1957/58	109.2	19.1	128.3	29.7	98.6	128.3
1958/59	116.9	19.7	136.6	30.7	105.9	136.6
1959/60	125.1	23.5	148.6	34.9	113.7	148.6
1960/61	133.9	18.7	152.6	30.5	122.1	152.6
1961/62	155.2	31.9	187.1	45.1	142.0	187.1
1962/63	179.9	32.2	212.1	47.0	165.1	212.1
1963/64	208.5	43.4	251.9	60.0	191.9	251.9
1964/65	241.7	50.0	291.7	68.5	223.2	291.7
1965/66	280.2	44.5	324.7	64.4	260.3	324.7
1966/67	322.0	65.1	387.1	88.2	298.9	387.1
1967/68	370.1	90.0	460.1	115.9	344.2	460.1
1968/69	425.3	115.3	540.6	144.2	396.4	540.6
1969/70	488.8	129.7	618.5	162.0	456.5	618.5
1970/71	561.8	121.2	683.0	157.3	525.7	683.0
1971/72	647.9	150.9	798.8	194.0	604.8	798.8
1972/73	747.0	165.7	912.7	216.8	695.9	912.7
1973/74	861.5	181.3	1042.8	242.2	800.6	1042.8
1974/75	993.5	195.8	1189.3	268.2	921.2	1189.3
1975/76	1135.7	204.8	1340.5	280.7	1059.8	1340.5
1976/77	1307.7	214.4	1522.1	304.8	1217.3	1522.1

Source: Ministry of Finance.

Income Inequality and Poverty

Beracia's population, forged into one nation at the time of independence, comprises three major ethno–cultural–linguistic groups. The Blē, who constitute about half of the population, are primarily rural and engaged in various agricultural activities. The second largest group is the Aspro who form about 35 percent of the population and are heavily engaged in the manufacturing and commercial sectors of the economy. The Kokkina, the third major group, constitute about 10 percent of the population and are more evenly represented in nearly all economic activities*. *Table 1* shows the composition of Beracia's population. While the process of urbanization has continued since 1970, the next census will not be undertaken until 1980 and no more recent demographic data are available.

TABLE 1 Population by location and ethnic grouping: 1970 (percent)

Population group	Urban	Rural	Total
Blē	14.8	85.2	100.0
	(20.9)	(63.5)	(48.7)
Aspro	56.3	43.7	100.0
	(56.4)	(23.2)	(34.7)
Kokkina	31.6	68.4	100.0
	(10.0)	(11.5)	(11.0)
Others	78.7	21.3	100.0
	(12.7)	(1.8)	(5.6)
Total	34.6	65.4	100.0
	(100.0)	(100.0)	(100.0)

Source: Central Bureau of Statistics (1974) *Census of Population (1970). Vol. I.* Summary Characteristics of the Population of Beracia.

---

* The remainder of the population consists of non-Beracian residents, minor ethnic groups and a sizeable Lebanese trading community. See *Census of Population of Beracia (1970)* **XIV,** Definitions of Terms Used in the Census Questionnaire. Central Bureau of Statistics, 1976.

Data on income distribution in Beracia have only recently been made available. Despite this, policy-makers have long felt that income was maldistributed and poverty rampant. It was known that rural incomes were lower than urban incomes; this suggests that the average income for the Blē, who are concentrated in the rural areas, must be lower than the incomes for the predominantly urban Aspro and perhaps even lower than that of the Kokkina. Such a pattern of income distribution has obvious political repercussions since the Blē, by virtue of being the largest ethnic group, dominate the political structure and are heavily represented in the civil service. Hence any concrete evidence that incomes are maldistributed along ethnic lines, or that poverty is heavily identified with one ethnic group, would give weight to those who have argued not only for specific programs aimed at redresssing poverty but for programs aimed at accelerating the economic development of one specific ethnic group over the others.

During 1975, the Central Bureau of Statistics conducted a Household Income Survey (HIS), the results of which have just been made available to the Ministry of Economic Planning, which has constituted a small working group to analyze the data and make policy recommendations. In addition, a Household Expenditure Survey (HES) was conducted in 1977. Some very preliminary tabulations from that survey have also been made available to the working group.

TABLE 2 Number of rural and urban households by income classes

Household income class (Lp/month)	Rural	Urban	Total
No income	232	109	341
1–125	1 588	459	2 047
126–250	3 574	1 075	4 649
251–400	3 113	1 195	4 308
401–550	2 356	1 099	3 455
550–700	2 709	1 497	4 206
701–700	1 953	1 221	3 174
1 101–1 700	807	535	1 342
1 701–2 300	386	284	670
2 301–3 000	184	140	324
3 001–4 000	145	118	263
4 001–6 000	68	59	127
6 001–8 000	35	35	70
8 001–12 000	16	14	30
12 001+	10	9	19
All income classes	17 176	7 849	25 025

Note: Urban areas are defined as all cities with a population of over 100 000 inhabitants. All other areas are considered 'rural' although it should be noted that a number of good sized cities are thus defined as rural.
Source: Central Bureau of Statistics, 'Household Income Survey for Beracia, 1975' unpublished.

A summary tabulation of the HIS data, showing the distribution of incomes in the urban and rural areas is given in *Table 2*. More detailed tables, which also provide data on the highly sensitive topic of ethnic income distributions, are shown in Appendix *Tables A.1–A.4*, while the preliminary tabulations from the HES are shown in Appendix *Tables A.5* and *A.6*.

To estimate the household income distribution we need to know the actual income of each household. Unfortunately this is no longer available because the income data were coded into intervals. The problem then is to reassign an income level to each household in each interval. One assumption, often used, is to assume that each household receives an income equal to the mid-point of the income interval. This assumption is reasonable for fairly small (and dense) income intervals but is less likely to be a correct representation of reality for large income intervals with few observations and is totally inapplicable for open-ended classes. One solution is to fit the mean incomes for each interval from the parameters of that distribution [see equation (C11.1)].

The mean household income in any interval (x, z) is given by:

$$\text{Mean income } (x, z) = \frac{b}{(b-1)} \frac{(z^{1-b} - x^{1-b})}{(z^{-b} - x^{-b})}, \tag{C11.1}$$

where b is the Pareto distribution parameter. Once the means of the income classes have been calculated, various measures of income distribution can be derived, including the Gini and Theil coefficients.

There is also a need to define some target poverty level so that specific policies can be formulated to assist the poor. An obvious first step is to define poverty. One choice is to define the poor as those who fall below the 40th percentile in the income distribution*. Alternatively one can estimate a poverty line income level. The Ministry of Social Development recently undertook a study of the 'income required to maintain a family in good nutritional health'†. The minimum food budgets, shown in *Table 3*, are based on the recommended calorie and protein requirements for third-class hospital patients. These dietary requirements, separately available for males, females and children, were converted to food items by assuming that the calorie and protein

TABLE 3 Cost of minimum food budget by ethnic groups (1975)

	Blɛ̃		Aspro		Kokkina		Children	
Stratum	Male	Female	Male	Female	Male	Female	0–6	7–11
Rural	53.34	50.69	51.60	48.93	53.93	51.28	31.41	44.20
Urban	54.31	51.66	52.52	49.87	55.48	52.83	32.12	45.08
Average (unweighted)	53.83	51.18	52.06	49.40	54.71	52.06	31.77	44.64

Source: Ministry of Social Development, unpublished memoranda, 1978.

---

*   The popularity of this particular figure seems to stem from a speech by Robert McNamara, president of the World Bank, who noted that development often seemed to by-pass the lowest 40% of the income distribution in developing countries. Cf. Robert S. McNamara (1972). *Address to the Board of Governors*. Washington, D.C. the World Bank

†   Ministry of Social Development, unpublished memoranda, 1978

needs would all be met by purchasing the lowest cost food items. The differences by ethnic group reflect differences in consumption habits, while the urban–rural difference is a result of the lower food prices prevailing in rural areas. All food items were costed at 1978 prices. Since no separate cost-of-living indices are available for urban and rural areas, let alone by ethnic groups, the various food budgets were deflated to 1975 prices using the 'food' component of the cost-of-living index.

An estimate of non-food expenditure is also required to calculate the poverty line budget. Two different methods are proposed. In the first, suggested by Orshansky*, the proportion of total expenditure on food is estimated for all families with monthly incomes less than some arbitrary level (say, the lowest 40th percentile). The poverty line is then calculated by multiplying the reciprocal of this proportion by the minimum food budget†.

The second alternative adds an estimate of non-food essential items to the food budget. Such non-food essential purchases are estimated below:

	Cost/person (Lp/month)
Clothing and footwear	3.27
Rent, fuel, power	12.97
Household equipment and operations	1.38
Transport and communication	2.37
Total	19.99
Say	20.00

Given this data it is possible to derive an alternative measure of the poverty line in Beracia and thus estimate the number of poor.

The Cabinet Economic Committee requests from the Ministry of Economic Planning a comprehensive report on the distribution of income in Beracia, including measures of the distribution by ethnic group and by location, and an analysis of the extent of poverty. In order to help focus the work, the Principal Secretary has prepared terms of reference for the report. These are essentially a series of questions aimed at providing a focus, but the report can range well beyond these terms of reference. One point is critically important: because the issue of ethnic group income disparities and poverty is potentially so explosive, care must be taken to support all statements concerning this aspect of Beracia's development with careful analysis based on data.

---

* M. Orshansky (1965). Counting the Poor: Another Look at the Poverty Profile. *Social Security Bulletin* **28**, 3–29

† The expenditure data from the Household Expenditure Survey (HES) are shown in Appendix Tables *A.5* and *A.6*.

Questions

1. Are the data generated by the HIS and the HES consistent with the known macroeconomic data for the economy?

2. The HIS income refers to gross or pre-tax income for the 'average' month while the HES survey, carried out over a full year, asked only one question relating to income. What effect will these methodological problems have on the results? Is income, or household income, the correct variable for measuring income distribution? Which distribution is more relevant: household income or the distribution of individuals by per capita household income?

3. What are the distributional characteristics of the various income distributions? What has happened to income inequality over time? How does Beracia's income distribution compare to that of other countries at a similar stage of development?

4. To what extent is the ethnic income difference a consequence of non-group factors? For example, it has been argued that differences in family size, participation rate and location (urban vs rural) explain ethnic income differences. Is this a feasible explanation?

5. What would be a reasonable poverty income line for Beracia? What are the policy implications of each of the methods suggested for calculating a poverty level?

6. What policy measures might be put forward to achieve the dual aims of poverty eradication and income redistribution? Over what time period might such policies be effective? Would such policies be consistent with Beracia's national development policies?

7. If a 'basic needs' approach were to be adopted, what specific measures would be included? How would this approach differ from other poverty redressal programs? Do conditions in Beracia warrant a basic needs planning approach? If so, what are the benefits and costs of such a policy?

Further reading

AHLUWAHLIA, M. (1974). Income Inequality: Some Dimensions of the Problems. In *Redistribution with Growth* (H. B. CHENERY *et al.*). London, Oxford University Press

AHLUWAHLIA, M. (1974). The Scope for Policy Intervention. In *Redistribution with Growth* (H. B. CHENERY et al.). London, Oxford University Press

BELL, C. L. G. (1974). The Political Framework. In *Redistribution with Growth* (H. B. CHENERY *et al.*). London, Oxford University Press

BELL, C. L. G. and DULOY, J. H. (1974). Rural Target Groups. In *Redistribution with Growth* (H. B. CHENERY *et al.*). London, Oxford University Press

BRUNO, M. (1977). Distribution Issues in Development Planning—Some Reflections on the State of the Art. Paper presented at the Workshop on Analysis of Distributional Issues in Development Planning. Bellagio, Italy

FEI, J. C. H., RANIS, G. and KUO, S. W. Y. (1979). *Growth With Equity: The Taiwan Case.* New York, Oxford University Press

FISHLOW, A. (1972). Brazilian Size Distribution of Income. *American Economic Review* **62,** 391–402

ORSHANSKY, M. (1965). Counting the Poor: Another Look at the Poverty Profile. *Social Security Bulletin* **28,** 3–29

PAO, D. C. (1974). Urban Target Groups. In *Redistribution with Growth* (H. B. CHENERY *et al.*). London, Oxford University Press

SEN, A. K. (1976). Poverty: An Ordinal Approach to Measurement. *Econometrica,* **44–2**

Appendix to Case 11

TABLE A.1 Number of households, average household size, average number of income earners, mean household income, participation rates[a] and dependency ratios[b] by household income class all ethnic groups, including 'others'[c]

Household income class (Lp/month)	Number of households	Average household size	Average number of income earners	Mean household income	Average participation rate	Average dependency ratio
No income	341	4.51	0	–	–	–
1–125	2 047	2.84	1.12	62.5	0.39	2.54
125–250	4 649	4.27	1.25	188.0	0.29	3.42
251–400	4 308	4.95	1.37	325.5	0.28	3.61
401–550	3 455	5.44	1.52	475.5	0.28	3.61
551–700	4 206	6.05	1.75	625.5	0.20	–
701–1 100	3 174	6.57	2.06	900.5	0.31	3.19
1 101–1 700	1 342	7.12	2.38	1 400.5	0.33	3.00
1 701–2 300	670	7.46	2.69	2 000.5	0.36	2.77
2 301–3 000	324	7.14	2.76	2 650.5	0.39	2.59
3 001–4 000	263	7.46	3.22	3 500.5	0.43	2.32
4 001–6 000	127	6.90	3.09	5 000.5	0.45	2.23
6 001–8 000	70	7.34	3.06	7 000.5	0.42	2.40
8 001–12 000	30	8.16	3.77	10 000.5	0.46	2.16
12 001+	19	13.11	8.37	15 130.0[d]	0.64	1.57
All income classes[e]	25 025	5.363	1.63	649.1	0.30	3.26

Notes are found after Appendix *Table A.4.*

TABLE A.2 Number of households, average household size, average number of income earners, mean household income, participation rates[a] and dependency ratios[b] by household income class ethnic group: Blē

Household income class (Lp/month)	Number of households	Average household size	Average number of income earners	Mean household income	Average participation rate	Average dependency ratio
No income	190	4.24	0	–	–	–
1–125	1 762	2.94	1.13	62.5	0.38	2.60
126–250	3 841	4.53	1.28	188.0	0.28	3.54
251–400	2 830	5.37	1.44	325.5	0.27	3.73
401–550	1 780	5.68	1.56	475.5	0.27	3.64
551–700	1 716	6.05	1.70	625.5	0.28	3.56
701–1 100	1 061	6.43	1.87	900.5	0.29	3.44
1 101–1 700	395	6.56	2.20	1 400.5	0.33	2.99
1 701–2 300	152	6.83	2.34	2 000.5	0.35	2.94
2 301–3 000	66	7.01	2.44	2 650.5	0.35	2.87
3 001–4 000	41	7.75	3.36	3 500.5	0.43	2.31
4 001–6 000	19	8.21	3.43	5 000.5	0.42	2.39
6 001–8 000	5	8.8	3.40	7 000.5	0.39	2.59
8 001–12 000	3	6.67	1.67	10 000.5	0.25	3.99
12 001+	2	11.00	2.00	15 130.0[d]	0.18	5.50
All income classes[e]	13 863	5.084	1.46	432.4	0.29	3.38

Notes are found after Appendix *Table A.4.*

TABLE A.3 Number of households, average household size, average number of income earners, mean household income, participation rates[a] and dependency ratios[b] by household income class ethnic group: Aspro

Household income class (Lp/month)	Number of households	Average household size	Average number of income earners	Mean household income	Average participation rate	Average dependency ratio
No income	110	5.16	0	–	–	–
1–125	150	1.91	1.03	62.5	0.54	1.85
126–250	515	2.72	1.12	188.0	0.41	2.43
251–400	910	3.98	1.25	325.5	0.31	3.18
401–550	1 070	5.03	1.42	475.5	0.28	3.54
551–700	1 831	5.93	1.75	625.5	0.30	3.39
701–1 100	1 718	6.64	2.15	900.5	0.32	3.09
1 101–1 700	766	7.63	2.55	1 400.5	0.33	2.99
1 701–2 300	428	7.99	2.86	2 000.5	0.36	2.79
2 301–3 000	198	7.72	2.96	2 650.5	0.38	2.61
3 001–4 000	164	7.90	3.20	3 500.5	0.41	2.47
4 001–6 000	78	7.32	3.18	5 000.5	0.43	2.30
6 001–8 000	40	8.48	3.25	7 000.5	0.38	2.61
8 001–12 000	11	9.09	4.18	10 000.5	0.46	2.17
12 001+	14	14.79	10.50	15 130.0[d]	0.71	1.41
All income classes[c]	8 003	5.839	1.90	908.6	0.32	3.06

Notes are found after Appendix *Table A.4.*

TABLE A.4 Number of households, average household size, average number of income earners, mean household income, participation rates[a] and dependency ratios[b] by household income class ethnic group: Kokkina

Household income class (Lp/month)	Number of households	Average household size	Average number of income earners	Mean household income	Average participation rate	Average dependency ratio
No income	32	4.47	0	–	–	–
1–125	90	2.00	1.05	62.5	0.50	1.90
126–250	263	3.66	1.16	188.0	0.32	3.16
251–400	551	4.41	1.24	325.5	0.28	3.56
401–550	596	5.40	1.55	475.5	0.29	3.48
551–700	647	6.39	1.89	625.5	0.29	3.44
701–1 100	384	6.76	2.23	900.5	0.33	3.03
1 101–1 700	169	6.23	2.07	1 400.5	0.33	3.04
1 701–2 300	77	6.08	2.39	2 000.5	0.40	2.70
2 301–3 000	46	5.70	2.63	2 650.5	0.46	2.17
3 001–4 000	44	6.70	3.57	3 500.5	0.53	1.88
4 001–6 000	16	6.94	3.75	5 000.5	0.54	1.85
6 001–8 000	10	6.70	4.30	7 000.5	0.64	1.56
8 001–12 000	9	10.22	4.78	10 000.5	0.47	2.14
12 001+	2	4.50	2.50	15 120.0[d]	0.56	1.80
All income classes[e]	2 936	5.453	1.72	704.1	0.31	3.2

Notes. [a]Average participation rate = $\dfrac{\text{Average number of income earners}}{\text{Average household size}}$

[b]Average dependency ratio = $\dfrac{1}{\text{Average participation rate}}$

[c]'Others' includes Beracian citizens who are not members of three major ethnic groups *and* are permanent residents.

[d]Mean household income approximated using 'Van der Wijks law' with g = 1.24. See Jan Pen (1971), *Income Distribution* (Harmondsworth, Penguin)

[e]Average totals are weighted averages.

Source: Department of Statistics, 'Household Income Survey for Beracia, 1975', unpublished.

TABLE A.5 Distribution of monthly expenditure per rural household: 1977 (Lp/month, 1977 prices)

	Expenditure per household	Income classes								
		Below 140	141–280	281–400	401–550	551–800	801–1100	1101–1400	1401–1900	1901+
Number of households	5 190	398	1 276	954	709	807	398	204	202	242
Number of members	26 415	816	4 798	4 512	3 857	4 890	2 627	1 416	1 586	1 913
Average number of member/households	5.09	2.05	3.76	4.73	5.44	6.06	6.60	6.94	7.85	7.91
Average number of earners/household	2.89	1.49	2.15	2.47	2.82	3.13	3.39	3.56	4.36	4.75
Average household expenditure (Lp/month)	600	85	213	348	482	679	958	1 228	1 598	3 005
Expenditure on:					(percent)					
Group 0: Food, of which	41.3	53.7	56.8	53.0	50.2	45.8	42.3	39.9	36.0	24.1
Rice	(28.8)	(46.6)	(41.7)	(37.0)	(33.9)	(29.6)	(26.3)	(23.2)	(22.3)	(17.1)
Bread and cereals	(8.8)	(7.5)	(8.0)	(8.6)	(8.7)	(8.8)	(9.1)	(9.3)	(9.5)	(8.3)
Meat	(11.6)	(4.0)	(3.6)	(5.2)	(6.7)	(10.0)	(12.5)	(15.4)	(16.4)	(24.4)
Fish	(13.6)	(15.8)	(14.6)	(14.7)	(14.1)	(14.3)	(13.5)	(12.9)	(12.8)	(10.9)
Milk, cheese, eggs	(6.3)	(1.5)	(3.3)	(4.4)	(5.5)	(6.2)	(6.9)	(7.7)	(7.9)	(8.8)
Oils and fats	(4.3)	(3.9)	(4.0)	(4.0)	(4.1)	(4.4)	(4.4)	(4.6)	(4.7)	(4.2)
Fruit and vegetables	(15.1)	(8.3)	(11.3)	(13.2)	(14.3)	(15.1)	(16.2)	(16.5)	(16.3)	(17.4)
Sugar	(5.6)	(8.3)	(8.2)	(7.5)	(6.9)	(5.8)	(5.1)	(4.2)	(4.1)	(2.6)
Coffee, tea, cocoa	(2.7)	(2.4)	(3.0)	(2.8)	(2.8)	(2.7)	(2.7)	(2.7)	(2.7)	(2.3)
Other foods	(3.2)	(1.7)	(2.3)	(2.6)	(3.0)	(3.1)	(3.3)	(3.5)	(3.4)	(3.9)
Group 1: Beverages and tobacco	4.2	4.0	5.1	5.3	4.8	4.4	4.1	3.8	3.9	3.1
Group 2: Clothings and footwear	6.1	1.1	3.3	4.5	5.9	6.2	6.4	6.7	7.9	6.4
Group 3: Gross rent, fuel, power	12.7	28.0	18.0	15.3	14.2	13.4	12.0	12.3	10.6	10.0
Group 4: Furniture, household operations	4.0	1.3	1.9	2.9	3.3	4.0	3.9	4.0	4.7	5.2
Group 5: Health services	1.5	0.4	0.8	0.9	1.2	1.2	1.6	1.8	2.0	1.8
Group 6: Transport and communication	11.9	2.5	4.0	5.5	6.5	9.0	10.7	11.1	12.6	24.7
Group 7: Recreation	5.5	0.6	1.3	2.3	2.9	4.9	6.3	7.0	8.2	7.5
Group 8: Miscellaneous, of which	12.8	8.4	8.8	10.3	11.0	11.1	12.8	13.4	14.2	17.2
Food away from home	(36.0)	(60.5)	(41.9)	(37.5)	(34.5)	(34.0)	(36.4)	(37.5)	(40.7)	(32.5)
Beverages/tobacco away from home	(19.6)	(21.5)	(21.8)	(23.5)	(21.9)	(22.1)	(20.8)	(21.4)	(20.7)	(13.4)
Other miscellaneous expenses	(44.4)	(18.1)	(36.3)	(39.0)	(43.6)	(43.9)	(42.8)	(41.1)	(38.5)	(54.0)

Source: Department of Statistics, Preliminary Tabulation 1977 Household Expenditure Survey.

TABLE A.6 Distribution of monthly expenditure per urban household: 1979 (Lp/month, 1977 prices)

	Expenditure per household	Below 140	141–280	281–400	401–550	551–800	801–1100	1101–1400	1401–1900	1901+
									Income classes	
Number of households	2 632	28	123	251	266	470	331	283	270	340
Number of members	12 835	40	328	870	1 115	2 346	1 879	1 853	1 897	2 507
Average number of members/household	5.43	1.43	2.67	3.47	4.19	4.99	5.68	6.55	7.03	7.38
Average number of earners/household	3.17	1.18	1.70	2.03	2.35	2.71	3.14	3.67	4.28	4.74
Average household expenditure	1 166	102	218	346	481	673	936	1 201	1 577	3 286
Expenditure on:					(percent)					
Group 0: Food, of which	30.1	40.5	40.8	38.8	39.8	39.3	37.1	34.9	32.2	23.0
Rice	(16.4)	(26.5)	(23.2)	(23.2)	(21.2)	(19.2)	(17.2)	(18.6)	(14.7)	(12.5)
Bread and cereals	(9.6)	(12.1)	(11.9)	(10.8)	(11.2)	(9.7)	(9.7)	(9.0)	(10.1)	(8.8)
Meat	(19.9)	(9.7)	(13.5)	(14.1)	(15.4)	(17.1)	(20.3)	(17.6)	(20.7)	(23.4)
Fish	(14.1)	(16.4)	(16.8)	(16.3)	(14.5)	(15.1)	(13.7)	(14.6)	(14.3)	(12.9)
Milk, cheese, eggs	(9.1)	(4.8)	(6.4)	(8.0)	(9.1)	(8.7)	(8.9)	(9.3)	(8.9)	(9.9)
Oils and fats	(4.2)	(2.7)	(3.7)	(3.6)	(3.8)	(4.0)	(4.3)	(4.7)	(4.2)	(4.3)
Fruits and vegetables	(17.3)	(18.7)	(15.2)	(14.8)	(15.1)	(16.9)	(17.0)	(16.8)	(18.2)	(18.1)
Sugar	(3.0)	(3.1)	(4.3)	(4.1)	(3.9)	(3.6)	(2.8)	(3.3)	(2.7)	(2.4)
Coffee, tea, cocoa	(2.8)	(2.8)	(2.4)	(2.3)	(2.6)	(2.8)	(2.9)	(2.8)	(2.8)	(2.9)
Other foods	(3.6)	(3.3)	(2.8)	(2.6)	(3.1)	(3.0)	(3.2)	(3.3)	(3.3)	(4.8)
Group 1: Beverages and tobacco	3.5	1.3	5.4	4.1	4.7	4.0	3.5	3.7	3.6	3.0
Group 2: Clothing and footwear	4.9	1.5	2.3	3.0	2.9	3.8	4.1	5.1	6.1	5.3
Group 3: Gross rent, fuel, power	17.5	30.0	23.5	20.0	18.5	18.7	18.0	17.3	17.0	16.5
Group 4: Furniture, household operations	4.3	0.8	1.2	1.9	2.2	2.9	3.4	3.7	3.9	5.5
Group 5: Health services	1.9	—	0.8	1.1	1.3	1.7	1.9	2.0	2.0	2.1
Group 6: Transport and communication	12.7	0.8	3.5	3.8	5.4	6.6	7.9	8.6	8.9	18.7
Group 7: Recreation	8.1	4.1	2.4	4.3˙	5.9	6.3	7.4	9.0	9.4	9.0
Group 8: Miscellaneous, of which	17.0	21.1	20.2	23.0	19.3	16.5	16.7	15.7	16.8	17.0
Food away from home	(48.2)	(65.0)	(65.6)	(66.4)	(59.9)	(54.5)	(50.8)	(52.8)	(52.6)	(41.0)
Beverages/tobacco away from home	(16.5)	(23.6)	(21.7)	(18.7)	(19.4)	(20.3)	(18.8)	(19.6)	(19.2)	(13.8)
Other miscellaneous expenses	(35.3)	(11.5)	(12.8)	(14.9)	(20.7)	(25.2)	(30.4)	(27.7)	(28.3)	(45.2)

Source: Department of Statistics, Preliminary Tabulation 1977 Household Expenditure Survey.

Index

Index of Persons